Redrawing the Historical Past

Redrawing the Historical Past

History, Memory, and
Multiethnic Graphic Novels

EDITED BY
MARTHA J. CUTTER &
CATHY J. SCHLUND-VIALS

The University of Georgia Press • Athens

Publication of this book was made possible, in part,
through the support of the University of Connecticut.

© 2018 by the University of Georgia Press
Athens, Georgia 30602
www.ugapress.org
All rights reserved
Designed by Melissa Bugbee Buchanan
Set in 10/13 Minion Pro

Most University of Georgia Press titles are
available from popular e-book vendors.

Printed digitally

Library of Congress Cataloging-in-Publication Data

Names: Cutter, Martha J., editor. | Schlund-Vials, Cathy J., 1974– editor.
Title: Redrawing the historical past : history, memory, and multiethnic
    graphic novels / edited by Martha J. Cutter and Cathy J. Schlund-Vials.
Description: Athens : The University of Georgia Press, [2017] |
    Includes bibliographical references and index.
Identifiers: LCCN 2017042875| ISBN 9780820352015 (hardcover : alk. paper) |
    ISBN 9780820352008 (pbk. : alk. paper) | ISBN 9780820352022 (ebook)
Subjects: LCSH: Graphic novels—History and criticism. | History in literature. |
    Memory in literature. | Minorities in literature. | Ethnicity in literature. |
    Narration (Rhetoric)—Social aspects. | Comic books, strips, etc.—
    History and criticism.
Classification: LCC PN6714 .R43 2017 | DDC 741.5/9—dc23
    LC record available at https://lccn.loc.gov/2017042875

CONTENTS

Coloring a Planetary Republic of Comics

Frederick Luis Aldama

SINCE THE APPEARANCE MORE than a century ago of Asian Americans as monstrous swarms invading the lands in San Francisco's *The Wasp* (1880) or Frederick Burr Opper's Happy Hooligan (1900) as a thick-accented, Irish American buffoon, much has changed in the U.S. comics landscape. Civil rights tugs-of-war together with demographic weight have engendered a huge number of multiethnic creators and consumers reading and working in the United States today. African Americans, Native Americans, Latinos, and Asian Americans—ethnic groups that had traditionally been kept in the penumbra—have pushed their way into the light. While it took a century, perhaps we can say that in terms of multiethnic representation in the comic book and graphic narrative world, we have arrived.

For today's authors of comics and graphic novels by and about racial or ethnic groups, even the sky does not seem to pose any limits. Multiethnic comics and graphic novels presently appear in and vitally give form to all the genres. Independent practitioners such as Cuban American Frank Espinosa created *Rocketo* (2006) and Chicanos Mario and Gilbert, of Los Bros Hernandez, crafted *Citizen Rex* (2009) in order to take readers into the future with their variously realized sci-fi epics. Others might choose the crime/noir storytelling envelope. I think of John Layman and Rob Guillory, who invented the so-identified cibopath detective, Tony Chu, who solves crimes by tasting the flesh of organic matter, people included, or Gilbert Hernandez's nihilistic stand-alone graphic novels such as *Chance in Hell* (2007), *Speak of the Devil* (2008), and *Troublemakers* (2009), among others. There are those who ink more youth-oriented, coming-of-age (and coming-out) stories, such as Ivan Velez with his *Tales of the Closet* (1987) or Grasiela Rodriguez's *Lunatic Fringe* (2010). And there are many who choose the life-education journey format (or bildungsroman), such as Rhode Montijo with his underworld journeying child-protagonist in *Pablo's Inferno* (1999–2001); Wilfred Santiago's contemporary 9/11-set, urban-dwelling twenty-something Omar Guerrero *In My Darkest Hour* (2004); Gilbert Hernandez's angsty suburbanite Latino in *Sloth* (2006); or Adrian Tomine's late-twenties Ben Tanaka in *Shortcomings* (2007).

Long the bastion of the swarm of mainstream Anglo-American superheroes, today we see more and more superheroes of color. Especially interesting developments include Robert Morales and Reginald Hudlin's introduction of an African American Captain America figure with *Isaiah Bradley in Truth: Red, White, and Black* (2004); Brazilian Gabriel Bá and Gerard Way's introduction of the eye-patched, knife-throwing vigilante Diego (along with the ultimate other, the hybrid gorilla-Martian/human, Spaceboy) in the *Umbrella Academy* (2007–8); and U.S. Latino Fernando Rodriguez's kinetic, modern-day Cuauhtémoc incarnation in construction-worker-by-day Tony Avalos as *Aztec of the City* (1993–). In the maxi-series 52 (issues 1–52, 2006–7) Geoff Johns and Grant Morrison develop the out-lesbian relationship between Latina Renee Montoya (former Gotham City police detective) and Kate Kane (Batwoman). In *Daredevil: Father* (2004) former editor-in-chief of Marvel, Joe Quesada, introduces his readers to the Vodun-practicing Afro-Latino team "The Santerians"; in *Exiles* (2001) Judd Winick brings to life the lesbian Asian émigré superhero Sunfire; Robert Kirkman creates Asian American Dupli-Kate, her brother Multi-Paul, and well-heeled Black Samson in *Invincible* (issues 2 and 6, 2003). In *Kato, Origins* (2010), Jai Nitz turns Anglo Green Hornet's Asian sidekick Kato into the dexterously smart and athletic central protagonist who sleuths out then defeats the baddies.

Multiethnic comics and graphic novels run the gamut of storytelling format, theme, and characterization, including the autobiographical, biographical, historical, satirical, erotic, and pedagogical formats. The crisscrossing of history with autobiography is found among others in Latina Iverna Lockpez's *Cuba: My Revolution* (2010), Filipina Lynda Barry's *One! Hundred! Demons!* (2002), and Percy Carey's *Sentences: The Life of M. F. Grimm* (2007). Ho Che Anderson and Wilfred Santiago use the biographical format in their various highly stylized biographical portraits: Anderson's *King* (1993–2003) and Santiago's *21: The Story of Roberto Clemente* (2011); Kazuki Ebine, on the other hand, chooses to use the manga format to create a biography of *Gandhi* (2011). Others create historical fictions, such as Derek McCulloch and Shepherd Hendrix with *Stagger Lee* (2006) and Ben Katchor with *The Jew of New York* (1998). Some choose to add to the multiethnic comic book canvas by creating extremely satirical comics and graphic novels that aim to reteach us history, including Lalo Alcaraz and Ilan Stavans's *Latino USA* (2000, 2012) and *A Most Imperfect Union* (2014). Yet others such as Gilbert Hernandez (*Birdland*, 1990–94) and Sandra Chang (*Sin Metal Sirens*, 2001–2) choose the riskier and risqué format of erotica.

Within all these genres, we see comics and graphic novels by and about race and ethnicity mixing up the genres. For instance, in *Secret Identities* (2009) the various independent and mainstream Asian American authors/artists situate their superheroes within significant historical moments for the Asian American community, including the building of railroads, the internment camps, and the murder of Vincent Chin. Jason Aaron and R. M. Guéra blend crime noir with the western in *Scalped* (2007–12), and Rafael Navarro mixes the gothic with horror and the noir formats in *Sonambulo* (1996). I mention these few examples to give a sense of the many multiethnic comic books and graphic novels from which today's readers can choose, as well as to suggest that there is much terrain to be covered by critical inquiry and scholarly work.

Martha J. Cutter and Cathy J. Schlund-Vials bring together essays that consider the link between graphic novels by and about multiethnic U.S. experience and history. In each essay we witness the rich and varied interplay between history, memory, and multiethnic graphic novels. The collection opens all our senses to how this visual-verbal format can and does give shape to racial and ethnic identities and experiences in ways that engage audiences anew.

Redrawing the Historical Past wakes us to the vibrant pulse of the multiethnic comic book scene today. We learn how Mat Johnson and Warren Pleece (*Incognegro*, 2008) use the verbal (dialogue) and visual (shading that sidesteps black or white racial identifications) to positively deploy a racial passing narrative where the protagonist does not need to choose between white or black but rather embraces several racial identities at once. We learn of how Jeremy Love (*Bayou*, 2009) draws inspiration from literature (Uncle Remus stories) and early twentieth-century photographs of African Americans to create a comic that conveys a disquieting aesthetic: the art comforts while the theme of lynching shockingly disturbs us. We learn, too, how an "orientalist" aesthetic in the hands of Asian creators Gene Luen Yang and Sonny Liew (*The Shadow Hero*, 2014) can become a powerful means to undo stereotypes of Asian American identity. During this journey we learn how the civil rights struggle and queer racialized subjectivity intersect in the work of Howard Cruse (*Stuck Rubber Baby*, 1995) and about Art Spiegelman's commitment to complicating racial identity in his post-*Maus* works. Other historical topics analyzed include Lila Quintero Weaver's Latina *testimonio* of race wars in the deep south (*Darkroom*, 2012), the Vietnamese experience (Clément Baloup's *Mémoires de Viet Kieu*, 2006–17 and GB Tran's *Vietnamerica*, 2010), and so much more. Taken as a whole, *Redrawing the Historical Past* demonstrates how graphic novelists from a wide variety of ethnic planetary experiences use visual-verbal formats to enrich our understanding of individuals weighed down and destroyed by the past along with those who overcome histories of racial oppression.

Certainly, Cutter and Schlund-Vials and their cadre of scholars included herein do not pretend that this visual-verbal storytelling format is a cure-all to our social ills—nor do they see it as historical document. However, they do powerfully persuade us to consider how graphic novels by and about the multiethnic experience in the United States can open our eyes wide to deliberately erased chapters from our past. I think of Jim Crow segregation or the Holocaust, the forced relocation of Native peoples, or the Japanese American incarceration/internment, for instance. In the hands of graphic novelists attuned to the multi-ethnic experience, new ways of looking back to the past are offered in order for us to act progressively for humanity today and tomorrow. Finally, *Redrawing the Historical Past* invites us all to join in the interpretive work necessary to thicken and solidify the presence of the multicolored, manifold branches growing from comic books and graphic novels today.

ACKNOWLEDGMENTS

FROM THE VERY BEGINNING, Walter Biggins at the University of Georgia Press has been enthusiastically supportive of *Redrawing the Historical Past*; he was able to see the value of the project and pushed us, as editors, to complete a volume of essays that would forge new ground in terms of field, discipline, and use of complex analytical modes. Such provocations were buttressed by the expert advice we received from anonymous readers, who—at different points—offered critical suggestions that strengthened the stakes of the project's engagement with history through the rubrics of graphic narrative, literary analysis, and visual culture. Last, but certainly not least, the University of George Press is in many ways a model home for this project: we are honored to join other authors and editors whose work in graphic narrative has been foundational, inspirational, and aspirational. We are especially appreciative of the press's staff, who patiently answered our inquiries and helped us bring *Redrawing the Historical Past* to completion.

As evidenced by the essays that comprise *Redrawing the Historical Past*, this project is very much a sustained collaborative conversation about multiethnic graphic narrative. The project began as a discussion that followed a 2015 Modern Language Association panel focused on comics, which featured Julie Armstrong and Taylor Hagood (who are both in this anthology). We are therefore thankful for the opportunity to harness these conversations in one place, and *Redrawing the Historical Past* is very much a dialogic space. We are indebted to each of the contributors, whose pieces make visible the ways in which historically situated graphic narratives have increasingly become a central aspect of what previously has been characterized as an experimental, popular form. Our contributors exhibited a rare generosity of spirit with regard to revision and editing; indeed, they promptly answered our multiple inquiries and exhibited unparalleled commitment throughout the publishing process. We are especially thankful to Frederick Aldama for encouraging us to pursue the project and for his excellent foreword to the volume. In a more local register, Hayley Stefan deserves special commendation for the large amount of work she did under a tight deadline to prepare the manuscript in its final stages. We are also thankful for the financial support we received from the University of Connecticut's Fund for Interdisciplinary Research Endeavors (FIRE), Scholarship Facilitation Fund, and the College of Liberal Arts and Sciences Book Fund. A special word of thanks also to our copyeditor Rachel Van Hart and to Alexis Boylan.

Martha Cutter would personally like to thank her parents, Eve and Phil Cutter, and her partner, Peter Linehan. She also thanks her friends and colleagues from ARG (Americanist Reading Group) who read parts of her essay in an earlier form, including Shawn Salvant, Kate Capshaw, Sherry Harris, Chris Vials, and Jerry Philips. She also thanks Derek Parker Royal for his enthusiasm for this piece and for the serious study of the graphic novel.

Cathy would like to personally thank her parents, Charles and Ginko Schlund, who set both a high bar and model example; her twin brother, Charles, whose sense of humor is rooted in an unmatched wit; and her husband, Chris Vials, whose unending support, gentle guidance, and keen intellect are foundational.

Redrawing the Historical Past

INTRODUCTION

Redrawing the Historical Past

History, Memory, and Multiethnic Graphic Novels

Martha J. Cutter and Cathy J. Schlund-Vials

ON MAY 30, 1975, IN A PORTLAND State University speech titled "A Humanist View," Toni Morrison provocatively averred, "No one can blame the conqueror for writing history the way he sees it, and certainly not for digesting human events and discovering their patterns according to his own point of view. But it must be admitted that conventional history supports and complements a very grave and almost pristine ignorance."[1] Morrison's critique of history—predicated on a reading of state-authorized narratives that eschew individual accounts and familial remembrances in favor of "large distinctions" and strategic omissions—coincides with the post–civil rights movement "ethnic turn" in literary studies and anticipates a particular historical preoccupation in multiethnic American literature. Indubitably, multiethnic American literature—since the arrival of the likes not only of Morrison but of Maxine Hong Kingston, Philip Roth, Sandra Cisneros, Junot Díaz, and Sherman Alexie, among other prominent writers—has emerged as a significant site to "revise" *and* "rewrite" previously held notions of U.S. history. Such revisions often take the form of narratives that detail disremembered accounts of exclusion, ethnoracial violence, and systemic oppression. These forgotten histories have repeatedly been reclaimed in works that challenge and resist dominant narratives of assimilation and accommodation. Morrison's initial call against official history has, as many literary scholars rightly note, repeatedly been answered by novelists, autobiographers, and poets who are included in what is now a firmly established and recognized multiethnic American literary canon.

If Morrison's mandate to revise history has resounded in multiethnic American literature in the decades following the civil rights movement, this historically driven imperative has—as this collection maintains—assumed an even more vehement register in turn-of-the-twenty-first-century multiethnic graphic novels. Such works, on the one hand, require readers to cross gutters between graphic narrative frames in order to make meaning. On the other hand, these multivalent projects prompt readers to participate in a diegetic world of text and image that more often than not tactically rehearses, reimagines, and replays

1

"dark moments" in history. From Jim Crow segregation to the Holocaust, from the forced relocation of Native peoples to the Japanese American incarceration/ internment, and from de jure discrimination to systemic state violence, multiethnic graphic novels represent a unique and increasingly popular genre on which to map alternative political genealogies and critical historiographies. As suggested by Art Spiegelman's celebrated investigation of a paternal past in *Maus* (volume 1)—subtitled *A Survivor's Tale: My Father Bleeds History* (1986)—history exists at the forefront of "marginal" accounts and is a predominant emphasis in multiethnic graphic narrative. Using the open and flexible space of the graphic narrative page—in which readers can move not only forward but also backward, upward, downward, and in several other directions—contemporary multiethnic writers present history as a site of struggle where new configurations of the past can be manipulated and alternate conceptualizations of present and future histories might be envisioned.

Redrawing the Historical Past: History, Memory, and Multiethnic Graphic Novels takes seriously such historical movements and historiographical revisions in multiethnic graphic narratives. This collection focuses exclusively on the interplay between history, memory, and graphic novels. Such an approach is necessary because of the historically driven imperative of these texts themselves; these evaluations of graphic form and function bring to light new critical insights and reflect innovative engagements with literary theory and visual culture. Joseph Witek, in his influential book *Comic Books as History: The Narrative Art of Jack Jackson, Art Spiegelman, and Harvey Pekar* (1989), has argued that historical graphic works deal with "an event that is 'already told,' already weighted with cultural significance" (17), although it can certainly then be retold with a difference (4). However, we—along with our contributors—contend that history itself is fluid, unstable, and polyphonic in multiethnic graphic novels. Following Hayden White's theory of history as a constructed narrative more akin to a mode of storytelling, as opposed to an account of set events, *Redrawing the Historical Past* concentrates on the ways in which the past is evocatively renarrated, provocatively reconfigured, and strategically remade in multiethnic graphic novels.

Such reflections on the past, as narrated through graphic means, build on previous scholarly work and fill a specific gap. To wit, despite the prominence of history in contemporary U.S. multiethnic graphic narrative, to date there has yet to be a single study exclusively concentrated on representations of history in multiethnic graphic novels. Only a few book-length studies deal explicitly with history in graphic narrative, and they do not focus specifically on multiethnic narrative; these include Witek's aforementioned *Comic Books as History*, Richard Iadonisi's edited collection *Graphic History: Essays on Graphic Novels and/ as History* (2012), and Annessa Ann Babic's edited *Comics as History, Comics as*

Literature: Roles of the Comic Book in Scholarship, Society, and Entertainment (2013). Several new works also concern ethnic or postcolonial narrative yet do not make history an overt focus, such as *Multicultural Comics: From* Zap *to* Blue Beetle (edited by Frederick Luis Aldama, 2010), Adilifu Nama's *Super Black: American Pop Culture and Black Superheroes* (2011), the Eisner Award–winning *Black Comics: Politics of Race and Representation* (edited by Sheena C. Howard and Ronald L. Jackson II, 2013), *Drawing New Color Lines: Transnational Asian American Graphic Narratives* (edited by Monica Chiu, 2014), *Postcolonial Comics: Texts, Events, Identities* (edited by Binita Mehta and Pia Mukherji, 2015), and *The Blacker the Ink: Constructions of Black Identity in Comics and Sequential Art* (edited by Frances Gateward and John Jennings, 2015). To be sure, *Redrawing the Historical Past* is very much in conversation with these works and is indebted to the significant scholarly interventions contained in a 2007 *MELUS* special issue edited by Derek Parker Royal (*Coloring America: Multi-Ethnic Engagements with Graphic Narrative*). The collection quite substantively and substantially follows in the analytic footsteps of studies such as Hillary L. Chute's *Graphic Women: Life Narrative and Contemporary Comics* (2010), Michael A. Chaney's edited collection *Graphic Subjects: Critical Essays on Autobiography and Graphic Novels* (2011), and *Comics and the U.S. South* (edited by Brannon Costello and Qiana J. Whitted, 2012). Notwithstanding the undeniable strengths of each of these respective studies, at stake in *Redrawing the Historical Past* is a divergent and capacious sense of what constitutes historical narrative, of what history itself means, and how multiethnic subjects can engender alternative histories that are more open and dialogic than dominant chronicles of events.

Accordingly, *Redrawing the Historical Past* presents an innovative body of criticism about recently published works that have, to date, received scant scholarly attention. While many of the essays deal with U.S. history, several expand the terrain of this history internationally and geographically to include groups affected by U.S. militarization (such as Vietnamese refugees in France and the United States) and places considered origin points for diasporic migration (for instance, Poland, China, and Southeast Asia). Correspondingly, *Redrawing the Historical Past* is a uniquely cartographic project insofar as it not only maps historical developments but also follows the transnational movements of individuals, groups, and ideas to the United States; it similarly charts—through visual medium and mass culture—contemplations of the past relevant to contemporary debates over U.S. nationhood, selfhood, and belonging. The writers and artists whose works serve as the basis for the critical essays in *Redrawing the Historical Past* are identifiably "American" with regard to nationality; with the exception of Scott McCloud, these cultural producers by and large fall neatly into the now-established category of "multiethnic," as an unavoidably heterogeneous, authorial designation made up of first- and second-generation immigrants, African Americans, Latino/as, and Asian Americans.[2] In the face of such diverse cultural productions, and despite varied engagements in terms of theme and schematic, *Redrawing the Historical Past* on one level contemplates the ways in which the very histories that bring such groups "into being" (for instance, disastrous U.S. foreign policies in Asia, immigration law shifts, and state-sanctioned segregation) continue to shape their present-day livelihoods.

On another level, *Redrawing the Historical Past* seizes on what has become a recognizable graphic movement in U.S. literary studies and multiethnic American literary studies; such a focus is evident in the increased scholarly attention paid to text/image productions and the concomitant emergence of "comics studies" and "graphic narrative studies" as interdisciplinary sites and curricular emphases in humanities departments across the country. Even so, we as editors have mainly limited this collection's purview to works that are not intended to be consumed in excerpted format or read in serial form (e.g., our essays mostly do not discuss "comics proper," texts that appear sequentially week to week or are published monthly as issue to issue). We use the terms "graphic novel" and "graphic narrative" to describe this body of work, which primarily includes long-form contemporary graphic novels and autobiographical works intended to be read pictorially and thematically as *integrated texts*. Central to *Redrawing the Historical Past*'s essays are holistic reading practices that reflect and refract those associated with long narrative retellings in novels and multidecade remembrances in full-length memoirs. Of course, this distinction is not a hard and fast one, and many works originally published in part in serial form (such as Spiegelman's *Maus*) are ultimately collected and read in book form. However, we would suggest that the very act of collecting such works into a volume on one level indicates a reading practice that focuses on integration of excerpts into something like a complete novelistic whole.[3]

On another level, "collecting" as narrative act instantiates an ineludible attention to archives (as assembled, collated, and curated historical artifacts). Suggestive of "collections of historical documents or records providing information about a place, institution, [and/or] a group of people" and indicative of "places where historical documents or records are kept" (*Oxford English Dictionary*), "archives" (as collected notion and collective site) concomitantly occupy a peculiarly vexed location and particularly prominent position in many contemporary graphic novels. As Hillary L. Chute notes in her evaluation of Alison Bechdel's *Fun Home: A Family Tragicomic* (2006), much of the novel's narration pivots on "acts of looking at archives" (182), which through reiterative observation bring to light familial, social, and political traumas (involving the father's suicide, familial dysfunction, and the ongoing marginalization of LGBT subjectivities in the United States).

Given the visual registers of medium and historical preoccupations of form, as well as the focus on collecting and archiving experiences that have been fissured and broken, it is not surprising that several of the graphic novels and memoirs discussed in this volume accordingly include photographic replications and representations. Integral to many multiethnic graphic novels is a re-seeing of history, and central to these revisionist works is an archival project of reassemblage. Therefore, the strategic utilization of photography on the one hand affords author-artists an opportunity to engage what Charles Hatfield characterizes as "ironic authentication." As Hatfield maintains, in such authentication (as manifest in *Maus*), photos seem to "offer a value-neutral, purely denotative vision of persons and places" that operates in stark contrast to the connotative dimensions of drawn illustration and individuated characterization (145). On the other hand, this reading of photography in graphic novels corresponds to what Elisabeth El Refaie characterizes as the "myth of photographic truthfulness," which is "based not so much on the 'lifelikeness' of the images the camera produces but rather on the photograph's apparent indexical referentiality" (159). Taken together, such idiosyncratic negotiations of dominant history, which intersect with the radial contours of memory, render visible the wide-ranging critical possibilities of multiethnic graphic narrative, which—as the contributors to this collection make clear—indefatigably challenge myths of "truthfulness" in terms of established accounts of U.S. exceptionalism. Such exceptionalism—which repeatedly asserts the endurance of democratic virtue and the constancy of wholesale tolerance—is potently undermined when situated adjacent to the experiences of those who struggle with basic rights recognition and political enfranchisement. In terms of both genre and content, then, multiethnic graphic novels are uniquely focused on the gaps of traditional U.S. historical narrative and a reparation of these fissures through unique artistic endeavors that piece these fragmented histories back together.

History and Memory:
John Lewis, Andrew Aydin, and Nate Powell's *March*

Incontrovertibly, graphic narratives dealing with history have proliferated since *Maus I* and *Maus II* were published in the late 1980s and early 1990s. Similarly, graphic accounts that marry the personal to the political, and works that link the political to the autobiographical, have increased exponentially in the first two decades of the twenty-first century.[4] On that last point, the production of personal autobiographical works that use graphical narrative to investigate historical events would certainly be a rich vein of study; one could analyze how the genre of autobiography is, like the novel, being remade in graphic narratives, which are deeply embedded in questions of memory and historiography. But leaving that for another collection to investigate, *Redrawing the Historical Past* scrutinizes what the writing of history within multiethnic graphic novels does to the conception of history itself. If history is already, in White's terms, a type of narration, or, worse yet, "a nightmare" from which we are trying to "awake" (in James Joyce's infamous 1922 declaration in *Ulysses*),[5] what is the point of integrating historical narration and historical events within multiethnic graphic novels, or of even trying to piece this nightmare back together?

History itself is undeniably textualized and textual. We *read* histories. And we also *see* them via famous iconography, such as photographs of Martin Luther King Jr., of the Hiroshima atomic blast, or of Phan Thị Kim Phúc as a young girl, running naked with peeling, charred skin after her clothes have been burnt away by napalm, a now emblematic image of the American war in Vietnam. Photographs of such famous events are, within the dominant imaginary, fixed and unchanging—it is in fact hard to recall that Phúc survived this iconographic image; she went on to study medicine and create the Kim Phúc Foundation, which provides medical and psychological assistance to child victims of war. By contrast to photographs, which frequently and mechanically capture moments in time, multiethnic graphic novels are able to revise the static iconicity of such famous historical images by making them mobile and fluid within the space of the graphic narrative page, while at the same time harnessing the synergetic power that images and texts together can create. Such dynamism is evident in a number of primary works included in this collection, which tactically "redraw" photographs as a means of reimagining and re-mediating the historical. These revisionary aspects are by no means limited to artists and writers; indeed, as a reader moves across, down, or over such mobile accounts, s/he is taught that history is a multifaceted, polyvocal story that requires the reader's engaged investment to rescript and complete.

This conceptualization of history as polyvocal, intertextual, and metatextual, mediated through the act of "redrawing" and comprehended via the public practice of reading, is evident in *March*, a multiethnic three-volume graphic memoir cowritten by John Lewis and Andrew Aydin and featuring Nate Powell's visually stunning artwork. Lewis was originally moved to write his autobiographical history of the civil rights movement after reading *Martin Luther King and the Montgomery Story*, a ten-cent comic book published by F.O.R. (the Fellowship on Reconciliation). A recruiting tool for the civil rights movement, the comic had a global impact, inspiring similar protest movements around the world: as Lewis and Aydin recall, "F.O.R. had also published a popular comic book called *Martin Luther King and the Montgomery Story*, which explained the basics of passive resistance and non-violent actions as tools for desegregation" (1: 77). In volume 1, Lewis and his fellow congregants at the First Baptist Church in Nashville conduct workshops on nonviolent protest using techniques outlined in the comic, and in volume 3 the F.O.R. comic book is recalled again on the final page as a specific prompt for the writing of *March* (3: 246). But *March*'s integration of this comic book, as will subsequently become apparent, is more than merely pedagogical or honorific.

When examined closely, it becomes evident that *March* is a complex and careful contemplation of the status of history in written texts and visual ones (such as comics, newspapers, photographs, and books). *March* places itself within a textualized narrative universe of histories, opening up in the process a concurrent meditation on the ways in which written and visual texts can serve underrepresented groups. "Let the spirit of history be our guide," comments Lewis toward the end of volume 1 (113), as he leaves his congressional office to attend the January 20, 2009, presidential inauguration of Barack Obama. Admittedly for Lewis, history is no simple matter. In fact, all three volumes of *March* indicate that history is a multidimensional and dynamic system composed of oral and textual elements, indicative of the past and suggestive of the present, which converge on personal stories and political events. These elements culminate into a dialogue between what constitutes official "authentic" history (as manifest in speeches, written journalistic accounts, and photographs) and what is silenced or unspoken because it is does not fit neatly within a dominant chronicle as shaped by human interlocutors, writers, journalists, and politicians.

Thematically, there are many examples (beyond the integration of the F.O.R. comic book) that attest to how history is textualized in *March* as a dialogue between past and present, the spoken and the silenced, and the oral and the written. First, all three volumes are narrated as flashbacks—flashbacks that begin on the day of Obama's inauguration and stretch back as far as 1947, with the first Freedom Riders (2: 133) who rode on the CORE (Congress on Racial Equality) Journey of Reconciliation. Lewis is both storyteller and chronicler in *March*, a work that visually and chronically flips between historical civil rights events and moments in the present, inclusive of the mundane and significant. As a historically inflected text and personally driven reflection, *March* presents its readers with a multilayered, Janus-faced treatment of U.S. history that at the level of plot and by way of characterization refuses facile linearity while engendering a profound sense that past is indeed "prologue." All three volumes are dedicated "to the past and future children of the movement," suggesting that for the authors of *March* history is not linear. Such historical layerings are by no means limited to narratival emplotments; they are analogously replicated in formalistic features such as the absence of gutters between panels. If, as Scott McCloud observes, gutters function to delineate the passage of time (*Understanding Comics* 101), their omission in key junctures of *March* enables a crucial juxtaposition of the civil rights past and the Barack Obama present, which on one level makes possible a palimpsestic assessment of history.[6] On another level, the simultaneity of past and present—which productively situates the race-based struggle for rights alongside the election of the nation's first African American president—destabilizes teleologies of racial progress that privilege an understanding of U.S. history as an ascendant, progressive movement forward.

In turn, such destabilizations render visible an ongoing dialectic between what is recorded by the press as official history and what remains on the margins. For example, in volume 1 an unnamed librarian tells Lewis, "Read. Read Everything" (1: 49), yet when Lewis wants to know more about Martin Luther King Jr., his research in the library uncovers only one article about him (1: 56). This event occurs in 1955, but the attempt to keep King in the shadows of history will not succeed, as the novel tellingly comments with this visual and graphic metaphor: "Lines had been drawn. Blood was beginning to spill" (1: 56). As Lewis as narrator subsequently makes clear, contrary to revisionist arguments that emphasize the power of media in the making of the movement, the press at times figures keenly as a troubling apparatus of biased white hegemony. For instance, the killers of Emmett Till go free and even confess to the murder in *Look* magazine (1: 57). King's famous "Letter from Birmingham Jail" was composed on scraps of newspaper and "smuggled out of his cell" (2: 129); after King's lawyers reassemble this letter, the *New York Times Magazine* refused to publish it, though extensive excerpts were published without King's consent in 1963 in the *New York Post Sunday Magazine*. In volume 3, the press is ubiquitous and now largely seems to side with the civil rights movement; for example, the press has shifted to covering important civil rights events such as Fannie Lou Hamer's riveting 1964 address to the Democratic National Convention (DNC) (3: 107–11). Yet this volume also notes the way that the press tends to identify white civil rights workers by name but not black workers (3: 53) and tends to give credence to incendiary claims by individuals such as J. Edgar Hoover, as in his insistence that civil rights workers are "being exploited by communists to generate racial tensions" (3: 82). By referencing the press's haphazard and often biased coverage/noncoverage of important civil rights events, Lewis challenges its authority with regard to accurately recording civil rights history.

Perhaps more importantly, running through all three volumes is a recognizable deep skepticism about how key civil rights events are incompletely recorded by the press, which is depicted as an entity that often must be manipulated to cover the movement. As a civil rights leader surmises, "In a movement, you **don't** deal with the press—you **act** like there **is** no press. Otherwise you end up staging it" (2: 131). Authenticity is created, it seems, by acting like the press does not exist—which then generates more press coverage that (ironically) appears to be covering unrehearsed events. There is a sense as well by volume 3 that many events are being staged specifically for the press, such as the replica of the burnt-out car in which three civil rights workers were killed that is brought to the DNC convention by the SNCC (Student Non-Violent Coordinating Committee) and receives a good deal of press coverage (3: 105–6).

March's critical engagement with civil rights history as engineered chronicle is by no means limited to press coverage; tellingly, the graphic narrative provides other movement stories that highlight fissures and ruptures omitted from its master narrative. While Lewis remains the work's primary protagonist, *March* features various vantage points, which include the movement's leaders, children engaged in protests, individuals who actively impede its activities, and individuals who are cast outside its discursive and political parameters. For example, Malcolm X is not invited to the famous 1963 march on Washington, D.C. (a fact highlighted in a full-splash page in *March*, 2: 149); he is, however, given space within volume 3 to expound on his ideas (133–37). In this way the text allows for oppositional voices and points of view. Lewis himself is pressured to tone down his somewhat militant speech for the march on Washington (2: 164), and he reluctantly does so—yet he includes the original version of the speech in volume 2's back matter. Such inclusions position dominant narratives of the civil rights movement alongside marginalized accounts as a means of recovering—via image and text—a more complete portrait of the movement.

This impulse to recover alternate perspectives is also epitomized by the narrative's visual characterization of individuals who impede the civil rights movement. Volume 2 highlights Bull Connor's controversial decision not to have policemen on hand when the Freedom Riders' bus rolls into Birmingham, Alabama. Officially, Connor is shown saying on television to a reporter, "Mother's Day. We try and let off as many of our policemen as possible so they can spend the day at home with their families." Yet this "official history" is punctured in the panel below, where the real reason is stated in a banner headline superimposed over Connor's face: "We found out later that he'd promised the Ku Klux Klan fifteen minutes with the bus before he'd make any arrests" (2: 48). Similarly, volume 3 begins with the September 1953 Birmingham, Alabama, church bombing that killed four little girls, an event much chronicled in official histories of the civil rights movement. But it also contains a less chronicled comment by then-governor George Wallace, which may have incited the bombing: "two weeks before the bombing, [Wallace] was quoted in the paper saying, 'what this country needs is a few first-class funerals'" (3: 18). Visually, this comment is placed below drawn framed photographs of three of the girls who were murdered; it is also located within a round panel that shows a representation of the three girls' coffins, shrouded in flowers, wreathes, and leaves. In so doing, *March* visually puts the blame for the death of these girls not only on the murderers but also on elected officials such as Wallace. In addition, it juxtaposes the personal history of the murdered children with Wallace's official history to suggest the ways in which marginalized parts of history can be brought to the foreground, both literally and pictorially. In sum, *March* visually and lexically validates the ways in which alternative chronicles of the civil rights movement can refigure and replay the dominant narrative and the "official" voice of history.

While *March*'s strategic uses of text and viewpoint attest to a desire to reveal revisionary perspectives about the movement, its tactical utilization of photography—which involves both the camera and its produced images—reconfirms *March*'s overall skepticism toward official history. Entities such as SNCC hire their own photographers, and sometimes it is these photographs that become iconic. Illustratively, a picture taken by Danny Lyon in Cairo, Illinois, of children and adults praying before they try to integrate a segregated swimming pool becomes "probably the most popular poster of the movement." *March* integrates a *drawn* representation of this photo (2: 120) that, when juxtaposed with text, instantiates a postimage reflection; as Lewis notes: "what a lot of people **don't** know is what happened just after the photo was taken," when the little girl from the photo is almost run over by an irate driver (2: 121). The press also has a penchant for photographing "moments of drama and violence," such as the march on Selma, but as the narrative voice notes, "it tends to be forgotten . . . just how many days of **uneventful** protest took place" before this more famous event (3: 150). *March* persistently reintroduces "forgotten" events to elide the photographic and historical vacuity surrounding them.

March also incorporates instances of real photos (redrawn by Nate Powell) into the text on numerous occasions (1: 19, 61; 2: 131, 154; 3: 18, 190), thereby providing a sort of metacommentary on photography, which encompasses both its limits and its values in the representations of history. Early in volume 2, when Lewis is trying to desegregate a movie theater showing *The Ten Commandments* in Nashville, he depicts a photographer taking pictures as protesters are violently attacked. Yet what remains unclear is the photographer's intended focus. Specifically, in the panel the camera faces *out of the picture*, so the reader is uncertain as to whether the photographer is taking pictures of the demonstrators, the local white teenagers who are beating them up, or the police who are doing nothing (2: 18). Such ambiguities reiterate critiques of the press while providing readers with a more expanded and expansive narrative of the movement's visual and pictorial history.

Furthermore, *March* engages history through acts of memory, which time and again privilege the protagonist's recollection of events; such recollections occur at the behest of individuals who visit Lewis's office, who serve as a key audience for these alternate perspectives on the movement. Rather than concentrating on what "actually happened," *March* engenders through personal reflection and multiple viewpoints a different way of reading and subjectively thinking about history in a manner that eschews ostensible certainty, seeming neutrality, and a master narrative. History becomes a narrative created in front of an audience, something that is constantly and consciously staged. It also has elements of call-and-response in that Lewis's own stories are only called forth by the presence of various visitors to his office. In this way, *March* presents a performative version of history, one that is more fluid and open than the dominant narratives of this era and of the civil rights movement generally presented by mainstream books, media, and newspapers.

Redrawing the Multiethnic Contours of the Historical Past: Chapter Overview

Like *March*, *Redrawing the Historical Past* is first and foremost concerned with the graphic representation of history. The essays in this volume are ordered chronologically; such an ordering—which privileges historical event over publication date—is intended to highlight the collection's overall focus on the ways in which the past is radically recollected and remembered. To reiterate and expand, the essays included in *Redrawing the Historical Past* take on the issues of history, memory, and multiethnic graphic narrative using diverse methodologies and approaches; they are also guided by three specific inquiries. In particular, the editors have prompted each author to consider, in a more global vein, the concept of history and how it is manifest in their chosen texts. Equally crucial is a concurrent evaluation of the ways in which the graphic novel as distinct genre can *formally* renovate or intervene in notions of the historical past. Last, but certainly not least, the editors have urged authors to take seriously the possibilities and limitations of these historical revisions with regard to envisioning different, new, or even more positive versions of both the present and the future.

Such considerations are at the forefront of Martha J. Cutter's "Redrawing Race: Renovations of the Graphic and Narrative History of Racial Passing in Mat Johnson and Warren Pleece's *Incognegro*," which opens *Redrawing the Historical Past*. Published in 2008, *Incognegro*—as Cutter maintains—is a work that is in dialogue with what is now recognizable as the genre of the passing narrative, which has origins in the nineteenth century. Set in the Jim Crow South, with nods to nineteenth-century passing texts as well as twentieth-century ones such as George Schuyler's *Black No More* (1931), and with specific allusions to Jean Toomer, *Incognegro* nevertheless militates against the narrative's dominant script, which time and again reaffirms racial identities by returning characters to identities that are either black *or* white. Cutter maintains that by incorporating historical figures into a fictional narrative about racial passing, Johnson and Pleece play with past history; in so doing they produce a more fluid and open racial system in which everyone is a potential incognegro or unknown when it comes to racial identity. This chapter also argues that by designing a series of passing figures who cannot be visually recognized, the novel deconstructs the longer history of the portrayal of racial identity in comics as a whole. These meditations on what W. E. B. Du Bois noted was the "problem of the color line" are differentially explored in Taylor Hagood's "Nostalgic Realism: Fantasy, History, and Brer Rabbit–Trickster Ambiguity in Jeremy Love's *Bayou*." Bringing together the corpus of Joel Chandler Harris's Uncle Remus stories (as cinematically manifest in Disney's 1946 *Song of the South*) and a turn-of-the-twentieth-century African American photobook, *Bayou* (2009) offers its readers an uncanny engagement with the racial and racialized historical past. According to Hagood, Love's juxtaposition of the fictional and stylized, along with the photographic and realistic, creates a narrative text/image production that negotiates the historical past via a powerful blend of nostalgia and realism. This blending, drawn and colored with the warmth of a children's book, foregrounds a monstrous reimagining of Brer Rabbit and minstrel stereotypes, which renders visible a complex engagement with early twentieth-century southern racism and racial violence.

Such critical juxtapositions between realism and fantasy similarly presage Caroline Kyungah Hong's "Teaching History through and as Asian/American Popular Culture in Gene Luen Yang's *Boxers* and *Saints*." Concentrated on Yang's 2013 two-volume graphic narrative about the Boxer Rebellion (circa 1899–1901), Hong begins with a consideration of two distinct genres: historical fiction and fantasy. Noting that Yang's engagement with the historical past intersects with allusions to Chinese opera, Chinese mythology, and U.S. superhero comics, and maintaining that its doubled narration brings to light past/present ambivalences, Hong argues that integral to *Boxers* and *Saints* is a dialectical relationship to history that is ostensibly about the past yet encompasses political and ethical questions relevant to a present marked by war and terror, nation and empire, religion and ethnicity, violence and justice. Another Yang text serves as the textual basis for Monica Chiu's "Who Needs a Chinese American Superhero? Gene Luen Yang and Sonny Liew's *The Shadow Hero* as Asian American Historiography," which situates his 2014 collaborative publication within a history of comics publishing and mid-twentieth-century representations of race. Through references to graphic narrative form and methodology, Chiu's essay addresses iconicity and Orientalist humor as a means of mapping the work's political investment in what she identifies as a racialized historiography within polemical comics representations.

The concomitant engagement with midcentury politics and historical representation in Chiu's investigation into *The Shadow Hero* overlaps with Julie Buckner Armstrong's "*Stuck Rubber Baby* and the Intersections of Civil Rights Historical Memory," which marks a narratival return to the civil rights movement. Armstrong's essay focuses on Howard Cruse's *Stuck Rubber Baby* (1995) and asserts that the text is marked by a queer intervention that, analogous to the previously discussed *March*, fractures consensus recollections of the protest movement. Emphasizing the simultaneity of multiple binaried subjectivities (black/white, queer/straight, drag queen/preacher), Armstrong maintains that *Stuck Rubber Baby* paves the way for a more dynamic, inclusive story of the movement as marked by multiple stakeholders, liberation agendas, and freedom visions. The deconstruction of what has become a master narrative of the movement by way of "other" bodies is echoed in Jorge Santos's "On Photo-Graphic Narrative: 'To Look—Really Look' into Lila Quintero Weaver's *Darkroom*," which features a Latina protagonist who comes of age during the civil rights movement. Published in 2012, *Darkroom* draws on the author's familial history, particularly as it involves her father, a photojournalist. Analyzing Weaver's contrasted utilization of actual photographs and drawn images, Santos argues that Weaver blurs the line between photographic realism and graphic narrative; in so doing, she introduces a "sliver of gray" vis-à-vis the dominant black/white narrative about race and the movement. Such "slivers," Santos concludes, reflect and refract the vexed experiences of Latino/as during the civil rights era.

Moving next to the Vietnam War era (or Second Indochina War, 1955–75), the subsequent two essays consider ways in which the historicization of this transnational conflict needs to be reconfigured by the integration of alternate perspectives. Jeffrey Santa Ana's "Environmental Graphic Memory: Remembering the Natural World and Revising History in *Vietnamerica*" focuses on the memory and reenvisioning of imperialism's destruction of land and people during the Vietnam War; this chapter considers the ways in which GB Tran's *Vietnamerica* (2010) is first and foremost a postcolonial graphic novel. Drawing on what ecocritic Rob Nixon calls "slow violence" to encompass delayed destructions in the formerly colonized regions of the Global South dispersed across time and space, Santa Ana examines Tran's graphic representations of slow violence. Such evaluations are, as Santa Ana subsequently argues, intended to change how readers perceive, recall, and respond to a variety of social crises in the present historical moment, inclusive of environmental calamities produced by centuries of plunder, conquest, and war that have ravaged the Global South's native habitats. Tran's graphic memoir and Vietnam remain central critical sites in Catherine H. Nguyen's "Illustrating Diaspora: History and Memory in Vietnamese American and French Graphic Novels." In particular, this comparative chapter reads *Vietnamerica* and Clément Baloup's three-volume *Mémoires de Viet Kieu* (2006, 2012, 2017) to argue that the graphic memoir uses personal history and autobiography to open up a collective, polyphonic account of displacement and immigration.

Moving from the 1970s into the contemporary period, Angela Laflen's "Punking the 1990s: Cristy C. Road's Historical Salvage Project in *Spit and Passion*" examines the ways in which Road's graphic bildungsroman (published in 2012) rescripts the history of the early 1990s to explore the experiences of her protagonist, a lesbian of color. Situated adjacent to debates over gay marriage (which culminated in the 1994 passage of the Defense of Marriage Act, or DOMA) and set within the context of a reinvigorated punk movement, Laflen contends that *Spit and Passion*'s skepticism with regard to consumer culture and protest concerning U.S. conservatism renders visible a history of feminist activism and queer of color critique. Such consumer critiques and their connections to identity politics are also at play in Cathy J. Schlund-Vials's "Speculative Fictions, Historical Reckonings, and 'What Could Have Been': Scott McCloud's *The New Adventures of Abraham Lincoln*." Published in 1998, *The New Adventures of Abraham Lincoln* represented a "field first" insofar as it innovatively combined computer-generated and manually drawn digital images. Characterized by McCloud as both his "first attempt at computer-generated artwork" and an unassailable "flop," *The New Adventures of Abraham Lincoln* follows African American protagonist Byron Johnson and his friend Marcie in the contemporary moment as they attempt to thwart a simulacra version of the sixteenth president. The product of an alien conspiracy, the imposter Lincoln attempts to reclaim his executive position and finish his presidential term; armed with historical facts, Byron eventually exposes this planetary plot and saves both nation and the world. According to Schlund-Vials, it is Byron's historical cynicism—which occurs within an imaginary wherein racial conflict and racialized disparity is troublingly elided in favor of symbolic declarations of progress—that provides a significant foundation on which to critique turn-of-the-twenty-first-century multiculturalism and U.S. exceptionalism.

Rounding out this focus on the last decade of the twentieth century is Katharine Capshaw's "Fractured Innocence in G. Neri and Randy DuBurke's *Yummy: The Last Days of a Southside Shorty*." Written and illustrated by African American men and addressed to adolescent readers, *Yummy* (2010) depicts the life and death of an eleven-year-old black gang member in Chicago. Set in 1994, *Yummy*—as Capshaw notes—employs the visual to depict fractured points of view—of childhood at once politicized, pure, and abject—on the protagonist's relationship to innocence. In so doing, Neri and DuBurke uncover the ways in which constructions of black childhood embody irreconcilable concepts about innocence, subjectivity, and the value of human life while pushing the reader to consider the insufficiency of the historical record. As in the case of Emmett Till and consistent with the more recent Black Lives Matter movement, *Yummy*'s narrative makes clear the limitations of historiography, arguing that black male childhood becomes legible through only a few unsatisfactory narrative pathways: either naïve innocence, profound violence, or death. Fittingly, given the prominence of *Maus* within the study of graphic narrative, *Redrawing the Historical Past* concludes with Jennifer Glaser's "Art Spiegelman and the Caricature Archive." As a number of critics have noted, Art Spiegelman's decision to use animals to represent national, racial, and ethnic identity in *Maus* dramatizes both the role of the animal in the long history of anti-Semitic caricature and the ethical (and representational) problems attendant to racial essentialism. Few scholars have extended this analysis of race into Spiegelman's post-*Maus* work. From his critique of racism in Robert Crumb's representation of African American identity in 1995 to his investment in the aftermath of the Danish Muhammad cartoon controversy in 2005, Spiegelman has manifested a profound engagement in investigating the relationship between comics and caricature. Glaser considers this particular "caricature archive" to engage a wider meditation on the complex inheritance of caricature for comics artists and the necessary grappling with this history of racial (and often racist) caricature around which many contemporary comics pivot. As a look not only at the past of graphic novels but also at the present (with reference to Spiegelman's post-9/11 work *In the Shadow of No Towers*, published in 2004, and the 2011 and 2015 attacks on the satirical French magazine *Charlie Hebdo*), we consider Glaser's essay to be an excellent summarization of many of the themes raised in the collection as a whole regarding memory, multiethnic graphic narrative, and the redrawing of the historical past.

Redrawing History and Producing Flexible Constructions of the Past

Our current era evinces both immense fascination with history and pronounced skepticism toward it. In one of our classes we recently asked students to pick from various definitions of history at the start of the semester, expecting that many would choose something neutral such as John Anderson's 1876 definition: "History is a narration of the events which have happened among mankind, including an account of the rise and fall of nations, as well as of other great changes which have affected the political and social condition of the human race" (1). Yet class consensus leaned much more heavily toward a more quixotic definition of history, such as Ambrose Bierce's definition from 1911 (in *The Devil's Dictionary*):

"HISTORY, n. An account mostly false, of events mostly unimportant, which are brought about by rulers mostly knaves, and soldiers mostly fools" (188). We did not have to introduce Hayden White's idea that historical writing often mirrors literature, sharing a robust dependence on narrative and storytelling to create coherence ("Interpretation"). Our students understood that history is *what gets remembered and written down* rather than what *really* happened. Moreover, as one student commented, because history is usually written by the "winners," by those who hold power, it leaves little space for those who typically have not held social, legal, or linguistic authority. For such individuals history is often nightmarish and violent. Indeed, a character such as Sethe in Toni Morrison's *Beloved* (1987) finds herself trapped and traumatized by the history she engendered and created as the infamous "Modern Medea." Sethe cannot awaken from the nightmare of the past and is, quite literally, traumatized by history, which Morrison both invokes and refigures in her reading of the historical personage of Margaret Garner.

And yet, as this collection of essays demonstrates and as the many recent graphic works that take history as their subject attest, history, though nightmarish, violent, and most often written by the dominant hegemony, still continues to *matter* as a space to reclaim the past. By introducing a sense of history as multivocal, unstable, slippery, and always mediated by human consciousness, these essays foreground the need to not only redraw history but also redress it. Holocaust survivors have affirmed that if we cannot remember the past, we are doomed to repeat it. Yet for the authors and illustrators discussed here, it might instead be averred that those who do not remember the past *differently*—from the point of view of the oppressed and with attention to what White calls its metafictional qualities—are doomed to repeat it. These writers and illustrators, then, unearth and remake aspects of history in order to provide a more productive, mobile, and fluid relationship with our pasts.

Historical graphic novels have the ability to return to the traumatic past and construct a new reality that acknowledges the dehumanizing nature of much of what we consider history. Graphic novels, in their nonlinear and often fragmented visual spaces, which require the reader to create what McCloud calls "closure," also allow for contradiction and paradox to become tools in sorting out and establishing some control over the past. These texts turn to the past not only or necessarily to create a new factual history but instead to ask readers to resist stabilizing the past's meaning as a totalizing narrative about what "really" happened. In so doing, these authors and illustrators urge readers to envision polyphonic, diverse, complicated narratives of history—versions of history that enable not only recitation of past trauma but also a reevaluation of what is at stake in the envisioning of history itself.

NOTES

1. From Portland State University's Oregon Public Speakers Collection: "Black Studies Center public dialogue. Pt. 2," May 30, 1975 (http://bit.ly/1vO2hLP). Part of the Public Dialogue on the American Dream Theme, via Portland State University Library (http://pdxscholar.library.pdx.edu/orspeakers/90/).

2. While Scott McCloud does not fit the rubric of "multiethnic" author, his *The New Adventures of Abraham Lincoln* features an African American protagonist who contends specifically with the legacies of the slaveholding past. The inclusion of McCloud in this collection speaks to his prominence with regard to graphic narrative/novel scholarship and is intended to expand the purview of "multiethnic graphic novel" to involve a larger discussion about McCloud's graphic storytelling perspective (as one that features as key figure an African American subject negotiating the racialized past).

3. Even with John Lewis, Andrew Aydin, and Nate Powell's *March*, released in three volumes over a period of four years (2013–16), a reader is encouraged to read the *whole* work rather than a single volume; on sale in August 2016 was a "Trilogy Slipcase Set" that retailed for much less than individual volumes. Similarly, Jeremy Love's *Bayou* (discussed in chapter 2) was originally distributed as an online comics series, from 2007 to 2010, but is now *only* being sold in book form (and is now described by DC comics as a "graphic novel"); this suggests that Love's work is now meant to be read in a holistic manner as an integrated textual artifact.

4. Recently works that use graphic narrative to teach history have proliferated and include titles such as Wayne Vansant's *Grant vs. Lee: The Graphic History of the Civil War's Greatest Rivals during the Last Year of the War* (2013); Jonathan Fetter-Vorm's *Trinity: A Graphic History of the First Atomic Bomb* (2013); Alan Cowsill's *World War One: 1914–1918* (2014); Jonathan Fetter-Vorm and Ari Kelman's *Battle Lines: A Graphic History of the Civil War* (2015); Wayne Vansant's *Normandy: A Graphic History of D-Day, the Allied Invasion of Hitler's Fortress Europe* (2012) and *Gettysburg: The Graphic History of America's Most Famous Battle and the Turning Point of the Civil War* (2013); Dwight Jon Zimmerman and Wayne Vansant's *The Vietnam War: A Graphic History* (2009); and Harvey Pekar, Ed Piskor, and Paul Buhle's *The Beats: A Graphic History* (2009). There has also been a proliferation of historical, biographical, or autobiographical graphic memoirs such as Ho Che Anderson's *King: A Comics Biography* (2010), Olivier Morel and Maël's *Walking Wounded: Uncut Stories from Iraq* (2013), and Riad Sattouf's award-winning *The Arab of the Future: A Childhood in the Middle East, 1978–1984* (2015).

5. See chapter 2 of *Ulysses* where Stephen Dedalus (who in many ways is Joyce's alter ego) states, "History . . . is a nightmare from which I am trying to awake" (33).

6. See, for example, pages 176–77 of volume 2, where words from Obama's 2009 inauguration speech bleed over into a scene that takes place on September 15, 1963—the bombing of the Sixteenth Street Baptist Church that killed four little girls.

CHAPTER 1

Redrawing Race

*Renovations of the Graphic and Narrative History of
Racial Passing in Mat Johnson and Warren Pleece's*
Incognegro

Martha J. Cutter

THE PUBLICATION OF MAT JOHNSON and Warren Pleece's graphic novel *Incognegro* (2008) marked the first time that a graphic narrative entered and attempted to transform the vexed terrain of the literary and autobiographical passing narrative.[1] Historically, the genre is fraught with questions about how race is "read," what it means, and how unstable or stable it is: If the "black" racial passer can "pass" for white, is race only a social construction? Johnson and Pleece's text complicates this question of the meaning of race by refusing to shade as dark the vast majority of its characters (whether they are black or white). The novel—set in the early 1930s—concerns Zane Pinchback, a reporter of African American family background who can pass for white and does so in order to collect the names of individuals who have been instrumental in lynchings in the South, writing about what he discovers under the pseudonym "Incognegro." The novel's plot centers on a passing mission in which Zane goes into disguise to save his brother Alonzo from lynching; Alonzo is, in theory, darker skinned and so cannot pass. Yet Zane, who sits on the left, is drawn with the same skin color as his brother Alonzo, who sits on the right (see figure 1.1). In this black-and-white graphic narrative about racial passing, then, it would seem that nothing—including physical skin color—is in fact black or white.

The illogicality of racial taxonomies in which one can look white but be coded legally or socially as black is also a crucial historical component of written passing narratives, so Johnson and Pleece's graphic narrative complements and indeed extends innovatively many concerns of this genre. Yet the text has received little critical attention in terms of its engagement with either the historical genre of the passing narrative or, for that matter, the history of the production of race and racial passing within comics.[2] *Incognegro*'s creators clearly are engaged in an intertextual dialogue with the rich literary and lived history of the passing genre, especially with texts published when this novel is set (in the early twentieth cen-

Figure 1.1. Mat Johnson (writer) and Warren Pleece (illustrator), *Incognegro* (2008): 30.

tury); this essay investigates the graphic novel's transformations of passing narratives from this era.[3] It also situates the novel within a longer historical tradition of representations of blackness and passing in comics, within an archive of mid- to late twentieth-century cartooning. In this archive, black or passing individuals are often portrayed in a stereotyped or stereotypical mode, even when created by African American cartoonists.

Incognegro must therefore be understood as both a redrawing and a redressing of several types of historical texts. Through intertextuality Johnson and Pleece move from a readerly to a writerly approach to prior textual and visual historiographies of blackness and passing; in so doing, *Incognegro* creates something that exceeds the referents on which it is built: a writerly passing narrative—a text that the reader might consent to actively write and rewrite. Roland Barthes describes a "writerly text" as one that makes the reader "no longer a consumer, but a producer of the text" (4), describing such texts as plural, open, and infinite in the number of readings that can be produced (5). In such texts, reading becomes an activity that does not consist of stopping the signifying systems at work but of "coupling these systems . . . according to their plurality" (11); these works therefore encourage a reader to rewrite and revise them. The primary impulse of *Incognegro* is to open up and liberate the history of racial passing from the limited historical configurations of this genre and their encoded representation of racial subjectivity. By incorporating real historical figures into a "fictional" text about racial passing, and into their signifying network, Johnson and Pleece play with past history itself, formulating a new racial system in which we are all (black and white) potential incognegros—or unknowns—when it comes to racial identity. Furthermore, by creating a plethora of passing figures—white and black ones—who cannot be visually demarcated from "real" blacks, they also intervene in the longer history of the portrayal of race in comics, redressing this visual legacy as well.[4] In finally leaving open the question of what Zane himself will be—black, white, both, or neither—and of how race itself can be visually portrayed, the authors create what Scott McCloud would call a "silent accomplice" (*Understanding Comics* 68) in the reader, who may also be able to hold open the historical narrative of racial passing in his or her writing and rewriting of the graphic narrative.

Historical Intertexual Referencing: Moving the Passing Narrative from a Readerly Signifying System to a Writerly One

A reader knowledgeable about the history of racial passing in the early twentieth century might experience a degree of familiarity when encountering *Incognegro* because the novel is filled with, and indeed boldly usurps, the plot and action of other passing narratives from this era. Of course, as Charles Hatfield notes, many alternative comics often highlight their status as a text "through embedded visual references to books, other comics, and picture-making." Beyond emphasizing "the materiality of texts" (Hatfield 65), the creators of *Incognegro* have a larger purpose. Many passing narratives of the early twentieth century have a familiar trajectory: the passer decides to pass, moves to a new location, takes on a new name, and then either dies, returns to his or her "true" race, or stays outside the United States (mainly in Europe).[5] There is also an insistence, frequently, that the passer has to choose one race—he or she cannot be mixed race, or on both sides of the color line, without tragic consequences. For example, a passing character in Alice Dunbar-Nelson's "The Pearl in the Oyster" (1900) states: "we will go away somewhere where we are not known, and we will start life again, but whether we decide to be white or black, we will stick with it" (64). There are exceptions to these narrative trajectories, of course, but many passing narratives from this historical era follow them to some degree, constituting a genre unto itself—a genre that questions the meaning of race, even as it often concludes by suggesting that one must be *either* black or white, at least to survive in the United States during this time period. These types of denouements can be construed as readerly (rather than writerly) articulations of racial passing. Barthes argues that the readerly is based on "operations of solidarity," on repetitions of meanings that ultimately allow them to "stick"; he notes that the ideological goal of this technique is to "naturalize meaning and thus to give credence to the reality of the story" (23). Some passing texts from this time period conclude, then, by stabilizing the plot in ways that may close down the plurality of questions the text as a whole raises about what race really *is*.

There are a number of intertextual references in *Incognegro* that refer to this narrative trajectory but also open up its history—sampling, remixing, parodying, and remaking it. For instance, *Incognegro* loosely follows the life of a real racial passer, Walter White (1893–1955), a very light-skinned African American who considered himself a "voluntary negro."[6] As a national staff member of the NAACP from 1918 onward and its executive secretary from 1931 to 1955, White often passed for white to investigate racial lynching in the 1920s and 1930s and was nearly lynched himself on more than one occasion when his true identity was almost discovered.[7] Mat Johnson's author's note mentions that *Incognegro* is in part inspired by his learning about Walter White's journalistic work, "posing as a white man in the deep south to investigate lynchings," and indeed, in *Incognegro* Zane takes on a Walter White type of persona (4). As most readers of the passing narrative would know, Walter White was not only famous for his journalism but also for his fiction about passing, for he wrote a passing novel called *Flight* (1926). This novel features a female persona who boldly experiments with a white identity and business career, only to eventually and rather unconvincingly return to the "black" race, which has rejected her because of an out-of-wedlock pregnancy. *Flight* therefore reinserts "black" passing characters into a black social milieu; this reinsertion is unconvincing as the character was rejected due to reasons that still exist (her conception and raising of a child outside of marriage). White's heroine, Mimi Dauphin, also sees herself as "'Free! Free! Free!'" when she rejoins the black race, configured as "her own people" and her "happiness" (300), but there is little evidence for this in the text. The text as a whole does show the color line to be incoherent, yet in the end it unexpectedly redraws it, placing the heroine, who is of mixed-race Creole background, on the colored side. As we will see, *Incognegro*, which is set in a similar time period, keeps open the possibility of multiple racial alliances and identities in its ending.

Incognegro also samples features of White's writings that are more writerly, in Barthes's terms. White also wrote his own autobiography, *A Man Called White: The Autobiography of Walter White* (1948), which by title, of course, plays with the fact that a man "called white" is not really "white," at least by the codes of this time period and by his own self-identification. Interestingly, at the end of this volume, White articulates his multiracial heritage: "I am white and I am black, and know there is no difference. Each casts a shadow, and all shadows are dark" (366). Shadows play a significant role in the obscuring of race in *Incognegro*, as Tim Caron has pointed out, rendering some characters who seem to be black in shadow so that a reader cannot discern their skin color, even in bright sunlight (195). Both White and Johnson/Pleece play with the racist terminology of blacks as shades or shadows, of course. Yet in the novel as a whole, Johnson and Pleece displace the rather shallow notion of race as stable that we see in a character such as Mimi with a more Walter White–like and open idea of race as mutable and unstable. Shadows, after all, are ineffable, and we all (black and white) cast them.

Moreover, at the conclusion of *Incognegro* the central character does not decide to be *one* race; instead he chooses to have several racial identities at once. In response to his brother's question, "So what Negro you going to be, then?" the main character, Zane, responds, "That's the best thing: identity is open-ended. Why have just one?" (129). Zane also implies that he will still "keep going incognegro. Somebody has to. I can"—that is, he will still pass for white—but he will also have an arts column "in [his] own name" (130). He will be both Zane Pinchback, a black writer in the New Negro movement; Incognegro; and perhaps other selves. Through these mechanisms, the novel illustrates that race does not exist as a coherent visual or psychological identity, as Zane states earlier: "That's one thing that most of **us** know that most white folks don't. That race doesn't really exist. Culture? Ethnicity? Sure. Class too. But **race** is just a bunch of rules meant to keep us on the bottom. Race is a strategy. The rest is just people acting. Playing roles" (19, emphasis in original). In scenes such as this, *Incognegro* rewrites the readerly quality of the ending of some early twentieth-century passing narratives by sampling them and then producing something new—a passing narrative set in the same time period in which the passer refuses to be fixed into one identity. At the text's end, then, the reader is asked to keep open the multiple possibilities of racial identity that the passing plot raises, to create a writerly conclusion that does not immobilize the open textual universe the graphic narrative attempts to create. Some versions of the text are subtitled "a graphic mystery," and indeed the real mystery of the text may not be who killed whom but what race *is*. This particular mystery is never clarified but kept open through Zane's refusal to pick just one racial persona.

Incognegro likewise directly references and samples a passing novel by the author, journalist, and social commentator George Schuyler (1895–1977), integrating the author's own name: "George Schuyler, the columnist from the Messenger, even he's got a *novel* coming out" (13). This satirical novel—*Black No More* (1931)—tells of a process wherein black characters are lightened to whiteness by a special scientific procedure. This procedure results in racial and social chaos until it is revealed that the "New Caucasians" are in fact "whiter than white"; in theory they therefore can be distinguished from the "true" Caucasians by their too-pale skin. This upends the hegemonic binary in which white skin is valued over black skin, yet it also leads to an outpouring of products and practices intended to transform skin that is too light to skin that is dark enough to be truly white (or Caucasian).

The satire is clear; however, the novel also makes the point that in the United States race is still very real, and the color line is constantly being drawn and redrawn in an anxious effort to fix it, with dangerous results. At the end of *Black No More* a mob lynches a white Ku Klux Klan character because they have learned that he has the proverbial "one drop" of black blood. The ending of *Incognegro* mirrors the ending of *Black No More* in that the "black" character who has been passing for "white" manages to have a KKK grand wizard marked out for lynching in his stead. Yet, as Theresa Fine has pointed out, readers never see this actual lynching, as they see several others in the text, so the Klansman's fate is put into the hands of the reader (119). This is another aspect of the graphic novel's writerly ending, for it is up to us to decide whether we will imaginatively deliver the final blow, whether we will (in our minds) lynch the KKK man or set him free.

Another aspect of the graphic novel's rewriting of the ending of *Black No More* is that the KKK man in Schuyler's text is discovered to have the proverbial "one drop" of black blood that makes him black. Conversely, the Klansman in Johnson and Pleece's text is never shown to have any "black" blood. Blackness and white-ness are therefore depicted as permanent and abiding illusions, pushing beyond Schuyler's text, where it appears that racial lines are redrawn at the text's end to some degree. *Black No More* also concludes with an interracial family composed of the main character (a "whitened" Negro) and his white wife and mixed-race child in France (not the United States), suggesting that it is only outside the United States that the racial line can cease to be drawn. Johnson and Pleece, conversely, have the central character choose to remain in the United States, maintaining identities as both black and white, despite its history of pervasive racial violence. *Incognegro*'s revision of *Black No More*, then, provides no end to racial violence, but it also keeps open the possibility of a color line that is more permeable and fluid than fixed and closed, even in the United States in this his-torical era.

A third intertextual reference point is present in the main character's name—Zane Pinchback—which alludes to another famous racial passer, Jean Toomer (1894–1967), born Nathan *Pinchback* Toomer. While there has been some con-troversy about how and when Toomer passed for white, it is certain that he was light-skinned enough to do so; there is also ambiguity about whether his grandfa-ther—P. B. S. Pinchback—who did identify as black, was in fact of African Amer-ican descent. By simply calling their central character Zane Pinchback, Johnson and Pleece draw on a complicated history of racial mixing and crossing of various color lines. Toomer's text *Cane* (1923) also features a number of characters who pass across various color lines, only to be reprimanded by society for this; for example, in "Bona and Paul," Paul, who seems to be passing for white, is a subject of ridicule and curiosity: "Suddenly, he knew that he was apart from the people around him. . . . Suddenly he knew that people saw, not attractiveness in his dark skin, but difference" (75). Paul is leered at by a black doorman and abandoned by his white girlfriend, Bona. Paul is ultimately and (it seems) against his will forced into the category of "black." Zane Pinchback, unlike Paul in Toomer's short story, manages to keep his racial identity open and plural.[8]

The graphic novel thus transforms early twentieth-century passing texts, playing with them, turning historical figures such as Walter White and Jean Toomer into fictional ones and placing the names of actual people (such as George Schuyler) into the mouths of fictional characters. The graphic narrative also undermines the line between "fact" and "fiction" by mixing "real life," "authentic" narratives (such as Walter White's investigative journalism about lynching) with fictional ones such as the plot of Schuyler's *Black No More*. In so doing, it attempts to open up the history of racial passing in this time period and to turn it into a more writerly signifying system in which "fact" and "fiction" cannot be easily drawn apart.

Thematically, the graphic narrative also attempts to create a new racial logic in which anyone, black or white, can be a racial passer, an incognegro, a racial unknown; it therefore plays with the signifying system that creates race itself. There are at least three incognegros in the book: the white-looking black man Zane; his friend Carl, who attempts to take over this role to impress a girlfriend; and, finally, the Ku Klux Klan man who is supposed to be lynched in Zane's place at the end of the novel (and a photo is then printed in the newspaper listing him as the *real* Incognegro). All three characters thus take on the signifier of the "Incognegro." That a white man also fulfills this role suggests, as does the shading of the characters within the frames themselves, that race is not real but performed. To fully understand this redrawing of the passing genre, however, a closer examination of the way blackness and passing are presented from a graphic point of view is necessary.

The Visual Rhetoric of Passing in *Incognegro*: When Black and White Is Not Black and White

As Caron has noted, because most of the characters in the text are drawn in a way that makes their racial identity indistinguishable (that is, the text does not shade or shadow most black characters to suggest their race), in many instances it becomes impossible to determine race visually. Furthermore, because the text contains no color illustrations, skin tone is not usually rendered—that is, it is not possible to tell whether someone has skin that looks light brown, dark brown, coffee-colored, tan, pink, white, and so on. Race therefore must be discerned through action, dialogue, character speech, context, or other *nonvisual* markers—a point that coheres with the way passing narratives often undermine racial visuality (the passer "looks white") but also complicates it, since the majority of individuals in the book (those who can and those who cannot pass for white) are drawn as racially ambiguous. In this regard, the visual illustrations undermine one strand of the hegemonic logic of racial rhetoric in the time period depicted, a time period that saw the codification of the "one drop" rule in census taking and legal discourse, the rise of eugenics, and the passage of laws such as Virginia's Racial Integrity Act of 1924.[9] In various ways, these historical developments tended to focus on racial segregation and difference, as well as the idea that race could be discerned through visual tests or cues such as bluish half-moons on fingernails, pinkish palms, or a "'telltale kink in the hair'" (Sollors 145; see also 142–62). The hegemonic ideology of race in this time period insisted that, no matter how minute, racial differences would manifest themselves, and the "one drop" of black blood would somehow become evident.

Incognegro, set directly in the time period of the rise of the one-drop rule and of racial eugenics, tends to work against racial separation and difference by refusing visually to portray black racial difference and by turning the gaze of the "black" racial subject back onto the viewer (see figure 1.2). In figure 1.2, for example, all the characters consider themselves to be African American, but none of them carry characteristics that mark them as such: by skin color, way of speaking, and hair styles and texture they appear to be white, or perhaps Spanish, Italian, or Greek.[10] Moreover, most of the frames on this page focalize faces—each frame contains at least one face looking directly forward at the reader, as if daring them to see blackness in these "black" faces. Blacks are the object of the reader's gaze, but they are not visually black, as the buildings, coats, hair, and even the walls of the flat are. The page achieves a kind of chiaroscuro effect, especially in the second top panel, where the face of the character is clear and highlighted and functions as a kind of visual hook, while the background is dark. Here, black (racial) characters do not in fact appear black (visually), and in the work as a whole "whites" are drawn in the same style as blacks, further eroding the logic of racial visibility. McCloud argues, "When you enter the world of the cartoon—you see yourself," and "the cartoon is a vacuum into which our identity and awareness are pulled" so that "we don't just observe the cartoon, we become it" (*Understanding Comics* 36). We can see this process at work in figure 1.2, as both white and black readers could project themselves into these faces, which mostly lack visual particularity. Carl is shown with a mustache, but in many of the panels the faces look like masks into which a reader—black or white—could easily project him or herself.

Moreover, the scene in which Zane "transforms" also makes the point that visual racial categories are constructs and again encourages what McCloud would call viewer identification and involvement (204) through a certain level of facial nonparticularity. In figure 1.3, Zane moves from being a "black" person to a white

Figure 1.2. Mat Johnson
(writer) and Warren Pleece
(illustrator), *Incognegro*
(2008): 14.

Figure 1.3. Mat Johnson
(writer) and Warren Pleece
(illustrator), *Incognegro*
(2008): 18.

one, yet he looks little different in the first shot (top left-hand corner) versus the last shot (bottom right-hand corner). As Zane steps "outside of history" (Johnson and Pleece 18) by becoming white and therefore invisible, we see that his transformation from a visible black man to an invisible white one is really no transformation at all. And indeed, the very small gutters between the frames of this page—and the flipping from past to present—assume a permeability of racial identities across time. Black is white here and white is black, as the page plays with historical and visual boundaries; as the reader moves across the page (from left to right) horizontally, he or she also moves historically through hundreds of years of racial formation, from past rapes of black women (upper right panel) to the production of someone like Zane, a "white Negro."

The page, then, quite literally forces a contemporary reader to *see* history, to see a history that has been erased. This erased history is Zane's protection, but its erasure does not mean that it has ceased to exist. "Since white America refuses to see its past," comments Zane, "they can't really see me too well, either" (18). Zane's face also appears particularly blank in the top and bottom panels, encouraging a reader (whether black or white) to see Zane and comprehend the history to which he alludes—a history of rape and miscegenation that produces not only the specific reporter Incognegro but a whole nation of (white and black) incognegros. The panels themselves initially are small and confining, and of uneven sizes, leading to a feeling of claustrophobia and even fear, until we get to the final panel, which stretches across the page, revealing Zane looking at himself in the mirror. Clearly, the authors mean to hold a mirror up that reflects backward into history but also forward into the present moment, at readers who may see themselves in Zane or in his mirrored reflection.

In figures 1.2 and 1.3, the text's visual rhetoric—its words and pictures and the interactions between them—thus imply that black is white and white is black in an endless cycle of racial construction and deconstruction. The text balances its meaning between the visual (image) and rhetorical (language) poles, giving primacy to neither. However, complicating the idea that race is meaningless is the fact that Zane's identity as "black" is "discovered" at one point in the text by a black man who distinguishes Zane from his brother Alonzo, who (it seems) looks exactly like Zane except that his skin is somewhat darker. In figure 1.4 we see this "recognition" scene.

There are several interesting aspects of this page. First, the wagon driver—Josiah Ryder—is clearly identified as black through his reference to "white folks" as an othered group who are "damn dangerous" (64). It is also evident that Zane actually believes in the ideology that his one drop of black blood will manifest itself somehow when he asks Josiah: "How did you know [my race]? . . . Is my kink showing?" That Zane to some extent believes in the ideology of one drop,

Figure 1.4. Mat Johnson
(writer) and Warren Pleece
(illustrator), *Incognegro*
(2008): 64.

Figure 1.5. Mat Johnson
(writer) and Warren
Pleece (illustrator),
Incognegro (2008): 62.

even while the text as a whole works to dismantle the concept, shows the fixity of this idea within consciousness in this historical moment. The last panel's layout—with Zane's white, clear features outlined in the bottom left and Ryder's darker arms and face taking up roughly three quarters of the frame—visually emphasizes the symbolic presence of a racial darkness that threatens to engulf the whiteness of the racial passer. So some characters, it appears, believe they have a real racial marker that threatens to overshadow their putative "whiteness."

Blackness as such also manifests itself in other ways. As mentioned previously, Zane's brother Alonzo is never shaded as dark in the text, as some of the other African American characters are. But it is not entirely true, as one reviewer claims, that the novel lacks "distinguishing color cues" regarding race (Gustines) in terms of all characters. In figure 1.5, for example, we see Johnson and Pleece playing (again) with shade, putting a woman who *appears* to be black under an umbrella that *appears* to shade her dark skin, but we also see an unambiguous shot (in the second panel) of a man sitting in sunlight whose face is specifically colored as black. These frames stretch across the page at an almost leisurely pace, mirroring the pose Zane assumes as he watches the magic of the South—its calmness and peace, which only hides a deep racial violence—unfurl.

As viewers, we are therefore given plenty of time to observe the "black" characters. Zane's perspective seems to be the organizing one in this scene; as we see in the second, third, and last panel, he is the one viewing the man fishing and the woman selling corn. Perhaps the graphic narrative means to show here how Zane sees blackness in the South, the land of his birth, and how he reads race into various figures of the rural landscape. But if a goal of this text is to undermine and remix the visual logic of race, why include figures that are drawn as black, such as the man fishing in the water in the second panel? To understand the meaning of this particular detail we must look at other graphic narratives that portray blackness and passing. *Incognegro* also redresses these visual traditions to produce a text in which racial identity *is* written into the text in a nonstereotypical way, even as its stability is questioned. As such, the graphic narrative moves beyond the historical time frame in which it is set to take on a broader history of the portrayal of African Americans within comics in the latter half of the twentieth century.

Representations of African Americans and Passing in Comics: Always Already Stereotyped?

As many critics have noted, until recently African Americans have been represented only in stereotypical ways in comics (Aldama, *Your Brain* 30; Wanzo 95–96). Some authors have even claimed that a type of stereotyping—or "simplification"—is necessary for comics to make meaning. Will Eisner has argued influentially and infamously, "Comic book art deals with recognizable reproductions of human conduct. Its drawings are a mirror reflection, and depend on a reader's stored memory of experience to visualize an idea or process quickly. This makes necessary the simplification of images into repeatable symbols. Ergo, stereotypes" (*Graphic Storytelling* 11). Of course, there is a great deal of debate about this practice, with some critics contending that these stereotypes are only conventions (Barker 127), while others assert that they embody ideological beliefs about race (Gordon 62).[11] Leaving aside for a moment whether it is true that cartoons *must* rely on stereotypes, it is certainly clear that many early classic cartoons—including those by Eisner—deploy stereotypes in their representation of African Americans. For example, Eisner's Ebony White in his 1940s comic book series *The Spirit* (1940–52) is an example of how blacks become symbols of bestiality and simplicity. Ebony White's age is ambiguous; he sometimes appears to be a young boy, while at other times he is an adult who drives a taxi.[12] Nonetheless, he wears the visage of a monkey and has big bulging eyes and red lips that perhaps allude to the minstrel show's caricature of blackness. Classic comics are filled with such racist depictions, as has been argued many times before.[13]

The tradition of portraying blackness in exaggerated or stereotypical ways is not the domain of white cartoonists only, however. African American cartoonists have sometimes reacted against this buffoonery by overemphasizing blackness and by turning blackness into a type of textual blankness in which faces cannot be seen at all. Such seems to be the case in Kerry James Marshall's *Rythm Mastr* (1999–) comics series. His figures seem stock and primitive, and emotions cannot be easily written onto their black, dark faces. Undoubtedly, as Rebecca Wanzo argues, Kerry is aware that historically "caricature has been one of the most important aesthetic modes of comic production, but the phenotypic excesses of caricature produce challenges for creators of black characters, who recognize that blacks are always already stereotyped when their bodies are represented" (97).[14] Other African American authors of graphic narratives have portrayed blacks in a hyperbolic fashion that seems to be straight out of blaxploitation filmmaking. For example, this hyperbolic representation of blackness is present in the 1990s *Brotherman* comics series created by the artist/writing team of Dawud Anyabwile and Guy A. Sims. Each character in the series—including Brotherman himself— is larger than life and exaggerated. The characters are also sexualized in ways that fit with historical portrayals of African Americans. Lola Hubris/The Seductress is able, for example, as her "superpower" to "render men her puppets" and force them to succumb to the "veil of her beauty," echoing the historical stereotype of the Jezebel.[15] These images seem to harp heavily on stereotypes of blackness: the Jezebel, the Bad Man, the sexualized predator, and so forth. Of course, as Leonard Rifas observes, "merely noting the presence of images of racial difference fails to account for the ways that cartoonists use these images, which might be satiric, ironic, parodic, or even idiotic" (35). Even today, however, comics often perpetuate stereotypes of the past. As Marc Singer notes, they may contain either "token characters who exist purely to signify racial clichés," or there may be a "more subtle system of absence and erasure that serves to obscure minority groups even as the writers pay lip service to diversity" (118).[16] But must African Americans be always already stereotyped in comic books?

This is precisely why *Incognegro* does include some visually black characters— the text explores nonstereotypical representations of blackness and is in an intertextual graphic dialogue with this historical tradition in the comics. Characters that are drawn as black in *Incognegro* therefore are not portrayed in exaggerated or stereotypical ways, either physically or linguistically (see figures 1.4 and 1.5). Moreover, the black wagon driver, Josiah Ryder, in figure 1.4 is portrayed as intelligent enough to pick out Zane's race, and he is also given dialogue that refutes the more educated, supposedly more sophisticated Zane:

> ZANE: White folks see what they want to see. That's what makes them so easy to fool with this passing thing.
> RYDER: White folks do see what they want to see. And that's what makes them so damn dangerous. If you going to help Pinchy, or even help yourself, you best not forget that. (64)

In a certain sense this is the message of the book as a whole: that race does and does not exist. For Ryder, who is dark-skinned, race *does* exist as more than mere "role playing"—whites see his physical difference, and that makes them dangerous; and yet it does not exist physically for someone like Zane who can pass, who can play the role of whiteness. The fact that such a complex message about ideology is put into the mouth of a man who is dark-skinned (Ryder cannot pass for white) is telling in light of the historical stereotyping of blackness in comics. This gesture goes against a visual and rhetorical tradition in which blacks often play the roles of Sambos, too simple to understand the complexities of the world grasped by whites with their supposedly more sophisticated intellect. Giving Ryder these words also functions as a remix of previous texts in which blackness was used to reify racial categorizations.

Incognegro also samples and remixes a prior comics tradition in which the subject of racial transformation or racial passing (from black to white or vice versa) is treated in a way that reifies and stabilizes whiteness, in opposition to a blackness that is portrayed as bestial, servile, or disempowered. For example, C. C. Beck, the creator of Captain Marvel (Billy Batson), depicts Billy going into blackface and becoming a parody of a black man (see figure 1.6). We must note Billy's stereotypical language here: "is you sho' we is gonna be all right, mistuh bossman?" to which Edward Smith responds, "why certainly, Rastus. You're just

Figure 1.6. C. C. Beck (artist), Pete Costanza (penciler), and Bill Parker (writer), "Captain Marvel Rides the Engine of Doom," *Whiz Comics*, no. 12 (Jan. 1941), rpt. in *The Shazam! Archives*, vol. 1 (1992): 168.

as safe as if you were in bed in your own little cabin in the cotton" (168). Racial transformation thus replicates, verbally and pictorially, stereotypes about whiteness and blackness.

The subject of racial passing has also been treated in comics in ways that support stereotypes and stereotyping. For example, in the lead story, "I Am Curious (Black)" in the comics magazine *Superman's Girl Friend, Lois Lane* (1958–74), no. 106 (1970), Lois Lane tries to understand the lives of the black citizens of Metropolis by asking Superman to use Kryptonian powers to transform her into a black person. In so doing, she echoes a group of actual white reporters who "became black" in order to investigate racism from 1940 to 1970—journalists such as Ray Sprigle (1886–1957), Grace Halsell (1923–2000), and (most famously) John Howard Griffin (1920–80). If we compare Lois's scene of transformation (the cover image) in figure 1.7 with Zane's (see figure 1.3) we can see the racial logic at work here. For the creators of *Superman's Girl Friend* race is an essence—her breasts

Figure 1.7. Robert Kanigher (writer), Werner Roth (penciler), and Vince Colletta (inker), *Superman's Girl Friend, Lois Lane,* no. 106 (Nov. 1970): cover.

become larger, her thighs heavier, and her hair curlier in this transformation from white to black—whereas Zane's transformation is really no transformation at all.

Moreover, in the narrative, the impetus for Lois's transformation is a stark division between black and white—no black person will speak to her when she is white and trying to investigate their lives. This division only ends when Superman saves the day, rescuing both Lois and a black man who has reviled her (in her white self). The implication is that black and white are separate and that blacks need whites to help them with their racial struggle. The text does end with Lois (returned now to whiteness) shaking hands with the black man who once reviled her, but it seems that only the deus ex machina of Superman's arrival can achieve this reconciliation between black and white. This is an imperative of classic comics as a whole, of course—the superhero generally arrives to "save the day," but in this particular narrative this denouement tends to stabilize the meaning of whiteness and blackness, a point that Pleece and Johnson may wish to redress.

More recent comics have also treated passing and passers in a somewhat stereotypical manner. For example, Kid Quantum (James Cullen) in *Legion of Super-Heroes* (1989–2000), no. 33 (1992), created by Tom Bierbaum et al., appears to be a young black man but is actually an alien Protean, a shape shifter (see figure 1.8). However, the race that Kid Quantum comes from—the Proteans—are described as being viewed "for decades . . . as unintelligent house pets" (Singer 111). Moreover, Kid Quantum is less a singular identity than an amalgam of the Protean race who has shape-shifted into a human form. Last, although viewers know that he is a shape shifter, we do not see Cullen shift from race to race. He may be an amalgamation of minds and races, but visually he remains black, only transforming into other black identities.

Comics that feature the subjects of black-white passing therefore often repli-

Figure 1.8. Tom Bierbaum et al., *Legion of Super-Heroes*, no. 33 (September 1, 1992): 18.

cate stereotypes of blackness and whiteness and a color line that separates both groups. Johnson and Pleece, on the other hand, refuse to draw a visual color line over which Zane must cross in order to pass for white; therefore, they imply that white is black and black is white, and the identities are the same visually for Zane, Carl, and others. On a deeper level, the text also struggles to remix comics featuring blacks by undermining stereotypes of blackness itself. Caron does not read the images in *Incognegro* as a "direct response to or rebuttal against the myriad racist caricatures to be found in the work of various cartooning giants" but posits instead that "Johnson and Pleece take as their subject the very act of representing race" (139). I would argue that both these goals are at work. Johnson and Pleece's black characters do exist in the text, outside of the shadows to which Caron draws attention (155), yet they are not "simplified" or stereotyped. In fact, they are quite varied. We see black, white, and mixed-race characters; we see working-class, upper-class, and educated African Americans; we see people who speak in dialect and people who do not; we see both southern and northern blacks. Both the passing plot and the text's portrayal of black characters therefore diversify representations of blackness.

We can also see Johnson and Pleece using a characteristic convention of comics—the split persona—to dramatize the instability of racial and gendered identity: Zane has two personas, his black one and his role as the reporter Incognegro; his friend Carl switches places with him and so becomes both Carl and Incognegro; the gender passer Francis/Frances Jefferson-White has both a male and female identity; and so on. Singer argues that comics "possess a highly adaptable set of conventions" and that a few titles "display the genre's and medium's potential by using the generic vocabulary of the secret identity to externalize and dramatize the conditions of minority identity in America" (118). Johnson and Pleece use this convention of the split or dual identity—a convention that we might also note is embedded in the passing narrative—to a similar end. The citing, quoting, and remixing of the passing narrative as a literary genre and of comics portraying blackness and passing through a visual-verbal text thereby moves toward a new and more open and writerly construction of the meaning of race. The text also uses past cultural productions to comment on the present-day meaning of race. It samples and remixes passing narratives of the past, in other words, to show how they are not truly in our past but are also an erased part of our present history.

The visual rhetoric of *Incognegro*—its words and pictures taken together—attempts to create a blackness that is *not* stereotypical but does exist. In so doing, Pleece and Johnson also address the current state of race relations in the United States—a state of race relations in which race as color still does matter very much, despite the fact that we are supposedly "postracial," as the recent deaths of Trayvon Martin (1995–2012), Eric Garner (1970–2014), Michael Brown (1996–2014), Sandra Bland (1987–2015), Alton Sterling (1979–2016), Philando Castile (1983–2016), and so many others illustrate. Pleece and Johnson reclaim the history of African American portrayal in the comic book tradition through characters who are visually black, mixed race, and white, but they revise this history so that blackness is not represented in a stereotypical way. They also remix the passing narrative, moving it toward an open and writerly system in which individuals can choose multiple racial identities. Yet by creating some characters who are marked visually as black (and who cannot pass for white), they also speak to the current context of race in the supposedly postmodern, postracial, and even posthuman moment we live in *now*, in which race both does and does not matter, and both is and is not written onto the skins of individuals as visual blackness. Conventional history may be, as Toni Morrison has commented, written by the "conqueror" in such a way that it "supports and complements a very grave and almost pristine ignorance" about the past.[17] However, Johnson and Pleece's graphic mystery attempts to use the passing narrative to open up this "innocence" and to allow a reader to *see* invisible aspects of this past history. Perhaps most importantly, the text redraws this past history in order to create a more open conceptualization of the ideologies that subtend formations of blackness, whiteness, and race itself— and to create a signifying system that a reader not only can consume, but also can write, rewrite, and redress.

NOTES

A shorter version of this paper was delivered at the American Literature Association Conference in Boston, Massachusetts, on May 28, 2011; I thank my fellow panelists—Danny Anderson, Jorge Santos, and Tof Eklund—for helpful feedback. The following individuals also offered extremely helpful suggestions on various drafts: Anna Mae Duane, Shawn Salvant, Kathy Knapp, Michael Gil, Alexis Boylan, and especially Cathy Schlund-Vials.

1. Of course, Mat Johnson is well known for his novels about individuals who identify as African American yet can pass for white, such as his most recent book *Loving Day* (2015), in which a mixed-race father learns he has a daughter who does not know she is biracial and believes herself to be white. *Incognegro*, however, is the only graphic novel in which Johnson deals with the subject of racial passing.

2. Critical essays on *Incognegro* by Kenji Gonda, Tim Caron, Theresa Fine, and Robert Loss do not address the subject of racial passing per se but tend to focus either on the portrayal of lynching or race. Still, I am indebted to many of Caron's insights about the meaning of race in the text and Fine's and Loss's about the text's portrayal of lynching. Frederick Luis Aldama also briefly mentions *Incognegro* in "Multicultural Comics Today" (14).

3. The text is written by Mat Johnson, with art by Warren Pleece.

4. For another essay that uses the concept of remix, see James Braxton Peterson.

5. Well-known examples from this era include Charles W. Chesnutt's *The House Behind the Cedars* (1900) and Nella Larsen's *Passing* (1929), in which passing characters die; Frances Harper's *Iola Leroy, or Shadows Uplifted* (1892) and Walter White's *Flight* (1934), in which passing characters refuse to pass or ultimately go back to their "true" race; and William Dean Howell's *An Imperative Duty* (1891), James Weldon Johnson's *Autobiography of an Ex-Colored Man* (1912), and Jessie Redmon Fauset's *Plum Bun* (1928), in which passing characters stay in Europe.

6. For a more detailed discussion of the relationship between Zane and Walter White, see Fine 117–18.

7. These details are taken from White's autobiography, *A Man Called White*.

8. A whole strand of texts in the passing narrative tradition feature female-to-male gender crossing, and *Incognegro* also samples this tradition through several female characters who pass as male. There is a blurring, then, of both racial and gender boundaries in *Incognegro*.

9. The language of "one drop" was codified in 1920 by the Census Bureau. The term "mulatto" was eliminated, and the bureau stipulated that "the term 'white' . . . refers to persons understood to be pure-blooded whites. . . . A person of mixed white . . . and Negro . . . is classified as . . . a Negro . . . regardless of the amount of white blood" (Bureau of the Census, 1923).

10. This is not to imply that the novel uses no visual markers of race for its passing (or near-white) characters. For example, fashion choices such as clothes, hairstyles, facial hair, and so on sometimes provide visual markers within the story, especially when contrasted with those of white characters. But it is to state that race is not generally written onto the skin of the passing characters (it is not an epidermal characteristic). Moreover, as I show elsewhere, in the novel darker-skinned characters who cannot pass are often shaded with darker hues of ink.

11. For an excellent discussion of this debate, see Singer 108–10.

12. Eisner has acknowledged that Ebony White is a stereotype and explained his creation this way: "The only excuse I have for [that portrayal] is that at the time humor consisted in our society of bad English and physical difference in identity. Later I attempted to depart from it by having a black character, a detective, who spoke proper English and I had an airplane pilot that was black" ("Never Too Late").

13. One particular issue of *Batman* (1940–2011) features a black waiter who also looks simian-like. See "Addressing Ebony White."

14. Also see Wanzo's discussion of how Marshall incorporates "aspects of African American history, African mythology and aesthetics, and Bunraku puppetry" into this series (97–98).

15. See *Brotherman*.

16. For a longer discussion of these images, see Fredrik Strömberg. With few exceptions, until the late 1960s classic comics featured images that, according to Strömberg, "often simplify and stereotype their subjects" (23). More recently, some cartoon lines have sought to create nonstereotypical versions of blackness. In 2010 DC Comics's *Action Comics*, no.

9 presented a black Superman who was not drawn with stereotypical features. See also Singer's discussion of Tony Isabella's *Black Lightning* (1995) series and Chris Cross's *Xero* (1997–98) series. For a longer discussion of recent comics featuring African American superheroes, see Adilifu Nama.

17. From Portland State University's Oregon Public Speakers Collection: "Black Studies Center public dialogue. Pt. 2," May 30, 1975 (http://bit.ly/1vO2hLP). Part of the Public Dialogue on the American Dream Theme, via Portland State University Library (http://pdxscholar.library.pdx.edu/orspeakers/90/).

CHAPTER 2

Nostalgic Realism

Fantasy, History, and Brer Rabbit–Trickster
Ambiguity in Jeremy Love's Bayou

Taylor Hagood

THE GRAPHIC NOVEL *Bayou*, created, written, and illustrated by Jeremy Love from 2007 to 2009, is a uniquely hybrid production on many levels, from its digital-print publication history to its content and style that blend the edginess of an independent comic with the slick look of a DC "property." This hybridity extends to *Bayou*'s treatment of the history of race and violence in the U.S. South. Love's approach to history is distinctly postmodern, ranging through images and themes with a lurking awareness of the simulacra from which they emerge and viewing history through cultural mythologies and stereotypes instead of under the pretense of a "straight-ahead" treatment. As Qiana J. Whitted explains it, "Such visual and verbal codes allow *Bayou* to signify southern history not merely as a series of cultural scripts . . . but as a microcosm of competing fictions the reader is forced to negotiate" (208).[1] What is surprising and brilliant about *Bayou*—what sets it apart—is that it appropriates some of the most powerful and pernicious elements of southern white figuration in a way that is violent yet simultaneously beguiling. Specifically, this comic, created by an African American author/artist, unsettlingly casts racist stereotypes as signifying in both negative *and* positive ways. The ambivalence created by this technique creates a tension that might be thought of as a kind of nostalgic realism in that it fearlessly treats "real" themes of violence and cruelty within the glowing atmosphere of fantasy inherent in the graphic novel's literary ancestor and model: the Uncle Remus tales, written by Joel Chandler Harris in the late nineteenth century and embodied in the Walt Disney film *Song of the South* (1946), which center on the highly problematic trickster Brer Rabbit. Unsurprisingly, Brer Rabbit plays a central role in *Bayou*, and his trickster ways, with their irresolvable embracing of seeming binaries, mirror the comic's paradoxical blend of nostalgia and realism. The resulting text is one that finds magic in a simultaneous recuperation and deconstruction of a racist past.

Nostalgia and Realism, Sources and Intentions

Neither "nostalgia" nor "realism" is an absolute with simple functions in *Bayou*. In fact, I apply these terms idiosyncratically as labels designed to identify movements and strategies rather than as clearly defined concepts. In the schematic I am employing to track the complex dynamics of the comic, the terms "nostalgia" and "realism" might best be thought of in the same way that the "debit" and "credit" columns of double-entry bookkeeping function. These two terms, "debit" and "credit," do not signify as they do in everyday language but instead operate functionally to follow the movement of money in regard to assets and liabilities. Just as an entry in the debit column necessarily precipitates an entry in the credit column with the two working to identify movements in a constantly maintained equilibrium, elements of nostalgia and realism function together in *Bayou* and do not necessarily identify an essential type. Such elements can actually perform as both, so that an image that might be thought of as functioning nostalgically at one point might operate as an element of realism at another. It is because images, elements, and characters can cross the line between a nostalgic function and a realistic function so seamlessly that *Bayou* creates its unsettling effects. An item's function derives not from inherent value but rather from its play within the textual fabric.

While the movements I am calling "nostalgia" and "realism" do not function as absolutes, Love nevertheless mobilizes elements in relation to the binary they represent, which makes it advantageous to identify their contours. I thus designate "nostalgia" as referring to aspects of an element, image, character, or dialogue that present from a past that lays claim to an existence outside of historicity, while "realism" gestures to a feasible historical specificity. This does not imply that something performing as nostalgic in the graphic novel is necessarily ahistorical or that something identifiable as realistic must necessarily be characterized by rigorous historical marking. For example, a panel rendered in a more exaggeratedly cartoonish style might well perform realistically while a panel drawn in a style that approaches realism, or even photorealism, may operate nostalgically. Again, I employ these terms in order to identify an element's performance in a given textual moment.

These performance-movements of nostalgia and realism map onto two additional binary spectrums. The first corresponds most readily to nostalgia, and I am designating it the spectrum of comfort-horror. Nostalgic aspects can slide along the spectrum between evoking a sense of delight and comfort or of horror and disdain; the power of *Bayou* resides in its tendency to strike the middle of that spectrum so deftly that it can emerge as both horrifying and comforting simultaneously. The other spectrum, which corresponds with realism, is that of fantasy-actuality. I use the term "actuality" here partly to avoid the confusion of reusing "reality" but also to designate a different value of "realness" than the effective one of the larger nostalgia-realism binary; "actuality," for my purposes, *does* refer to an absolute in referencing specific place and time.[2] Unlike the comfort-horror spectrum, the gradation zone between fantasy and actuality features a line of demarcation in the form of a nominal border between what might be thought of as the realm of the fantastic and the realm of the actual historical Mississippi of 1933. While the fantastic and the actual serve as ostensibly static places, the line between them is hardly fixed because throughout the graphic novel characters cross that line, and plenty of elements from the realm of the fantastic appear in the realm of the actual.

Bayou plies this array of spectrums to generate tensions of ambiguity, conflicting emotive effects, and ambivalence of evident intention, all of which derive from the graphic novel's sources and Love's complex engagement with them. Love has cited two major sources: one is photographic, as he has explained that when he was a child his family had a book of photographs of African Americans taken during the first half of the twentieth century.[3] This book made a deep impact on his imagination and visual register. Apparently, the book was lost at some point, but when he was an adult Love found a copy, and it served as an important guide for many of the drawings in *Bayou*. A number of the images in the graphic novel actually replicate those in the book. It is difficult to discuss such a source without access to it, impossible to know if it presented Love with positive or negative images of African American life or both. It would appear that such a source would enforce the graphic novel's realism in its presentation of images of the actual.

Even though this source primarily offers the precedent and medium of "photorealism," however, it is also affected by subjectivity and even nostalgia. It must be acknowledged that photographs are more complicated than the simple realism they are capable of projecting, carrying the elements of posing, lighting, angle, and so on. Beyond these built-in complexities, though, Love intimates that the photographs signaled more than a simple realistic visual engagement, for the book was a family possession and thus one deeply connected in Love's mind with his family's roots in North Carolina, which existed as a fascinating and romantic place for him—a romance Love assigns to the South generally. In an interview with John Hogan, Love answers the question, "What is your experience with the territory you depict in *Bayou*?" with, "My extended family and ancestry are southern. I was able to draw on the rich family history, stories, and anecdotes I've heard since I was a child. The smell, the wet heat, the food, and the general character of the south will always be a part of me. I think the fact that I see it as more of a childhood memory informs the dreamlike quality I'm trying to achieve with

Bayou" (Love, "Jeremy Love's"). This is a striking statement—evoking a romance of the South that often becomes associated with neo-Confederate nostalgia, but Love's understanding of the region is based on a southern African American store of experiences. It also speaks to the ways in which even elements of "realism" are ensconced in memory and emotion.

The other source of *Bayou* is distinctly nonrealistic and is instead a source of nostalgia par excellence: the Uncle Remus tradition. Love first encountered this source in childhood in the form of the Disney film *Song of the South*; despite its presentation of African American stereotypes, the film's lush animation and music apparently captured Love. The film, of course, distills the Uncle Remus stories of Joel Chandler Harris, and at some point Love began to read those as well so that by the time of his creating *Bayou*, Love was at least reasonably if not well acquainted with this nostalgic body of work. This tradition centers on the interaction of a community of talking animals, the most clever and dynamic of whom is Brer Rabbit, who repeatedly outwits his adversaries, most famously Brer Fox and the Tar Baby he creates to catch Brer Rabbit. Brer Rabbit is uncontainable and unpredictable, bringing all the unsettling qualities of one who moves in and out of legality and between the poles of ethical/unethical behavior. When Brer Fox cannot keep Brer Rabbit pinned down to Tar Baby because Brer Rabbit tricks him into throwing him in the briar patch, we might champion the rabbit as an underdog, but the line between resourcefulness and roguery is fine, and tricksters, including Brer Rabbit, always pose some level of danger.

The Uncle Remus tradition presents as vexed a source as the book of photographs seems to have been, not only because of the paradoxes of Brer Rabbit but also because of the tradition's material history. The original stories, penned by a white man from northern Georgia, are clearly part of the local color moment that made use of dialect generally considered demeaning to African Americans.[4] But, as Elizabeth Ammons and Valerie Rohy argue in the introduction to their anthology of local-color writing, frame narratives often functioned to center ostensibly marginal characters, giving a voice to regional figures otherwise not available to them. Harris, in particular, was dedicated to preserving African American dialect as "scientifically" as possible, and he includes in his second collection, *Nights with Uncle Remus* (1883), a semischolarly introduction attempting to parse the connections between African mythologies and the fables Remus tells. Moreover, in Remus's stories, not only do the animals such as Brer Rabbit, Brer Fox, and Brer Bear outwit each other, but they find themselves pitted against Mr. Man, who represents empowered whites, most specifically the white aristocratic southern class. This subversive element arguably sets Harris's work apart from that of, say, Thomas Nelson Page, who employs former slaves to perform the labor of narrating the nostalgic memories of the white aristocracy and former slaveholding class; R. Bruce Bickley Jr. observes, on the other hand, that "critics of the day saw Harris as the more authentic artist" (48).[5] As it is, though, Harris is a white writer presuming to write black people, and the 1946 film *Song of the South* that makes use of the Uncle Remus character and the animals he describes has been even more problematic for increasing numbers of viewers, far removed from the racial politics of Harris's post-Reconstruction moment. That this source serves Love in creating *Bayou* is thus vexed since its nostalgia is so fraught with the painful history of racism and race-inflected politics.

Taken together, these two sources—the one "realistic" yet tinged with nostalgia, the other nostalgic yet fraught with pernicious politics—display the irresolvability of *Bayou*'s two fundamental movements. The reader confronted with Love's lush illustrations in a story that features terrible violence might find herself positioned oddly. It is presumably easy to dismiss Harris's stories and the Disney film as creations of a white establishment (not just the authors and producers but the dominant culture of the moment in which they lived and which they upheld), and the reader might wonder why this resuscitation of those characters should be at all acceptable in the early twenty-first century. Presumably a white writer/artist producing such a creation would encounter serious suspicion, but even though an African American man's creation of such a graphic novel probably invites readers to look for its deconstructionist purposes, questions about the effects (looked for and unlooked for) of the work still might arise. *Bayou*'s unflinching treatment of lynching and its careful subversion of multiple racist stereotypes well show that Love means to turn the Remus tradition on its head. Indeed, as we shall see, Love explores the darker implications of Remus's animals and even Remus himself. At the same time, however, the overall visual style of the graphic novel evokes the color and magic of *Song of the South*, which readily accentuates its comfortable aspects but jars with the horror of the realistic history it engages. Where the reader might look for the jagged-line inking that signals a no-frills serious engagement with the dark shadows of history, instead he encounters a seductive warmth and glow in much if not most of the imagery in *Bayou*, even in the most ghastly scenes.

While I do not mean for my reference to Love's race to reduce him and his work to essentialized notions of authorial intent based on race, Love's authorship plays a role in how readers understand the text. In the earlier-cited interview, Hogan asks Love, "Where did you grow up?" to which Love answers, "I was born in North Carolina and grew up in Philadelphia, Pennsylvania, and Sacramento, California." Hogan follows up with, "How did you make sure you were accurately depicting the early 1930s in Mississippi?" to which Love rejoins with, "I have my parents and family members for small things, and I am a student of Southern history and folklore. It was something I was always interested in. However, I am not trying to create a docu-drama here. As long as it feels right, I'm fine" (Love, "Jeremy Love's"). This querying of autochthony commonly occurs regarding authors writing about the U.S. South; Hogan does not pursue the discussion based on race or possession of or entitlement to the topic of southern culture, and in fact the easy evocation of "southern" in the interview to refer to black culture in the South appears to be far from the conventional popular (and for many decades even academic) silent assumption that "southern" means "white." Still, the question about history seems odd in a graphic novel that does not present as purely historical—is Hogan asking Love if his depiction of talking animals is an "accurate" representation of "reality"? Or does his question pertain to "actual" race relations in 1930s Mississippi? The ambiguity of the question ultimately reflects the ambiguity of the comic itself, drawing as it does on both "history" and "folklore." At the heart of it, too, persists curiosity and perhaps assumption about what Love, as a black writer, is trying to accomplish.

Love himself foregrounds his positionality in creating *Bayou* in a way that conveys its hybridity, doubleness, and ambiguity. He tells Hogan,

> I've always been interested in the mythology of America. The south, in particular, seems like a haunted place. You have this region that is covered with blood but produces so much beauty. I never really felt connected to African mythology until I started reading Joel Chandler Harris' Uncle Remus tales. Seeing how elements of African mythology were interwoven with American folklore was the spark. What led me to the Uncle Remus tales was Disney's *Song of the South*, a film I've always had mixed feelings about. I felt I as an African American creator could reclaim that mythology.

Curiously, it is through the white writer Harris's work that Love finds his way to "African" mythology, hinting at the always already compromised nature of African American culture that has conventionally been presented by white writers, artists, and performers. Love's statement that he seeks to "reclaim" the mythology created by Harris, Disney, and the history of white racial hegemony is thoroughly keyed to his being a black man. One is reminded of Charles Waddell Chesnutt's efforts to appropriate and claim Thomas Nelson Page's techniques, exposing the plantation nostalgia of Page as a farce; as Keith Byerman has argued, however, Chesnutt's efforts largely failed because his appropriation looked to many readers of his moment like the real thing. In walking a vexed line between realism and nostalgia, Love's reclamation runs the same risk, which would presumably be best avoided by keeping always in the reader's view the fact that the comic is created by an African American man.

I choose to focus on Love's comments about the Remus tradition also and, finally, for the ways they work the term and concept of "mythology," since myth functions uniquely in relation to nostalgia and realism and can be seen as a force that steers elements into their varying performances. Love is answering Hogan's question about what inspired the comic, and after offering the above comments he adds, "I thought this world would be the perfect place to stage an epic fantasy tale. I could mash up elements of the Civil War, blues, African mythology, Southern Gothic and American folklore and show how they form a tapestry that is the American South." Despite his use of the word "fantasy," this "mash-up" more readily approaches the blend of history and fantasy that "myth" comes closer to describing. "Mythology" for Love seems to refer to legends, myths, and images that bear a tangential relationship to history per se yet at the same time have historical traction. The line between "history" and "myth" is very thin for Love (myth might even be thought of as carrying history with it as a kind of silent partner), and these two ontologies are especially problematic when appearing in comics and graphic narratives (especially one published by DC), given the fact that comics' legacy of sensationalism tinges even the most serious of productions. The actual history of the Civil War, folklore, mythology, and so on somehow come together to form a "tapestry," a figuration that suggests a number of varying threads making up the larger pattern or image and that together forge a fabric. If I may continue my evocation of that material, the idea of threads of a tapestry best approaches this comic's complexity and describes the somewhat elaborate schematic I am presenting.

Myth and its nominal opposite—history—describe the final operative force I seek to identify in *Bayou*. It is not difficult to discern in Love's rhetoric Claude Lévi-Strauss's "bricolage," and we might understand *Bayou* as operating within the kinds of strictures of myth that the structuralists identified. But Love is more postmodern than structuralist, and he seems to see these elements as historically tied and historicizable and yet also free-floating bits to seize and incorporate into his vision. He is offering a "fantasy epic," but it possesses the teeth of historicity and claims of authenticity. Love thus faces the same dilemma that Joseph Witek has seen in other creators presenting historical comics in that they must create narratives that "deploy the conventions of each medium to make truth claims about an event that is 'already told,' already so weighted with cultural significance that any telling risks the loss of its individual rhetorical force in the face of previously established readings and individual associations. Each teller must hew closely enough to the 'known' story to seem factually accurate while at the same time presenting a narrative emotionally compelling enough to be worth the retelling" (*Comic Books as History* 17). The "already told" for Love is never simply something told in the form of history nor even in any unproblematic way in the form of myth, since both are fraught with elements of each other.[6] The doubled logic of mythology (myth/history) guides the comic's elements through varying shades of comfort-horror and fantasy-actuality that resolve into the larger levels of nostalgia and realism.

The Graphic Style of *Bayou*

With these sources and the dynamics of nostalgic realism and their interconnections with comfort-horror/fantasy-actuality/mythology(-history) in mind, we can turn to the comic itself and see that it opens with a triad of panels/pages that sets the comic's visual tone via a group of images that appropriate white southern nostalgic motifs in unsettling ways. The opening panel takes up the entire first page and initiates the tense balance of comfortable fantastic nostalgia with reality (see figure 2.1). It presents a yellow sky with two large umbrella-shaped trees dominating the entire left side. They are set in the background and loom over a small black sharecropper cabin with a spindly disheveled fence surrounding it. The sun sits low and white just off center. The middle ground is made up of a cotton field, and in the right corner making up the extreme foreground a cotton stalk juts, adorned with cotton bolls. The panel evokes the opening scenes of the film *Gone with the Wind* (1939), with their painted image of Tara set far back against a dramatic orange sunset. But where Tara stands as the white Big House conventionally symbolizing slaveholding, the hut in Love's panel is black. Where the sanguine sky of *Gone with the Wind* heightens the drama of the operatic film it begins, the yellow sky here might be seen as either morning bright or perhaps indicative of neither morning nor evening but rather a kind of sick perpetual midday. In short, Love evokes an image from the visual history of southern plantation mythology and culture but reorients it into an image that foregrounds the classic elements of cotton and a house in a long shot into something seemingly pointing in a different direction. It is, as it were, the other side of the plantation, at once horrible and realistic yet strangely capable of evoking the nostalgic comforts of the fantastic.

The second panel (see figure 2.2), which solely occupies page 2, again presents ambivalent images of long-established signifiers of the South. The sky appears as a peaceful blue with a few light, white, fluffy clouds. A rust-colored pickup truck speeds past a sign bearing the Confederate flag with the words "Welcome to Charon, Mississippi" written across it. Under the sign, in grass of a smoky gray-green hue, are huddled three white rabbits and a gray one. A box in the bottom right corner states, "Charon, Mississippi 1933." The image offers a strange contrast of the innocent and noninnocent—the rabbits may or may not be aware of the truck or of the import of the sign underneath which they sit, although their presence (especially that of the gray one) foreshadows the centrality of Brer

Figure 2.1. Jeremy Love, *Bayou*,
vol. 1 (2009): 1.

Figure 2.2. Jeremy Love, *Bayou*,
vol. 1 (2009): 2.

Rabbit and the Remus tradition to the comic. Interestingly, the gray rabbit is the largest, and he is turned away from the other three and from the roadway where the truck is entering town; this rabbit signals hybridity and the manner in which a trickster figure "looks away" from convention. Meanwhile, conflict reigns in the image, for the Confederate emblem glares in what might without it seem a benign scene.

The third page of the comic rounds out this stage setting for the comic's vexed treatment of conventional southern signifiers in the text (see figure 2.3). It, too, is composed of a large single panel. In the print version of the comic, this page seems to point back to the previous panel on the page to the left: literally, an arrow in a sign mounted on a brick wall points to the "Colored Entrance." A crow stands on the sign, its head pointed the same direction as the gray rabbit in the panel before. Both point to an inset panel, which features five faceless white men and a white boy looking at the blood-dripping feet of a lynched black male.[7] The foot of the tree trunk on which the body hangs is the same color as the victim's skin, and it descends into what looks like a large foot that clutches into the grass. What look like black insects flit about the hanging body against the yellow sky (the larger panel features a blue sky). These insects again create a strange juxtaposition: at first glance, they appear to be flies surrounding the dead body, but closer inspection shows their shape to be butterfly-like, and the appearance of such hybrid flying insects in incongruous moments continues throughout the comic. What seems to be a stock image of racist terrorism might also be understood as an evocation of a magical albeit dystopic fairyland, with butterflies and a possibly humanoid tree changed from enchanted images to images of horror. Such appearance of elements from the realm of the fantastic into the realm of the actual typifies what Farah Mendlesohn refers to as a "liminal fantasy," which she sees as being "perhaps the most interesting because it is so rare [and can be characterized by a moment when] . . . the fantastic leaks back through the portal [dividing the realm of the fantastic from reality]" (xxii). With this panel, the reader encounters some of the central elements of the comic: racism, violence, children and their place in regard to that violence, and animals that signify in important ways. The South the reader encounters in *Bayou* is terrible, to be sure, and yet oddly enough a reader might be tempted by its lush colors and enchanted elements to want to go there despite its dangers.

These panels typify the nimble play of myth and history, comfort and horror in the realm of the actual, although there are moments when the text moves even closer to realism. A notable example is the newspaper story section titled "Tragedy on the Bayou," a kind of illustrated prose piece that includes a statue of the Confederate general Douglass M. "Hellhound" Bogg, which Love renders in a realistic style. Another identifiably realistic approach appears in the backstory

Figure 2.3. Jeremy Love, *Bayou*,
vol. 1 (2009): 3.

that Uncle Bedford offers the comic's heroine Lee Wagstaff when he gives her
a tomahawk belonging to his great-grandfather. The panels switch to a sepia
monotone that makes use of pencil work as well as inking, which signals a real,
true, historical moment.[8] The story tells of Uncle Bedford's heritage as a black
Choctaw. As he explains, "Way back, I reckon more than 100 years ago, Enoch
lived in an old Spanish fort in Florida. Injuns, Choctaw, Seminole, and Negroes
who run off from slavery, that was a safe place for them. They made a good life
for themselves in that swamp." The panels then show an image of the fort, which
presumably references Saint Augustine's Castillo de San Marcos, where the Seminole chief Osceola was held captive (see figure 2.4). Uncle Bedford narrates the
story of his great-grandfather Enoch's escape with the Seminole warrior (pictured
in two panels) who gave him the axe, as it is called, and a panel shows Enoch in
a Union uniform during the Civil War with a rifle in one hand and the blood-
dripping axe/tomahawk in the other. This scene differs from the standard mode
of presentation in *Bayou* because of the predominance of pencil work, which in
this case signifies a less "comic" aesthetic. At the same time, when Uncle Bedford
makes mention of "Old Hickory," a sketched portrait of Andrew Jackson appears.
Love sticks close to history in evoking hybrid Native and African Americans, in
yet another element of hybridity in the text, and the story seems fully anchored
in the historical. Yet Love places the entire story within the narrative voice of

Figure 2.4. Jeremy Love, *Bayou*,
vol. 1 (2009): 68.

Uncle Bedford, which works not exactly to compromise its historical accuracy
or historical truth value but does keep it from being in any way an unmediated
presentation of history.

Again, though, more often than not Love weaves the fabric of his narrative
in a more consistent albeit ambiguous blend of actuality-fantasy/history-myth/
comfort-horror. The bayou—the actual slow-moving body of water—serves a
vital function in this blend. On one hand, it exists both as a "real world" place that
harbors bodies and giant catfish and is the site of such events as body dumping
and abduction: "The Bayou is a bad place, Ain't nuthin' good ever happened
around there," Lee says in the comic's opening dialogue. At the same time, the
bayou harbors the border between the actual world of the comic's setting of 1933
and the realm of the fantastic. Although Love does not present the bayou as a
full-fledged swamp, he means for it to be the ungovernable space of horror that
Anthony Wilson has seen southern swamps as representing in literature and
film. The bayou also can be seen as being an actant in the comic in the way that
Jane Bennett describes compost to function, and this acting aspect of the bayou
finds incarnation in the fact that the titular character of the novel is a black man
named Bayou. Whitted is especially attuned to this aspect of Bayou when she

writes that his "immense stature, gentle manner, and green skin connect him to hybrid monsters like Swamp Thing whose physiology acts as an extension of their natural surroundings" (203). Bayou, the character, is a giant black man whose clothing suggests that he might more readily belong to the nineteenth century than to the early twentieth. A defender of Lee, even at terrible cost to himself (at the end of volume 2 he gets maimed and perhaps even dies), he functions as a bridge between the realm of the fantastic and the realm of the actual. He is both a figure enslaved to Bogg and a man who can cross over into the "real world." He might even be thought of as a kind of Remus figure in his relationship with Lee that might be seen as similar to Remus's relationship with children. Indeed, when Uncle Remus actually does appear in the comic, he resembles Bayou, although significantly he appears in a dream, where he attempts to lead Lee into trouble and turns into another golliwog-type monster when she does not acquiesce.[9] Unlike the Uncle Bedford section, however, the bayou and the character Bayou (with a few exceptions) all appear drawn in the same ways and in the same coloring, making it difficult for the reader to be sure exactly which world Lee is moving in, just as it is difficult for Lee to determine this herself.

Brer Rabbit, Trickster-Complicator

Central to all of the ambiguity of form and content in the comic is the character who shares the center of the story with Lee: Rabbit. Again, it is unsurprising in a comic so indebted to Harris's stories that Brer Rabbit should figure so largely, but what is interesting is the series of ways in which he does. After the initial image of the four rabbits huddled under the "welcome" sign to Charon, a rabbit next appears about a third of the way into volume 1 in the middle of Lee's dream, when she has been knocked out by white men who have come to arrest her father. The image appears in two panels on a single page, the top one revealing Lee facing a giant rabbit and the second offering a close-up of the rabbit (see figure 2.5). The figure of the rabbit is uncanny, occupying an unsettling liminal space between being alive and dead and creating a kind of horror that is attractive even as it is repelling. Obviously not a "real" rabbit, it might be the kind of talking rabbit that appears in *Alice in Wonderland*, or maybe it is a stuffed toy rabbit: it is unclear whether in the lower panel the question "where's Lily?" is being asked by the rabbit or by Lee. The rabbit's misspelling Lilly's name highlights the doubleness of the trickster and of the tendencies of the comic as a whole. If understood as a still and silent stuffed animal, the nostalgia and play suggested by the toy transforms, via the uncanny, into an image of horror. It is difficult to tell if this rabbit represents a friendly figure or a threatening one.

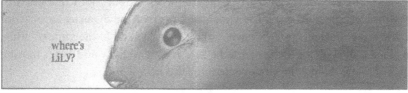

Figure 2.5. Jeremy Love, *Bayou*,
vol. 1 (2009): 62.

    This lack of clarity about whether the rabbit is good or bad, friend or foe, takes
center stage in volume 2. Just five pages in we see Brer Rabbit himself dressed
in convict's clothes, working on a chain gang with other animals that directly
evoke the stories of Harris. This moment blends into one of Lee's dreams in
which she encounters her mother, who tells her that people call her "Tarbaby,"
the name of the tar doll Brer Fox creates in order to trap Brer Rabbit in what is
surely the most famous of the Uncle Remus tales (and which recalls the image
of the possible stuffed toy rabbit as representing a kind of tar baby to which Lee
gets stuck).[10] Back in the waking world, Lee and Bayou are looking for Rabbit to
see if he can help them find Lilly; they go to his wife's house and find that he has
not been around in three months, at which point they go to his girlfriend's house
and see that his girlfriend and children have been murdered. Lee and Bayou then
proceed to Tarrypin's Juke Joint, which is peopled with characters straight out of
the Remus tradition. Finally, Lee and Bayou find Rabbit on the chain gang and
free him, for which Rabbit is not at all thankful, since he had found "peace" from
troubles on the chain gang. When Lee tells him, "I was thinking you can dig up a
story out yo' noggin that tells you where my friend is," Rabbit simply laughs and
says, "You fools came all the way here on the count of my stories? Ha ha ha!! I
lost dem stories in a dice game in Nawlins to Brer Fox!" The comic then moves

into a flashback of Charon, Mississippi, 1922; now Rabbit is not a talking cartoon rabbit but a (cartoon version of a) black man, who emerges from the bayou with none other than Bayou himself, drawn now not as a friendly monster but likewise as a man. Despite Bayou's concerns about what might happen if "Bossman find out we comin' topside," the two get dressed up to go to a juke joint to play blues (Bayou on the harmonica, Rabbit on the guitar) while Tarbaby sings. During a break in the music Tarbaby and Rabbit are making out backstage when Stagolee, the hammer of the Bossman, appears to punish Rabbit for coming to the "real" world. Stagolee tells him, "Bossman tried to fool you wit the Tar Baby before. Never figured it work the second time round. Ain't no Briar Patch to save you dis time." As Stagolee starts to cut Rabbit with a straight razor, we realize that just as in this comic there is no difference between Mr. Bossman the white writer (presumably Joel Chandler Harris and the white-dominated literary tradition) and Remus himself, we also can see how Brer Fox may well be an agent of the white power structure, as Stagolee is.

We might begin to think that Rabbit is essentially a "good guy" who suffers at the hands of the Bossman and his agents, but true to the form of Love's comic (and arguably to the trickster character of Brer Rabbit as Harris conceived of him) Rabbit's character is elusive. Rabbit leads Lee, Bayou, and a talking raccoon (who is a woman dressed as a man) to the house of a now-reformed prostitute named Miss Meadows that he would visit in the past, where he cooks a stew that he laces with drugs, putting everyone to sleep so he can make his getaway. It is at this point that Uncle Remus appears in Lee's drugged dream, and even as she sleeps Rabbit attempts to leave the group behind and go his own way. However, Miss Meadows, who has not fallen prey to Rabbit's trick, confronts him with the revelation that Lee is actually his child, saying, "You mean you don't know? Dat nappy headed-pigmeat. Her hide is black like Tarbaby, but she got da eyes of Bruh' Rabbit!" Suddenly, Stagolee appears again to kill Rabbit, only to be thwarted this time by Bayou and the raccoon—who shoots him down with a tommy gun. What resonates at the (current) stopping place of the story is Miss Meadows's revelation: just as *Bayou* is the descendant of Harris's stories and *Song of the South*, so the heroine of the book is the descendant of the trickster Brer Rabbit.

And yet Lee, despite bearing the name of the most famous Confederate, General Robert E. Lee, does not seem to have either the trickster traits of her father or the rambling traits of her mother. She wholeheartedly embraces people and things in her life, searching for Billy Glass, being friends with Lilly despite the girl's racism and betrayal of her, and fighting for her father with energy and devotion. If we accept the parallelism of Lee and the comic of which she is a part being the "children" of the Uncle Remus tradition, then we can access not just the similarities but also the *differences* between the descendants and their ancestors. The Brer Rabbit of Harris's work is a trickster figure in a body of literature that performs its own kinds of ventriloquist tricks, a group of stories designed to enlist the reader into sympathy with a stereotype of African Americans that even when rebelling against it perpetuates the division between the empowered white world and the black world thought to be made up of people conniving against each other. (Another version of this appeared famously in the radio and television program *Amos 'n' Andy* [on radio 1928–55, then as *The Amos 'n' Andy Music Hall* 1954–60; on television as *The Amos 'n Andy Show* 1951–53], in which African Americans swindle each other as they spin out quips all within the bubble of their own black world.) While Love could be understood as playing his own trick on that tradition, that very act of rewriting depends on a kind of simple honesty that works to expose the trick. Lee's uncompromising goodness serves to reflect on and define the comic's underlying goal of reclaiming the Uncle Remus tradition.

This reflection and defining is important to follow because, as noted earlier, Love's work runs the risk of seeming to promote the Uncle Remus tradition it is working to problematize. While some if not many readers would presumably perceive the ways Love works against the tradition, it is not at all inconceivable that readers of a background that cherishes *Song of the South* and perhaps even Harris's stories themselves could see in it a celebration of the Remus tradition. These latter readers might welcome the return of characters to whom they have formed emotional attachments, characters who signify not as creations of a rac-ist/racialist literary history but adorable animals who sing "Zip-a-dee-doo-dah, zip-a-dee-ay" and who populate the Disney World ride Splash Mountain. The matter of readership seems especially pertinent precisely because this produc-tion is a comic and not a work presenting itself as "literature," by which I mean a work that is strictly verbal and clearly aimed at a literate and literary audience. Certainly it is a complex and artistic work of literature, but it walks a thin line in parading figures from such a controversial background, especially when there are plenty of arguments for letting those rest in old trunks somewhere in back storage rooms of the minstrel tradition.

The current ending of the comic highlights the questions surrounding the soundness of such a production as this one. As Bayou helps fight off Stagolee when the latter attacks Rabbit, there suddenly appears a flock of black birds that attack him. These are "Jim Crows" sent by the Bossman, Bogg, and they repre-sent an unsurprising figuration in that they are an incarnation of segregation just as Bayou is an incarnation of the bayou. But this is not the first time they have appeared. As mentioned earlier, the third page of the comic features a crow sitting on the "Colored Entrance" sign, an animal brought into play in opposi-tion to the rabbits on page 2; in this case, the crow seems to be the "real-life" one that registers on the realistic level instead of the fantastic one, although later we realize that it symbolizes and embodies the white tradition Rabbit/rabbits must deal with. The first time the actual "Jim Crows" appear in the comic is when Lee and Bayou find Cotton Eyed Joe at his home and confront him to find Lilly. Cotton Eyed Joe chases Lee out of his house, trying to kill her. Just as he does so, suddenly the Jim Crows appear to attack, not Bayou or Lee but Cotton Eyed Joe himself. The problem here is that Cotton Eyed Joe is the son of Bogg. It seems strange that the Jim Crows should attack a white character when clearly Bayou and Lee are the ones who are causing disruption in this parallel world. In the first appearance of the Jim Crows it would seem that Love has a perfect opportunity to present a physical incarnation of the unfairness of the Jim Crow laws in which black characters find themselves constantly confronted with a nonlevel playing field (literally so in the opening section of that book). Yet, in a somewhat baffling move, Love's having the Jim Crows attack Cotton Eyed Joe, who is most definitely a monster, goes against the very historical precedent to which they refer.

Indeed, the agents of Bogg are themselves often African American or signi-fying in an African/African American cultural context. Bogg's three principle henchmen who appear in the first section are somewhat predictable: a hound dog (think blood hounds chasing runaway slaves) and two hooded figures who recall Ku Klux Klan members. But these characters are finally inept compared to the nastiest figure of all, Stagolee, who is a black man in the service of Bogg. Certainly the classic Stagger Lee stands as a folk figure significant as a black man who kills other black people, but Love puts him in the service of the white powers that be. Love also casts his Stagolee character as a type reaching back to Africa when he shape-shifts into a half panther and half African warrior, with golden earrings, a feather armband, and tattoos. This moment may confuse the reader when it appears in volume 2 because of the similar moment that occurs in volume 1, but this time in what is evidently a positive connection with African imagery and myth: when Bayou accompanies Lee to Cotton Eyed Joe's house, she suddenly appears in his eyes as a young African girl, wearing a white robe, and with a gold neckpiece, earrings, and hair dressing holding her hair in an African style. Bayou responds by calling her "Nuh-Nandi," to which Lee, appearing as herself again, turns and asks, "Who?" This moment differs from the Stagolee one because it happens in the eyes of Bayou, where the reader sees the African appearance of Stagolee directly. But the reader may nevertheless be left wondering whether to understand African tradition to be a positive or negative thing in this comic.

And in a larger sense we might ask exactly on which side the comic itself is on; should it be seen as an agent of the white racialist/racist tradition in which it is based, or of an antiracist ethic that intuition insists it at least seek to be? To some extent, of course, my raising this binary could be unfair, not only because of the artificiality of binaries themselves but also because the comic so foregrounds hy-bridity and liminality on so many levels. At the same time, though, so much is at least potentially at stake in the existence of such a comic, and however delicately and carefully it may position itself along the color line, the attendant histories and oppositions of both sides of present-day culture, with its acts of violence, show us that for many people in U.S. culture the us-versus-them mentality of racial warfare remains persistent and deadly. Perhaps Love employs the Uncle Remus tradition precisely to woo readers otherwise resistant to the historical realities of racist violence and/or committed to promoting white-dominant visions of southern history. By giving such readers characters and visual cues of nostalgia, the logic may go, the comic can enlist them in an understanding of the history of murder and cruelty. But these same readers might just as quickly point to the violence that takes place among African Americans in the comic and bring up age-old arguments about black-on-black violence as evidencing racial "inferiority."

History and/in *Bayou*: Unfinished Business

Where does all of this, then, leave us concerning history and/in *Bayou*? Set in 1933 Mississippi, with flashbacks to earlier moments, it is a de facto historical work that, despite its postmodern techniques, nevertheless must lay claim to a certain level of authenticity, which resides most conspicuously in the "topside" of the bayou's Charon, Mississippi, lynching narrative. The fantasy side of the comic also addresses history, including the history of racial stereotyping, but it does so according to a different set of rules: where the political positioning of the lynching narrative is clear—lynching and those white people who are responsible for it are evil (although not all the white people in this narrative are completely "bad," all of them *are* caught in system)—and the moral compass in the realm of the fantastic is haywire, spinning all over the place. In a sense, the comic as it presently exists victimizes itself because the frame has not been closed, and we the readers do not yet know what will happen with the lynching story. Will Lilly emerge finally to save the day, making the story a triumph of solidarity between a black girl and a white girl, fighting against not only the racist establishment but also the patriarchal tradition? Will Bogg in the end come topside and direct a lynching of Lee's father, confirming the reality of history that so often lynching was not averted? Will Bayou, whom the Jim Crows have at least maimed and may have killed, turn out to be resilient enough to rush in and save the day, smashing the white lynchers topside? Or is the story moving toward a conclusion in which Lee's alleged father is lynched and Rabbit steps in to be the father he actually is and become vindicated as finally an agent of good despite his trickster tendencies while the man who raised Lee never has to know he was never actually her father?

Perhaps, in our present moment, when no more answers to the problem of the color line seem to be available, *Bayou* functions most provocatively *unfinished*.

Fans have been clamoring for years now for Love to finish the comic, and Love has claimed that he knows how it will end. It may be that property issues complicate its completion, since the "property" of *Bayou* is presumably owned by DC, which gives the company control of it. But then, DC's owning properties has not particularly thwarted their continuance in other cases. At any rate, whether Love is doing so intentionally or not, *Bayou*'s real historical significance may ultimately be more about the early 2000s than the early 1900s, more about the competitions for and conflicts within the ownership of historical narratives in our moment than about whatever history is, was, or could be regarding the actual Depression-era South. I am particularly struck by some of the marketing language connected with volume 2: the back cover announces, "Lee Wagstaff continues her perilous journey through the eerie parallel world of Nawlins," and the biographical statement about Love at the end of the book states, "In *Bayou*, Love weaves an epic and haunting fantasy set in the Reconstruction-era South." Both of these statements are patently untrue. While Rabbit closes the volume *talking* about the need to go to New Orleans to find Brer Fox, none of the characters actually go there. And the comic has no connection with the Reconstruction era. What one *does* encounter in volume 2 are storms that include flooding—storms that key into images of Katrina and might cause a present-day reader to think of the disaster in the Crescent City—and characters that form the stock core of the comic who derive from the immediate post-Reconstruction moment. I am not willing to go so far as to suggest that Love and/or whoever else involved in generating the marketing language necessarily seeks to extend the trickster hybridity of the comic into the cover text, but I find these elements in that text revealing for the complexities of history and myth, nostalgia and realism at work in the comic.

For readers looking for resolution and wondering why it has been so long in coming, it might be that the very tension of that waiting is Love's goal, a tension that could be ended by bringing the story to a close. On the other hand, Love's deft hand at employing hybrid elements to build and maintain that tension suggests that he may be able to "conclude" the story without necessarily obliterating the tension that drives it. For resolution to questions about the comic, as with questions about the direction of interracial tension and violence in the United States in our moment, we must continue to wait and see.

NOTES

1. Whitted's essay explores haunting and postmodern historiography in *Bayou* and Alan Moore's *The Saga of the Swamp Thing* (1984–87). In this essay, I seek to build on Whitted's work as well as Rain Prud'Homme C. Gomez's discussion of *Bayou*'s treatment of Native American history. Whitted mentions in passing "the paradox of pleasure and pain that

distinguishes the Deep South" in *Bayou* (203), and I am deepening and expanding the focus on that aspect of the text.

2. I should say that despite this specificity, I am not under the impression that Love means to evoke anything particular about the year 1933 in Mississippi; at any rate, it is beyond the scope of my argument to prove that possibility.

3. Love has mentioned this source often in lectures. I cite his keynote at the Comics Studies in the South Symposium at the University of South Carolina in 2013.

4. Even as I identify Harris as a white writer who ultimately supported segregation and racist/racialist views, I would note that Harris himself was the illegitimate child of a seamstress who went to work for a plantation owner in Georgia to learn the printing trade and there met the people who would be the models for Uncle Remus and other African American characters. As R. Bruce Bickley Jr. asserts, Harris "instinctively recognized a strange similarity between the deprivations of his own past and those of [African Americans]" (36). I am not suggesting that Harris could fully enter into or grasp the experiences of black southerners, but as Bickley and other biographers sense, ambiguities persist in Harris's writing that suggest some level of awareness and perhaps identity with the African American efforts to resist white aristocratic power structures. This ambiguity is significant for the ways it transfers through the stories to the ambiguity and hybridity of *Bayou*. On Harris, see also Wiggins; Cousins.

5. In fact, Harris's intentions can be difficult to read, and at times his work can be seen as being more closely aligned with that of Paul Laurence Dunbar and Charles Waddell Chesnutt.

6. For further discussion of comics and history that plays on the concept of the "already told" in the context of comics and history, see Berlatsky; Duncan and Smith.

7. Love's pencil work is faintly visible in the forms of crosses on these white faces, suggesting a connection to the Ku Klux Klan.

8. Concerning the function of color versus monotone, Scott McCloud writes, "The differences between black-and-white and color comics are vast and profound, affecting every level of the reading experience. In black and white, the ideas behind the art are communicated more directly. Meaning transcends form. Art approaches language. In flat colors forms themselves take on more significance. The world becomes a playground of shapes and space. And through more expressive colors, comics can become an intoxicating environment of sensations that only color can give" (*Understanding Comics* 192).

9. The blurring of dreams and the real world is yet another ambiguous and hybrid element in the comic that takes on particular importance in the second volume.

10. My referring to this moment as a "dream" is problematic, for it is not purely confined to the realm of dream since any injury she or anyone else suffers in the dream affects the person's actual body. Whitted refers to these occasions as "moments of 'rememory' that are not quite dreams or flashbacks, but material traces of the past" (208).

CHAPTER 3

Teaching History through and as Asian/ American Popular Culture in Gene Luen Yang's *Boxers* and *Saints*

Caroline Kyungah Hong

THIS ESSAY EXAMINES HOW Gene Luen Yang's *Boxers* (2013) and *Saints* (2013), as Asian/American graphic narrative works of historical fiction/ fantasy, engage in the important cultural and political work of telling and teaching history.[1] The two-volume set, written and illustrated by Yang and colored by Lark Pien, garnered Yang his second nomination as a finalist for the National Book Award in Young People's Literature and also earned him a 2014 *Los Angeles Times* Book Prize. The pair of graphic narratives reimagine the history of the Boxer Rebellion from two seemingly opposed perspectives. Imagined as a war epic, *Boxers* is the origin story of the Boxers and the coming-of-age narrative of Little Bao, a Chinese peasant boy who leads the violent uprising against foreigners and Chinese Christians. It culminates in the Boxers' siege of foreign legations in Peking, their defeat, and Bao's apparent imminent death. Alternatively, *Saints*, modeled after autobiographical comics, is told from the perspective of Four-Girl/Vibiana, a young Chinese convert to Christianity who is eventually killed by Bao during the uprising. It concludes with an epilogue that reveals Bao has survived.

What can graphic narratives such as *Boxers* and *Saints* contribute to the teaching of history and historiography, especially in light of recent national and global conversations about the challenges therein?[2] The hybrid visual-verbal form of graphic narratives is effective not only in teaching specific histories but also in teaching *how* to "think historically" (Brozo et al. 57). For one, the medium is instructive in its negotiation of "the visible and the invisible," the "silent dance of the seen and the unseen" (McCloud, *Understanding Comics* 92), highlighting gaps quite literally in the gutters between panels on the page. Jared Gardner argues, "Of all modern narrative forms, comics are the most compressed, the most dependent on ellipses and lacunae; comics, that is, must always show and tell only a fraction of the information required to make narrative sense of the information being presented" ("Same Different" 138). Furthermore, as Rocco

Versaci observes, "one can never completely 'escape' into a comic book, because its form—impressionistic illustrations of people, places, and things—reminds us at every turn (or panel) that what we are experiencing is a representation" (6). This form thus makes visible notions of history as representation, the interconnectedness of "story" and "history," and history as always incomplete, in process, and interpretive.

Boxers and *Saints* engage in precisely this kind of complex historical thinking, as does much of Yang's oeuvre. In his best-known graphic novel, *American Born Chinese* (2006), Yang reimagines the popular Chinese mythocultural figure of the Monkey King, revives nineteenth-century U.S. images of the "heathen Chinee," and alludes to pop-cultural phenomena such as the Transformers, William Hung, and the Back Dorm Boys, all in service of an Asian American bildungsroman. In weaving together these transhistorical, transnational, and cross-cultural elements, Yang illustrates the interplay of history and popular culture.

In *Boxers* and *Saints*, Yang not only uses popular culture to teach history but also considers how history itself is pop cultural. To this point, I begin by briefly discussing the Boxer Rebellion as a significant historical context. I also look at how Yang takes liberties with this history—for example, by incorporating Ch'in Shih-huang and Joan of Arc in his fictional rendering of the Boxer Rebellion. Then, I analyze panels that demonstrate Yang's engagement with pop-cultural forms—such as U.S. superhero comics, Chinese opera, and mythoreligious narratives—to think about the mutually constitutive nature of history and popular culture.

As Hillary L. Chute observes, graphic narratives are "not only about events but also, explicitly, about how we frame them" (Chute, *Graphic Women* 2). In the final section, I focus on how Yang frames his versions of the Boxer Rebellion as two volumes and how that frame relates to his gendered representations. The dual structure can be read as a powerful statement about the necessity of telling a "people's history" from multiple perspectives—history as heteroglossia. The doubled and dialectical structure also underscores the ambivalence surrounding this historical event, and history in general, contributing to an understanding of history that is not reducible to dichotomies of good and evil, right and wrong, winner and loser. At the same time, I contend that Yang's linking of gender and genre in this diptych is problematic in its seemingly oppositional framework and underpins some of the very binaries it aims to deconstruct, particularly in reinforcing the dominance and value of certain historical perspectives and narratives over others.

The Boxer Rebellion as Historical Context and
as Historical Fiction/Fantasy

As is clear from interviews, Yang intended *Boxers* and *Saints* in part as pedagogical tools for teaching a historical event seldom taught in U.S. schools, a
history he finds meaningful and relevant to our contemporary world.[3] The Boxer
Rebellion (also known as the Boxer Uprising or the Yihetuan Movement, circa
1899–1901) was a consequential turn-of-the-century global conflict that shapes
China's foreign policies to this day. Amid European, U.S., and Japanese imperialism in China, a secret society calling itself the Righteous and Harmonious
Fists (*Yihequan*) was formed in northern Shandong Province in the late 1890s.
The Boxers, as they were named by foreign missionaries for their martial arts
training, were mostly young peasant men who practiced rituals they believed
possessed them with spirits and made them invulnerable to weapons. They traveled north, destroying churches and foreign properties and brutally attacking
and massacring foreigners and Chinese Christians. In the summer of 1900, with
the support of Empress Dowager Cixi, the Boxers besieged the foreign legation
district of Peking, until the arrival of troops from the Eight-Nation Alliance
of Japan, Russia, Great Britain, France, the United States, Germany, Austria-
Hungary, and Italy subdued the uprising. The Boxer Protocol officially ended the
Boxer Rebellion in 1901, and its terms included steep war reparations, execution
of officials, stationing of foreign troops in Peking, prohibition on importing arms,
and destruction of forts, leading to the weakening of the Qing Dynasty and the
beginning of the end of imperial China (Cohen 54, 56).

The Boxer Rebellion as historical context is productive for teaching complex
historical thinking in a number of ways. First, the event's origins, import, and
effects were contested from the beginning and continue to be debated. Historian
Joseph Esherick supposes that "there is no major incident in China's modern
history on which the range of professional interpretation is as great" (xiv), which
emphasizes the fact that history does indeed require interpretation. The Boxers
have been condemned as ignorant, barbaric xenophobes on the one hand and
glorified as protonationalist, anti-imperialist heroes on the other.[4] The dual perspectives of *Boxers* and *Saints* are able to convey both of these interpretations.
Second, the globally mediatized nature of the Boxer Rebellion is historically significant: "The Boxer Rebellion marks a special point in the history of media and
war because all major powers of that time were involved in it. . . . Consequently,
the worldwide presence of the Boxer Rebellion in the media surpassed that of
previous conflicts" (Knüsel 51). Yang often calls attention to this aspect of the
uprising in interviews, calling it "the first truly global conflict" and "the first war

in the age of mass media" ("The Boxers"). Third, the Boxer Rebellion played a critical role in spreading the insidious image of the Yellow Peril throughout Europe and the Americas (Knüsel 58), an essential historical and cultural context for Asian and Asian American studies. Finally, the Boxer Rebellion illuminates the formative role of popular culture in shaping history, a point I expand on in the following section.

Yang is not the first to reenvision this historical context, but he is the first to depict it using the graphic-narrative form in the United States.[5] In doing so, he did not simply "cartoonify" this history, nor did he try to faithfully illustrate an extant eyewitness or journalistic account for the sake of historical accuracy. As with any fictional representation of history, Boxers and Saints focus on some aspects of the Boxer Rebellion and exclude others. For example, while Japanese imperialism played a prominent role in China at the time, Yang largely erases Japan from his versions of this history.[6] One effect of this gap is that it draws a clearer divide between the Boxers and Westerners, between Asians and non-Asians, a conflict that is perhaps more legible from an Asian American perspective.

In his historical fiction/fantasy, Yang also adds elements that were never there, creating linkages across a variety of historical contexts: for instance, in his fictional protagonists' interactions, real and imagined, with historical icons from other eras. In Boxers, Bao is possessed by a powerful and vicious black-robed figure who he later learns is Ch'in Shih-huang (or Qin Shi Huang), the first emperor of China. In interviews, Yang describes Ch'in Shih-huang as an ambiguous and controversial figure: "He united seven separate kingdoms into a single nation. He built the Great Wall and was buried with the terra-cotta soldiers. The Chinese have mixed feelings about him. They're proud of the nation he created, but he was a maniacal tyrant. He slaughtered thousands of people. He buried scholars alive and burned entire libraries of books. I feel like his spirit has haunted China over the centuries, especially during China's darkest decades" (N. Clark). Yang links the histories of Ch'in Shih-huang and the Boxers, the former literally haunting the latter in Boxers. Not fully in control of his actions and pressured into increasing brutality by the emperor, Bao describes the process of transforming into Ch'in Shih-huang as a momentary feeling of drowning (Boxers 129) and repeatedly dreams of being dragged underwater by the emperor against his will. Their transhistorical relationship is fraught and unstable, though no less impactful as a result.

By contrast, in Saints, Four-Girl/Vibiana finds a more supportive historical guide in her visions of Joan of Arc, who inspires more than she haunts, though she is also an ambiguous figure, as I discuss below.[7] Yang sees Joan of Arc and the Boxers as mirror images, which also implicitly connects his two protagonists: "Joan was basically a French Boxer. She was a poor teenager who wanted to do something about the foreign aggressors invading her homeland. She found power in strange (to the modern mind, anyway) spiritual beliefs. And she was an underdog all the way through, just like the Boxers were. So in the stories told by the Boxers' enemies was a figure very much like themselves" (N. Clark). Yang draws transhistorical, transnational, and cross-cultural connections between the Boxers and Joan of Arc and, I argue, in his thinking about history more broadly.

Both Ch'in Shih-huang and Joan of Arc are thoughtfully chosen by Yang as historical icons who reveal parallels in history across time and space. But historical figures on their own are not enough to tell the whole story. Though *Boxers* and *Saints* are populated by characters based on historical figures—Red Lantern Chu, Master Big Belly, Father Bey, Dr. Won, Prince Tuan, the Kansu Braves, Baron von Ketteler (Mozzocco)—the protagonists are necessarily fictional: as Yang notes, "Nobody really knows for sure how the Boxer Rebellion started. It began among the poor, and the history of the poor is rarely written down" (N. Clark). And it is imperative that Bao and Four-Girl/Vibiana are connected to but are not the same as these historical figures; they are not mere incarnations of the cliché that history repeats itself. I contend that Yang is teaching about history in the tensions and negotiations between the "real" and the fictional/fantastical. Min Hyoung Song argues, "Yang stands out for his willingness to bend the conventions of genre storytelling to contribute to his realist aspirations" (Song, "'How Good'" 76). It is precisely this interplay between an "emphasis on the day-to-day, which is the hallmark of 'serious' graphic narratives, and the fantastical, which is an aspect of mainstream comics" (77), that I find exciting about Yang's approach to history. Thinking about history as a kind of fiction or fantasy crafted out of a multiplicity of "bits and pieces of history" (Solomon), "constructed by authors who have biases" (Brozo et al. 57), rather than as complete, continuous, linear narratives that can be true and objective, is part of what *Boxers* and *Saints*, and graphic narratives in general, can contribute to the teaching of history and historiography.

Yang's use of magical realism precludes us from reading his work within the rubric of historical accuracy. Though magical realism risks exoticizing and Orientalist readings, it also challenges the tendency to read Asian American literary and cultural texts for their "authenticity" and social realism. Blurring the lines between history and fantasy forces us to rethink a myopic view of history through the limits of a realist lens, to recognize how the fantastical and phantasmic are always already present in history. This shapes the very form and content of *Boxers* and *Saints*: Yang explains, "The facts around the Boxers suggest a blend of magic and history. They believed that the gods possessed them, that the gods gave them superpowers. They believed warriors could spring from magic beans. They believed charms would make them bulletproof. They gave me a theme to carry through the entire project" (N. Clark). Yang's commitment to both history and fantasy is also why he avoids answering questions about whether the magical-realist elements of *Boxers* are intended to be read as "real" and actually happening to these characters (e.g., does Bao really become Ch'in Shih-huang, or is it all in his head?). This is indicative of his critical approach to historical thinking: Yang leaves these questions open, resisting foreclosing readers' disparate interpretations and cultivating instead an "in-between space of not knowing" (Spurgeon).

In the following two sections, I examine more of these open-ended questions and the choices Yang makes in asking them, in particular his linking of history and popular culture, and his approaches to gender and genre.

History as Asian/American Popular Culture

I agree with Yang that "one of the most compelling reasons to study the Boxer Rebellion is that it demonstrates the power of pop culture" (Yang, "The Boxers"), and *Boxers* and *Saints* prompt readers to see history through the lens of pop culture, to see history itself *as* pop culture. The Boxers, arguably "best understood as having grown out of the popular culture of the North China plain" (Cohen 38), were especially influenced by Chinese opera, a complex yet accessible pop-cultural form with more than three hundred different regional styles (Goldman 2). Andrea Goldman notes, "Before the twentieth century, opera in China was the mass-communication medium of the times, as powerful in shaping and reflecting popular imagination as television and cinema are in our own times. Opera suffused the very fabric of life. . . . It was one of the key mediums through which ideas about the self, family, society, and politics were transmitted over time, over space, and across class" (3). In sum, "in late imperial China . . . opera was the medium that shaped and expressed most people's understanding of history and culture" (3). This was true for the Boxers, who "imitated the martial arts performers they had so often seen in village operas" (Cohen 39).

Yang describes the Boxers as looking to opera for inspiration and empowerment in ways analogous to "modern day geek culture" (G. L. Yang et al. 131): "Chinese opera told epic tales of colorfully-costumed heroes who fought evil with superpowers and magical weapons. The heroes of the Chinese opera were not unlike the heroes of modern American comic books, only instead of capes, flags flapped at their backs" (Yang, "The Boxers"). On his blog, he discusses a number of similarities between Chinese opera and U.S. superhero comics, such as the importance of colors and costumes, the centrality of choreographed battle scenes, and so forth (Yang, "How Chinese Opera"). He acknowledges that, in his renderings of opera figures, he endeavored "to evoke American superheroes" and "blend traditional Chinese imagery with a Jack Kirby/Bruce Timm sensibility" (Goellner). Yang's use of the visual vocabulary of mainstream U.S. comics and the superhero tradition, as well as martial arts films and manga, is a key transnational feature of his historical fiction/fantasy that hybridizes Asian and U.S. pop culture to tell a history that was already transnational and hybrid.

Boxers opens with a sequence of panels depicting the significance of the Chinese opera for the protagonist (Yang, *Boxers* 4–5; see figure 3.1). The individual panels that portray Little Bao watching the opera, as well as the mise-en-page,[8] highlight the role of the spectator, emphasizing our shared position as audience with Bao: as Bao puts it, "and together we *watch*" (4). There are no other words in the four wide panels that show Bao watching the opera, aside from the "bing dak dak" of the music. The absence of speech and thought draws us into the opera along with Bao and underscores its affective impact on him; his facial expressions and body language convey a range of emotions and responses. And while the staged opera is contained within the panel frames, Bao stands in front of and beyond the frames, alongside a statue of Tu Di Gong, the local earth god. The panels thus become the stage, the proscenium. This meta move accentuates the presence and effects of the panel frames. The same frames, of course, go on to border and contain the story of Bao and the Boxers, the history of the Boxer Rebellion becoming a cultural production not unlike the opera, as we take Bao's place as the captivated audience. The impact of pop culture thus exceeds the literal frames of this graphic narrative.

Pop culture also figuratively frames Bao's world and worldview, which become increasingly "operaticized" (Cohen 113). A narrative box states that "the opera lingers" (Yang, *Boxers* 6), and we see how Bao measures just about everything in his life against the opera, seeing opera figures everywhere, from his daily work (6–7), to his first encounter with Four-Girl (9), to his perception of his father as "a hero they could compose operas about" (14), before he becomes a pitiful figure after being beaten nearly to death by foreign soldiers. And these imaginary visions foreshadow Bao and the Boxers ritually summoning and becoming these opera gods in battle.

Bao's relationship with Mei-wen, his romantic interest and the main female character in *Boxers*, is also framed by their engagement with pop culture. Before the climactic battle in Peking, Bao and Mei-wen are taken to a puppet show by Bao's childhood friend Bing Wong-bing (265–66; see figure 3.2). These panels visually echo that first scene of Bao viewing the opera. The use of repetition with a difference is one of Yang's most effective visual and narrative techniques, in *Boxers* and *Saints*, as well as in earlier works.[9] Like the previous scene, the three spectators are drawn over and outside the panel frames. Bing Wong-bing's facial

Figure 3.1. Gene Luen Yang,
Boxers (2013): 5.

Figure 3.2. Gene Luen Yang,
Boxers (2013): 266.

expressions call to mind Bao's childhood reactions, but the most dramatic gaze in these panels is not their watching of the puppet show but Mei-wen's turning to look affectionately at Bao. The following page portrays the young couple holding hands for the first time and blushing. This happy scene conveys how pop culture facilitates recognition and connection, even love, in shared cultural experiences and pleasures.

A key difference from the former scene is that this is not the opera but a puppet show version of the opera. Though Bao exclaims, "It's just like an opera, only smaller!" (265), the details suggest that they are actually quite different. The puppets are diminutive versions of opera figures and therefore less impressive, more like child's play, underscored by the naïve enthusiasm of Bing Wong-bing. This is reinforced by the dialogue, which was absent earlier and here makes the performance seem corny and melodramatic. Moreover, these panel frames do not serve as stage or proscenium, as the puppets are framed by a puppet theater drawn inside the right half of the panels. This extra level of mediation, the double frame, is a reminder that this is a representation within a representation, confronting us with the complex and palimpsestic workings of pop culture within and as history.

The sites and forms of pop culture in *Boxers*, like the histories they inform, are ambiguous and in process, often contested and challenged. It is no accident that the icon of Tu Di Gong, whom Bao associates closely with the opera, is broken, degraded, and/or deformed in both *Boxers* (19, 30) and *Saints* (8), these disrespectful acts catalyzing Bao's desire for justice and revenge. The unstable and contested nature of pop culture and history is also apparent with the mythoreligious narratives in both volumes. In *Boxers*, not long after the puppet show scene, Mei-wen and Bao sneak into the Hanlin Academy Library, the most prestigious, elite scholarly institution in China at the time. Mei-wen views the library as a repository for narratives: "Just think, Bao! We're surrounded by stories!" (*Boxers* 276). Because Bao is illiterate, Mei-wen reads him a story. (And before she begins to read, Mei-wen and Bao repeat the word "story" four times in three panels.) Again, this scene repeats visual elements of the earlier scenes of the opera and the puppet show. Mei-wen reads aloud, while she and Bao are depicted over and outside the panel frames that illustrate the story of the princess who becomes Guan Yin, the goddess of compassion (277–80). Mei-wen and Bao are shown in front of the wide panels at the bottom of each page telling the story, their bodies bleeding to the bottom edges, but not in front of every panel as with the opera and the puppet show. And unlike those preceding scenes, they do not actually "see" this story, except in their imaginations, and this is marked by the rounded corners of panels that contain moments of storytelling (Dooley). Mei-wen's eyes are focused on the book, while Bao's eyes are closed, presumably engrossed in the story. But the last panel of this series shows that Bao has fallen asleep and missed the crucial denouement of the story, when the princess shows compassion for her father and becomes Guan Yin. This suggests that the violent culmination of the Boxer Rebellion is connected to an inability to see and hear the lessons apparent in such mythoreligious narratives. (It also seems to imply that visual and performative cultural forms have more of an impact than the literary, which is unable to sustain Bao's attention.) On the following page, composed of three wide panels with Bao and Mei-wen drawn on the left side, against a backdrop of library shelves, Mei-wen appears to find this endearing and kisses the sleeping Bao on his cheek. But the rows of darkened, untitled books in the background of this scene appear ominous, especially when juxtaposed with the bright colors and dynamic images from the opera, puppet show, and Guan Yin's story.

These books, as is Bao and Mei-wen's relationship, are indeed doomed. Despite Bao's promises to Mei-wen to preserve the library, Ch'in Shih-huang provokes Bao into setting fire to the building. Bao proclaims this act is "for *China*" (Yang, *Boxers* 312), and Mei-Wen responds, "What is China but a people and their sto-ries?" (312). Mei-wen tries to save the burning books and dies off-page when the library collapses in flames, and all Bao can do is shed a single tear (315). While the impact of Bao's brutal killings of soldiers and civilians is somewhat softened by their cartoonification, this is portrayed as perhaps his greatest crime, not only in his betrayal of Mei-wen but in the destruction of the very stories and cultural forms that empowered him in the first place. Yang suggests there can be no more redemption for Bao, a failed nationalist hero, once he burns down a bastion of Chinese culture, a culture that had already been under attack.

These scenes of the opera, puppet show, and library are not incidental or di-gressive to Yang's version of the Boxer Rebellion. These moments are formative and essential to moving forward the historical-fictional narrative. The focus on the position of the audience/spectator in particular depicts the power of pop culture to influence and move historical agents.

In *Saints*, Four-Girl/Vibiana's major pop-cultural influences are religious fig-ures and biblical tales. And just as Yang draws parallels between the Boxers and contemporary "geek culture," he makes analogies between the Chinese Chris-tian converts during the era of the Boxer Rebellion and "modern-day American manga fans" (Z. Smith), for how they take foreign stories and apply them to their own lives. Though this analogy elides the uneven ways in which these stories are circulated, through acts of colonization or cultural appropriation, the com-parison does serve as a reminder of the multidirectional transnational flows of cultural forms.

As aforementioned, Four-Girl/Vibiana is inspired by her imagined encounters with Joan of Arc. With visual cues, Yang makes clear that we are to read religious figures and narratives in *Saints* as functioning similarly to the opera and stories in *Boxers*. For one, just as the opera's bright colors contrast those of Bao's dingy and muted reality, Joan of Arc's appearances are also contrasted in color with Vibiana's world, though within a more limited palette: Joan glows in golden yellow tones, suggesting a dreamlike or otherwise unreal quality. And like *Boxers*, *Saints* also emphasizes Four-Girl/Vibiana's position as audience, in her case as a witness to, rather than a participant in, Joan of Arc's history. One wide panel literally frames Vibiana as a spectator of Joan (*Saints* 97; see figure 3.3). We see Vibiana on top of the village wall, looking down on Joan in combat. She, and we, cannot see Joan, as the battling figures are drawn too small and without detail, indicating just how far we are from the action, while the distant onomatopoeic sounds of "Clang!" ring across the battlefield. This panel is reminiscent of the panels depicting the opera and the puppet show: the village wall frames the scene below, a proscenium or window into the action, as if Vibiana is watching a play on stage from the balcony. On the following page, she sighs, "So glorious," and contemplates how boring her life is in comparison. When she is caught where she is not supposed to be and asked what she is doing, she replies, "Nothing," as the scene below disappears with a "Poof!" (98). This confirms that these visions are figments of Vibiana's imagination, foreclosing the kind of ambiguity we see around the fantastical scenes in *Boxers*.

As I noted earlier, Yang uses rounded panel corners to signify metatextually when stories are being told within the larger narrative, in contrast to sharp panel corners that indicate action as well as performances (creating an interesting distinction between stories and cultural forms such as the opera and puppet show). Bridget Dooley points out that the rounded corners are used not only for stories

Figure 3.3. Gene Luen Yang,
Saints (2013): 97.

and accounts told firsthand by the characters but also for mythoreligious narratives, such as the biblical tales Four-Girl is told by Dr. Won, suggesting "that the religious narratives being told are just that: stories" (Dooley).

As Dooley notes, Yang subtly plays with the panel corners in significant moments in both volumes. Before Bao kills Vibiana toward the end of *Saints*, Joan of Arc appears to her one last time, as she is burning at the stake (Yang, *Saints* 153). Tears stream down Joan's face, but these are revealed to be tears of hope and humility, not of pain and fear, because Jesus has appeared to her, and by extension to Vibiana, a vision within a vision. Jesus tells Vibiana the story of the Good Samaritan over several wide panels, slowly raising his arms (154–56). In a large, full-page panel, he concludes the story in the crucified position, hanging against a plain gray background, the cross an absent presence (156). The wounds on his hands are shown in close-up, opening up slowly over another three wide panels to reveal an eye (157), known as the *hamsa* in some cultures, like the ones portrayed in *Boxers* as belonging to Guan Yin, "the goddess with one thousand eyes to look for suffering and one thousand hands to relieve it" (Yang, *Boxers* 280). This is then followed by another full-page panel depicting a resurrected Jesus, surrounded by dozens of *hamsa* symbols radiating out from his body (Yang, *Saints* 158; see figure 3.4). The corners of this particular panel are sharp-edged, signaling that this moment is real, that Vibiana truly sees Jesus. Yet Vibiana is also depicted over and outside the panel frame, her body bleeding to the bottom edge of the page, as we saw in the opera, puppet show, and library scenes, which suggests that she is the spectator of a cultural production, outside of what is happening within the panel frame. And though this moment is what prompts Vibiana's genuine conversion and her final, quietly heroic act of prayer, we know Jesus is not physically present in that alleyway, where Bao executes Vibiana just a few pages later.

This panel from *Saints* ties Chinese and Christian mythology together, drawing parallels between Guan Yin and Jesus Christ, both figures of sacrifice and compassion. Again, this is a feature of Yang's historical fiction/fantasy, to make transhistorical, transnational, and cross-cultural linkages. Yang expounds, "I hope that my books aren't just about the clash between religions—I wanted to explore their overlap too" (Liu). In the repetition of imagery used to portray Jesus and Guan Yin, Yang offers an accessible anti-Orientalist critique, illustrating the ways in which the "East" and the "West" are interconnected and mutually constitutive. Toward the end of the library scene in *Boxers*, there is another full-page panel of Guan Yin, standing majestic and statuesque, her palms touching, *hamsa* radiating out from her body (282; see figure 3.5), similar to the panel depicting Jesus in *Saints*. Mei-wen and Bao are centered in front of the panel, in what has been the spectator position, though neither sees Guan Yin, as both

Figure 3.4. Gene Luen Yang,
Saints (2013): 158.

Figure 3.5. Gene Luen Yang,
Boxers (2013): 282.

their eyes are closed, the only closed eyes in a sea of open eyes. This panel frame is different from every other panel in both volumes in that its corners are *both* rounded and sharp edged. This lends further ambiguity to the meaning of this moment, suggesting numerous possible interpretations of these mythoreligious stories, multiple and even contradictory roles that these stories, as pop culture, might play in individual lives and in the broader histories they inhabit. It also further blurs the lines between fantasy and reality, story and history, as I have been discussing throughout this chapter.

Gender and Genre: The Limits of Historical Fiction/Fantasy

Along with Yang's signature minimal, clean-lined, accessible cartooning style and Pien's coloring, Yang makes a number of noteworthy stylistic choices to frame this history and center non-Western perspectives (e.g., the decision to render non-Chinese languages untranslated and in scribbles). The most significant of these is the structure of the two separate yet linked volumes, which can be purchased and read separately but are mostly sold together in a slipcased edition and read as a pair. For Yang, the fantastical history of the Boxer Rebellion had to be told from two perspectives, as an expression of his own ambivalence and a reflection of his Asian American and Catholic identities: "The more I read about the Boxer Rebellion, the more conflicted I felt. Who were the protagonists here? Who was more deserving of our sympathy? The Boxers or their Chinese Christian victims? . . . In many ways, the Boxer Rebellion embodies a conflict that some Asian and Asian American Christians struggle with, a conflict between our Eastern cultural heritage and our Western faith. The two volume structure is meant to reflect this conflict" ("Exclusive"). The doubled and dialectical structure of the graphic narratives and their cross-gendered, cross-genre perspectives are central to Yang's approach in telling this complex history. And yet Yang has talked about "hoping that [the two volumes] would be separate, that they would be able to stand . . . as separate narratives" (Solomon), that "each would represent a complete, cohesive worldview" (Mayer). It was actually his editor who first suggested releasing the volumes together (Mayer).

Although it is possible to read them as standalone works, it is hard to imagine why anyone would (and not only because *Saints* reveals the ending of *Boxers* to be misleading). As the prior section demonstrates, numerous threads and tropes are carried across both volumes. Violence is one of the strongest through-lines linking the two works. Yang confesses, "I made a choice early on to make this my most violent book" (G. L. Yang et al. 129), even as he tried to "'cartoonify' the violence to make it more palatable" (Mozzocco). We see this early on in *Boxers*: the panel that reveals Red Lantern's fate—the close-up image of his severed head, bloody and bruised, on a stake—is graphic and chilling, however cartoonified (Yang, *Boxers* 104). In *Saints*, the violence appears less extreme and graphic but is no less disturbing. This violence is explicitly patriarchal in nature, evident in scenes such as Four-Girl/Vibiana being slapped by her grandfather (Yang, *Saints* 40), being beaten by her cousin Chung at her Uncle Jong's orders because of her decision to convert to Christianity (71–72), and ultimately her execution by Bao. The violence perpetrated by Bao and the Boxers is obviously central to both volumes, and Yang's visual strategy of repetition with a difference is used to great effect to connect yet also distinguish the two works, especially in their depictions of violence. We see this, for instance, in another pair of visually repetitive panels, in which the Boxers are preparing to attack the Christian stronghold where Vibiana lives. The Boxers stand ready in rows and are chanting in unison, "Kill! Kill! Kill! Kill!" this chant filling the panel, arranged behind the Boxers and their weapons. In *Boxers*, the panel, which takes up two-thirds of the page, shows the Boxers as the opera gods, dressed in their bright costumes and masks (224; see figure 3.6). But the same moment looks very different in *Saints* (132; see figure 3.7). The panel in *Saints* takes up the whole page and is filled with even more rows of the chant "Kill! Kill! Kill! Kill!" And we see not the opera gods but ordinary young men, without costumes or masks, colored in the muted brown and gray hues of the rest of *Saints*. These changes transform this image from a heroic and fantastical battle scene to a disturbing portrait of bloodthirsty young men, their collective murderous drive overshadowing them as individuals. This duo of panels is more evidence that something is lost if we read these volumes as separate, as they comment on and complete each other throughout, offering conflicting but also overlapping interpretations of history.

An emphasis on the volumes' repetitions and connections is not to deny their differences. These distinctions are necessary and strategic in order for Yang to represent the history of the Boxer Rebellion from differing perspectives: one "a story about heroism," an "epic journey," "like the comics version of a Chinese war movie, long and bloody with a tragic ending," and the other "about sainthood," "much more limited in scope," "shorter, quieter, more humble" (Goellner). Formal and stylistic differences serve to distinguish these two perspectives and approaches. For example, the panel frames of *Boxers* are drawn with crisp, straight lines, while the frames in *Saints* are drawn without a ruler, appearing hand-drawn and thus conveying the idea that *Saints* is more intimate and personal (Liu). And for Four-Girl/Vibiana's narrative boxes in *Saints*, Yang uses his wife's handwriting to similar ends (Liu). Pien's coloring, which I mention above, is another significant difference. The palettes of both books are muted and share tonal similarities, but the colors are even more subdued in *Saints*, which is primarily colored in grays, with the exception of Vibiana's visions of Joan of Arc and Jesus, which are

Figure 3.6. Gene Luen Yang, *Boxers* (2013): 224.

Figure 3.7. Gene Luen Yang, *Saints* (2013): 132.

colored in shades of gold, yellow, and brown, brighter and more textured in contrast to Vibiana's world but still limited in its range of hues. *Boxers*, on the other hand, is in "full color" (Liu). Bao's world is colored in browns, beiges, grays, and blues to represent an "impoverished landscape," but it is injected with the bright color palette of the opera costumes, "unbridled rainbow anarchy," their heroic and fantastical adventures contrasting but also interacting with the harsh lives of Chinese peasants (Gilly).

An unfortunate consequence of these thoughtfully stylized differences as they play out across the dual-volume format is that they set up a binaristic and hierarchical framework. The two book covers mirror each other and suggest a kind of symmetry: each cover features half of that volume's protagonist's face, with their respective historical mentors, Ch'in Shih-huang and Joan of Arc, in the background. Laid side by side, the halves of their faces line up, suggesting a kind of equivalence in their stories, each telling one half of the history of the Boxer Rebellion. But the two volumes are obviously not equal or symmetrical. For one, *Boxers* is much longer than *Saints*. Yang admits, "part of the reason the two volumes are of different lengths is that it's not a perfect match-up. Like, a better match-up would be if I told the Boxers' stories in one volume, and then the stories of the Europeans in another" (Z. Smith). There is a tension between the desire to do equal justice to both Bao's and Four Girl/Vibiana's narratives and the acknowledgment that it is not possible in the way the stories are structured in relation to each other: "the two books weren't competing on the same level" (Goellner). There is a primacy to *Boxers* over *Saints*, which has to do with length, with the way their narratives are told and structured, with *Saints* adding to and extending the ending of *Boxers*, but which also has to do with how the two volumes have been marketed and read. Though Yang "was hoping you could read them in either order," he admits, "it sounds like—for most people at least—it works better if you read the bigger one first" (Spurgeon). Even the way the set is named, usually referred to as *Boxers* and *Saints* but sometimes as one title, *Boxers and Saints*, indicates a prioritizing of the first volume.

The distinct genres of the graphic narratives and the ways these genres are gendered further this sense of a binaristic and hierarchical relationship between the two volumes. As a comics version of a Chinese war epic, *Boxers* is intended as a heroic and tragic tale not only of one peasant boy but of a more sweeping nationalist history. To that end, it is told in the present tense from a male point of view, its chapters marked by place and year, and is full of movement and action. *Saints* is a shorter, more intimate narrative of a female protagonist, chapters marked by her age, and written like a journal or diary, borrowing from the conventions of American autobiographical comics (Goellner). Designed to look and feel "like an old-timey film" (Gilly), it is told in the past tense, and it is revealed in the end that our protagonist is actually dead, that this has been the story of "how [she] died" (Yang, *Saints* 162), that what we have been reading has been narrated essentially by a ghost. Yang attempts to convey the import and value of both narratives. However, *Boxers* and *Saints*, I am sure unintentionally, harken back to tired ideas that Asian/American men's stories are heroic, action-packed, worthy of longer and more present narration, while Asian/American women's stories are more internal, less public and political, and therefore less timely. Thus, especially within the contexts of Asian American literature and culture, this gendered genre structure is troubling, though it is instructive in getting readers to confront the ways in which history is always gendered.

It is not just form but also content that reveals the gendering of this history. *Boxers* is primarily and unselfconsciously a story about brotherhood, about the filial and communal bonds among men. This is made clear throughout, from Red Lantern Chu's mentoring of Bao, at a moment when Bao's father is lost to him, to the oath of brotherhood he and his brothers make, in homage to the Peach Blossom Tree Oath from the Chinese classical novel *The Romance of the Three Kingdoms* (Yang, *Boxers* 137–38). Women play a secondary and limited, though important, role in *Boxers*. Mei-wen, Bao's love interest, transforms into the woman general Mui Gui-ying, and she and her Sister-Disciples, who are named the Red Lanterns, actually come to Bao's rescue. But the creation of the Red Lanterns is necessitated by the Boxers' rejection of women from their brotherhood—Bao leaves Mei-wen behind because of his jealousy over her relationship with his brother Chuan-tai, whom I discuss more below. And though Red Lanterns was the historical name for groups of women who fought alongside the Boxers, and Yang believes the connection to the historical Red Lantern Zhu to be coincidental (Solomon), in *Boxers* he has Bao suggest the name to Mei-wen, inspired by his friend/mentor Red Lantern, who, he recalls, "had a particular appreciation for women" (Yang, *Boxers* 254). Women characters in *Boxers* may be heroic and powerful, but they are relevant only insofar as they are instrumental to and supportive of the men's narratives; their stories remain in the background.

Yang offers a critique of the Boxers' treatment of women in this volume focused on men, but this critique doesn't go far enough. He cites historical evidence of the Boxers' misogyny: "The Boxers had this weird relationship with women. Like, they really believed in yin, which is a Chinese concept of female energy, and the Boxers were really suspicious of it and afraid of it" (Solomon).[10] This is reflected in the laughable character of Lu Pai the magistrate, who tells bizarre, misogynistic stories of the "foreign devils" being tainted by yin. The narrative makes clear that Lu Pai is not to be believed or taken seriously: "His stories are filled with outlandish lies" (*Boxers* 179), as Bao knows. But ultimately Bao and the Boxers are accepting of Lu Pai and see his stories that feminize the foreigners and demonize the feminine as "amusing" (179), not harmful.

The primary function of women in *Boxers*, to go back to the subtext of Red Lantern's "particular appreciation for women," is to serve as objects of romantic and sexual desire, evident in the heteronormative romance plot concerning Bao and Mei-wen. Red Lantern, usually a figure who commands respect, acts out of character, goofy and juvenile, when he talks about women, anticipating Lu Pai's absurd comments: "I need to be careful. They say that if a man desires a woman too strongly, he will be polluted by her Yin. / But maybe some of us don't mind a little pollution, eh? Ha ha!" (58). He also talks about women as if they are otherworldly: "Even when they stink they smell like heaven! Women are something else! They're . . . they're *magic!*" (57). Women are thus seen as part of the realm of the fantastical, much like the opera gods, rather than part of the Boxers' reality, their history. These sexist ideas about women—as secondary to men, as variously monstrous, polluting, and objectified—are replicated without enough explicit critique for the readers. And the claim that this is just a reflection of something that was "historical" seems a cop-out.

The most troubling aspect of the treatment of women portrayed in *Boxers* is the culture of sexual harassment and abuse, perpetrated primarily by Bao's brother Chuan-tai. When Mei-wen claims she can never repay the men for their help, Chuan-tai leers, "Oh, I'm sure we can think of something" (134). He also objectifies women in statements like, "I mean, did you see that one girl in the last village? When she walked, the way her——" (194). Most disturbingly, toward the end of *Boxers*, Bao comes across Chuan-tai attacking Vibiana. When Bao inquires as to what Chuan-tai is doing, Vibiana exclaims, "What do you think he's doing?!" (242), implying that he's trying to rape her. But we don't witness the attempted rape, only its interruption, and the threat of sexual violence is never actually named. And in the statements above, Chuan-tai doesn't actually say what he wants Mei-wen to do and is cut off before naming the unnamed woman's body part. Yang portrays the Boxers' violence against women, and his critique of that pervasive violence, with ellipses and gaps. As a result, it's easy to ignore or gloss over this gendered violence and to subsume its significance in relation to the main storyline.

In *Saints*, the female protagonist's narrative is obviously foregrounded, although, as described above, it is a very different kind of story, narrow in scope, imagined as personal and private. Four-Girl/Vibiana turns to Christianity in order to escape her life as an unwanted and abused child within a patriarchal family. Her struggles are figured as individual and internal, rather than reflecting the broader struggles of a community or the nation. This is reflected in Yang's inspiration for the character, which came from his personal family history: "Vibiana was inspired by a relative of mine, a convert to Catholicism. She was born on a bad day according to traditional Chinese beliefs, and as a result, her grandfather treated her horribly. She was considered bad luck. She never connected her conversion to her childhood experiences, but to me the connection is clear as day. She couldn't find a place for herself in Eastern stories, so she turned to Western ones" (N. Clark). The other likely source of inspiration for Yang's female protagonist is Saint Vibiana, a third-century Roman martyr and the patron saint of the Roman Catholic Archdiocese of Los Angeles. Four-Girl chooses the name Vibiana for herself when she is baptized, another transhistorical, transnational connection.[11] It also seems no accident that she is named after a saint whose life story is unknown, who is absent from history, though her martyrdom and sainthood suggest she was important: "we know next to nothing about Saint Vibiana. . . . She is nobody and everybody" (Stoltz).

Unlike Bao in *Boxers*, who embarks on a hero's journey, even if it ends in failure, Four-Girl/Vibiana is depicted as a kind of antihero. Whereas Bao is empowered by his training to become a warrior for China, Four-Girl/Vibiana's religious education appears much less noble and agentive. Her initial attraction to Christianity is spurred by superficial reasons—by cookies, for example—and a misguided desire to embrace what she believes is her devilhood. And once she is baptized, none of her potential vocations are workable, whether becoming a priest, marrying seminarian Kong, or becoming a "MAIDEN WARRIOR" like Joan of Arc (Yang, *Saints* 103). The reality of her Christian life is not miraculous or magical but utterly ordinary, routine, and unfulfilling, as we see in a series of six square panels, laid out on one page, that depict a day in her life working at the orphanage. The first and last panels are nearly identical drawings of the orphanage, one taking place in the morning and the other at night, and the panels in between illustrate her routine of reading to the orphans, preparing their meals, feeding them, and putting them to bed (89). The life of a "saint" in this case is nothing more than the repetition of feminized labor. Though the mise-en-page shows us the passage of a single day and its work, it also gives the sense of multiple and never-ending days, all the same. There are subtle clues—her mouth set in a thin line or turned downward, her back turned to us as she prepares food—that signify the toll this monotonous domestic work has on her.

Even Vibiana's interactions with Joan of Arc, a more traditionally heroic figure, emphasize her disempowerment. Unlike the Boxers as opera gods, the fact of Joan's unrealness, her imaginariness, is confirmed and emphasized. And unlike Bao's encounters with Ch'in Shih-huang, Joan offers Vibiana very little in the way of guidance, drawing a clear boundary between them by saying things such as "Orleans is my destiny, Vibiana. Yours lies elsewhere" (91), and "I have my day's work, and you have yours!" (108). Joan remains distant, not the kind of

Figure 3.8. Gene Luen Yang,
Saints (2013): 160.

hero we can identify with as readers. Joan is also portrayed as somewhat gender
nonconforming. Vibiana initially thinks Joan is a boy and first refers to "him"
as "the skinniest boy I'd ever seen" (49). The narrative does not really comment
on why she makes this assumption. Even after she learns that this is Joan of Arc,
when she witnesses Joan's conversion moment, she asks herself, "How in the
world did this frightened little girl grow up to be that boy-girl dressed in metal?"
(56). What is it about Joan that makes Vibiana unable to imagine her as a girl or
woman? In these moments, *Saints* appears to support the idea that heroism, the
kind that involves action and violence, is always at least partially gendered male,
while faith, martyrdom, and sainthood are feminized.

Vibiana's most legibly heroic act in *Saints* comes at the end of her story and
life. In the moments before she is killed, Vibiana teaches Bao a prayer. She tells
him to "just *listen*" (159), and then there is a stark full bleed of Vibiana praying
on her knees, eyes closed, as Bao stands behind her (160; see figure 3.8). We know
this scene is crucial because, in the almost six hundred combined pages of *Boxers*

and *Saints*, Yang uses full bleeds—when the image runs all the way to the edges of the page, without borders or gutters—very sparingly. When he does use full bleeds, they are not necessarily at the most dramatic or climactic moments but seem to signal imminent change, such as Bao's embodiment of the element of fire before he kills Vibiana and massacres the remaining Christians in the church (*Boxers* 238), or the two-page spread depicting their arrival in Peking (256–57), which marks the beginning of *Boxers'* denouement. This moment in *Saints*, just a couple pages before the end of Vibiana's narrative proper, precedes her murder at the hands of Bao, an event that is much more quickly dispatched in *Boxers*. It is significant that there is no text on this page. On the page following the bleed, Vibiana says to Bao, "So that's what you say when you pray" (*Saints* 161). But the reader has not been privy to this prayer. As Douglas Wolk notes, "readers tend to hit the brakes when they encounter wordless sequences" (129). As readers, we linger in this moment of prayer with Vibiana, attending to her quiet act of heroism, as the angle of the image visually aligns our perspective with hers. Unfortunately, it appears to have little consequence, as Vibiana is murdered by Bao two pages later. Her story ends with the following short sentences in three small, separate narrative boxes: "And that was it. / That's how I died. / Unable to protect anyone" (Yang, *Saints* 162). Of course, Yang reveals that this is not entirely true and that there is indeed something heroic and saintly in Vibiana's actions.

Still, thinking about the conclusions of both volumes in tandem reinforces the primacy of Bao's story over Vibiana's, as Bao's actions and failures become a crucial part of this history, while Vibiana's death appears less historically meaningful. The epilogue to *Saints*, a volume ostensibly about Four-Girl/Vibiana's journey, returns us to Bao's narrative after Vibiana's death. This epilogue makes *Boxers* and *Saints* a true diptych, where the latter volume radically reframes the former. At the end of *Boxers*, it appears that Bao is dying, as he watches the opera gods fly away into the sky. But this epilogue fades in on a still-living Bao (165), who saves his own life by reciting the beginning of the Our Father prayer he had just learned from Vibiana (167–68). After his life has been spared, he is reunited with his brother Chuan-tai.

It is important to note that *Saints*, too, minimizes Chuan-tai's attempted rape of Vibiana, even more so than *Boxers*. In *Saints*, we see Chuan-tai sexually harassing Vibiana, her punching him, and him taking her, and then several pages later he is portrayed as reluctant to continue his attack. He says to her, "I thought I wanted . . . something from you, but not like this . . . This isn't what I want at all" (Yang, *Saints* 150). Again, the "something" Chuan-tai wants from her remains unspoken, and his hesitation is perhaps meant to be read as redeeming him in some way. This prepares the reader for the epilogue, which concludes both volumes with the reunion of the two brothers, both compromised but recommitted in their brotherly oath (169). Though it is clear that neither Bao nor Chuan-tai are good guys or heroes in the end, nonetheless they get to live and walk away from the violence they have wreaked, whereas the women, Mei-wen and Vibiana, are dead.

These interworkings of form and content, of genre and gender, remain a troubling aspect of Yang's retelling of the Boxer Rebellion. But even these gendered problematics in *Boxers* and *Saints* have something to teach us—the understanding that history, like popular culture, and indeed *as* popular culture, is always contested and in process, a site of constant struggle and contradiction, ambiguity and ambivalence. These two volumes are effective not only in teaching specific historical content but also in teaching nuanced approaches to historical thinking. In encouraging his readers "to look into the actual historical event" (Mayer) and "to look at both sides of every argument" (N. Clark), Yang reminds us that history is never complete or finished and must always be told from multiple perspectives.

Boxers and *Saints* are ostensibly about a moment in China's past, but the political and ethical questions they raise—about war and terror, nation and empire, religion and ethnicity, violence and justice, coming of age and gender—are of course central to our global present and future. And though these graphic narratives are clearly inflected by twenty-first-century Asian/American experiences and frameworks, they also tell a history that was already transnational and global, already raced, gendered, sexualized, and classed. Yang effectively draws such connections across time and space, taking seriously the task of interpreting and portraying the history of the Boxer Rebellion, while remaining committed to using pop culture to make his work accessible and relatable to contemporary readers. To borrow the words of comics scholar Joseph Witek, "this is history with a difference" (*Comic Books as History* 4).

NOTES

I wholeheartedly thank the editors, Martha J. Cutter and Cathy J. Schlund-Vials. Their generous and thoughtful feedback and guidance were of tremendous help in revising this piece.

1. For other Asian/American historical graphic narratives, see, for example, Henry (Yoshitaka) Kiyama's *The Four Immigrants Manga: A Japanese Experience in San Francisco, 1904–1924* (1931); Miné Okubo's *Citizen 13660* (1946); Ann Marie Fleming's *The Magical Life of Long Tack Sam* (2007); GB Tran's *Vietnamerica: A Family's Journey* (2010); David H. T. Wong's *Escape to Gold Mountain: A Graphic History of the Chinese in North America* (2012); and Thi Bui's *The Best We Could Do: An Illustrated Memoir* (2017).

2. See Conway; Wong. On the teachability of graphic narratives, see, for example, Hong 11–12. See also J. Clark on teaching nonfiction graphic narratives (though note the absence

of Asian/American texts). There are, however, valid concerns about the "'cartoonification' of history" and how it can reinforce certain modes of learning like rote memorization (Ford 125).

3. For teaching guides to *Boxers* and *Saints*, see Kelley; Jaffe.

4. See Cohen 286.

5. In Asia, the Boxers were glorified in films such as *Boxer Rebellion* (1976) and *Legendary Weapons of China* (1982), produced by the prolific and influential Shaw Brothers studio of Hong Kong cinema. In the West, "in film, fiction, and folklore, [the Boxers] functioned over the years as a vivid symbol of everything [we] most detested and feared about China—its hostility to Christianity, its resistance to modern technology, its fiendish cruelty, its xenophobia, its superstition" (Cohen 15). See also Forman on British adventure novels about the Boxers.

6. Japanese soldiers may have made up as much as one-third of the foreign troops that quelled the uprising. See Cohen 54.

7. When writing about this character in general, I refer to her, awkwardly, as Four-Girl/Vibiana. When discussing specific scenes, I refer to her as either Four-Girl or Vibiana, depending on how she self-identifies in those moments.

8. Mise-en-page refers to "page layout," or "the arrangement of elements in the space of the page" (Cohn 45).

9. See, for example, Cong-Huyen and Hong 83.

10. For more on the Boxers' relationship to women, see Cohen 119–45.

11. Many thanks to Cathy Schlund-Vials for pointing out this connection.

CHAPTER 4

Who Needs a Chinese American Superhero?

Gene Luen Yang and Sonny Liew's The Shadow Hero
as Asian American Historiography

Monica Chiu

AMID AN ENDURING RACIAL homogeneity visually evident in a history of superhero comics, Gene Luen Yang and Sonny Liew's graphic narrative *The Shadow Hero* (2014) boldly illustrates a visual history of difference by limning Chinese immigration, acculturation, and race consciousness in its introduction to the nation's first Chinese American superhero. Surprisingly, the unusual origin story resonates exceedingly well with themes typifying recognizable superhero figures. It does so by visualizing what is alien and what is native and by the process of animating masking and revelation. More provocatively, however, *The Shadow Hero* intertwines comics' superlative heroism with past derogatory Oriental references in an attempt to revise or reimagine both—what is heroism and its relation to Orientalism?—in the contemporary moment. *The Shadow Hero* limns a history of Chinese Americans in comics against the evolution of American superheroes, always looking backward to move forward.

Generally, mid-twentieth-century representations of the broad category of Asians in popular culture have been offensive. Theodor Seuss Geisel, for example, well known for his beloved *The Cat in the Hat* (1957) children's book, is less famous for his disparaging World War II cartoon editorials, such as that featuring a slant-eyed Emperor Hirohito in cahoots with Adolf Hitler. John Kuo Wei Tchen and Dylan Yeats provide a comprehensive collection of such racist images in their edited collection *Yellow Peril! An Archive of Anti-Asian Fear* (2014), cataloging historically typical anti-Asian imagery in American popular culture since the mid-nineteenth century.[1]

In the growing medium of comics, such objectionable caricatures disparaging racial and cultural differences have largely disappeared from print—despite occasional vicious recurrences—as the industry transitioned from serialization to what we now call the graphic narrative.[2] But the superhero genre's emphasis on contrasting native and immigrant or earthly and alien being endures. As a case in point, Yang iterates that Superman, debuting in 1938, "spends his whole life in between . . . cultures," that of the American one and that of the alien one

(Yang, "Interview").[3] Likewise, the twenty-first-century "*Shadow Hero* is really [also] about the immigrant experience" (Yang, "Interview"). States Gerard Jones of *Superman*, the series is "an allegory that echoed for immigrants and Jews [who dominated in early comics production]: the strange visitor who hides his alien identity so as to be accepted by a homogeneous culture" (173).[4] In this essay, I inquire if the Shadow Hero, featured in a narrative published by a mainstream comics press and created by an author (Yang) well respected for former publications debunking pervasive myths about Chinese Americans—and who is currently writing DC's Superman storylines—can be culturally (re-)imagined and accepted as a mainstream superhero in our current culture.

The Shadow Hero is Yang and Liew's invented backstory to Chu Hing's 1944–45 six-issue-only *Blazing Comics* series featuring an assumed Chinese superhero called the Green Turtle, a masked, caped guardian who assists China against Japan during World War II. Significantly, Chu was one of the first Asian Americans working in the Golden Age of comics, the name given to the first era of superhero comics that was ushered in by *Superman*'s 1938 debut and lasted through the mid-1960s. *The Shadow Hero*'s back matter contains a color reproduction of the first issue of *Blazing Comics* accompanied by Yang and Liew's unconfirmed speculation that because Chu's publishers doubted the commercial success of a Chinese American superhero among mostly non–Chinese American readers his face is always obscured by his swirling cape, his mask, his own arm, or another character (*Shadow Hero* 155). Furthermore, his skin is "an unnatural pink," write Yang and Liew, "as if to emphasize just how Caucasian this [masked, thus assumedly non-Chinese] hero is supposed to be," further prohibiting the possibility that an Asian/yellow superhero might be accepted by a mass, white readership (156). In *Blazing Comics*'s pages, raced characters appear only as expected and accepted slant-eyed, buck-toothed caricatures. Burma Boy, Green Turtle's accomplice against national and political imperialism but certainly not visual imperialism, frequently asks the Green Turtle for his origin story but is never afforded the luxury of a response (*Shadow Hero* 156). More than seventy years later, Yang and Liew's *The Shadow Hero* envisions the missing story as a historical addendum against Orientalized visual inscription.

Yang's former well-received graphic narratives, discussed at length later in the essay, iterate a commitment to re-visioning related issues of historic Orientalist types, recasting them as more socially ridiculous than perilous. In Yang's latest graphic narrative—throughout, I will distinguish between author Yang and artist Liew as needed—he casts the cape of the American superhero (a hero routinely perceived as a white man) over Depression-era Chinese American protagonist Hank Chu to fashion a Chinese American superhero who battles literal (embodied) stereotypes (such as dragon ladies, Fu Manchu–like types, Nehru suit-wearing henchmen), all of which appear in the visual archive of the history of Chinese Americans in popular culture. His characters perform so-called natural, embodied Orientalisms) modifying seemingly solidified visual inscriptions to demonstrate how the images exceed, or play with, originary or seemingly naturalized meanings. However, Yang and Liew's post-Orientalist humor is troubled by an enduring "Asiatic form"—a figure defined by Colleen Lye as embodying representations of Asians as Yellow Peril and model minority—because it resists assimilation into an American comics form that has been occupied by a traditionally white superhero. The form of the Asiatic masses encounters the masses of the comics form, two histories converging in a comics idiom.

I argue that *The Shadow Hero*'s revelation of a Chinese American superhero once doomed to anonymity by editorial decree is less engaging than its evocation of a historiography of Chinese Americans in comics. Examining Yang and Liew's *The Shadow Hero* through the failed *Blazing Comics* invites a dialogue about the cultural history of comics and graphic narratives in relation to the rise and fall of superheroes in mass culture. This essay examines the depiction of a history of race and immigration through the production of popular culture. Yet while Yang and Liew's narrative gestures toward Chinese (racial) affirmation, my argument suggests that we may not need a Chinese American hero, or that we may not need *this* Chinese American hero, at this cultural juncture.

Back Matter, Race Matters:
Superhero History and the Chinese in America

Joseph Witek contends, "Comic books as narrative and as cultural productions merit serious critical analysis" (*Comic Books as History* 3). His argument invites a reading in which the successional (progressive) histories of both comics superheroes and Asian Americans in U.S. politics and culture are juxtaposed against a so-called backward glance—to Golden Age heroes and to a 1930s Chinatown life—as prevalent in *The Shadow Hero*. Jerry Siegel and Joe Shuster's creation of *Superman* denoted a physically and ethically strong man *for* the people. Issue after issue, he defended Depression-era common folk against greedy corporate types, dangerous working conditions, or risky foreign entanglements, passing along to his successors a modus operandi to protect the weak. This prototype came to represent the typical superhero of the Golden Age of comics. Superheroes marketed during World War II participated in fierce patriotism and overseas support for the Allies, "sacrificing their freedom and individuality" for national and domestic policies, thus moving beyond the realm of a confined Metropolis toward national defense (Wright 207). Superhero comics confronted a slump during the panics of the 1950s, when publishers were charged with promoting youth violence, sexual desire, and xenophobia. But after World War II and amid a new atomic age, self-introspective heroes emerged—in contrast to the demigod heroes of yore—from the late 1950s to the 1970s. Spider-Man, for example, who debuted in 1962, accepts his awesome power as a great responsibility to those he protects and serves. During the Vietnam War protests and the civil rights and women's movements, however, superheroes, like many American citizens, noted hypocrisy in what increasingly was viewed as outdated narratives of patriotism, duty, and the rituals of domesticity (especially for women comics consumers) to which they had been tethered for so long. Scrambling for innovative characters during a period of comics censorship and a changing market, "reluctant" superheroes debuted, such as the Fantastic Four (1961) and the Hulk (1962) (Wright 207). Twenty years hence, after national civil rights eruptions and a nation on edge over policing communism, Wright argues that comics entered a "cynical era" in which the superhero, generally known for "good citizenry," became an "aberration" (266). The period gave rise to the aging, brooding *Batman: The Dark Knight Returns* (1986), with its right-wing Dark Knight (Batman) accompanied by his sidekick Carrie Kelley (the new, woman Robin), and the antiheroes of Alan Moore and Dave Gibbons's *Watchmen* (serialized from 1986 to 1987).[5] Yang and Liew's *The Shadow Hero* encompasses characteristics from each of these progressive periods. Like the original Superman, the character the Shadow Hero is dedicated to protecting the common folk of Chinatown while also endowed with keen self-consciousness, often self-doubt, in his sensitivity to race and gender ("I can't hit a girl!" he retorts to the fighting Chinese American Red Center [*Shadow Hero* 110]).

Related historical progressions and regressions are evoked in the narrative's 1930s Chinatown location, where residents are hemmed in by laws (such as the 1882 Chinese Exclusion Act, later bolstered by the 1892 Geary Act). Additional social restrictions bar them from citizenship, from owning land, and from marrying outside their race until tensions with China ease in the 1940s. In the same manner that Yang combines superhero characteristics from the advent of Superman to the present day, so too does he anachronize the teleology of Chinese American history: first-generation immigrants are embellished with twenty-first-century race consciousness; Depression-era Chinese gangsters are self-consciously aware of their own cartoon performativity, a racial a-formation of sorts.[6] *The Shadow Hero* looks backward and forward, simultaneously extrapolating from superheroes' origin stories, from Chinese American history, and from an archive of visual history, one to which Tchen and Yeats admonish us to "take notice of these [Oriental] ephemeral fragments and turn them into [critical] stories" (27). *The Shadow Hero* is thus both a cultural product of comics' history and a critique of it. Untethering history from its (progressive) sequentialism may be representative of the trajectory of Asian American subjectivity that has moved from exclusion and prohibition to the "liberation" and progress of the model minority. In my reading of *The Shadow Hero*, I question if it recovers from a racist past or relapses into a modern version of it.

Concomitantly, the superhero genre is the origin story for long-form, non-serialized graphic narratives such as *The Shadow Hero*. Such narratives evolved from the consternation over comics' so-called appalling representations of crime (as acceptable), horror, women, and race in the early and late 1950s, outlined above. Subsequent publishers' self-censorship contributed to a profound sense of innovation suffocation among comics artists, providing the impetus for underground comix, a short-lived phenomenon (from approximately 1968 to 1975), in which works were self-published or produced by small presses such as Last Gasp, Print Mint, or Kitchen Sink. From this movement for freedom of graphic expression arose graphic series and graphic narratives intentionally rendered ineligible to receive the medium's Comics Code Authority stamp of approval, such as Justin Green's seminal *Binky Brown Meets the Holy Virgin Mary* (1972), an autobiographical (nonserialized) tale of religious guilt, sexual thoughts, and obsessive-compulsive disorder. According to Hillary L. Chute, *Binky Brown* paved the way for Art Spiegelman's serialized *Maus* (1980–91) (Chute, Review 414), eventually a Pulitzer Prize–winning narrative, among other radical texts such as Harvey Pekar's *American Splendor* (1976–2008) and Phoebe Gloeckner's *A Child's Life and Other Stories* (1998). These groundbreaking texts and their successors—graphic narratives—highlighted a wide range of heretofore less accentuated themes in the medium, from illness and sexual trauma to adolescent angst and homosexuality. Subsequently, they provided more opportunities in the 1990s and the twenty-first century for an influx of graphic narratives by and about Asian Americans.[7]

Siegel's original Superman wrestled with assimilation and identity issues that continue to pervade Asian American graphic narratives, many of which, such as *The Shadow Hero*, address themes of identity, emasculation, model minority expectations, difference, immigration, nationalism, and transnationalism. Comics narratives in the groundbreaking *Secret Identities: The Asian American Superhero Anthology* (2009) follow a historical trajectory of Asian immigration and Asian Americans in popular, social, and legal culture, from depicting their contributions to building the transcontinental railroad and the internment of Japanese Americans to Wen Ho Lee–influenced allegations of espionage.[8] Cathy J. Schlund-Vials argues that the anthology is "a capacious revisionist project concerned with 'rectifying' . . . the paucity of Asian American superheroes" and an "'unmasking' of Asian America by way of 'Yellow Power' politics" ("Drawing from Resistance" 7, 10). Yang and Liew's "The Blue Scorpion and Chung" collected in *Secret Iden-*

tities is a fascinating precursor to *The Shadow Hero* because it revises superhero and Asian American idioms, foremost as a parody. In "The Blue Scorpion and Chung," the strong and agile masked Korean American chauffeur Chung protects his non-Asian employer, the Blue Scorpion, an impulsive, racist, and alcoholic masked "hero." In Yang and Liew's hands, the brave sidekick Chung shows up his boss, a comics caricature of the 1966–67 television series *The Green Hornet* in which martial arts–wielding sidekick Kato (represented by Chung), played by Bruce Lee, takes screen precedence over protagonist Green Hornet (represented by the Blue Scorpion), played by Van Williams. One assumes this outcome occurs repeatedly, cued to readers when a criminal, handcuffed in the back seat, casually remarks to Chung, "The news reports always make like you're Chinese. . . . You do all the work, he [Blue Scorpion, currently passed out in the front seat] gets all the glory" ("Blue Scorpion" 70). Chung's response, that "sometimes justice requires . . . sacrifices" (74), is illustrated by a series of flashbacks in which readers come to appreciate just the sacrifices Chung makes in pairing up with his pathetic boss, including the loss of his girlfriend and his identity as the true hero. Behind every successful white superhero, Yang intones, is a racial shadow. This comics one-off thus predetermines *The Shadow Hero* in which Yang dispenses with the Asian sidekick to explore the potential of a Chinese American superhero: the powers he possesses, what he lacks in cultural capital, and if, given a cultural climate in which heroes are assumed to be non-Asian, he can lead us from Superman to the Shadow Hero and beyond.

Updating American Superheroes

Yang and Liew's protagonist Hank Chu/Shadow Hero, emerging five years after the publication of "The Blue Scorpion and Chung," appears at a moment when graphic narratives by Asian Americans, often but not always featuring Asian American heroes, suddenly boast some recognizably complex heroic personalities whose powers often assist them in critiquing their (racial) place and depiction in America) Brian Lee O'Malley's Scott Pilgrim (2004–10) in his eponymous series (author O'Malley is Asian Canadian, but his protagonist Scott is not necessarily so); Suresh Seetharaman, Jeevan J. Kang, and Sharad Devarajan's Pavitr Prabhakar (the South Asian version of Peter Parker) in their *Spider-Man: India* (2004–5),[9] and writer G. Willow Wilson and artist Adrian Alphona's Kamala Khan in *Ms. Marvel* (2014–17). But despite this new cast of Asian American characters, typing (a reliance on caricatures) and not the advent of innovative heroes is *The Shadow Hero*'s currency. Liew's familiar Orientalist figures gloss, or perhaps defang, the aforementioned archive of anti-Asian fear mined by Tchen and

Yeats in which, as W. J. T. Mitchell states about the study of figures and symbols, "iconology recognizes itself as an ideology, that is, as a system of naturalization, a homogenizing discourse" (30). This ideological iconography drives how comics work, for as Derek Parker Royal argues, comics stereotypes "communicate quickly and succinctly" but can fall "into the trap . . . of inaccurate and even harmful representations" (68).[10] Interestingly, he never answers the important questions about who decides which images become harmful and offensive and which images serve to reimagine staid visual types.

On the one hand, the ideologically infused icons of Liew's *Shadow Hero*—a tong (gang) master and a tiger mother raising her model minority son—rewrite racial invisibility by granting superhero Hank a recognizable Chinese physiognomy against that of the traditionally white superhero; and more importantly, he is given a quotidian Chinatown family life. Yang visually asserts that Orientalist types in *The Shadow Hero* are endowed with other lives (maternal, familial, emotional lives) that typically have remained buried beneath the static representation of the stereotype. Thierry Groensteen's discussion in *Comics and Narration* (2013) of how a single-panel image "can *evoke* [but not necessarily tell] a story" endows Liew's seemingly flat (stereotyped) Orientalist images with storied depth, a progression that might explode stationary representations (23). On the other hand, as a revisionist history, *The Shadow Hero* assumes that readers understand the images' hyperbole as racial critique and thus trades on these Orientalist stereotypes for laughs. According to Henry B. Wonham, "the insubstantiality of the caricatured image [as deviation], its exaggerated artificiality, is itself a rebuke to the very idea of the norm" (32). Yet because the jokes rely on the social stability of the exaggeration, repetition of caricature stalls progress into a different future for the Chinese American image.

That said, when outdated images meet politically and socially updated characters in *The Shadow Hero*, they are viewed as both charming and problematic. In a discussion of a history of types and their possible destruction, I begin with Hank's mother Hua, whose character addresses issues relevant to immigrants, to women immigrants, and to assumptions about Chinese American women. Hua is deeply disappointed on her arrival into the fictional American coastal city that Yang calls San Incendio, what she views as a dirty, smelly, noisy place so unlike the one embedded in her vivid imagination delineating a cleaner and literally brighter nation; that said, flashbacks to her immigrant youth are rendered in gray and brown tones. Disappointment fosters her resignation to marriage, motherhood, and domesticity, the latter playing out both in her own home and in her role as a maid and chauffer to a wealthy white woman. Seemingly docile to her employer, she exhibits defiance and bravery in the white woman's absence. Part resourceful first-generation immigrant and part twenty-first-century pop-culture tiger mom, she represents the juxtaposition of anachronistic images that range loosely along Robert G. Lee's trajectory of the "six faces of the Oriental" (8–12).[11]

Hua's humdrum life experiences an exciting jolt when she is dramatically rescued from a gun-toting thief by the Anchor of Justice, a caped, flying superhero who happens to be hovering about San Incendio when she finds herself face to face with the thief's gun. While Yang intimates Hua's own desire to become a superhero[12]—undoubtedly an exciting break in the monotony of her days—she understands the restrictions to such a fantasy imposed on her gender and her race: white women citizens had only recently received suffrage in the 1920s, and Chinese women, whether citizens of America or not, were subject to patriarchal strictures that too often forestalled their potential beyond domestic duties and employment. From that day forth, Hua dedicates herself to fashioning a superhero from her average son Hank, also an unlikely hero candidate. The vividly iconoclastic Hua again resigns herself to occupying the role of a typical, self-sacrificing Chinese mother as well as an overpowering, zealous tiger mom who, in this humorous version, idealizes a profession for her son not in the expected fields of law or medicine but in superheroism. In her determination to endow Hank with a superpower, she kicks him into a toxic spill, after which he gains the culturally advantageous ability to turn pink when wet—to become visibly Caucasian—which is Yang's reversal of the so-called contagious Asian immigrant (a "condition" whose condemnation involves the entire white/pink race) and his comment on the cultural power of whiteness.[13] If Hua herself cannot become a (white) woman superhero, her pink Chinese son has a chance. Thus, the origin of one of Hank's so-called superpowers is a humorous riff on the serious phenomenon of race as a visible entity, or race *as* empowering or disempowering.

Hank's second superpower animates Orientalist mythology: he inherits his father's shadow from the "old country," a Chinese turtle spirit, one of four, all of whom were "born with China, and throughout the centuries they had watched over her [the nation]" (Yang and Liew, *Shadow Hero* 1). After his father's murder by a local tong, the shadow endows Hank with the ability to be unassailable, literally, by guns and, metaphorically, by snide remarks about his identity, not as a Chinese American—Yang suggests we have moved beyond such affronts—but as a Chinese American superhero. Villain Mock Beak's Chinese henchman states, "Ha ha ha! I thought only *gwailo* [foreigners] were shameless enough to dress up like that!" (133), intimating that the Chinese American Shadow Hero cuts a ridiculous figure, to the Chinese themselves, in his cape and tights. Indeed, perhaps a Chinese American woman superhero would have been less incredulous and whimsical, as Hua is naturally endowed with an amazing strength of spirit that

Hank must slowly, painfully earn through physical training. Playing with cultural myths such as superheroes, Chinese animal spirits, and tiger moms, Yang and Liew attempt to defuse the ideology behind them.[14]

Subversions as Merely More Oriental Versions

Two superheroes work amiably in *The Shadow Hero*, the domestic Hank Chu and the extraterrestrial Anchor of Justice, the latter exposing Hank's continued feelings of alienation as a visibly and culturally different racial subject. The sentiment harkens back to Superman as "the strange visitor who hides his alien identity so as to be accepted by a homogeneous culture," as quoted earlier, and further associates the seemingly disparate areas of science fiction culture and immigrant assimilation. Justice's planetary alienation from earth assists us in understanding the Shadow Hero's cultural alienation from the dominant society. Justice removes his fleshlike (pink) mask in a near-concluding panel to reveal the metal visage beneath it. He confides to the Shadow Hero, "my parents aren't from around here, either" (152).[15] Lan Dong argues of this sequence, "Some masks, just like some racial registers, are more visible than others. It is their differences as much as their common identities that connect the Green Turtle [so called before Hank's adoption of the name the Shadow Hero] to the Anchor of Justice. It is through such 'productive interaction' that the book destabilizes the historical racialization of Asian Americans as well as the convention of white superheroes in American comics" (Dong 16). Yang's hero, rooted in a Depression-era past, encounters a future being who helps him assess his existence in the present. At narrative's end, however, the Shadow Hero declines Justice's invitation to fight evil the world over, settling on protecting the more circumscribed population of Chinatown. Similar to Superman's circulation in Metropolis and Batman's in Gotham City, Yang limits the novelty and cultural power of a Chinese American superhero to a Chinese American location. Progress and regress go hand in hand in *The Shadow Hero*: one step forward through a Chinese American superhero, one step back in twenty-first-century self-confinement to a limited arena.

In contemplating *Blazing Comics'* possible deliberate concealment of the Green Turtle's racial identity, Yang and Liew wonder if Chu and his publisher "are wrestling [over the superhero's identity] within the art itself" (*Shadow Hero* 157). *The Shadow Hero* emphasizes notions of duality, perhaps most simply through a narrative background that traces the history of Chinatown and superheroes and through a foreground, or what I argue is the effect on the reader of Yang and Liew's comics' reimaging of historical representation. All of *The Shadow Hero's* main characters suffer from duality, possessing one mundane and one exaggerated personality. Yang accepts the hierarchy that the mundane is expected while the exaggerated is imagined. While Emperor Ten Grand, for example—a white man in yellow face who serves as the emcee of the opulent Palace of Forbidden Fortunes Bar and Casino—is composed of such a duality, the fact remains that M. Bender, the failing actor behind the mustache and face paint, can summarily dismiss his act as merely lucrative play in tough financial times and still be taken seriously as a white man in his natural face. Hank as superhero and Hua as an immigrant/tiger mother are clearly not to be taken seriously, yet, unlike Ten Grand, they also are not conveniently exchanged for financial gain. Hank and Hua always play into societal expectations even when they do not intend to.

The Shadow Hero's fight scenes, certainly an expectation in a superhero narrative, pulse with energy, but the narrative's assertive emphasis on literally shattering stereotypes is more funny than aggressive. Interspersed among onomatopoetic comics' whacks, whaps, whumps, kapows, and gongs reside other such clichéd language, all of which announce a focus on play: the lovestruck Shadow Hero wooed into a literal trap (door) by the beautiful, Chinese cheongsam-wearing Red Center; the flail-wielding henchman in a Nehru suit; the good Justice who appears more like a floating high priest with a receding hairline than a superhero. A cute turtle divides the book's chapters. If, as Sandra Oh argues, the cloying film featured at the start of the graphic narrative *Shortcomings* (Adrian Tomine, 2007) and vigorously critiqued by the narrative's protagonist assures us that author/artist Adrian Tomine's representations of race will not be equally as "corny" (130), *The Shadow Hero*'s reliance on a racist archive turns this tack on its head. Liew visualizes, playfully and charmingly, Asian American visual inscriptions to re-animate and retell the already hypervisible. The upshot is an unabashed and intended corniness through which *The Shadow Hero* repossesses a century of Asian American racial injury, embodied by culturally and politically alienated subjects, an insurmountable racial melancholy, as argued by Anne Anlin Cheng. In the realm of the mawkish, what undergirds Hank's superpower subjectivity is his turtle spirit, the one who goes rogue by departing from his beloved China, first hitching a ride across the ocean in the shadow of Hank's father, then occupying Hank's shadow. Thus embodied, the turtle spirit first endows Hank's father with the ability to resist alcohol or a propensity to drink. This is just the personal downfall that brought him unintentionally to America, as in this inebriated state he accidentally stumbles onto a ship bound for America, Yang's jab at an accepted history of willful Chinese immigration to Gold Mountain.

When the turtle spirit occupies Hank's shadow, he grants him the ability to resist bullets. This power accords with other of the narrative's race politics in which reappropriating the derogatory by projecting its comic side is one strategy for dodging racist bullets. If the aforementioned collection *Secret Identities: The Asian American Superhero Anthology* is committed to uncovering what

Schlund-Vials calls "shadow histories," or the "shameful concealment and en-compassing narratives of exploited labor, racism, and war" that "are inextricably part of the larger 'unmasking' project" ("Drawing from Resistance" 15–16), then *The Shadow Hero* also clearly commits to a project of unmasking, but its Chinese "alien" is hardly the "disturbing and dangerous" Orientalist version referenced in Robert G. Lee's historical trajectory (3). Rather, it is a playful one whose powers to effect ideological change seem relatively benign.

In Yang and Liew's graphic narrative tack, historical origins are playful pop-culture objects. For Oh, on the other hand, Tomine's *Shortcomings* can unhinge Asian American racial identity from a preexisting social script to create Ben, a conflicted and contradictory protagonist who resists culturally prescribed Asian Americanness while coveting whiteness. *The Shadow Hero*, however, rescripts images to charm rather than complicate its characters or haunt its readers. Ulti-mately, the narrative's allure reminds us that under the cape and mask, Hank Chu is still a Chinese American man whose claim to superhero fame is stymied by negative assumptions about race and empowerment, in and out of comics.

The Shadow Hero shares iconic and narrative similarities to Yang's *American Born Chinese* (2006) in which protagonists Jin Wang (who attempts to become white) and the Monkey King (an animal in Chinese literary classics who attempts self-deification while abhorring his monkey state) eventually accept their inherent Chinese American and monkey (essentialist) selves, respectively. While *American Born Chinese* was praised for dismantling persistent and pervasive Chinese Amer-ican stereotypes through the same kind of visual humor used in *The Shadow Hero*, Michael Cadden argues convincingly that "In *American Born Chinese*, intentional transformation for change is never a real option. It is self-delusion," closing off the narrative from the transformative options proclaimed by Yang's reviewers. If the Monkey King expresses to Jin "how good it is to be a monkey" (Yang, *American Born* 223), it intimates that Jin must find self-satisfaction as a "racial minority," argues Cadden. He must accept that he always will remain "subordinate" to the likes of (white racial shadow) Danny. How, then, asks Cadden, is Jin to "move forward"?[16] This question haunts *The Shadow Hero* and scholars such as Min Hy-oung Song who inquire into where "race thinking" leads in the "unique" graphic form of *American Born Chinese*, given its origins and perpetuation in "a history of [Asian American] visual representation" (Song, *Children of 1965* 131). Indeed, where does Yang and Liew's race rethinking lead us? *The Shadow Hero* proposes Chinese American progress away from stereotypical origins in spite of Hank's evolution into a mythological hero because this hero's foundational roots lie, in-controvertibly, in the form of a revered white American Superman. But Hank, while toxically pink, will never be racially white.

The theme of Chinese American subordination is echoed in author Yang and artist Thien Pham's *Level Up* (2011), in which Chinese American protagonist Dennis Ouyang accepts the model minority identity against which he has been fighting his entire life by continuing his medical studies after a brief hiatus, during which he questions the impetus behind his studies: Is it his own or is it heavily encouraged by his father's desires for his son's future profession as a doctor? Yang suggests that the idea of the model minority inevitably lies within this and other of his Chinese American characters' essentialist cores. Dennis's self-acknowledgment that he is a model minority (and his decision to continue his medical studies) and Jin's self-acceptance as a Chinese American do little to change the types. The persistence of Asian American types is commensurate with the rigid trajectory of the publishing industry in which mainstream superheroes are never Asian American, and those artists who create them do so as flimsy counters to their absence in popular culture.

If *American Born Chinese* imaginatively recuperates stereotyping through the historical figure of Chin-kee, based on late nineteenth-century anti-Chinese cartoons, Yang again relies on history in his *Boxers* and *Saints* to dismantle ideologies and typing surrounding the 1900 Boxer Rebellion (circa 1899–1901). Yang illustrates that while Western missionizing was indeed a form of imperialism, inhumanity circulated among both the Chinese nationalists and the Christians against whom the former fought. Neither proponents or advocates of Christianity nor those of Chinese mysticism practiced acceptable human morality. This is a powerful revisionist history that speaks back to the cultural construction of Chin-kee and Chinese American Jin as well as to Dennis's expected model minority status in ways that *American Born Chinese* and *Level Up* cannot do alone. If Jin must accept "an inferior position relative to others of his kind," states Cadden, so, too, must Shadow Hero Hank Chu, for his is inevitably (racially) less "super" among a popular audience than he self-imagines. Perhaps not all revisions are possible: neither successful assimilation into America nor mass appeal among readers of superhero comics.[17]

The Asiatic Racial Form Meets the Comics Form

Yet mass appeal is comics' foundation, a medium grounded in the masses of its readership, affecting production decisions and those academics who repeatedly encounter the othering of comics as a second-class art, questioning their value as scholarly texts.[18] Moreover, Superman's intentions to protect America's common people, just those masses that uphold the medium, resonate with the popularized racial othering evident in the historic Yellow Peril illustrations that Yang revises in *The Shadow Hero*. These recognizable caricatures emerge from nineteenth-century magazines and newspapers, later appearing in cartoons and comics (see

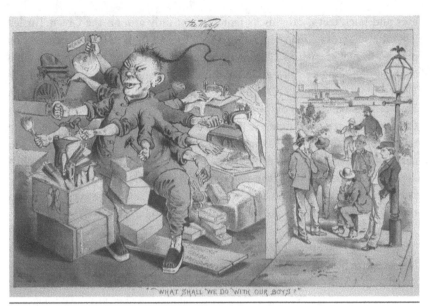

Figure 4.1. George Frederick Keller, "What Shall We Do with Our Boys?" for the *San Francisco Illustrated Wasp*, March 3, 1882.

figure 4.1). Before aggressive anti-Asian sentiment appeared in the United States, fascination over so-called curious Chinese immigrants and their quaint Chinatown quarters drove the "cultural inaccuracies" and "artistic license" that are depicted in images of the Chinese appearing in nineteenth-century publications such as *The Wasp* (1876–1941) or *Harper's Weekly* (1857–1916), consumed by a predominantly "white male readership," as argued by Philip P. Choy, Lorraine Dong, and Marlon K. Hom in *The Coming Man: 19th Century American Perceptions of the Chinese* (21, 22). Eventually, however, images of the exotic celestial devolved into "vicious political cartoons" amid increasing conflict between China and America (21). Such images often featured *throngs* of new overseas Chinese disembarking from sailing vessels or *masses* of Chinatown residents crammed into limited quarters, illustrating what Colleen Lye calls the Asiatic racial form: the swarms, hordes, and masses of Asian bodies that so threatened, and even now continue to alarm, the economic, political, and corporeal (physical and material) body of America. For embodied within this mass was a foreboding yet modernizing ability that might potentially crush a vulnerable West (17).[19] Asians were thus imagined as both threat and model to the Western world.

The anthropomorphic "venomous octopus . . . bent on ruthless conquest" featured in the first panel of *Blazing Comics* no. 1 metaphorizes an Asian imperialist reach, here that of the nation of Japan; the octopus's human face, with its slanted eyes and buck teeth, extends its tentacles not only around the Green Turtle's leg but also across a map highlighting locations of high Asian populations, or masses, in places such as China ("the oppressed Chinese" and "an incredible confusion of refugees"), Tibet, India, Burma, Thailand, Sumatra, and other Far East regions (see figure 4.2). The use of an octopus resonates well with the George Frederick Keller cartoon of the octopus-like Chinese laborer, in which vigorous Chinese industry—the figure is literally a jack-of-all-trades—results in white men's underemployment. Juxtaposed against the background of a rising sun clearly affiliated with Japan is the friendly looking Chinese turtle shadow/spirit depicted as an extension of the superhero Green Turtle. Within the comic, the poor Chinese *masses*, aggressively routed by "a large Japanese force," depend on this *solitary* superhero for their lives and their national security.

Keller's image also illustrates the two sides of the Asiatic racial form, efficiency and threat. Speaking through hundreds of Yellow Peril images, this form is a recognizable template, easily grasped by its non-Asian reading audience, so much so that Yellow Peril fears are "crystalized and embedded in the West," argue Tchen and Yeats (15). Yet they endure as visual ideology because such images so efficiently reflect recurring social attitudes, as in a 1997 *National Review* cover illustrating members of the former first family, the Clintons, in yellow face after political campaign contributor John Huang made headlines for his hefty but illegal donations to the Clinton administration. Concomitantly, the superhero is also an enduring and flexible formula. Initially marked by the mask and cape of Superman and his socially responsible work (Harvey 21), this version was significantly modified in subsequent superhero comics, discussed earlier, with the introduction of heroes who began to possess "distinct personalities as realistic and quirky as those of their readers," evidenced first in Jack Kirby's Fantastic Four, later in the X-Men and the Avengers (47). Mocking the superhero formula by endowing seemingly impervious strong men with psychological human frailties proved appealing, especially to the emerging collegiate readership of the time. In Yang and Liew's *The Shadow Hero*, the re-presentation of the superhero formula meets the enduring but flexible re-vision of the Asiatic form. The seemingly natural rippling musculature of Chu Hing's Green Turtle, for example, evolves only slowly in *The Shadow Hero*. Hank is a scrappy teen, typically emasculated as an Asian American male youth; only through daily physical training, accompanied by pain and bodily injury, can he evolve into the sculpted strongman Shadow Hero. In humanizing superheroes after what is called the Golden Age of comics (ushered in by Superman), a hero form or model came to be grounded in the notion of an evolution in which backstories provide the basis for the present and the future. Yang and Liew's *The Shadow Hero* speaks *back* to the formula of the

Figure 4.2. *Blazing Comics*,
no. 1. From the appendix of
Yang and Liew's *The Shadow
Hero*: n.p.

Asiatic other by eliminating the stereotypical Japanese enemy against whom the (1944) Green Turtle fights.

In animating the Green Turtle's imagined history, Yang and Liew single out Chu Hing from a vast collection of artists who once worked anonymously in comics' industrial production mode. *The Shadow Hero* endorses author-driven recognition against the character-forged or publisher- and later corporate-produced comics arena of the past, in which superhero characters were associated with corporate brands such as Marvel or DC. That *The Shadow Hero* is now incontrovertibly linked to comics "star" Gene Luen Yang and artist Sonny Liew endorses *The Shadow Hero*'s project of revealing the masked man in the early comics pages of *Blazing Comics*. It illustrates the importance of how Asian North American bodies and their racial inscriptions are envisioned and, conversely, how such visions can influence what we mean by individuality, nationality, and citizenship.

Small of Stature, Big on Solving Crimes: Future Asian American Superheroes

The Shadow Hero offers a rich, if brief, history of how race gets written into graphic narrative. It catalogs, broadly, Asian representations in popular culture at the same time that it questions the necessity for this Chinese American super-hero at this moment. That is, Yang and Liew's revisionist history that reinserts Chinese Americans into a comics past says little about Chinese American progression into the future. It delivers a Chinese American superhero but raises the uncomfortable proposition that perhaps we no longer need the Shadow Hero. Rather, the current comics market supports Chinese American characters, or more broadly Asian American characters, who need not be (super)heroes to be regarded as champions of Asian American causes or to battle against racist imagery in the cultural imaginary. And it supports the incorporation of Asian American comics' authors and artists. As a strong case in point, Yang recently joined the DC team, penning the script for, at this writing, *Superman* issue nos. 41 and 42 (2015). Consider also the graphic series *Chew* (2009–16) by John Layman and Rob Guillory, which intriguingly supports the notion that Chinese Americans are already grounded in their American nationality; they fit within the nation among other (nonracialized) misfits.[20] Protagonist Tony Chu, like Hank, is bandy legged and muscle deprived, but he is an excellent shot with his gun. Working first for the FBI, he eventually is transferred to the FDA for his ability to ascertain the history of any piece of food he ingests: the pesticides used on an apple, for example, or the orchard where it was grown, or the abattoir where a slaughtered cow eventually becomes the hamburger on his plate. That he is required in volume 1 to take a bite of both a corpse and a dog uneasily harkens back to Chinese types, but because his non-Chinese nemeses possess the same gustatory ability that Layman names "cibopathy," this unusual gustatory feature is de-essentialized, argues Jeanette Roan, shifting it from its accepted Chinese American practice. If eating dog or cannibalizing to solve crimes is naturalized in *Chew* across a range of raced cibopathic characters, so, too, are a host of other alimentary-related powers among a variety of racial, ethnic, and gendered characters. Small in stature but big on solving crimes, Tony—unabashedly and unassumingly Asian American—emerges as the undeniable hero among other of *Chew*'s principal and ancillary characters whose bodily physiques resemble those of Superman on steroids.

The Shadow Hero is less an attempt to map a history of Chinese Americans than to chart a history of Asian Americans in superhero comics. It deftly limns a collection of histories even if it falls short of challenging the racist hyperboles of racial representation. The stasis of the former argument grates against the focus on an origin story, an excavation resulting in a reincarnation. The narrative endeavors to look back in order to look ahead. But to what future such a narrative, such a superhero, points us is a vital question for superhero studies, graphic narrative studies, and Asian American and ethnic studies.

NOTES

1. Such types were the focus of a 2011 exhibition called "Marvels and Monsters in U.S. Comics, 1942 to 1986," curated by Jeff Yang. Its online version was managed by D. Daniel Kim (produced by the Asian/Pacific/American Institute at New York University).

2. The visual rhetoric of caricature surfaced in presidential campaign commercials as recent as 2012. I use Chute's term "graphic narratives" and not "graphic novels" (*Graphic Women* 3) to discuss nonserialized long-form works in sequential form while aware that so-called graphic narratives such as Art Spiegelman's *Maus* and Alan Moore and David Gibbons's *Watchmen* appeared serially before being collected into book-length narratives.

3. See Jean-Paul Gabilliet's *Of Comics and Men: A Cultural History of American Comic Books* (2009) and Gerard Jones's *Men of Tomorrow: Geeks, Gangsters, and the Birth of the Comic Book* (2004). Early comics production at DC and Marvel included what Gerard Jones calls prominent "Jewish kids," some of whom altered their names to mask their ethnic heritage, others to disassociate from the stigma of being a comics creator: Jack Liebowitz, Bob Kahn (Kane), Harry Donenfeld, Charlie Gaines, Stanley Lieber (Lee), Jake Kurtzberg, Will Eisner, Mort Weisinger, Julie Schwartz, and Bill Finger (Jones 135, 202, xiv, 129).

4. Jones goes on, "Secret identity stories always reverberated with the children of Jewish immigrants, of course, because they were so much about the wearing of the masks that enabled one to be an American, a Modern, a secular consumer, but still part of an ancient society, a link in the old chain, when safely among those who knew one's secret" (201).

Furthermore, Superman was inventor Jerry Siegel's imagined alter ego, the artist's own desires to be somebody with more magnetic talents and abilities than Siegel himself felt he possessed as an awkward high school student (Harvey 19).

5. According to Bradford W. Wright, the revised X-Men of the 1970s and 1980s, so unlike the everyman's Superman of the 1940s, were "outsiders . . . feared and hated by the society that they fought to defend" (263), while *Watchmen*'s societal "aberrations," forced out of retirement, are "a force for ruthless morality in a corrupt society that feared and despised them," thus marking the moral complexity of superheroes from around 1970 to the mid-1980s (266).

6. See Min Hyoung Song's "How Good It Is to Be a Monkey: Comics, Racial Formation, and *American Born Chinese*."

7. See my edited collection *Drawing New Color Lines: Transnational Asian American Graphic Narratives* (2015).

8. Following *Secret Identities*, the editors produced *Shattered: The Asian American Comics Anthology* (2012) featuring an expanded cast of characters in genres other than that of the superhero comic.

9. See Davé 130.

10. For more on this, see the introduction to my *Drawing New Color Lines*. Also see Joseph Witek's "Comics Modes: Caricature and Illustration in the Crumb Family's *Dirty Laundry*."

11. Min Hyuong Song introduces this juxtaposition as a critical element of the changing nature of racial typing in "How Good It Is to Be a Monkey."

12. Lan Dong points out that Hua wears the mask in the unpublished essay "Asian American Graphic Narratives: An Introduction" (11).

13. See Nayan Shah's *Contagious Divides: Epidemics and Race in San Francisco's Chinatown* (2001); a toxic spill in an immigrant community invokes arguments raised by Robert D. Bullard's *Dumping in Dixie: Race, Class, and Environmental Quality* (1990).

14. In this spirit of self-conscious play, the boat that takes Hank to Coolie Hat Rock, where the Palace of Forbidden Fortunes Bar and Casino stands, is named the "Caniff" after the creator of *Terry and the Pirates* (1934–76), featuring the first Dragon Lady of the comics.

15. Relatedly, the burden of history is so heavy for African Americans that any state of alienation by African American comics characters feels historically authentic. African Americans are no strangers to the surreal "as an everyday and historical experience," argues Adilifu Nama, for "what other group of people can lay claim to alien abduction and transportation on ships to strange faraway places as historical fact?" (11). Because contemporary African American artists are influenced by superhero and horror comics, the cosmic, and politics, they fashion "space"—both artistically and in time—to "critique the facile and crude representational clichés that have governed how blackness is presented and contrived in the American public imagination, television and film," argues Nama (11).

16. Cadden states, "While the narrative implies that racial denial is simply unacceptable, and makes a case for moving forward, it does not show us what moving forward looks like, which strikes me as much more important in this novel than in novels generally. The

Monkey King may offer Jin Wang acceptance of his racial identity, but Jin is left with really nothing but his racial identity." He concludes, "Jin is to make his peace with the fact that he is a lesser human as the Monkey King is a lesser deity, and that it begins and ends with race. The conclusion is that one is to be content as both separate and unequal, and that this is a divine arrangement. Be yourself."

17. While it is beyond the scope of this essay to discuss all of Yang's work, his *Animal Crackers* (2010) is another example revising Asian types.

18. When discussing early cartoons such as *Hogan's Alley* (1894–96), Jared Gardner points out that the first generation of comics' artists who were publishing in syndicated Sunday supplements reached a huge (nationalizing) readership (*Projections* 12). If, as Bart Beaty insists, comics are "the products of a particular social world" (43), it is understandable that early newspaper cartoons focused on "the grim realities of modern urban life," as Gardner illuminates (13), encompassing class and immigrant issues and poverty and thus choosing to create cartoon street kids such as Mickey Dugan (9). When Superman arrived on the popular culture scene, he came prepared to protect the common (American) man against corporate greed, mismanagement resulting in physically dangerous working conditions, and other precarious situations presenting potential dire consequences to the nation's everyman. Within the industry itself, comics were created through mass production, according to Bradford W. Wright, involving the collaborative efforts of script writers, illustrators, colorists, inkers, and letterers all working together in "an assembly-line production process" (22). And finally, in arguing how the vigorous work of fandom has elevated particular comics artists and authors (such as Jack Kirby and Robert Crumb) out of the industry's mass production morass into the more unusual phenomenon of comics stardom, Beaty demonstrates how this (mass) process of recognizing genius diverges from that established by the distinguished art world. In his study *Comics versus Art* (2012), he carefully charts the continued distinction, from as early as the arrival of Mickey Dugan, between the "low" comics audience and the "high" elite of the art world.

19. Lye draws examples of the evils of rapid industrialization from Progressive Era writers and journalists such as Jack London and Frank Norris. Within their journalistic and fictional depictions, the figure of the Asian takes a racial form: admired for its modernity (the construction of a city within a city, for example, referencing tunnels dug by the Japanese during the Russo-Japanese War, 1904–5) at the same time that their large numbers (as growing populations in their own countries, as a "mob" of protesters in others) come to represent the strong arm of industrialization/modernity itself, a faceless, nameless being crushing all within its path. In this sense, the East is seen as equal to the West; and sometimes, the capable East rendered the West in its "vulnerability to degeneration" (17).

20. Also consider Fred Chao's Johnny Hiro (2007–13) in his eponymous series, a scrawny, scrappy, and happy Japanese American kid working in a sushi restaurant whose adventures revolve around saving his girlfriend from Hollywood-inspired monsters such as Godzilla and King Kong. The creatures' cultural comment on nationalism, national antagonism, race, and gender undergird Johnny's battles against cultural imperialism, racism, and sexism.

CHAPTER 5

Stuck Rubber Baby and the Intersections of Civil Rights Historical Memory

Julie Buckner Armstrong

BIRMINGHAM, ALABAMA, PRODUCED some of the civil rights move-ment's most iconic words and images. During spring 1963, local and national activists joined forces in Project C, to "confront" this violently defended bastion of white economic and political power. In April, Martin Luther King Jr. out-lined the moral underpinnings of Project C's nonviolent protest with "Letter from a Birmingham Jail." Responding to the question of why movement forces had focused their efforts in that city, King's letter stated, "I am in Birmingham because injustice is here," and continued, "A threat to injustice anywhere is a threat to justice everywhere." Birmingham's commissioner of public safety, The-ophilus Eugene "Bull" Connor, embodied Jim Crow segregation. In May, when marchers—many of them children and teens—convened near the intersection of Sixteenth Street and Sixth Avenue North, the jowl-faced and pot-bellied Connor met them with a white armored tank and a bullhorn, barking orders to stop. After they did not, Connor had police dogs and fire hoses turned on them, making headlines around the world. Embarrassed city leaders wound up agreeing to hire black workers and to desegregate downtown stores and restaurants. The victory was short lived. Later that year, less than three weeks after the March on Wash-ington for Jobs and Freedom, events in Birmingham plunged the movement from elation to mourning. On Sunday, September 15, segregationists targeted the Sixteenth Street Baptist Church because of its civil rights organizational activ-ity. The bomb blast wounded twenty people and claimed four lives: Addie Mae Collins, Denise McNair, Carole Robertson, and Cynthia Wesley. The deaths of these "four little girls," as they are known collectively, generated a widespread outpouring of creative response that includes literary works, music, film, visual art, and public memorial. More than fifty years later, the church bombing—and Birmingham more generally—remains a significant moment in civil rights move-ment historical memory.[1]

Small wonder that Howard Cruse chose to set his 1995 graphic narrative *Stuck Rubber Baby* in a city where he, like his protagonist Toland Polk, came of age amid tumultuous civil rights developments. The plot centers on an older Toland's recount of a traumatic period from his past to a longtime, caring male partner. Toland's history involves not only wrestling with his sexuality during a dangerously homophobic time but also confronting the murder of his friend Sammy Noone, an openly gay man killed for speaking out against racist violence. The book "is a work of fiction, not autobiography," Cruse states in the acknowledgments (213), but lines between the two remain permeable. Events from Toland's life parallel those from Cruse's—including the birth of a daughter, the book's eponymous "baby." Although Cruse calls the town where Toland lives "Clayfield," its civil rights trajectory closely resembles Birmingham's. Demonstrators gather in a park where a commissioner named Sutton Chopper orders police dog attacks on them. Protest leaders coordinate activities from a motel rather than a church, and the motel is bombed shortly after Toland and his girlfriend—a folk singer named Ginger Raines—attend the March on Washington. The blast kills several young people and injures Ginger's friend Shiloh, an incident that sets in motion Sammy's death and, eventually, Toland's coming out. While many readers will recognize the historical basis of such details, other characters and places populating *Stuck Rubber Baby*'s Jim Crow–saturated landscape seem to be the stuff of what Cruse calls "fiction." However, the integrated mix of heterosexuals, gay men, lesbians, and drag performers who circulate through the book's parks, churches, motels, and bars has a direct autobiographical basis with clear historical roots. Such diversity may only seem unfamiliar because of the formal and thematic intersections that *Stuck Rubber Baby* inhabits: a graphic narrative that is also a work of movement fiction—where civil rights, usually coded as black, meets gay rights, mistakenly conceived of as white. Through those intersections the book creates a path where people and places from the margins move to center stage.

Reframing the Civil Rights Movement through Graphic Narrative

A variety of factors led Cruse to those intersections. Born in 1944, he grew up outside of Birmingham in a town called Springfield, smaller than the Clayfield that Toland inhabits. During the early 1960s, he attended Birmingham-Southern, a liberal arts college near Smithfield, where much of the racist violence occurred that gave the city its nickname, "Bombingham." Cruse's college years resemble Toland's early twenties in their broader outlines. The author refers to this period as his "youthful strggles [*sic*] to be heterosexual" ("Long and Winding"). The result of that struggle, for both, was a child given up for adoption. With the child's mother, called "Ginger" in the book, Cruse/Toland attended a party at a local motel (Birmingham's A. G. Gaston Motel, the book's Melody). The racially diverse group of bohemians and radicals he encountered was an eye-opener, Cruse explained in a telephone interview—making him feel "like it was possible for blacks and whites to mingle together. I got a chance to see that things could be more fluid." The process of illumination continued for Cruse and Toland through that crowd of "beatniks," as the author referred to them, who circulated in clubs that he represents in *Stuck Rubber Baby* as the Rhombus and the Alleysax. "The South was full of much more nuance," Cruse states. "In terms of the gay movement, this was six years before Stonewall. The South was thought of as very homophobic. . . . But I was there and I could contribute this picture" (Personal interview). The politicizing point for Cruse was not the murder of a Sammy Noone figure, as it was for Toland (the incident was fictionalized), but the Sixteenth Street Baptist Church bombing. An entry from Cruse's online chronology of the book, "The Long and Winding Stuck Rubber Road," explains: "It changed my life—not in an instant way but in a pivotal, long-term way. It made the tragedy and violence with which black people were living real to me in a deeply emotional way, and it forced me to ask myself why I was allowing myself to be a passive bystander while other people were making sacrifices in order to combat racism" (February 13, 1993). Cruse signals Toland's post-1960s activism through a "Silence = Death" poster in the background (207), a reflection of the author's own involvement in marches and the underground comix scene.

Cruse's experience in that arena and broader developments in the graphic narrative form made *Stuck Rubber Baby* possible. During the 1970s, he was known mostly for a strip called *Barefootz* (1975–79). In 1980 he took over editorship of the newly formed, and edgier, *Gay Comix* (1980–92), which he ran for several issues. Much of that decade found Cruse drawing *Wendel* (1983–89), a humorous yet outspoken cartoon that ran in *The Advocate* and addressed serious themes such as gay rights, gay bashing, and AIDS. Cruse began to get the idea for a longer project that would address his Birmingham experience in 1990 ("Long and Winding" Early March 1990). As Joseph Witek writes in *Comic Books as History* (1989), three developments made such a project conceivable. Jack Jackson's *Comanche Moon* (1979) and *Los Tejanos* (1981) offered, according to Witek, "revisionist historical tales . . . [that] reintroduce the stories of previously excluded figures of American history" (4). Harvey Pekar's *American Splendor* (1979–2008) used a comic book to tell the story of an individual life. And, most important, Art Spiegelman's *Maus* (1980–91) rendered both individual and cultural trauma in graphic narrative format, winning a Pulitzer Prize and opening up new possibilities for the form itself. If *Maus* played a small role in *Stuck Rubber Baby*'s birth, the book also provoked some anxiety on Cruse's part. Not long after he pitched the project to DC Comics, editors and friends began referring to it as "the gay *Maus*." "That makes me nervous," Cruse wrote. "My goal is to try and come up with a modest Howard Cruse story that makes sense and has some emotional authenticity" ("Long and Winding" November 21, 1990).

Cruse may have been too self-effacing. *Stuck Rubber Baby*, published in 1995, was so ahead of its time that some readers did not know what to make of it. A fifteenth-anniversary edition, released in 2010, capitalized on several developments: a growing market for graphic narratives, an increasing amount of scholarship on them, and an expanding national discourse about the rights of lesbian, gay, bisexual, and transgender (LGBT) individuals—especially as that discourse relates to the civil rights movement of the 1950s and 1960s.[2] The difference fifteen years makes can be seen in the contrast between Ray Olson's brief, but telling, 1995 *Booklist* review and Alison Bechdel's introduction to the anniversary edition. Although Witek notes that by the 1980s graphic works were understood as serious literature—no longer just for children and chuckles—*Booklist* classifies *Stuck Rubber Baby* among its young adult reads. The review does not mention that some of the book's scenes (including sex and violence) might be too "adult" for the "young" end of that age range, typically twelve- to eighteen-year-olds.[3] *Stuck Rubber Baby*, in Bechdel's assessment, is art for grown-ups. She praises its "formal virtuosity . . . its ambitious historic sweep, its rich characters, [and] its unflinching look at sex, race, violence, hate, and love." With respect to form, Bechdel elaborates, "Many of the pages are so densely cross-hatched with such delicate texture that they look as if they have a nap—as if . . . you ran your hand over them, you would feel velvet." Conversely, Olson's description of Cruse's technique is "busyness," although he does call *Stuck Rubber Baby*'s story "riveting." For Olson, the book's brilliance lies in the ways that Cruse shows how "the black civil rights struggle inspired the later gay one" (27). For Bechdel, those movements are more syncretic than distinct. She states, "Cruse deftly deconstructs race and sexuality more effectively than a shelf full of theory" (ii).

The difference fifteen years makes can also be seen in the small body of criticism that this "modest Howard Cruse" story has generated since 2010. Taking a cue from Bechdel, these works focus their analysis on the dynamics of race and sexuality. David Bordelon, for example, examines how reading materials act as more than just background. Print culture reveals the "nuance" that Cruse recalls. Bordelon explains, "In the hands of the prejudiced majority, [books, magazines, and newspapers] legitimatize and reify discriminatory racial and sexual codes; in the hands of Toland and others, they provide an escape from the segregation, violence, and social restrictions of the Jim Crow South" (108). Simon Dickel similarly looks at the ways music and visual style help *Stuck Rubber Baby*'s readers negotiate an axis of sameness and difference. Cruse connects "blackness, homosexuality, and Toland's coming of age," Dickel argues, but he does not conflate them

(620). Instead, he signals differences in narrative levels by using actual songs from the period in which the book's primary action takes place—such as "We Shall Overcome" and "Whatever Will Be, Will Be (*Que Sera, Sera*)"—versus those he makes up ("Love of a Lifetime," "Secret in the Air," "Can't Leave Me Behind") and by varying the ways he draws panels. Square frames with clear edges depict events from the early 1960s; frames with wavy borders show characters' imaginations and memories of those events (618). Gary Richards notes that Cruse intervenes in two specific forms: commenting on the white-authored coming-out novel's "silence about racial bias and privilege" and critiquing the white southern racial conversion narrative's "silence about sexuality and homosexuality in particular" (162–64).[4] Each of these perspectives provides a useful approach to *Stuck Rubber Baby*. What makes the book more than just a "gay *Maus*" is the artistry with which Cruse negotiates two specific forms.

In a volume devoted to one of these forms, graphic narrative, the other—civil rights movement fiction—needs further explanation. According to Sharon Monteith, the most specific definition of the term includes works that depict "civil rights organizations, voter registration and demonstrations, and activists in the African-American freedom struggle" ("Civil Rights Fiction" 161). Monteith explains that these works differ from literature that "locates 'civil rights' within a broad range of race relations" (ibid.).[5] The difference can be seen in a book such as Alice Walker's *Meridian* (1976), which centers on three characters involved in racial and social upheavals of the 1960s, versus Harper Lee's *To Kill a Mockingbird* (1960), which appeared during the movement but is set during a much earlier time period. Movement fiction emerged during the early 1960s, with stories such as Eudora Welty's "Where Is the Voice Coming From" (1963) and John O. Killins's novel *'Sippi* (1967), and continues with contemporary works that look back at this transformational historical period, including Anthony Grooms's award-winning *Bombingham* (2001) and Kathryn Stockett's controversial, yet popular, *The Help* (2009). Fiction constitutes one subset of a large body of creative work about the civil rights movement—including poetry, drama, graphic narratives, and other cultural productions—that has seen a recent growth in scholarship. One reason for that growth is the recovery of older works via anthologies, and another is a proliferation of more recent works.[6] With respect to graphic narratives, *Stuck Rubber Baby* paved the way for Ho Che Anderson's *King* (1993–2003); Lila Quintero Weaver's *Darkroom: A Memoir in Black and White* (2012); Mark Long, Jim Demonakos, and Nate Powell's *The Silence of Our Friends* (2012); and John Lewis, Andrew Aydin, and Nate Powell's *March* (2013–16).

The civil rights movement is the source of recent creative and academic attention because of the quest for nuance that Cruse mentions. Popular culture and public education have contributed to the creation of a movement narrative that civil rights scholars have come to call "consensus memory." Briefly, the story's trajectory goes from 1954 to 1965, from the Supreme Court's *Brown v. Board of Education* decision to the Voting Rights Act, where it gives way to Black Power (a supposedly different story). This version of events focuses on clear legislative aims, a distinct southern geography, a specific national leadership, and—as many have noted—a particular ideology.[7] This dominant narrative offers a "satisfying morality tale" about the "natural progression of American values," historian Jacqueline Dowd Hall explains (1235). The story "obscures and effaces as much as it reveals and illuminates," Peniel Joseph concurs (7). Some scholars see literature as the antidote to consensus memory. In "Making Civil Rights Harder," Christopher Metress argues for using creative works as a "valuable and untapped legacy for enriching our understanding of the black freedom struggle" (141). A book such as *Darkroom*, while set in Marion, Alabama, near the time of the 1965 Selma-to-Montgomery Voting Rights March, uses author Weaver's experiences growing up as a young Latina to complicate the strict divisions of black and white. Even a work such as Anderson's *King* adds significant depth to a national icon through its juxtaposition of perspectives and its collage of documentary-style drawing, imaginative renderings, color washes, and black on white.

Perhaps more important than any given work's ability to counter historical "facts" with more complex "truth" are the imaginative places it can take readers. A variety of civil rights scholars describe how the act of reading has the potential to change the ways that readers view themselves, their communities, and their relationships to the past. Margaret Whitt explains, "Literature can help us 'feel' history" (x). Richard H. King is more specific, explaining that fiction especially invites readers to ask wide-ranging moral and epistemological questions. In "Politics and Fictional Representations," King writes, "literature can inform us in the deepest sense about certain ethical and political dimensions of the way we 'are' in the world. . . . At its best fiction can illuminate certain dimensions of the experience of politics that otherwise might have remained hidden" (163). Literary representations of historical events such as the civil rights movement transport readers into spaces of critical thinking, feeling, and *being* in the moment—even more so when the work is a graphic narrative that combines the power of words and images.

Three pictures help explain. Figure 5.1 provides a familiar image from Birmingham's Project C to tell what seems on the surface a familiar story. The shot captures a white police officer grabbing a young black man, whose knees appear bent as if caught mid-sprint, while the officer's German shepherd lunges, about to bite the man's midsection. Another white police officer stands with his back to the camera, dog at bay. The action occurs at an urban intersection: the paved street is striped for traffic, a restaurant is visible in the background, and a vehicle

Figure 5.1. Walter Gadsden, a seventeen-year-old, is attacked by police dogs during a demonstration in Birmingham, Alabama, May 3, 1963. (AP Photo/Bill Hudson).

sits behind the crowd of black people—some watching, others moving hastily away. The clothes, especially the men's hats, place the setting in the 1950s or early 1960s. The emotions discernable on people's faces indicate that most are upset. The police officer facing forward wears sunglasses, but his gritted teeth reveal tension. The man he grabs looks determined rather than frightened, as one might think he would be when facing a dog attack. The scowling woman over the police officer's left shoulder appears angry, as do the people behind her. The man to her left seems concerned. Even if viewers miss details or see the photograph without much historical context, they are still likely to view it as a chilling scene of midcentury racial unrest.

When placed alongside other movement images (one typically sees the shot in a video montage) the story comes more clearly into focus. Consider these famous photographs: the casket containing Emmett Till's disfigured body; the Freedom Riders' burning bus in Anniston, Alabama; a quarter million people crowding the National Mall during the March on Washington; three men pointing from a hotel balcony in Memphis, Tennessee, at a fourth man lying in a pool of blood. Sharon Monteith calls such images "flashpoints" for the way they collapse the era into "television news sound bites that can be inserted into movies [and other cultural forms] quickly and efficiently" to provide a short history of civil rights ("Civil Rights Movement Film" 125). Flashpoints draw their power from two sources. Professional photojournalists shot and culled them from thousands of images for their compositional qualities and emotional appeal. More importantly, such representations tap into, and to some extent helped create, the civil rights consensus memory that viewers think they know. This tightly constructed consensus narrative, almost Aristotelian in its unities, connects civil rights to much older stories that also inform the Birmingham photograph in figure 5.1. This image depicts in microcosm a classic battle of good (the young man, Walter Gadsden, is engaged in nonviolent civil rights protest) versus evil (the unnamed white police officers who represent the system of Jim Crow segregation). The photograph thus transports viewers directly into the heart of a story familiar from classical mythology, religious texts, literature, and even comics books. Just before the tale's climax, evil appears to win. The enemy has the hero trapped, but the hero's eyes signal otherwise: that victory is assured.[8]

Figures 5.2 and 5.3, from *Stuck Rubber Baby*, rework the iconic Birmingham photograph and, thus, its accompanying narrative. In figure 5.2, a German shepherd lunges at a man who, unlike Walter Gadsden, shows fear in his face. Lines from "We Shall Overcome" indicate that protestors sing "We are not afraid," but captions belie that point. A caption overlapping two frames states that police officers taunted protestors with dogs, until one of them went too far. Close-ups of the dog on the next page explain even more than the interaction between Toland, Effie, and Marge (a lesbian couple that owns the Alleysax juke joint)—each of whom worries about Mabel, a character that plays piano at church on Sunday mornings and at the Rhombus bar on Saturday nights. The snarling dog that leaps out from between the frames at readers is also too much for Mabel, who slams her purse into the dog's head.

The graphic narrative's images, by taking readers places that the documentary photograph cannot, complicate civil rights consensus memory. In figure 5.1, the audience operates as relatively passive consumers of a story that—because of the image's composition and because of the context in which it usually appears—seems known. In figures 5.2 and 5.3, the audience becomes part of the action through various perspectives, including Toland's and Mabel's. In figure 5.2, readers approach the scene via Toland's confusion and fear. That fear increases as the dog appears to glare back from the page. In figure 5.3, it leaps out. Here, point of view—and, thus, reader sympathy—shifts from Mabel's anger to characters' concern for her to her act of fighting back. Figure 5.1 predicts an expected outcome (the nonviolent "good" hero wins), but in figures 5.2 and 5.3, the story takes an unexpected turn that also takes the reader to a potentially difficult place. One frame in this trajectory locates the audience in civil rights movement direct

Figure 5.2. Howard Cruse,
Stuck Rubber Baby (1995): 74.

Figure 5.3. Howard Cruse,
Stuck Rubber Baby (1995): 75.

action by quoting the lyrics to its most familiar song, "We Shall Overcome." Shiloh beseeches, "Don't worry." However, in the previous, more menacing frame, Commissioner Chopper warns (in a twist on Malcolm X) that he will use "whatever means are necessary." Cruse emphasizes Chopper's words over Shiloh's by mirroring the commissioner's figure and bullhorn with those of the glaring dog, held taut by a police officer wielding a billy club in his other hand. The dog attacks, all spittle and fangs, crashing through the chaotic crowd and directly into Mabel's anger: the two stand off with each baring teeth. Readers see the crowd's confusion (shown in the frame featuring Toland in the upper left) and Mabel's rage: the situation quickly moves from the nonviolence typically associated with direct action, "We Shall Overcome," and heroes such as Martin Luther King, who helped coordinate the Birmingham campaign. Mabel defends herself, as many readers would also—but as Walter Gadsden in figure 5.1 appears not to. Her act of self-defense, however, also puts us, the audience, in an uncomfortable or at least unfamiliar position. In a lower right frame, readers clearly understand that the dog is hurt ("Yip? Whimper"), and in the page's last image, Mabel confesses to Raeburn that her purse held a brick. The detail is key in civil rights movement fiction, recalling the flying debris that killed four black girls in a church bombing at the same intersection where this demonstration took place. Mabel's act thus comes to resemble something other than self-defense: retribution.

Exploding Heads, Magic Negroes, Violence, and Resistance

These chaotic scenes offer multiple viewpoints, but *Stuck Rubber Baby* is ultimately Toland's story. Cruse easily could have provided a "flashpoint" version of civil rights struggle and triumph as background for Toland's own coming-of-age. Why does the writer instead take readers to a new, different, and difficult place? Locating that place helps answer the question. With figures 5.2 and 5.3, he puts readers at the scene of a historical moment, at a literal intersection depicted in figure 5.1: Birmingham's Sixteenth Street and Sixth Avenue North, "ground zero" for Project C and many of the movement's iconic photographs (including, later, those of the church bombing). By placing readers at that geographic intersection, surrounded by images not typically associated with the consensus narrative—chaos, self-resistance, retributory justice—Cruse cracks open the narrative's nearly impermeable façade. As scholars of graphic narrative have discussed, such fracturing and refiguring is inherent to the form. Thierry Groensteen, for instance, explains in *The System of Comics* (1999) that "comics is not only an art of fragments, of scattering, of distribution; it is also an art of conjunction, of repetition, or linking together" (22). Derek Parker Royal, writing in a *MELUS* special issue on graphic narratives, states that such reworkings are particularly

Figure 5.4. Howard Cruse,
Stuck Rubber Baby (1995): 2.

vexed when dealing with multiethnic issues, for the possibilities and limits are significant. Because "comics rely on visual language that encourages a more immediate processing time within the reader," Royal states, their figures can reveal "the various assumptions, predispositions, and prejudices that author-illustrators may hold" (8). Conversely, Royal argues, comics also have the power to expose stereotypes more easily because they particularize the general, "thereby undermining any attempt at . . . erasure" (9). In the case of *Stuck Rubber Baby*, Cruse expands the visual frames of images that one typically sees at a specific geographic intersection in order to open up more imaginative intersections where new images and stories can emerge.

A series of frames from *Stuck Rubber Baby*'s page 2 can explain. In this scene, Toland picks up a copy of *Jet* magazine to read the 1955 story of Emmett Till's murder in Money, Mississippi (see figure 5.4). As with images previously discussed, this one reconfigures a civil rights moment often used as a "flashpoint." Emmett Till's death, which historian David Halberstam called "the first great media event of the civil rights movement" (437), galvanized a generation of civil rights movement and Black Power activists. Movement literature and film rely on scenes of reading such as the one depicted in *Stuck Rubber Baby* to signify instances of coming to political consciousness.[9] In three frames set midpage, Toland first starts to perspire as he reads *Jet*, explaining that he saw "a close-up photograph of a dead black person whose skull was all caved in" (Cruse does not replicate the famous photograph). The image troubles Toland's sleep: "something in my brain permanently blew a fuse," he says, as jagged lines emerge from his head in the second frame and bleed into surrounding ones. The third and final frame shows smoke spewing from inside his head and parts of his skull fragmenting as if it has exploded into the gutters. These panels are the first of several visually related depictions of violence, where Cruse fractures a panel into a pattern more closely resembling cubist art, with its geometric forms and misplaced body parts, than comic book grid. These images include a lynching (53), Sammy's confrontation with his homophobic father (164–66), and Toland's coming out, which is prompted by the memory of Sammy's lynching death (190–93). Drawing on the work of Martine Schüwer, Simon Dickel refers to this series of thematically connected images as "translinear intertextuality" (629). They are among the most significant visuals in the book, for they signal its key themes and plot developments. Dickel states, "The visual leitmotif of a crushed head emphasizes the political dimension of [Toland's] coming out because it not only links racism and homophobia but also connects the politics of the Civil Rights Movement to that of gay liberation" (627). Those connections are what help Cruse most effectively explode a civil rights movement consensus narrative.

One must note, however, that Cruse's explosion of the narrative remains problematic at times. For example, one key scene may be read in two different ways (see figures 5.5 and 5.6). Toland comes out at the funeral for his friend Sammy, killed after raging on television about bigotry when the Melody Motel is bombed. A local newspaper outs Sammy with an inflammatory headline, "Pervert on Payroll of Racemixing Church," and prints his address. Two unidentified men later come to the house—wounding Toland and hanging Sammy. At a memorial service, Toland's emotions get the best of him when he stands up to speak: he is traumatized by the violence, he feels survivor's guilt, he and Ginger have conceived a child, but he cannot publicly admit that he is gay. The page's middle frames show Toland overwhelmed. Shiloh, a mutual friend wounded in the motel bombing (and the same character who encourages marchers in figure 5.2), seems to stare at him with a hypnotic gaze in a frame that tilts on its edges to reflect Toland's own precarious state. The scene moves from a close-up of Shiloh, whose own head is safely bandaged, to one of Toland, whose head explodes as it did when he read the *Jet* article on Emmett Till. What follows is Toland's memory of what happened to him that night, as told through Sammy's perspective, an important shift in viewpoint for Toland. The scene unfolds via a page that operates on different visual levels. The background action is frozen in time: Toland is knocked out while hands grab Sammy about the legs and upper body to carry him away. The foreground action takes place through trapezoidal frames: the hands drag Sammy through thorns that tear his limbs, and they tie a rope around his neck. The scenes play out on the following pages with Sammy feeling a ferocious fire run through his neck then disappearing into a circle of light. Cruse returns to the book's regular rectangular panels, one of which spells out exactly why vigilantes attacked Sammy: he was a "nigger loving queer" (181). What Toland must wrestle with, when the page's background shifts from dark to light, as if a curtain pulls back to reveal his true self, is that "it could have been me." His confession is captured in a speech balloon that links his frame to one containing an image of Shiloh smiling. At issue is whether Shiloh's image, which also prompted Toland's confession, should be read in terms of service or solidarity.

Gary Richards would say service. His essay, "Everybody's Graphic Protest Novel," argues that Cruse's book is replete with such "magic Negro" figures that guide the white Toland through his developing political and social consciousness.[10] They include Les, his first male sexual experience; Les's parents, Harlan and Anna Dellyne Pepper, who mentor Toland on multiple occasions; and Mabel, "an oracular source of knowledge for the perplexed white boy" (173). So many black characters assist Toland that Richards cites Hillary Clinton's reference to the "African proverb that it takes a village to raise a child" and claims, "Cruse perhaps unwittingly suggests through his novel that it takes a village of black folks to raise a white homosexual in the U.S. South" (181). Simon Dickel takes issue with this sort of reading, arguing that Cruse's depiction of black queer life and his construction of black gay and lesbian characters seem consistent with available historical resources (218). Conversely, Dickel misses an important visual coding in the book's last pages. He notes that one gets the sensation of space and freedom at the end and that the last panel "does not fill the page. Instead, it is surrounded by a vast white space" (633). Readers should note, however, that on the penultimate page Anna Dellyne and Harlan, whose remembered figures deliver Toland to this sensation of space and freedom, are not dressed in their usual churchgoing attire but in that of servitude: as kitchen and lawn maintenance staff (see figure 5.7). Anyone who has read Toni Morrison's *Playing in the Dark* (1992) would find it difficult to see these figures as anything but the Africanist presence so common to U.S. literature, which facilitates and defines the white character's quest for freedom, itself represented by a "vast white space" as old as Edgar Allan Poe's Arthur Gordon Pym or Herman Melville's great white whale.

The images of Anna Dellyne and Harlan in the book's last pages, like that of Shiloh in figure 5.5, can also be read in a different way if approached—ironically—through the lens of civil rights movement literature. The Anna Dellyne and Harlan pictured in figure 5.7 link back to a conversation that begins on page 203, where Toland tells the older woman about the birth of his daughter and questions her on why she gave up her music career. The two drink coffee in the kitchen, where she has been working, while Harlan cuts the grass outside. Rather than seeing the two wearing the uniforms of servitude, as part of "the help" who guide Toland through a transitional time, readers might see them instead through the other, interrelated roles they play in the story: movement

Figure 5.5. Howard Cruse,
Stuck Rubber Baby (1995): 190.

Figure 5.6. Howard Cruse,
Stuck Rubber Baby (1995): 191.

Figure 5.7. Howard Cruse, *Stuck Rubber Baby* (1995): 207–8.

leaders, Les's parents, and mentors to Clayfield's grassroots activists. Their acceptance, much like Shiloh's smile, may stem from the fact that Toland has grown from the politically noncommittal character who first showed up at the Melody Motel party to one who has proven himself by putting his body on the line. He has marched in Russell Park and in Washington, D.C.; he has suffered violence and loss. Moreover, Toland has finally found the courage to stand up before others and articulate who he is and what he stands for at a time when such actions have deadly consequences. This scene also has the effect of placing civil rights leaders "at home"—showing that the Reverend Harlan Pepper and Anna Dellyne, a former jazz star, are regular people, like Toland. Much civil rights literature and history written today focuses on the change that everyday people, not unreachable heroes, created. At the March on Washington, Toland and Ginger sit with others at the reflecting pool and discuss civil rights activism. "Think about all the people who're here today, Toland," Ginger says. "Who knows how many of 'em are confused or fucked up inside. . . . What matters is that we all figured out it was important to be in Washington today" (102). Rather than Superman or Wonder Woman, Cruse's civil rights "comic book" illustrates that heroes can be flawed people just like its readers. Even Rev. Pepper, who leads Clayfield's troops against Sutton Chopper's dogs, remains Harlan, the "smart alecky little butter-ball [from] grammar school," as Anna Dellyne describes him (203).

If scenes of exploding heads visually connect Toland's coming out to Shiloh, Anna Dellyne, and Harlan as everyday people, then they also make visible the links between acts of violence committed against blacks and those committed against members of LGBT communities. Koritha Mitchell details those connections in "Love in Action: Noting Similarities between Lynching Then and Anti-LGBT Violence Now." The most visible and visceral forms of violence (murder, torture, rape, and beatings), Mitchell demonstrates, form a continuum with microaggressions (more fleeting, routine affronts, whether intended or not) to communicate that certain bodies have no place in the body politic. Mitchell calls that message "know-your-place-aggression" (701). Cruse depicts a range of these behaviors as they affect multiple individuals in his story. Blatant examples include the Melody Motel bombing and Sammy Noone's murder: acts intended to let members of politically marginalized groups know that they will meet serious consequences if they insist on standing up for their rights. Cruse demonstrates how aggression operates in other forms as well, whether through messages that occur in a frame's background (racist bumper stickers, Confederate flags, offensive speech that characters overhear), more direct interaction (Orley's assumption that everyone in the room is like him when he calls the Rhombus a "fag bar"), or Sammy's long catalog of failed attempts to fit into heteronormative society. As Dickel argues, "Cruse is careful not to equate racism and homophobia" (717). One might note the subtle links the author makes in figures 5.5 and 5.6, between the bomb blast that gave Shiloh a concussion and Toland's exploding memory. The trapezoidal images have parallel lines but unequal angles, much like the axis of sameness and difference that Cruse tries—not always successfully—to negotiate. Those parallel lines ultimately become a different kind of metaphor, for the interlocking structure of oppression that controls whose stories count, whose bodies count, who is allowed to occupy what space and why. Perhaps Shiloh smiles at Toland not in service of his coming out but to acknowledge a fellow traveler on the political margins.

From Margin to Center: A Deviant Civil Rights Movement History

Perhaps Shiloh also acknowledges a new comrade. One of *Stuck Rubber Baby*'s biggest contributions to civil rights historical memory is how it draws attention to daily forms of resistance against institutional power. By examining the intersections of civil rights and gay rights, Cruse opens a window onto understudied forms of fighting back. What makes his graphic narrative "novel" is the mix of gays, lesbians, drag performers, and heterosexuals who occupy the front lines and the secret spaces of struggle. Outside of Mississippi's 1964 Freedom Summer, the 1963 Birmingham Campaign may be one of the most heavily examined movement moments.[11] The literature on that moment has little to say, if anything, on LGBT participation. Conversely, scholars such as James Sears and E. Patrick Johnson have collected oral histories, mostly of white and black gay men, with minor attention to the civil rights movement. Bayard Rustin seems to stand alone at an intersection that Cruse has filled. Thaddeus Russell provides one reason why civil rights consensus memory sees that intersection as half empty, devoid of queers. Prior to the 1950s, Russell demonstrates, using a range of examples, "African American working-class culture was far more open to homosexuality and non-heteronormative behavior than was the black middle class, which led the movement." With the shift into high gear for civil rights, "the project of attaining citizenship was constructed upon heterosexuality," and public discourse squelched black queerness with black heteronormativity (103). Johnson explains why the intersection looks half empty from a different perspective. Queer studies, he states, "has often failed to address the material realities of gays and lesbians of color" ("'Quare' Studies" 129). With *Stuck Rubber Baby*, Cruse breaks down such barriers, queering civil rights movement history and integrating gay history. By doing so he provides a significant fictional intervention in the telling of consensus narratives, using Birmingham as a template for creating a more inclusive civil rights story. Bull Connor allegedly declared that blacks and whites were "not to segregate together." According to *Stuck Rubber Baby*, they did. The places where they defied those laws are worth investigating, because those places reveal that integration's front lines were not necessarily the more familiar bus depots and lunch counters, but the bars and the parties that the politics of respectability refuses to acknowledge. If such is the case, then how might that change ideas about civil rights history? Is consensus memory itself a form of "know-your-place-aggression," sending the message that some potential heroes and some forms of resistance do not merit recognition?

Scenes from *Stuck Rubber Baby*'s bars and juke joints provide a reference point. In one, Toland visits an integrated but mostly white gay bar, the Rhombus, for the first time and is shocked. "Where were the rednecks? Where were the cops?" he wonders. "Didn't they know that 'hallowed Southern traditions' were in danger of toppling?" (44). Later that night, Toland visits the Alleysax, which is located on Clayfield's outskirts, run by a black lesbian couple (Marge and Effie) and presided over by the black drag queen Esmereldus, who impersonates jazz great Anna Dellyne. Both the Alleysax and the Rhombus provide temporary respite, but neither is completely safe. The Rhombus, as its name implies, subverts a hierarchical, racist, and heteronormative social order as a space of equality: a rhombus has parallel lines and equal right angles. Rhombus customers can socialize, drink, and dance with whomever they please—to the tune of Mabel's piano (Mabel is the same character who wields the brick-filled purse in figure 5.3). When Commissioner Chopper's police force raids the bar, a red light goes off, signaling that patrons must switch dancing partners to heterosexual couples. (A later panel explains that the bartender keeps a mirror angled on the front door to alert him to approaching police.) Although Rhombus customers have developed tools of resistance, they are never completely free, as an earlier frame suggests. Toland enjoys a beer at the bar until he overhears a conversation in which one man says, "This place has sure gone down hill since they started lettin' so many niggers in" (43). A later scene at the Alleysax mirrors this one in the way it emphasizes freedom's contingency. After a night at the Rhombus, Toland's gang heads out to the Alleysax. A car with a "Keep America White" bumper sticker follows them. When they stop, the men who get out taunt them with homophobic slurs, offering something "lon-n-ng and . . . har-r-d": a switchblade (82). Toland's friends defend themselves by screaming, blowing car horns, and wielding a tire jack until Marge and Effie come out firing guns to run the toughs away.

These scenes, and others from the Rhombus and Alleysax, are particularly significant as specific historical reference points. Cruse links *Stuck Rubber Baby*'s bars to actual locations: the Rhombus is a composite of two Birmingham gay bars from the early 1960s (one of which, Tito's, was integrated), and the Alleysax is a fictionalized version of the Sand Ridge Country Club, a multiuse space outside the city limits that primarily served black patrons but operated as an after-hours bar welcoming everyone—including whites, gays, lesbians, and gender benders—as long as they did not cause police-attracting trouble (Cruse, Personal interview; Cruse, "Long and Winding"). Tito's and the Sand Ridge, like their *Stuck Rubber Baby* counterparts, offered temporary relief from the pressures of racism and homophobia, and—perhaps more important—they provide examples of local residents resisting the status quo by breaking a host of laws. Birmingham's General Code of 1944 (in place until civil rights changes of 1963 led to new codes in 1964) had multiple statutes that prohibited racial interaction in both public and private spaces, and each of those laws was reinforced by a general "Separation of Races" clause (Ch. 35, Sec. 359) that made it unlawful for blacks and whites to inhabit any public space that did not have separate entrances and exits as well as separate locations for seating and standing. The General Code had a similarly long list of statutes controlling sexual behavior, most of them defined under the vague terms "Disorderly Conduct and Obscenity." Chapter 16, Article I, for example, applies "community standards" of the "average person" to label anything "lewd, lascivious, filthy, or pornographic." Similar words apply to "disorderly conduct," which refers to the actions of "any person who shall commit any act or diversion tending to or calculated to debauch the morals of any person." If the city's laws seem vague, they were clear to Bull Connor, who ordered the vice squad to go after "perverts" and "deviants" in the early 1960s. The roundup targeted "exhibitionists, window peepers, homosexuals, and sadists" and swept through the downtown nightclubs, bus stations, and parks (Lankford 28).

Juxtaposing *Stuck Rubber Baby* against Connor's pervert purges suggests a deviant way to read civil rights movement history. On the one hand, Birmingham and other Jim Crow locations clearly were racist, homophobic places. Laws and customs were supported by violence that thwarted change. But changes were already taking place. Contemporary audiences are familiar with a story of change that starts with Rosa Parks sitting down on a Montgomery bus and ends with Martin Luther King Jr. falling down on a Memphis balcony. Pictures of Freedom Riders getting bashed in a Birmingham bus station and demonstrators getting attacked by police dogs and fire hoses in a Birmingham park have similarly become iconic—"flashpoints." Where are the parallel pictures of other rule breakers: queers getting pistol whipped in that same bus station, cross-dressers getting busted in a park five blocks away from its more famous sister, blacks and whites dancing at Tito's to an integrated jazz band, the Vic Cunningham Trio—everyone "segregating together" just blocks away from Bull Connor's office?[12] Where is the simple acknowledgment that the story of Birmingham, like the broader civil rights story, is multiracial, multiethnic, straight, gay, cross-dressed, conservatively dressed, and sometimes even *un*dressed. The absence of an iconic image does not signify the absence of a history. Some of the more famous civil rights photographs happened because movement organizers staged protests to get media attention and, thus, national sympathy. Likewise, many of Birmingham's LGBT rule breakers did not want media attention at all, especially if they were breaking racial codes as well. Cruse explains, "We benefited from the naiveté of most Birmingham people who did not know what was going on" (Personal interview). Birmingham's bars, juke joints, and gay ghettos exposed cracks in Jim Crow's armor. By centering on those marginal spaces where freedom was neither allowed nor expected, to exist, Howard Cruse asks readers to consider them as more than "modest" story—but as sites of an ever expanding, always inclusive historical memory.

NOTES

1. Extensive historical scholarship exists on the Birmingham Campaign. Excellent starting points include Eskew and McWhorter.

2. Discourse surrounding the relationship between the two movements, especially over whether gay rights constitutes a "new" civil rights movement, heated up during this fifteen-year period, which was flanked by several key events: President Bill Clinton's institution, in 1994, of the "Don't Ask, Don't Tell" (DADT) policy, which allowed gays and

lesbians to serve in the military but required them to keep their sexual orientation secret; President Clinton's signing, in 1996, the Defense of Marriage Act (DOMA), which banned federal recognition of same-sex marriage; the 2009 Matthew Shepard and James Byrd Jr. Hate Crimes Prevention Act, which expanded U.S. federal hate crimes law to include crimes motivated by an individual's actual or perceived gender, sexual orientation, or gender identity; President Barack Obama's reversal of DADT in 2010, allowing gays and lesbians to serve openly in the military; and, in 2013, the U.S. Supreme Court's recognition, in *Windsor v. the United States*, of same-sex marriage. A good historical overview of this discourse can be found in Stone and Ward.

3. That said, my son read it at thirteen. His review: "This is great! Buy me more books like it, please."

4. The white racial conversion narrative, as defined by Fred Hobson, refers primarily to autobiographical texts by southern writers such as Lillian Smith and Willie Morris, who move from complicity in a racist culture to enlightenment and describe that process using language similar to that of religious conversion (i.e., "sin" and "redemption"). Richards provides a detailed comparison of the coming-out narrative to the conversion narrative, using such southern examples as Truman Capote's *Other Voices, Other Rooms* (1948) and Rita Mae Brown's *Rubyfruit Jungle* (1973). A key difference, he explains, is that characters in the latter do not wind up at "redemption for past transgressions" but "insight and celebration" (163).

5. Ways of defining civil rights movement fiction can be fluid. For a breakdown of terminology, see Armstrong, "Civil Rights Movement Fiction," esp. 87–90.

6. Recent anthologies include Armstrong and Schmidt, Coleman, and Whitt. During the past decade, scholarship on civil rights movement literature has blossomed. See especially Gray, S. Jones, Metress, Monteith, Norman, and Norman and Williams.

7. For specific discussion of civil rights movement consensus memory, see Romano and Raiford. To understand the role of images and the media in constructing that "master narrative," see Ward.

8. The photograph, taken by Bill Hudson, ran above the fold on the *New York Times* front page on May 4, 1963, under the headline "Dogs and Hoses Repulse Negroes in Birmingham." Afterward, this shot and others taken during the protests circulated on national and international newswires, seriously embarrassing Birmingham's leadership and business elite. The city soon entered into negotiations with movement leaders, including Fred Shuttlesworth and Dr. Martin Luther King Jr. McWhorter discusses the photograph on pp. 373–76 of her book.

9. On the significance of Till to civil rights and Black Power, see Pollack and Metress. An appendix to that volume lists more than 150 literary responses to Till's death. Excerpts from some of those have been assembled in Metress, *The Lynching of Emmett Till: A Documentary Narrative* (2002).

10. Richards does not use this exact term, which traces back to Spike Lee's "the super-duper magical Negro" (Costello 162).

11. The literature on Mississippi is voluminous. Dittmer and Payne offer excellent starting points. The literature on Birmingham is equally large and includes detailed historical

overviews such as those by Eskew and McWhorter; oral histories such as those collected by Huntley and McKerley; a host of biographies and memoirs, such as McDowell's; and creative works such as Grooms's *Bombingham* and the multiple poems collected in Coleman's *Words of Protest, Words of Freedom* (2012).

12. For information about Tito's (which is now an abandoned building) and the Sand Ridge Country Club (which burned down), I would first like to thank Howard Cruse, who graciously granted me a telephone interview; Jim Praytor, a local jazz musician and early member of the Vic Cunningham Trio; and a group of men at a Birmingham bar, Al's on Seventh, who did not want to give me their real names but kept me company on a stormy night, buying me drinks and telling me stories.

CHAPTER 6

On Photo-Graphic Narrative

"To Look—Really Look" into Lila Quintero
Weaver's Darkroom

Jorge Santos

LILA QUINTERO WEAVER'S GRAPHIC memoir *Darkroom: A Memoir in Black and White* (2012) chronicles the arrival of her Argentinian immigrant family in Marion, Alabama, at the height of the 1960s U.S. civil rights movement. The narrative's subtitle highlights the ambiguous "sliver of gray" Weaver feels her Argentinean family occupied in Alabaman society—neither black nor white yet somehow, even paradoxically, defined by a juxtaposition between the two (19). The tenuous position of her family in a black/white society troubled Weaver's budding political consciousness, as her light skin often barred her from participation in the civil rights activism of her African American friends and classmates. The title of the memoir also indicates how indebted it is to an extensive, often black-and-white, photographic archive of the civil rights movement. In particular, photographs taken by her father, a pastor and photojournalist, appear recreated in Weaver's realistic aesthetic throughout the narrative. Initially, these recreated photographs chronicle the family's journey from Argentina to Alabama. They simultaneously corroborate her family's presence at various civil rights demonstrations—in particular those that led to the iconic Selma marches of 1965. By reproducing the documentary contributions of her photojournalist father, Weaver brings to the fore often unheard and unseen Latino/a contributions to the civil rights movement from outside a strict black/white positionality.[1]

Without deliberately differentiating between the two, Weaver blurs the line between photographs and graphic narrative as potential sources for articulating family history. *Darkroom*'s relationship to photography does more than simply borrow the implicit authority of photographs to document her family's immigration to the United States or authenticate her own narrative of civil rights activism. After all, if Weaver wished to simply detail her family's journey or substantiate her presence at these marches, she could have produced the actual photographs rather than pencil drawings throughout the memoir. Instead, Weaver's recurrent drawings of photographs pull together the varied personal and social themes the graphic memoir pursues. Photographs taken on school picture day frame Weaver's struggle to locate herself in a stark black/white dichotomy, bringing her work in line with Latino/a literary traditions exploring the racial binary of the midcentury United States.[2] Furthermore, Weaver's drawings of photographs pull from both real images (that exist outside of the narrative) and imagined ones. Drawing photographs also allows her to augment an already expansive civil rights photographic archive to highlight gaps in the historical record, particularly in regard to the Marion marches that resulted in the unseen death of activist Jimmie Lee Jackson. Through the symbolic rendering of photographs, Weaver interrogates perceptions of race and civil rights–era participation in order to create space for her Latina experiences within the larger narrative of 1960s activism. As the civil rights narrative is often remembered as a primarily black/white conflict, Weaver thereby expands the terrain of our cultural memories of the 1960s. I refer to Weaver's aesthetics as "photo-graphic narrative," a style that blends recreated photography with original drawings (also often depicted as photographs) to blur the line between photography and graphic narrative as methods for writing history.[3]

Weaver's concerns, however, are ultimately pedagogical, and the didactic nature of her memoir is only thinly veiled. In an early section titled "The Lesson," Weaver recounts her early art classes as a child in which she began to learn how to properly draw human bodies. Despite recounting a personal lesson she learned as a child, the section is narrated in the second person, coaching her reader to draw a human figure as an instruction manual might. Her takeaway from these lessons, Weaver writes, is that "As you learned to look—to *really* look—you began to see the wishful thinking behind the formula" (57). By using the second-person point of view, Weaver's imperative to her reader becomes clear. The symbolic representation of a human being through art, particularly in idealized ways, amounts to little more than empty artifices, one that constricts possibilities much in the same manner that race constricts the possible identity formations available to Weaver in Marion, Alabama. For Weaver, the photograph comes to represent how these idealized visions of race and history conspire to elide her potential contributions to the national narrative of civil rights, due in large part to her ambiguous position within a stark midcentury U.S. racial dichotomy. Consequently, Weaver's interrogation of the photograph simultaneously invokes the potential complicity of the viewer of the image in assigning racialized meanings to such representations. Weaver ultimately challenges her readers to "really look"—a signal to develop a self-awareness concerning their own interpretations of both race and history. She hopes to train her readers to see the necessarily constructed nature of race in the United States and to consider how race's accompanying historical narratives are likewise constructed (57).

Methodology: Weaver "On Photography" and an Ethics of Seeing

In order to elucidate the manner in which Weaver constructs her photo-graphic narrative, I draw from Susan Sontag's landmark essays collected in *On Photography* (1977). Like Weaver, Sontag frets over the fact that the photograph is "treated as a narrowly selective transparency," masking its artistic origins and political choices (6). Sontag reminds us that while photographs may function as "experience captured," they are also a product of artistic endeavor—that photographs are as much artifice as they are artifact. She argues that while the industrialization of the camera promises to "democratize all experiences by translating them into images," this still nonetheless occurs in the context of power, privilege, and access (7). She writes that to create a photographic record "means putting oneself into a certain relation to the world that feels like knowledge—and, therefore, like power" (4). Photographs, then, do not reveal the world as it is, but rather construct it according to the epistemology of the photographer. These insights, which align so well with Weaver's narrative goals, texture my reading of *Darkroom*. After all, drawn photographs cannot disguise their own artistic origins and can therefore address Sontag's concerns over transparency. The juxtaposition of Sontag and Weaver allows me to outline the representational strategies at play throughout *Darkroom*'s interrogation of the photograph.

Furthermore, both Weaver and Sontag are ultimately invested in the ethics of what art historian John Berger has referred to as "ways of seeing" in his own collection of essays. "In Plato's cave," Sontag writes, "in teaching us a new visual code, photographs alter and enlarge our notions of what is worth looking at and what we have a right to observe. They are a grammar and, even more importantly, *an ethics of seeing*" (3, emphasis added). Sontag's ethical concerns over what the viewer has the right to observe are grounded in her interrogation of the inherent power dynamics of who is permitted to direct the camera's gaze. She writes, "A photograph is not just the result of an encounter between an event and a photographer; picture-taking is an event in itself, and one with ever more peremptory rights—to interfere with, to invade, or to ignore whatever is going on" (11). Weaver's memoir shares similar concerns, as the memoir climaxes with the death of activist Jimmie Lee Jackson—a murder at the hands of an Alabama state trooper that went unphotographed. Due to her investment in the writing of history through the graphic narrative form, my work also draws from that of historians Michel de Certeau and Joseph Witek, supplemented by graphic narrative theorists Thierry Groensteen and Scott McCloud. Ultimately, Weaver's work foregrounds an explicit ethics of seeing, at which point I draw from Jacques Rancière's *The Emancipated Spectator* (2009) to illuminate how Weaver's work with photography hopes to bring the reader's own implicit ethics into focus.

The Family Photo Album as Historical Narrative

Vacillating between art styles that often juxtapose a photorealistic aesthetic with flat, two-dimensional outlines, Weaver sketches a vision of the 1960s that illustrates the role of the photograph in crafting her immigrant memoir. Repeatedly, *Darkroom* acknowledges the project's indebtedness to photography, as the book's epilogue confesses that "every image I have of Argentina is faded, borrowed, outdated, or imagined" (246). The line itself is superimposed over the family photo album, which itself contains a series of overlapping and presumably recreated family photographs (see figure 6.1). Like the photo album, *Darkroom* seeks to arrange images into a narrative that documents her family's personal history of immigration to the United States. The comic functions as a sort of meta–family album in this respect, one that tacitly acknowledges its own construction. For Weaver, the visual motif of the family photo album also underscores how the photograph interacts with other images to create an arranged and constructed narrative of both personal and political histories, much like the graphic narrative form itself. The family album first appears in the narrative when Weaver recounts her father's departure from Argentina and arrival in the United States. The page that recalls her father Nestor's journey features nine images arranged in three even rows, conjuring for the reader the image of a page from a family photo album. The individual snapshots are drawn with white borders and shaded underneath to evoke a sense of tangibility—the images appear to be photographs placed on a page as opposed to drawn panels. The cartoonish nature of the snapshots themselves belies their fictional nature as the final panel—that of Nestor's first photographic camera—reveals that these are not actual photographs but imagined images. The organization of the snapshots into neat rows simultaneously evokes the graphic narrative form, as the arrangement of the images strongly resembles the arrangement of individual panels on the page of a comic (which, of course, this is). In doing so, Weaver employs the photo-graphic narrative as simply another form of family history, which augments an existing record by filling in for Nestor's unavailable camera.

The image of the family photo album can also be read as a visual commentary on the relationship between photography, documentation, and narrative. Sontag insists that while we might "know the world if we accept it as the camera records it," photography ultimately atomizes the world, denies interconnectedness, and obscures possible continuities; in so doing, photography is "the opposing of understanding" (23). Weaver, then, must contend with the limitations of the photograph for her narrative to proceed. As we turn the page, we encounter a full-page image of a closet with boxes upon boxes of photographs followed on the next page by multiple and overlapping photorealistic recreations of family photographs (22) (see figure 6.2). Weaver writes that "the camera didn't miss

UP TO 1961, WHEN MY WHOLE FAMILY CAME TO AMERICA, MY FATHER'S LIFE CAN BE SUMMARIZED IN A SERIES OF SNAPSHOTS:

BORN IN ARGENTINA AT THE FOOT OF THE ANDES

ORPHANED AT AGE NINE

LEFT HOMELESS ALONG WITH HIS BROTHER

RESCUED BY AMERICAN MISSIONARIES

TAUGHT HIMSELF TO READ

CALLED TO PREACH

WED TO MY MOTHER

IMMIGRATED TO AMERICA

ACQUIRED THE FIRST OF MANY CAMERAS DESTINED TO RECORD MUCH OF OUR LIVES

21

Figure 6.1. Lila Quintero Weaver, *Darkroom* (2012): 21.

EVERY HOUSE
WE EVER LIVED IN HAD A
MAKESHIFT DARKROOM.

CONSEQUENTLY,
WE WERE OVERRUN
WITH PHOTOS.

22

Figure 6.2. Lila Quintero Weaver,
Darkroom (2012): 22–23.

much," evidenced by the fact that the page seems overwhelmed by the images themselves. Gone is the neat 3 × 3 panel arrangement of the previous page, exchanged for a visual cacophony of individual snapshots practically demanding to be arranged—to be narrativized. As if responding to her own artwork's plea for structure, the following page begins to organize the images into a narrative of her family's arrival in the United States. Placed over a pencil drawing of a globe, the reader's eye moves across the family's history even as the Quinteros move across continents—a move that places their story into a transnational context of arrivals and departures. The accompanying narration explains that despite her family's extensive photographic record, gaps in the narrative remain and that certain key moments "exist only in my mind's eye," reminding the reader of the limitations of photographic documentation (24). Sontag contends, "only that which narrates can make us understand" (23). For Weaver, photo-graphic narrative not only augments the family's photographs of their journey but also arranges, revises, contextualizes, and narrativizes them as well.

Darkroom's prologue immediately signals the memoir's interrogation of the relationship between photographs, narrative, and history as she seeks to document a personal familial history alongside the national narrative of the civil rights movement. Titled "Home Movies," the prologue reflects on the family's home movie nights and explains that Weaver's favorite moments came at the end of the night, when her father would rewind the films and let the children watch them in reverse (see figure 6.3). Much like her father, Weaver also manipulates the home movie by converting it into the visual grammar of graphic narrative; for example, each film cell appears as a separate panel in a drawn filmstrip. In doing so, Weaver reminds us that film is essentially a series of photographs, manipulated only to give the appearance of narrative progression. The page is arranged in four linear strips: the first two contain only one panel, the second of which has its bottom border interrupted by an overlaid drawing of a filmstrip winding through the page. The linear arrangement of these scenes moves the reader through the individual shots one image at a time as they invoke the physical filmstrip itself. By choosing to draw these panels as a filmstrip, Weaver is able to depict the temporality evoked by film in the atemporal medium of graphic narrative. Subsequently, rearranging the panels to reverse this temporality disrupts the teleology evoked by film, that is, that one moment leads directly to another from one known starting point to a predetermined destination.

The motif of the filmstrip implies a reading practice—the page aims to evoke the rhythm of film by mimicking its appearance—at a pace Weaver herself determines. This allows Weaver to slow the pace of her own history in order to distill her family's home movies down to their essence—a series of photographs

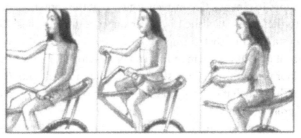

THE BACKWARDS
PEDALING OF A BIKE

THE BACKWARDS
DIGGING OF A HOLE.

HILARIOUS

BUT NOT EVERYTHING TICKLED OUR FUNNY BONES.

3

Figure 6.3. Lila Quintero Weaver,
Darkroom (2012): 2.

arranged and constructed to give the appearance of a holistic narrative. In *System of Comics* (1999), Thierry Groensteen refers to the arrangement of panels to evoke a sense of time as "the rhythmic function," as he compares the use of panels to frames in cinema. Groensteen argues that the content of panels is subordinated to the pace established by its arrangement. He writes: "The 'text' of comics obeys a rhythm that is imposed on it by the succession of frames—a basic heartbeat that, as is seen in music, can be developed, nuanced, and revered by more elaborate rhythmic effects stressed by other 'instruments' (parameters), like those of the distribution of word balloons, the opposition of colors, or even the play of graphic forms" (45). Groensteen is, of course, commenting on how panel work and frame arrangement influences the pace and rhythm at which a reader can engage with a novel, similar to film in this regard. More importantly, the graphic narrative form allows Weaver to make the distillation of her family's home movies visible to her reader. Symbolically, these initial pages serve as a microcosm for Weaver's entire project—which reveals the constructedness of civil rights narratives that owe so much to photography and film, not to counter them but to expand their scope.

Furthermore, these panels also call our attention to the role of film in recording both personal and national histories, as the following page recreates family recordings of African American protests in Marion, at the height of the civil rights movement. The following page contains only a single, full-page panel portraying a gathering of Marion protestors marching on their local courthouse. The subsequent pages again reverse the flow of the action, as Weaver comments that they would play the film in reverse over and over, that "the march took them around the courthouse I don't know how many times" (7). Weaver's narration slyly notes the cyclical nature of African Americans' struggle for civil rights, hinting at the potentially Sisyphean nature of their endeavors. Yet these pages remove the filmstrip motif in lieu of traditional comics panels while still slowing the rhythm for the reader, inviting us to dwell on their significance. Her comment on the following page that "the movie doesn't show how white people reacted" to the Marion marchers highlights the medium's limitations—film and photography may evoke an evidentiary air of fact or truth, yet they cannot possibly hope to portray the entirety of the civil rights movement. Rather than complete the picture, Weaver's implicit argument is that her photo-graphic memoir can highlight the incompleteness of even such highly documented eras in U.S. history. Photo-graphic narrative offers Weaver a narrative form that can uniquely complement and complicate popular recollections of the civil rights movement and introduce, as she puts it, the "sliver of gray" that represents her Latina perspective (57).

Racial Identity in Two Dimensions

Weaver's memoir, however, maintains a much more complicated relationship to the photograph. Rather than simply borrowing its implicit authority or offering her photo-graphic narrative as a corrective, a supplement, or an alternative, the photograph itself carries multivalent possibilities in Weaver's text. It functions not only as artifact or point of reference but as object of scrutiny and racial signifier as well. This is perhaps best represented in the interplay between the memoir's narrative content and its photorealistic aesthetic. Weaver casts her father, Nestor, a part-time pastor, teacher, and photojournalist, as both mentor and source of the family's political history. The opening image of the first chapter, "In the Dark," depicts Weaver in her father's workspace where she dutifully follows her father's instructions for developing photographs (14–15). This opening scene contains a partial splash page—a large image that encompasses two pages—of Nestor working diligently in his darkroom as Weaver looks on. The page contains small panels on the far right, each detailing one step in the film development process before finally "transferring the image onto the paper" (15). Weaver's narration draws the reader's attention to her highly symbolic use of the idea of the photograph, as she tells her reader that in her father's darkroom "much came down to the interplay of light and dark" (14). Since *Darkroom* also details the author's developing racial consciousness, "the interplay of light and dark" signals how her budding cognizance of the differences between black and white Americans—both in appearance and in social standing—frames her perception of Latina identity. Consequently, Weaver's desire to create space for her Latina identity within the larger narrative of the civil rights movement necessarily forces her to reconcile her position outside the racial dichotomy of Alabaman society. In doing so, Weaver also interrogates the role of photography in shaping her vision of the United States and her place within it.

Weaver's anxieties over how to articulate an identity in a white/nonwhite dichotomy into which she does not neatly fit are ultimately emblemized in the act of taking a photograph. While woven throughout the memoir, Weaver's struggle is confronted directly in chapter 5, "Ancestral Lines," which outlines her inability to articulate a Latina subjectivity in an Alabaman society that cannot recognize such an identity formation. The title of the chapter also signals the racial battle lines being drawn in her recently desegregated high school and the liminal space she, as a Latina subject, occupies between those lines. In one particularly revealing moment, Weaver struggles to mark her racial identity on a grade school form in which only "White" and "Negro" are options (see figure 6.4). Weaver comments in the accompanying text that "I'm certainly not a Negro. That only leaves one choice. But I don't really *feel* white" (86). Weaver casts racial identity as not only a legal or phenotypical distinction but as a formation residing somewhere at the intersection of privilege and consciousness. The text, depicted in small round bubbles that represent thought rather than speech, is not completely contained by the frame. These bubbles mirror Weaver's own budding recognition of her place outside the stark racial dichotomy in the United States as represented by the form. This symbolic placelessness is prefaced by her fellow classmates, as a white female student dismissively wonders, "Argentina. Hmm. . . . Oh! Is that in South Alabama?" Put more succinctly, an exacerbated white male student demands to know "WHAT are you?" (86). These are only two of many such moments in which Weaver is displaced socially, visually, and racially throughout the memoir. Such moments of misidentification are not limited to the perceptions of white students. Her older sister Lissy is taken for "Eye-talian" by the young African American men in her high school (216). That these boys took Lissy's non-Anglo appearance as an indication that "she didn't seem to be off-limits" adds a distinctly gendered quality to Lissy's racial experiences. Weaver also includes an anecdote of a black classmate asking to feel her hair, inverting a trope typical of African American female experience to accentuate both her proximity to and distance from any steady racial identification (216).

In the context of Lissy's ambiguous position within the U.S. racial hierarchy, photographs frame the narrative's discussion of the development and construction of subsequent identities. For example, the chapter "Passage" (a clever double entendre both for traveling to the United States and the desire to be viewed as white) highlights how photography influences narratives of Americanness. Weaver recalls how women's magazines such as *McCall's* influenced her perceptions of whiteness and beauty as an American flag waves proudly in a large panel overhead that dwarfs the figure of Weaver underneath (38). This scene is filled with images of a scantily clad woman, suburban houses, jewelry, and fancy automobiles—the expected consumerist trappings of midcentury America. The images are scattered about the page without panels or borders, an atomized arrangement that mirrors Weaver's own scattered sense of self. This scene tacitly indicts photography-based popular magazines that obscure as much as they highlight, as the children of the family are actually surprised to encounter African Americans once they have moved to the United States. Weaver recalls wondering "Where did all the black people come from? The magazines had never shown them" (42). Later, the photograph's ability to either highlight or obscure race drives her older sister Lissy's anxiety about being seen in school as "the girl with nigger lips," leading her to tuck her lips back in order to approximate an "'Anglo' grin" for her school picture (81). Lissy's anxieties about race are emblemized in the act of

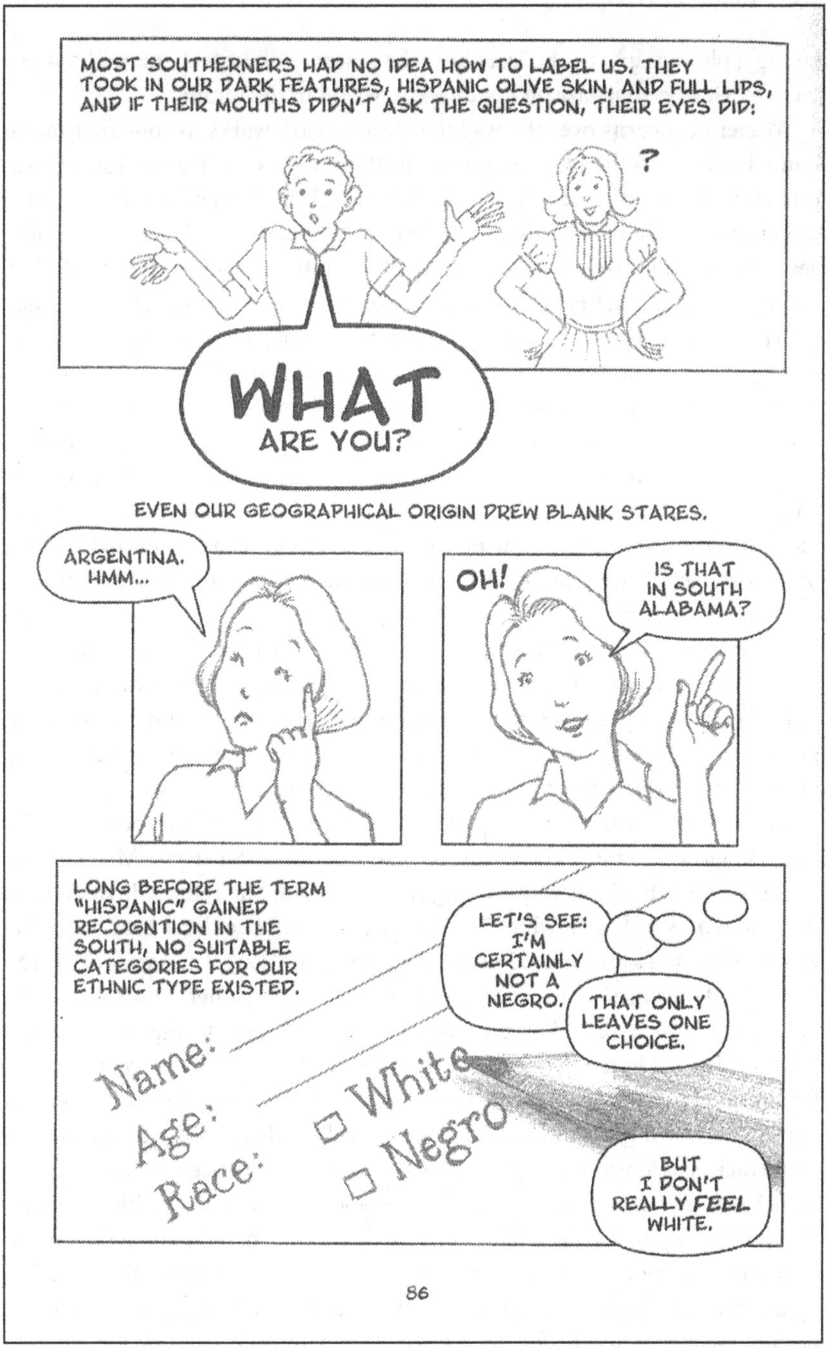

Figure 6.4. Lila Quintero Weaver, *Darkroom* (2012): 86.

taking a photograph, as she fears how she *is* seen, *will be* seen, or, perhaps, *not* seen, by viewers that gaze on her image now and in the future.

Weaver's concerns over the way the viewer's gaze works to construct race is limited neither to the photograph nor to those who view Weaver through the problematic lens of race. Flat, unshaded, two-dimensional line drawings are present throughout the memoir, standing in stark contrast to the photorealistic aesthetic present throughout so much of the narrative. Typically, Weaver deploys this style to highlight those with shallow perceptions of race, marking individuals with a "two-dimensional" racial consciousness in that it only considers white and black as available options, typically reducing one to an overly simplistic, typically racist caricature. For example, Weaver draws the classmates that wonder what her racial identity might be in this style, which mirrors their overly simplistic racial perspective (see figure 6.4). Weaver also uses this style when Lissy is accused of having "nigger lips" (80). By depicting people with a two-dimensional view of race with these simple line drawings, Weaver reduces the individual to his or her own worldview. Stated simply, she has us see them as they might see others.

Weaver's most damning use of these two-dimensional drawings indicts not only the racist whites of Alabama but herself and her readers as well. When recounting the moment Weaver receives her first pair of glasses as a young schoolgirl, Weaver tell us that her corrected vision was still imperfect in one very important sense (see figure 6.5): "*What a discovery.* The visual world was a thing of wonder. I hadn't suspected its breadth and richness. But now I saw. Still, my eyeglasses didn't correct a particular blindspot: the faces of black people looked interchangeable to me. I knew only one black person those days—Mrs. Jackson, the lady that helped out with ironing now and then. She refused invitations to join the family at lunch, which left me asking, *why?* I couldn't bear to see her eating alone, so I sat with her. But neither of us spoke" (74). The narration is scattered about the page, some words in text boxes or circles, others borderless, as the text struggles to be placed on the page as much as Weaver struggles to interpret the "blindspots" in her newfound field of vision. The prominent, central image features a group of four African Americans walking down the street. The four figures are drawn two-dimensionally, the same flat style typically reserved for the white racists of Marion. The panel is placed beneath the image of Weaver trying on her new glasses for the first time, indicating to the reader that this represents Weaver's perception of these four figures, who are drawn in the simple line drawings usually meant to represent someone with a shallow perception of race. Yet, by placing the image in sequence after the image of Weaver trying on her new glasses, Weaver indicts her own reductive, even if juvenile, view of race. After all, in this moment the four African Americans are not two-dimensional themselves but only perceived as such by the younger Weaver present in the memoir. With

74

Figure 6.5. Lila Quintero Weaver,
Darkroom (2012): 74.

this inversion, Weaver acknowledges her own limited perceptions of race and, in so doing, recognizes her own need "to look—really look." This scene is rife with implications for her reader as well, as the opening panel draws the glasses facing toward the reader. Symbolically, the reader sees the world through Weaver's eyes in this moment, as it prompts him or her to consider his or her own potentially problematic ways of seeing.

Weaver's story indicts her younger self not only for how she sees African Americans but for how she regards herself as an activist for their cause, as well as how her efforts are perceived. These insights prove particularly resonant in the book's discussion on the politics of participation in civil rights activism, even on the relatively low scale represented by Weaver's high school. Inspired by her father's activism, Weaver begins to flout the cultural mores that insist on the cultural segregation of African Americans from the white population of Marion—in outright defiance of the integrationist mandates of *Brown v. Board of Education* (1954). At school, she begins to befriend her black classmates, despite calls home from concerned (white) parents in the neighborhood who are worried that fraternizing with the implied sexual threat of African American males would ruin her future before she reached it (222). Rejecting her school's demands that she "restrict [her]self to bona fide academic activities," she begins to pride herself on standing on her activist bona fides instead. Yet the indeterminate nature of Weaver's racial identity—particularly her light skin—disrupts her newfound progressive politics as her African American friends still regard her with guarded skepticism. In one particularly tense high school scene, Weaver attempts to break up a fight between two African American girls, both of whom she considers her friends. One of the girls shouts angrily that Weaver should mind her own business, calls her a "cracker," and demands that she "go back to her own kind" (227). Taken aback, Weaver defends herself by claiming, "I've taken a stand for equality, and I've lost most of my white friends because of it!" The phrase "white friends" is perhaps the most telling, as it both implies a sacrifice to which her African American friend should be grateful and insists that Weaver, herself, is in fact not white (which is true).

Yet the design of the central panel of this scene, that of Weaver's high school identification card, immediately disrupts any potential earnestness we might bestow on Weaver's beleaguered younger self (see figure 6.6). On it, Weaver voices her demand that her social sacrifices be acknowledged from the photograph on the right. In this instance, the photograph voices how Weaver insisted that she be seen; it is this photograph that insists her African American classmates acknowledge her sacrifices. The background of the ID is emblazoned with Weaver dressed as a sort of civil rights Joan of Arc bearing the banner of progress ("Down with Racism") with her personal martyrdom etched haphazardly across her image

Figure 6.6. Lila Quintero Weaver,
Darkroom (2012): 227.

("Standing up! Hostility! Solidarity! Principles! Rejection! Lost Reputation!"). In stark contrast to her shaded photo, the image of Weaver as a civil rights martyr is drawn two-dimensionally, casting this vision of herself as little more than a shallow self-perception that subtly challenges the claims of her photograph. Further undercutting her assertion is Weaver's accompanying narration—"Blah Blah Blah!"—underneath the photograph on the right. On the following page, the reader is greeted by an angry set of eyes admonishing Weaver's claims to civil rights martyrdom. "We don't like you neither, cracker," her angry classmate yells. "You are not one of us! You got that? You are not one of us!" It is in this moment that Weaver faces a stark realization, as she is seemingly relegated to an unstable proximity to whiteness that she can neither fully claim nor truly inhabit.

Predictably perhaps, her very attempt to participate in her classmate's struggle for equality is met with hostility by her white peers, as a group of young boys threaten her brother with violence after he defends her reputation. Here, the reader encounters Weaver's younger brother, Johnny, directly for the first and only time in the narrative. She describes her brother's eyes as distant, containing the sort of "strange detachment" she has only seen in the eyes of desperate African American men (233). Johnny himself is drawn like a typical Latino boy—full lips (like Lissy's), thick black hair, with skin shaded slightly darker than the white boys that surround him. The implication is clear—Weaver and her siblings may not be black, but they certainly are not white, either. It is only after the fight is broken up that Johnny confesses to his sister that he was defending her against the accusation that she was a "nigger lover" (235). The reader is left to decide to what extent, if any, Johnny's reactions to this comment are charged with the same racial anxieties of his sister Lissy, who fears being seen as anything other than white. Weaver's recollections of her time in high school close on a now-familiar motif, with a two-page layout of Weaver reimagining the entire scene in reverse. Again, the reader witnesses the scene play out backward as the individual panels take Weaver back to the schoolyard to confront her accuser (236–37). In this imagined confrontation, Weaver responds to the accusation with a guffaw and dismissively calls her accuser an "idiot"—a cathartic fantasy made both possible and visible by photo-graphic narration. And while the photograph on Weaver's high school ID may represent an officially sanctioned identity (in that it is issued by a governing body—the high school), anxieties about how the image is interpreted by the viewer remains central to the narrative. Weaver's failure to have her high school activism acknowledged, as naïve as it might have been, in many ways motivates the memoir itself. She may not have been seen as an ally to the movement at the time, but photo-graphic narrative makes her contributions (and their incumbent angst) visible to her readers in the present.

All of these scenes preface one of the memoir's chief interventions by reminding the reader that to look on a photograph is not a passive act, as Weaver enacts Jacques Rancière's notion of "the emancipated spectator." Rancière claims that activist theater attempts to convert audiences from passive voyeurs to active participants in order to awake some form of new political, social, or intellectual consciousness. In as much as Weaver also hopes to awaken some latent political consciousness vis-à-vis the reader's gaze, comparisons resonate between Rancière and Weaver, as Rancière's activist theater uses human bodies as signifiers for the sake of storytelling and narrative. Conversely, it might be said that graphic narratives use signifiers to represent human bodies, in this case forgotten or disavowed by particular historical narratives. However, Rancière warns his readers that the dichotomy of the active versus passive spectator presumes that viewing is innately passive, denying its inherent potential for change. Rather, Rancière claims, the emancipation of the spectator "begins when we understand that viewing is also an action that confirms or transforms" (13). Weaver's photo-graphic narrative functions in much the same vein. As Lissy's previous anxieties about race highlight, to gaze on a photograph is itself an interpretive act—a reality often lost on the viewer due in part to the photograph's presumed evidentiary nature. One does not so much see a photograph as read it—the viewer implicitly interprets and constructs the image's meaning as opposed to simply receiving it. In other words, Weaver does not so much emancipate her spectators as she is reminding them of their already potentially emancipated state.

Darkroom's Ethics of Seeing: Witnessing and Testimony

Of course, *how* one "sees" is of equal concern to Weaver as *what* is seen. As Sontag insists, the photograph is not simply an artifact to be seen, but it concurrently induces an ethics of seeing, one linked to the performance of witnessing, documenting, and testifying. We might say that Weaver's own ethics of viewing are grounded not in the "right to observe" but in an obligation to bear witness. In this regard, Weaver's ethics echo Berger's assertion in *Ways of Seeing* (1972) that "we only see what we look at. To look is an act of choice" (8). Yet Weaver's emancipation of the reader also draws our attention to this deliberate process of seeing—to a conscious, willful, and ethical process of interpretive viewership. In order to illustrate this, Weaver's memoir features the recurrent images of eyes themselves, ubiquitous throughout the text—a motif present even on the memoir's cover. When Weaver is discussing her father's own history of activism, the reader encounters a splash page of repeating images drawing our eyes to her father's (see figure 6.7). The image of her father's eyes witnessing the brutal beatings at Marion foreshadow the riots of February 18, 1965, that resulted in the death of unarmed African American activist Jimmie Lee Jackson and inspired the iconic Selma

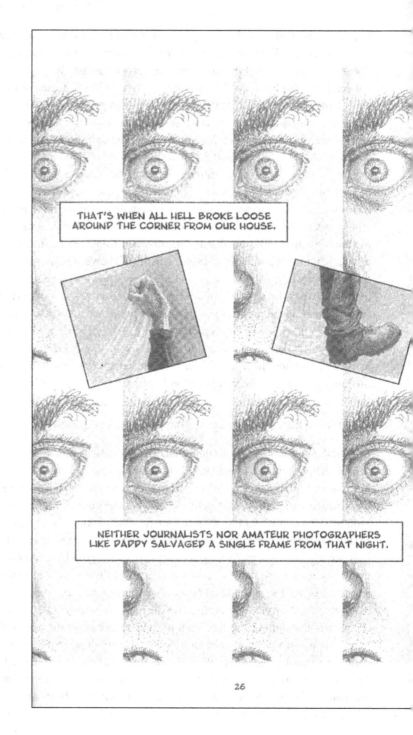

THAT'S WHEN ALL HELL BROKE LOOSE AROUND THE CORNER FROM OUR HOUSE.

NEITHER JOURNALISTS NOR AMATEUR PHOTOGRAPHERS LIKE DADDY SALVAGED A SINGLE FRAME FROM THAT NIGHT.

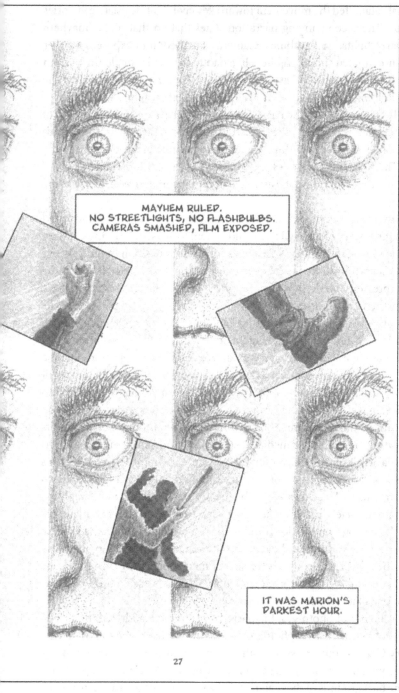

Figure 6.7. Lila Quintero Weaver,
Darkroom (2012): 26–27.

marches that catapulted the movement toward key civil rights legislative victories in the 1960s. The accompanying narration states that on that night "mayhem ruled. No streetlights, no flashbulbs. Cameras smashed, film exposed. Neither journalists nor amateur photographers like daddy salvaged a single frame from that night. It was Marion's darkest hour" (26–27). Nestor watches aghast at the brutality unfolding before his eyes as the violence itself is captured in a series of small panels scattered about the page. These small panels are overlaid on top of the repeating image of Nestor, as they disrupt the flow of the panels underneath in defiance of Groensteen's rhythmic function to become incorporated into the sequence. The repeating images of the beating suggest a trauma for Nestor—a disruptive memory that cannot be assimilated into the narrative structure of the piece itself.

Weaver's symbolic testimony takes the form of the photo-graphic narrative and fills gaps in the history of the civil rights movement by making "Marion's darkest hour" visible to her readers. The splash page of Nestor's reaction to the beatings contains no such transitions, as Weaver removes the gutter space between the panels, compressing the rhythm of time for the scene. The lack of gutter space and the consistency of the image suggests a moment frozen in a repetitious cycle. In *Understanding Comics* (1993), Scott McCloud has described the incremental, even infinitesimal, amount of time that passes from such frame-to-frame panel arrangement as "moment to moment," an arrangement that seeks to mimic the actual movement of time as much as possible (70). The fragmented images of the violence, depicted as photographs, defy easily placement on the page or into the narrative. In fact, without the accompanying narration by Weaver to contextualize the image, the reader might be put in the same position as Nestor—witness to an event that defies immediate comprehension. Yet these photographs also invoke a sense of immediacy for the viewer. Superimposed over Nestor's eyes, these snapshots depict acts of violence captured only in her father's memory, a documentary silence created not by the limitations of the photograph but by an Alabaman society unwilling to allow itself to be seen, as Weaver later reveals that Nestor's camera was destroyed in the riot by white supremacists. These scenes share Sontag's concerns about what the camera is permitted to purposely elide from the historical record. The recurrent images of eyes both in this scene and throughout the memoir remind us that to observe is itself a form of documentation, one that compels us to witness—and to testify.

Through the use of photo-graphic narrative, *Darkroom* addresses the brutal suppression of journalists and photographers at the hands of white supremacists at the Perry County courthouse in relation to a church-organized protest of incarcerated civil rights worker James Orange (see figure 6.8). Unlike the predominately white backgrounds of the majority of the memoir's pages, the scenes at the

Perry County courthouse are drawn on entirely black paper, highlighting what Weaver previously called "Marion's darkest hour" (162–63). Here, this comment takes on additional meanings, as the scenes open with white supremacists cutting the power to the streetlights illuminating the protest and smashing any cameras or flashbulbs that might document the ensuing one-sided attack on the protestors and journalists. In this sense, "Marion's darkest hour" refers both to the malicious nature of this event as well as the lack of corroborating physical documentation due to the darkness of the unlit street. The text marks this moment both as missing from the photographic record presented in the memoir and as an unavoidable stain on that very history. This scene even marks the physical book itself, as the pages are left unnumbered yet easily identified as the black pages stand out in stark relief, even when the book is shut, surrounded on all sides by the color white.

The second page of this scene returns the reader to a shot of Nestor's eyes, to he who "witnessed the madness" but was unable to record it. We also see Weaver employ snapshots to imagine the violence, which defy easy arrangement on the page—a visual signal to the difficulty of incorporating this violence even into her own overall narrative, echoing the previous image on pages 26–27. Weaver chooses to leave some of these imagined snapshots completely blank—a tacit admission of the limitations of even her photo-graphic narrative to recall or document these scenes of racial violence.[4] Initially, one might read these photographs as depicting a failed exposure as the physical film in the broken cameras are exposed and ruined. They also represent a sort of failure to expose, as these photographs would have been the sole corroborating evidence available to anyone hoping to reveal the identities of the perpetrators of these crimes. As these are not actual photos but recreations, readers know to interpret both the blacked-out images and the black frames and borders as deliberate aesthetic choices that replace the absence of evidence with evidence of the absence. In a manner of speaking, Weaver's memoir documents the darkness itself.

Nonetheless, these pages still enact Weaver's imperative to bear a continual form of witness in her present moment to the violence the camera missed in the past. The onomatopoeic text at the bottom of the scene—WHACKWHACK-WHACKWHACKWHACK—suggests a continuous violence enacted on African Americans that begins before this scene and continues beyond—violence that cannot be contained by the page. The following pages of this section vacillate between more traditional graphic narrative panel arrangements and a single image of a man with a can of black spray paint pointed evocatively at readers (165)—suggesting our own potential silencing. Eventually, Weaver's artwork returns to the disarray of scattered photographs from the initial layout (166–67), each representing a failed attempt to describe the madness of this racist rampage. At

MY FATHER WITNESSED THE MADNESS.

EEEEEEEK!

WHACK

WHACK   WHACK

WHACKWHACKWHA

Figure 6.8. Lila Quintero Weaver, *Darkroom* (2012): 162–63.

its climax, this section settles on two full-page images of Alabama state troopers chasing the unarmed Jimmie Lee Jackson and his parents into the infamous diner where Jackson will be murdered. Rather than take the reader with Jackson into the diner, Weaver chooses to leave the reader behind, as the final image closes on a "shot in the dark," leaving only an enigmatic BOOM to mark an all-too-familiar and predictably tragic conclusion to which Weaver's readers can only bear distant witness: "Jimmie Lee Jackson, dead at 26" (173).

Choosing not to depict the death of Jimmie Lee Jackson admits to the limitations of testifying to a murder unseen. Yet Weaver does not release herself or her readers from their obligation, as Nestor's eyes return to insist we bear symbolic witness to Jackson's tragic demise. Through Weaver's photo-graphic memoir, photography and graphic narrative function in concert as contrapuntal modes of documentation and expression that do more than verify events for their readers. It challenges them to be witnesses as well—a call to action emblemized by the woman on the lower right of the initial splash page who makes eye contact with readers and begs for their "help" (163). This simple present-tense imperative also reminds us that witnessing must be an active process, a skeptical act that acknowledges the limitations of documentation and representation.

Bearing Witness to "Events Already Told"

Weaver's narrative return to the protests of Marion prompts her readers to actively consider what the writing of political histories might elide or suppress. In *Comic Books as History* (1989), Joseph Witek claims that historical graphic novels and comic books may vary widely in perspective or point of view, but they do not exist primarily to counter dominant historical narratives so much as to reveal their ideological and narrative construction. Rather, Witek argues, historical comics reveal the innate constructedness of dominant historical narratives and that their authors must contend with the retelling of "an event that is 'already told,' already weighted with cultural significance that any telling risks the loss of its individual rhetorical force in the face of previously established readings and individual associations" (17). Witek's concerns over "an event already told" echo similar sentiments expressed in Michael de Certeau's analysis of the historical event as a concept in *The Writing of History* (1988). Rather than taking events as facts, de Certeau insists that events, even singular moments, are themselves smaller narratives that in total are woven together into the tapestries of history. He claims that so-called events do not explain history or delimit its ruptures but rather permit the intelligibility of historical narratives by providing the building blocks of teleology (96). For de Certeau, events represent historical moments imbued with meaning and arranged and contextualized into particular cultural narratives of said history. And, as Sontag claims, photographs might be thought of as such narrative events themselves, that "picture-taking is an event in itself" (11). In returning to the series of events on the night of February 18, 1965, Weaver manages to retell the story already told to ensure that the events of that infamous night in Marion survive to *be* retold after the suppression of journalists at the protests left Jimmie Lee Jackson dead with little corroborating evidence that this "event" ever occurred. Moreover, speaking from a Latina perspective also challenges any presumed concerns over who is allowed to testify, as Weaver refuses to be relegated to the racial sidelines of her youth.

While reflecting on the power dynamics implicit in photography, Sontag writes, "People robbed of their past seem to make the most fervent picture takers, at home and abroad" (10). In Weaver's case, we might say that she was not robbed of her past per se but that her ambiguous position as a Latina subject excluded her from participation in a larger national history. Relegated to the role of witness to the civil rights movement, rather than participant, Weaver nonetheless writes (or, perhaps, *draws*) her own history of activism in the movement. Through the concomitant narratives of her father's activism and her own difficulties joining her classmates' struggle, Weaver implicitly argues that bearing witness itself can be a form of participation.[5] Weaver's photo-graphic narrative allows her readers "to really look" at her subjective experience of a politicized Latina childhood, one invisible to both her peers at the time and absent in popular accounts of the civil rights movement, such as the recent film *Selma* (2014). The graphic form allows her contribution to be *seen*, not as a counter to these popular narratives but as a contribution. Furthermore, Weaver also reveals the innately racialized frameworks of such histories. Rather than deny or indict this reality, Weaver's work chooses to document it and, in so doing, forbids us from losing sight of histories themselves as constructed and interpreted. Ultimately, Weaver charges not the authors of history but the readers that receive them with developing an ethics of seeing. She reminds us that to look is to interpret, to imagine is to witness, and, finally, *how* we see matters just as much as what we *choose* to see. Or cannot.

NOTES

1. Of course, I do not mean to suggest that Latinos and Latinas were generally inactive during this time period. The Mexican American population in particular was quite active in the labor movement and the land grants movement, most famously Cesar Chavez and Reies López Tijerina. The Chicano art movement and the Nuyorican writers both produced novels, poetry, and art that explored what it meant to be Latino in a shifting U.S. racial landscape. Yet for the isolated Quintero family living in Marion, Alabama, without a strong Latino presence, allegiance with African Americans was the only available ave-

nue for activism. For more on Latino/a activity during this time period, see Lisa Sánchez González, *Boricua Literature* (2001); Marta Caminero-Santangelo, *On Latinidad* (2007); and Zaragosa Vargas, *Crucible of Struggle* (2010).

2. As Clara E. Rodriguez writes in her contribution to *Hispanic New York* (2010), Latinos in the United States were often forced to negotiate a "U.S. racial structure that assumed a white-notwhite division of the world" and were forced into an ambiguous "gray position" within this structure (184). It must be noted, of course, that Rodriguez is referring specifically to the experiences of Puerto Rican migrants moving to the mainland United States in this quote. However, difficulties in articulating Latino/a racial identity in the post–World War II United States, particularly in relation to the individual's proximity to whiteness, permeates both Latino/a ethnic memoirs and fiction. For example, Nuyorican authors Piri Thomas and Edward Rivera both attempt to articulate their own identities on a black-white spectrum. Chicano authors such as Rudolfo Anaya or Nash Candelaria negotiate their own potential whiteness against indigenous or Native American identity. However, locating one's self on a spectrum with (unattainable) racial and cultural whiteness at the top of a racial hierarchy is a consistent theme throughout this body of literature.

3. The way that graphic narrative blends word and image makes it an ideal medium in which to write the histories from otherwise omitted perspectives. From early work such as Jack Jackson's *Comanche Moon* (1977–78) trilogy to more contemporary works such as Marjane Satrapi's *Persepolis* (2000), graphic novels offer an alternative literary and intellectual space for the historically marginalized to write their own histories. In this sense, graphic narratives offer a space where the slivers (as Weaver puts it) of forgotten histories might be written into the larger collective narrative. In *The Writing of History* (1988), Michel de Certeau claims that these slivers, elements of the past sacrificed by dominant narratives to maintain their own intelligibility in the present, always "come back, despite everything, in the edges of discourse or in its rifts and crannies: 'resistances,' 'survivals' or delays discreetly perturb the pretty order of a line of 'progress' or system, of interpretation" (4). For her part, Weaver addresses these "rifts and crannies" (or gutters?) in the dominant cultural narrative of the U.S. civil rights movement as a black and white struggle by rendering both her family's personal and political histories as inextricably linked to this moment in U.S. history.

4. This might also explain why the memoir is relatively silent on the subject of Juan Domingo Perón's brutal regime as the president of Argentina in the 1960s—it only receives a single page of attention (Weaver 113). Since Weaver's memoir serves as a form of documentation, even if imagined, for events the family experienced, there would be little to help them account for this simultaneous dark time in Argentina's history. What little there is to know comes in the form of correspondence from her grandparents, which includes their photographs.

5. The fact that Lila is specifically a *child*-witness obviously shapes the memoir as well, an element I do not cover here. For more on Lila as a child-witness, see Breckenridge and Peterson, "Lila Quintero Weaver's *Darkroom: A Memoir in Black and White*: Envisioning Equality" (2013).

CHAPTER 7

Environmental Graphic Memory

Remembering the Natural World and Revising
History in Vietnamerica

Jeffrey Santa Ana

ONE OF THE MOST EVOCATIVE images in GB Tran's *Vietnamerica* (2010) is an enormous ancient tree (see figure 7.1). While the American-born Tran is on his first trip to Vietnam with his parents in 2006, his father, Tri Huu Tran, explains the tree's significance: "Local Vietnamese claim that the very tree Buddha meditated under is its ancestor. Monks carried a cutting of its root all the way from India, replanted it here, and built this temple around it. 2,500 years later, their disciples still care for it. Generation after generation have sat in its shade in pursuit of enlightenment" (9). Tri Huu Tran's explanation follows a life lesson from Confucius that Tran quotes on the preceding page: "A man without history is a tree without roots" (8). Tran's father inscribed this quote into a history book about the Vietnam War that he gave to his son as a high school graduation gift. To be sure, the quote respectively places the tree in the historical context of Tran's family in the United States, who are all Vietnam War refugees, as well as Tran's own place in a history of ancestry, origins, and migration within and beyond his family's Southeast Asian homeland. Yet the quote also implies the problem of historical erasure and alienation from ancestral origins for those Vietnamese Americans such as Tran who are American born, children of refugee parents born and raised in the United States after the Vietnam War's end on April 30, 1975.[1]

Together, the legendary tree and the Confucius lesson preceding it signify the collective history of the Vietnamese people both in Vietnam and in the diaspora. For Tran, this collective history includes his family history, inextricable from histories of colonialism and war in Vietnam that he must not only understand and remember as cultural inheritance but also retrieve and reconstruct as multigenerational ethnic history. And Tran does retrieve his family history by creatively reconstructing it through his comics art, which affirms his responsibility to know and culturally inherit the history of the Vietnamese people and assert his resistance to forgetting and losing this collective history in America.

Through both the Vietnamese people's ecological imagination and Tran's abil-

Figure 7.1. GB Tran,
Vietnamerica (2010): 9.

ity to visualize this imagination in his graphic memoir, the tree signifies a multivalent sense of place and history. For in *Vietnamerica* natural world imagery
implies remembering history and commemorating place, as well as origins and
belonging in an originary homeland from which all Vietnamese diasporic scat-
terings commence; it likewise exemplifies how the formal aspects of comics make
visible the physical and temporal displacements of violence that characterize a
diasporic subjectivity—a war refugee's psychological state when experiencing,
exhibiting, and reliving the trauma of losing home and self because of forced
relocation during the war and after. My examination of *Vietnamerica* focuses on
Tran's depiction of this diasporic subjectivity through his portrayal of his parents,
who tell him about growing up in rural villages when French and American
military forces occupied Vietnam. They remember experiencing the violence of
their homeland's "militarized physical environment" and feeling traumatized by
the furious transformation of the natural landscape into a war zone.[2] Forcibly
displaced within and beyond their own country by this violence, Tran's parents
suffer the loss of place and home that constitutes, in large part, their diasporic
subjectivity.

By illustrating his parents' memories of the war and their trauma from fleeing
destroyed homes and devastated landscapes, Tran depicts his parents' diasporic
subjectivity as the *outcome* of the war's militarized physical environment. Their
continuous manifestation of this subjectivity and enduring trauma as refugees
living in the United States manifests, in Rob Nixon's terms, the delayed and unseen effects of "slow violence." According to Nixon, slow violence is "a violence
that occurs gradually and out of sight, a violence of delayed destruction that
is dispersed across time and space, an attritional violence that is typically not
viewed as violence at all" (2). What Nixon's concept of slow violence registers
are consequential linkages between a past of "spectacular" military violence that
caused the war's environmental destruction *and* a present, as well as future, of
traumatized Vietnamese diasporic experience that continues as the psychological
aftereffect of involuntary migration, the "incremental and accretive" effects of
slow violence on the war refugee's psyche (2).

That the legendary ancient tree can be understood as a multivalent signifier
to reflect complexly the memory of place and ancestry in Vietnam's history of
war and forced relocation would further contextualize this tree within the traumatized Vietnamese diasporic experience. In this manner, the tree emblematizes
slow violence, and through this signification *resists* it as an "attritional catastrophe" that overspills "clear boundaries in time and space" marked by "temporal,
geographical, rhetorical, and technological displacements that simplify violence
and underestimate, in advance and in retrospect, the human and environmental
costs. Such displacements smooth the way for amnesia, as places are rendered

irretrievable to those who once inhabited them" (Nixon 7). Through the formal features of comics, Tran illustrates the tree image and other aspects of the natural world as environmental metaphors that draw attention to the pervasive but elusive effects of slow violence. By comprehending natural world imagery in graphic narrative as metaphors for remembering forced migrations that result from militarism's environmental ruin, this chapter argues that *Vietnamerica* envisions an ecological imagination as an intervention in Vietnam War history. Take again the legendary tree and other natural world imagery that begin *Vietnamerica*. These images depict what Tran remembers when he traveled to Vietnam with his parents to attend a memorial service for Thi Mot, Tran's maternal grandmother. Thi Mot has died in the coastal city of Vungtau, the place where Tran's mother, Dzung, left her when she fled Vietnam with Tri and their children after the communists seized control of the country in 1975. A two-page sepia-toned spread shows Dzung in a Buddhist temple leading Thi Mot's funeral procession while carrying a cremation urn that contains her mother's ashes. In this spread, which also depicts Vungtau's natural beauty (e.g., the city's mountainous seaside landscapes and the temple's luxuriant palms and bamboo architecture), Tran explains in a caption that Thi Mot's "elaborate memorial service gathered family from all over Vietnam, and as far away as the U.S., to the small beach community of Vungtau" (11). Together the caption and the image of Vungtau's natural beauty evoke the physical environment as intrinsic to both the ritual of cultural memory (the Buddhist memorial service) and the act of remembering a past event (Tran's own memory of the memorial service). That most of the image is colored a yellowish-brown tint, with the exception of Vungtau's azure sea and sky, gives the image a warm, antique feeling of an old family photograph. Like many other images in *Vietnamerica* that are also sepia toned, this image's monochromatic yellowish brown evokes the quality of remembering a past event that one feels when gazing at a historic photograph.

Through environmental metaphors for remembering the past and honoring cultural tradition, Tran articulates his sense of place in Vietnam within his family's history. Yet this sense of place is multivalent insofar as it is mediated by traumatized experiences resulting from diaspora and the war's destroyed landscapes that compel migration.[3] Tran indicates the psychological consequences of diaspora (e.g., Dzung's pain because she was away in America when her mother died) as an aspect of slow violence; however, he overcomes this violence's denial of persistent suffering by attending his grandmother's memorial to recognize and understand his parents' trauma. As Tran admits, "To be honest, I didn't fly across the world for Thi Mot. I did it for Mom. And Dad" (11).

Representing and resisting the delayed and unseen effects of slow violence, *Vietnamerica* evokes an ecological imagination to remember and historicize the Vietnamese people's origins and belonging in places from which they were forcibly removed because of the war's environmental destruction. U.S. military involvement in Vietnam, which attempted to extinguish the country's indigenous communist forces through an armed imperialist occupation that the Vietnamese call the "American War" (1955–75), lasted for twenty years and took a calamitous toll on the environment and people.[4] The human and ecological costs of the American War in Vietnam are immense. Between two and three million Vietnamese were killed by the war's end (Lawrence 168). The fighting destroyed millions of acres of farmland, wrecked Vietnam's industrial facilities, and devastated many villages and cities (167–68). Marilyn B. Young reveals that in South Vietnam

> 9,000 out of 15,000 hamlets, 25 million acres of farmland, 12 million acres of forest were destroyed, and 1.5 million farm animals had been killed; there were an estimated 200,000 prostitutes, 879,000 orphans, 181,000 disabled people, and 1 million widows; all six of the industrial cities in the North had been badly damaged, as were provincial and district towns, and 4,000 out of 5,800 agricultural communes. North and South the land was cratered and planted with tons of unexploded ordnance, so that long after the war farmers and their families suffered injuries as they attempted to bring the fields back into cultivation. Nineteen million gallons of herbicide had been sprayed on the South during the war, and while the long-term effects were unknown in 1975 (and are not clear now), severe birth defects and multiple miscarriages were apparent early on. (301–2)

Despite the American War's ending, then, its environmental and human consequences are clearly not over. Rather, they continue in the present as a complex outcome of slow violence. As Cathy J. Schlund-Vials maintains, "Dire consequences are ecologically evident in present-day considerations about Agent Orange usage. More than twenty-five years after the war's conclusion, the United States and Vietnam reached an agreement in 2001 to study the impact of the toxic defoliant, which to date has affected an estimated one million Vietnamese. The study highlighted the fact that Agent Orange is currently responsible for birth defects in approximately 150,000 Vietnamese children" ("Ecological Imaginations" 113). Along with the long-term neurological effects of chemical weaponry, the estimated 800,000 cluster bombs, M79 grenade bombs, and flechette bombs remaining buried underground in Vietnam and maiming and killing civilians is, as Ann Laura Stoler puts it, the evidential matter of the war's ecological "ruination"—the violent accrual of militarism's "imperial debris" that "remains in bodies, in the poisoned soil, in water on a massive and enduring scale" ("The Rot Remains" 26). Such imperial debris compels us to understand that the war's unending destructive impact on Vietnam's physical environment and health of the country's people reveals this war's history to continue in the present and into the future as a *longue durée.*

In *Vietnamerica*, the war's history as a *longue durée* may also be understood through the narrative's incorporation of various conflicts. For Tran's work insists on a *longue durée* reading of slow violence that renders discernable the catastrophic dimensions of multiple wars in Vietnam, beginning with the Resistance War against the French (1945–54) that opens Tran's graphic memoir and which bleeds into other conflicts, namely, the American War, the U.S. military invasions of Cambodia (1970) and Laos (1971) that were designed to destroy communist bases in both countries, and after the American War during Vietnam's reconstruction and reunification (1975–90).[5] After the war, the Vietnamese continued to suffer from a U.S. government that sought to punish the country for winning the war by reneging on promises of economic aid and extending an embargo that "had governed trade relations with North Vietnam during the war" to "all of Vietnam and Cambodia" (Young 301).

Revising History

As the Confucius quote and the tree image together illustrate in *Vietnamerica*, Tran's book is an intergenerational tale about how imperialist occupations and wars in Vietnam shaped his family's history and determined his own understanding of his place within this history. Told through an ensemble of perspectives in the past and the present, the narrative does not follow a linear temporality that is conventional to history's critical distance, documented explanation, and divisibility from the imagination (Misztal 99). Rather, it manifests the "plural, mediated, and fluid" process of remembering (106), specifically a process of generational remembering in which "the past is handed on via parents and grandparents and goes beyond the limits of individual experience" (84). Providing an artistic link between the generations of Tran's postcolonial and diasporic family, *Vietnamerica* is a graphic memoir that jumps dizzily amid Tran's experiences growing up in the United States and his family members who recount their lives during the French colonial era and American military involvement in Vietnam. Both a highly personal and a polyphonic story of generational memory in the diaspora, *Vietnamerica* employs unique features of sequential art narratives that "create suggestive but subliminal connections which need not correspond to the linear logic of the narrative sequence" (Witek, *Comic Books as History* 28). By using these unique features of the comics form to illustrate how memory's nonlinear temporality revises the past through the promotion of present events, Tran provides an imaginative intervention in Vietnam War history that augments historical knowledge of the war's impact on Vietnam's environments and the forced migration of its people.

Studies of comics as social documents and works of realism have shown that comic books and graphic narrative can reinterpret and revise history.[6] In this sense, *Vietnamerica* formally renovates Vietnam War history through verbal and visual elements that are unique to the ability of comics to create an atemporal sense of the past in the present. Capturing at once the living memory of forced relocations involved in the war refugees' experiences of violence and trauma, *Vietnamerica* elucidates these relocations as ongoing in the present—as the outcome of slow violence and hence refusing to render them over and done within a customary frame of history that discounts generational remembering in its attempt to represent and document only objective facts and events from the past. Because it employs deconstructive "visual grammars, image-texts, and graphic performances" that depict themes of dislocation, boundary traversal, and self/other oppositions (Mehta and Mukherji 3), *Vietnamerica* can likewise be understood as a *postcolonial* work that reenvisions Vietnam War history from a diasporic perspective in the present and the future. As a postcolonial comics text, it mediates the testimony of those Vietnamese who were forcibly relocated to America and the cultural transmission of this testimony to their progeny, to forthcoming American-born generations.

If, as Eileen Ka-May Cheng contends, "historical writing is as much a product of its time as any other historical development, and can therefore serve as a lens into major trends and developments in Western civilization" (1–2), Tran's graphic memoir shows that postcolonial comics as history and as a major artistic development that began in the twentieth century can revise Vietnam War history. As such, postcolonial comics bear witness—"to testify, to accuse, to archive" from and within a collective history of diaspora (Mehta and Mukherji 3). They reveal the continuing effects of *displacements* as the present inability to recognize and imagine war's destructive impact on the natural world that causally underlies these relocations in the past and which continues to do so in the present as slow violence. By making visible the physical and temporal dispersions of slow violence, *Vietnamerica* illustrates an ecological imagination from a postcolonial and diasporic perspective to remediate the history of the French colonial era and American military involvement in Vietnam. Accordingly, Tran's memoir assumes the registers of *visual* historical writing that characterizes primary features in postcolonial environmental criticism: to demonstrate that "the environment stands as a nonhuman witness to the violent process of colonialism" (DeLoughrey and Handley 8). As important, *Vietnamerica* documents the ecologically destructive consequences of imperialist militarization that evidences human beings as "geological agents" with "invented technologies that are on a scale large enough to have an impact on the planet itself" (Chakrabarty 207). To illustrate, an iconic image of the Vietnamese diaspora in the middle of the memoir demonstrates the war's devastating environmental impact (see figure 7.2). Entrapped people struggle to free themselves from inside a blackened gulf deeply cut by war technology, deep red colors at the top of the image suggesting a bloodied horizon. Vietnam is correspondingly depicted as a hemorrhaging wound within an Asian-Pacific region that has been eviscerated by imperialist intrusions and the successive wars. As Tran shows in this splash page, the geology and geography of Vietnam have been irrevocably shaped by the war's militarized physical environment. The country has figuratively become synonymous with war-induced devastation, an ecological ruin that is the primary cause of ongoing Vietnamese migration and refugeeism.

Ultimately, we can understand that *Vietnamerica* represents and resists the amnesia and invisibility of displacements that mark the attritional calamities and traumas defining slow violence in two specific ways. First, Tran uses the comics form to narrate his family's memories of the militarized physical environment during the war and does so within a critical frame through which to understand the slow violence of the environment's destruction and gradual decline. This ecological ruin is a primary cause of Vietnamese forced relocation both during and after the war. Tran's depiction of slow violence through illustrating his family's memory narratives that comprise *Vietnamerica* is what I call *environmental graphic memory*. The concept refers to an ecologically imaginative way that Tran is able to capture the pervasive but elusive effects of slow violence in his graphic memoir. In *Vietnamerica*'s postcolonial comics format, slow violence is visually narrated through specific interactions between text (captions, speech balloons, and sound effects) and picture (gutters, splash panels, and splash pages). I contend that these formal features of postcolonial comics exemplify the concept of environmental graphic memory as *resistance* to the memory loss of slow violence—a forgetting in which "distancing mechanisms" such as "the temporal distance between short-lived actions and long-term consequences" allow the "memory and body count of slow violence" to be "diffused—and defused—by time" (Nixon 41). And second, Tran's representation of slow violence revises traditional Vietnam War history through a comics form that counters this history's unified, linear, and restrictive time period. This is a simplifying temporal sense of the past that does not represent, nor even recognize as violence, the continuing traumas and forced relocations of diasporic Vietnamese. However, by illustrating his family's traumatized experience during and after the war, Tran lays bare the incremental processes of the war's ecological ruin that are typically overlooked in favor of a conventional history that renders over this form of ruination.

Figure 7.2. GB Tran,
Vietnamerica (2010): 158.

Remembering the Natural World

While on board a flight bound for Vietnam with her husband and her son, Tran's mother says to him, "You know what your father was doing at your age? He . . . WE left Vietnam. On the evening of April 25, 1975, our family crammed into a U.S. cargo plane bound for America. It was one of the last to take off before the Vietcong bombs destroyed the Saigon airport later that night. That was 30 years ago. Your father was the same age as you are now" (3–5). *Vietnamerica* thus opens with the mother's memory narrative about the family's escape from what Nixon would call the American War's "spectacular, immediately sensational, and instantly hyper-visible" violence (13).[7] The speech balloons containing her dialogue function as captions to narrate splash panels imaging the war's explicit, stunning violence: an airplane flies in a fiery blood-red sky while below it Saigon explodes and smolders, a city ablaze from bombings that Tran has drawn to nearly fill the page with thick black smoke billowing across the panels' gutters and right on through the panels' tiers (see figure 7.3).

Subsequent panels show the airplane to contain Dzung, Tri, their children, and Tri's mother (Le Nhi). They are all on board the plane while below them the airport from which they have barely escaped burns dramatically. A splash panel on the next page reveals Tran, who listens to his mother's story as he sits beside her on their flight to Vietnam. By this juxtaposition set up through both Tran's depiction of his mother's recalling the harrowing details of her escape and Tran's imagining these details as he listens to her, Dzung's graphic memory of the war's ferocious violence—in particular, the black and blood-red colors of combat—becomes his own.

What is significant about these beginning panels, which both unfold and encapsulate Dzung's act of remembering the war, is that they set up the contextual frame through which to understand how the war's spectacular violence and its environmental destruction (i.e., the bombing of Saigon and its environs) leads to slow violence, evident in Dzung's narration of her traumatized experience in being forcibly relocated away from her homeland to the United States. Tran's imaginary depiction of his mother's account of the war's militarized physical environment exemplifies resistance to forgetting the histories of colonialism and war in Vietnam, a characteristic feature of environmental graphic memory in his comics text. Insofar as Dzung highlights the war's environmental destruction in her story, her recalling this destruction can be understood as her environmental memory, which resists forgetting the war's militarized destruction of the land as a primary cause of her forced relocation. Because environmental graphic memory here conceives of representing forcibly relocated Vietnamese people as environmental migrants, it also implies an ecocritical lens through which to see

Figure 7.3. GB Tran, *Vietnamerica* (2010): 4.

and critique the physical environment's devastation and gradual decline as slow violence—a violence that becomes immediately traceable to the war's origins in French colonialism and American militarism.[8]

Situated relationally to one another, comics panels are "necessarily placed in relation to space and operate on a share of space" (Groensteen 21). Although the comics panel or frame structures space as a determinate element of the image's composition that the frame encapsulates and contains, it also connotes a multifaceted diegetic position in which a segment of action—the image—both acquires and produces meaning in *juxtaposition* with adjacent frames. In this way, comics indeed function as a specific language because, according to Thierry Groensteen, they simultaneously mobilize an "entirety of codes (visual and discursive)" that constitutes the multilayered and interactive vocabularies of the comics form (6). Situated relationally in apposition with other images, a single image within a panel or a page in comics is inflected with meaning that is always in association with a succession of other images coming before and after it. As Groensteen explains, "the juxtaposition of several panels of the same format will translate into a rapid succession of actions or of replies" (46). Through such a juxtaposition, then, a single image in comics will acquire, in associative relationship with other panels or images, a coherent and thematic context.

Through the frame's relational effect of spacing when images are read in juxtaposition with one another and through this spacing's effect to illustrate the generational remembering relayed in Dzung's narrative, *Vietnamerica*'s primary theme is the legacy of one's place in the history of the war and in the diaspora. Vibrant images of Dzung's recalling the Resistance War when the French military bombed the mountains surrounding Langson, the village where she was born, indicate Tran's endeavor to illustrate the harrowing details of his mother's childhood memories about this war's spectacular violence. In so doing, Tran implies that he inherits Dzung's traumatized experience of forced relocation—an implication of the consequential linkage between the war's spectacular destruction of the environment and his mother's diasporic subjectivity in the present. For example, a vertical tier of panels depicts French military planes dropping bombs onto the mountains and jungles where the Viet Minh hide (see figure 7.4). Sound effects of "THOOM" above red and orange colors that render the detonating bombs mimic the distressing reverberations of explosions in warfare. These volatile colors and sound effects contrast with the calm blue of an evening sky and peaceful green mountains and forests. Yet the consequential linkage between the spectacular violence of warfare and the slow violence of traumatized experience is especially signified in the tier's vertical arrangement of panels: the top panel shows a military plane dropping bombs that explode onto landscapes in the middle panels; the bottom two panels reveal a petrified family

Figure 7.4. GB Tran, *Vietnamerica* (2010): 31.

in their makeshift shelter as the bombings intensify around them, with the final panel depicting a young child whose large alarmed eyes clearly illustrate distress, her resulting traumatized experience. Descending the page in the tier's gutters, Dzung's narration further registers this consequential linkage between militarism's physical violence and its long-term traumatizing effect on civilians: "Trying to go on with their daily lives, families like mine got caught in the cross fire. Lucky for us, the North had a lot of caves. Especially around the village of Langson. The place where I was born" (31). Such juxtaposition in *Vietnamerica* that accentuates a causal relation between the explicit violence of warfare and environmental devastation that renders civilians homeless and forces them to relocate is evident in a series of panels that portray Tran's grandmothers in mourning.

The Memory of Trees

As these juxtaposed frames demonstrate, picture and text act together in *Vietnamerica* to reenvision Vietnam War history from a diasporic perspective. Central to this perspective is a multivalent sense of place that foregrounds remembering the natural world to imply an ecocritical account of colonialism and militarization. Such a reading is manifest in Tran's depiction of his mother's memory of trees at her childhood home three decades after the war has ended. Here, Dzung's remembering the natural world grounds her diasporic subjectivity in a post-reunified homeland that has changed forever because of the war. While talking to her son on the phone about their upcoming trip to Vietnam, Dzung tells him she has been dreaming about a tree that grew in the courtyard of her childhood home in Langson: "I had that dream again last night. . . . It was clearer this time. I could hear its leaves rustle and feel its rough bark" (49). For Dzung, this "tree dream" recalls its thriving life, a defining feature of her own life and her homeplace as a child. As a living creation of the natural world, the tree reflects Dzung's childhood body and embodies her "body memory" of home. As Janet Donohoe explains, "body memory and place memory cannot be separated. We have place memory precisely because we have body memory and we have body memory precisely because we have place memory. This allows us to recognize the importance of home as a foundational bodily memory. The body is how we make a place of our own and the central place of our embodiment is our home" (7). For Dzung, the courtyard tree in Vungtau is a multifaceted signifier of home, self-identity, and family history, much like the way the legendary ancient tree that begins *Vietnamerica* embodies the collective history of the Vietnamese people.

Because the tree serves as a palimpsest for Dzung's memory of her childhood home—a place essential to her self-identity before trauma—for her to find this tree gone on returning to Langson would therefore be an intensely upsetting event. In the page that shows Dzung's return to Langson, Tran depicts his mother's homecoming as a happy occasion that rejuvenates her until she arrives at her childhood home and discovers the courtyard has been "cleared out" (see figure 7.5). "Don't you remember?" her brother Vinh says. "That's where the family tree stood" (61). This vertical tier of panels that ends with a frame that splits Dzung's face in half—the left part illustrating her face as a child and the right part depicting her distress in the present—raises a host of questions. Is it significant the lost tree was "the family tree"? How are we to understand Tran's split image of his mother in the psychological context of her traumatized experience? How are we to comprehend the image in the historical context of Vietnamese forced migration and diaspora? How is the split frame to be understood within the critical frame through which to comprehend the slow violence of the environment's destruction and gradual decline?

As with the vertical tier of panels that depict French military planes bombing the mountains and jungles where the Viet Minh hide during the Resistance War (see again figure 7.3), the vertical tier of panels that show Dzung's distress over the loss of the tree in a post-reunified Vietnam also implies the consequential linkage between militarism's physical violence and its long-term traumatizing effect on civilians. In this regard, both tiers narratively indicate the war's environmental ruin as a primary reason for Dzung's and her family's forced migration and the slow violence of their ensuing trauma. Dzung is reminded of her trauma when she realizes the "family tree" has been lost, and further, Vinh implicitly demands this remembering when he asks, "Don't you remember?" The vertical and descending arrangement of the tier's panels is also important to narrate cumulatively the significance of the tree within a natural world setting for remembering place and affirming home. Beginning with the panel at the top of the tier, both text (caption and speech balloons) and picture (images of Dzung in livid blackish-blue colors) act together to demonstrate how creations of the natural world reflect Dzung's childhood body and embody her memory of home when she was a child. Tran's narration in the caption inside the top two panels ("Every sight, sound, and smell transported her further and further back" and "Unlocking long buried memories of her forgotten childhood") directs our interpretation of the panels' images in which Dzung smells cooking food and holds in her hands fruit she once ate as a child. The tier's third panel reveals Dzung as a young girl, rejuvenated by remembering the natural world—a remembering that is inseparable from her memory of home and that enables her to recognize the importance of home as a foundational bodily memory. The vertical layering of the panels in this tier, then, exemplifies the unique way in which a postcolonial comics form narrativizes remembering place and the natural world as a palimpsest of personal and historical memory for Vietnamese people, such as Dzung, who are diasporic.

Figure 7.5. GB Tran,
Vietnamerica (2010): 61.

And more obliquely, the vertical tier's layering evokes an imaginary inscription on the page that reflects the hybridity and "unhomeliness" of Vietnamese pasts, as well as an ecocritical acknowledgment of the indelible traces of colonialism, war, and diaspora on Vietnam's present.[9]

In the tier's bottom two panels that split Dzung's face in halves, Tran evidently intends to illustrate his mother's distress on realizing that her childhood home has been forever changed because of the missing family tree. However, what compounds her distress here is also what the vertical tier depicting Langson's battletorn environments implies: the war's destruction of the environment is why Dzung was traumatized as a child, because she was forced to leave her childhood home in consequence of this destruction. And in the present, despite Vietnam's post-reunification, the war continues to affect her sense of place and identity—an ongoing subjectivity of self-division and fragmentation implied by the marked contrast between Dzung's bluish-black face and the white outlines surrounding and splitting the panels. The war continues to affect Dzung to the extent that it has rendered the family tree lost, which triggers involuntary memories—like an "emotional flashback"—of Dzung's childhood trauma in which a French soldier killed her father, Thi Mot remarried, and her family moved away from "the volatile North" (44), abandoning "everything in Langson" (45).[10]

The tier's final frame of Dzung's split face has several meanings pertaining to the memory of trees as a primary theme in *Vietnamerica*. First, it is another example of the memoir's tree imagery as a multivalent signifier that reflects the memory of place and ancestry in Vietnam's history of war and forced migration. As such, it further expresses Tran's ecological imagination to reenvision Vietnam War history from a diasporic perspective. Second, as an environmental metaphor for the pervasive but elusive effects of slow violence, this final frame exemplifies how *Vietnamerica* recasts traumatized Vietnamese diasporic experience as both a story and a history about environmental migrants. And third, it illustrates the psychological costs of diaspora for Dzung: the slow violence of losing an ancestral home that had a fundamental influence on the manner in which she constitutes the world. In so doing, the frame effectively discloses this loss as the implication of Dzung's fragmented or divided self-identity, her "double (and even plural) identifications that are constitutive of hybrid forms of identity" (Braziel and Mannur 5). As Donohoe perceives, the loss that one feels when returning to an ancestral home that has changed "is intertwined with the narrative of one's self as well as one's community, [and] the experience is at the same time the quiet reminder of one's loss of self and loss of world and others" (79). Yet for Dzung, the implication of the lost family tree is much larger than realizing her childhood home has not waited for her unaltered, that it has not remained indifferent to her memories. For her, the consequence of losing the family tree means that *all* of

Vietnam's natural world that she remembers from her childhood has irrevocably changed. The country's mountains, beaches, and landscapes that she romantically recalls from her childhood—a time before the trauma of fleeing from Langson's battle-torn environments—are now irretrievable because of the war.

In *Vietnamerica*, tree imagery as a visual motif for remembering the enmeshment of Tran's family in the war's history is most evocatively pictured on a splash page in which a large tree both overlays and is partially superimposed by sepia-toned panels that reprise earlier panels, raising the memory of particular events depicted by these panels (see figure 7.6). Insofar as the purpose of a splash page is to establish time, place, and mood through page-spread frames that give special attention to particular events (Eisner, *Comics and Sequential Art* 62), the large tree eloquently highlights the memory of the war and Tran's family in Vietnam. It is, moreover, a remarkable example of what Thierry Groensteen would call the "quality of the *place*" in comics form—a distinctive spacing effect whereby the arrangement of superimposed images achieves "the effect of braiding" panels that are "distant by several pages, and that cannot be viewed simultaneously" (148). Groensteen explains:

> As it is articulated to several of its likenesses by a relation that comes under the jurisdiction of braiding, the panel is enriched with resonances that have an effect of transcending the functionality of the site it occupies, to confer the quality of the place. What is a place other than a habituated space that we can cross, visit, invest in, a space where relations are made and unmade? If all the terms of a sequence, and consequently all the units of the network, constitute sites, it is the attachment, moreover, of these units to one or more remarkable series, that defines them as places. A place is therefore an activated and over-determined site, a site where a series crosses (or is superimposed on) a sequence. Certain privileged sites are naturally predisposed to become places, notably those that correspond to the initial and final positions of the story, or the chapters that compose them. . . . But other places do not coincide with any privileged sites; it is the effect of braiding that brings them to our particular attention and constructs them as places. (148)

The "quality of the place" achieved by "the effect of braiding" within this page's tree image is an important formal aspect of comics in *Vietnamerica* for two key reasons, both of which underpin this chapter's argument that Tran's graphic memoir envisions an ecological imagination to intervene in Vietnam War history. The large tree reprises earlier tree imagery—in particular, the legendary ancient tree at the beginning of the memoir and Thi Mot's family tree (Tran 62), which immediately follows the page with the final frame of Dzung's split face. Echoing these earlier images that take place in a post-reunified Vietnam, the tree effectively braids together these images to confer the quality of place for

Figure 7.6. GB Tran, *Vietnamerica* (2010): 218.

Tran's family in both the historical context of the American War's conclusion—for example, four pages later a page spread announces "The Vietnam War has finished" (22)—and the memoir's narrative context of transitioning to the astonishing event of the family's flight from Saigon, just before the Viet Cong attack the airport from which they have flown.

The tree's braiding effect to confer the place of Tran's family within the narrative of diaspora is depicted climactically in a black and white spread that illustrates the family as they board the plane that will take them to the United States (see figure 7.7). The image of a small leaf here partially superimposes the plane and, subsequently, appears in six more pages but floats alone within these blackened pages. Evidently the leaf is a metaphor for the family's violently forced relocation to America. For they have been torn away from Vietnam and compelled to leave Thi Mot behind in Vungtau. The lone drifting leaf therefore implies the family's *place* in the Vietnamese diaspora through the simile of the tree's torn-off leaves, an environmental metaphor for positioning the family's migration and their ensuing traumatized experience within the critical frame of slow violence.

A second meaningful effect of braiding in the tree image occurs through a superimposed panel that illustrates Tri at work on his paintings during the American War. Other panels in the image depict the devastations of combat—destruction that will, in turn, destroy Tri's art after he flees Vietnam for the United States, a place where he will never again create his paintings. In a series of panels earlier in the memoir, Tran explains the content of his father's art: "French impressionist styled, romanticized Vietnamese landscapes" (24). In Saigon, Tri became "a rising star in Vietnam's art scene" because of his idyllic paintings (24). Panel sequences later show Tri as a young man who paints on a canvas while facing dramatic natural landscapes (80–81). Luminous colors in these frames render the ecological content of his paintings: blue and green hues depict Vietnam's lush mountains and forests and thus reprise the panels in which French warplanes drop bombs on the environments surrounding Langson during the Resistance War.

Near the end of the memoir, Tri's landscape paintings reappear in frames that narrate his reunion with his father, Huu Nghiep, who saved one of the paintings from destruction by the Viet Cong at the time of the country's reunification. In this sequence, Tri notices the painting in his father's house, but neither he nor his father mentions anything about it. Yet this painting in Huu Nghiep's home arouses in Tri upsetting memories about how the war terminated his artistic career and literally destroyed most of his art. A panel in this sequence shows Tri's landscape paintings on fire with the words "SNAP" and "POP" mimicking the noise of his burning canvasses and, more obliquely, replicating the panels at the beginning of the memoir depicting Saigon ablaze as the Viet Cong attack the city. Again, coloring and shading are significant here to indicate the war's graphic

Figure 7.7. GB Tran,
Vietnamerica (2010): 266.

violence and its traumatic impact on Tran's family. In addition to the sepia-toned color of the tree, which implies remembering family life and history during the war, the blasts of orange and cerise both partially covered by and overlaying the tree denote Vietnam's war-induced devastation and ecological ruin as a primary cause of the loss and trauma deeply embedded within Tran's family history.

To be sure, the effect of braiding achieved by Tri's paintings in the tree image confers the importance of connecting ancestry and origins (a multivalent sense of place) to Vietnam's natural landscapes. But the war's destruction of these landscapes extinguishes Tri's art and terminates his career as an artist, and as a result destroys connection to a sense of place as an aspect of slow violence. For Tri, then, the loss of his art and his career because of the war traumatizes him. In this regard, his loss brings to mind Dzung's distress over the loss of her childhood home—a loss implying the consequential linkage between militarism's physical violence and its long-term traumatizing effect on civilians.

That Tran both begins and ends his memoir with the Confucius quote, which his father inscribed into the Vietnam War history book that he gave to his son as a gift, indicates that Tran understands the parallel between his own labor as a graphic artist to creatively reconstruct his family history *and* his father's training as a painter to portray the historical sites and places of Vietnam's beautiful landscapes. Tran conveys this parallel playfully through the family tree that opens and closes *Vietnamerica*, likening his graphic memoir to a cinematic or televised production that introduces his family members as "The Cast" in a movie or TV sitcom (see figure 7.8). Among other things, this visual reconstruction of the family tree, which attempts to piece Tran's family history back together, connotes his admiration for Tri's career as an artist in Vietnam and, in turn, Tri's empathic recognition for his son as he attempts to succeed on his own as a young artist in America. By beginning and ending *Vietnamerica* with the Confucius life lesson that is figuratively braided with the family tree, Tran thus affirms his responsibility to understand and culturally inherit the history of Vietnamese people and avow remembering a connection with, as well as a place within, this collective history in America.

Visualizing an Ecological Imagination

Vietnamerica shows *and* remembers the violence wrought by the environmental destruction of colonialism and war. It illustrates the diaspora of people who were and continue to be dispossessed and displaced by the slowly unfolding ecological catastrophes of multiple imperialist incursions and the wars resulting from these imperialisms. As a unique genre of the comics form, Tran's work makes visible the temporal dispersions of slow violence and thus offers a way to change how we

Figure 7.8. GB Tran, *Vietnamerica* (2010): Color image that begins and ends novel.

perceive, recall, and respond to a variety of social crises in the present historical moment—crises such as the environmental calamities produced by centuries of plunder, conquest, and war that have ravaged the Global South's native habitats. By documenting his family's environmental memory to characterize their diasporic subjectivity, *Vietnamerica* reinterprets the hard facts of the war's "environmental issues"—specifically, its militarized physical environment—as historical matters that are "grounded in cultural memory" (Erll 173).[11]

Graphic memoirs such as Tran's are a compelling example of "comics journalism," which typically feature the memory of actual events put into comics form and give "voice to historic peoples who were treated inhumanely by the dominant ideologies of their times" (Duncan and Smith 266–67). Mediating the testimony of forcibly relocated Vietnamese through formal aspects that are unique to postcolonial comics, *Vietnamerica* offers a radical alternative to conventional Vietnam War history. By converting slow violence into image and memory narrative, Tran's graphic memoir formally renovates Vietnam War history through verbal and visual elements in comics that create an atemporal sense of the past in the present. In so doing, it visualizes an ecological imagination to recall, revise, and augment historical knowledge of militarism's impact on the natural world and engages with those we call environmental migrants: people displaced by colonialism, economic collapse, and ecological ruin, the outcome of human beings as geological agents within a *longue durée* of global environmental crisis.

NOTES

1. Tran was born in South Carolina in 1976, a year after his parents, siblings, and paternal grandmother fled Vietnam and arrived in the United States as refugees.

2. In her examination of environmental metaphors for a diasporic context of war and forced relocation in Vietnamese American texts, Cathy J. Schlund-Vials perceptively shows how these texts depict "an ecological pattern of images that is tied to a traumatized Vietnamese American experience and militarized physical environment" ("Ecological Imaginations" 112).

3. As Schlund-Vials contends, militarism's violence produces a multivalent sense of place for Vietnamese people who are forced to move in consequence of the war's destroyed landscapes. For instance, in Le Ly Hayslip's autobiographical *When Heaven and Earth Changed Places* (with Jay Wurts, 1989), Hayslip portrays destroyed environments in rural Vietnam as a "Janus-faced depiction of military space, which brings into play considerations of power and politics, [and] engages multivalent senses of place" (Schlund-Vials, "Ecological Imaginations" 115).

4. In the United States, the American War is known as the Vietnam War and also the Second Indochina War. Beginning with U.S. imperialist intentions to get involved militarily in the Indochina region, the war occurred in Vietnam, Laos, and Cambodia from November 1, 1955, to the fall of Saigon on April 30, 1975 (Neale 74).

5. Also known as the First Indochina War, the Resistance War was fought by the Viet Minh, a communist-dominated nationalist movement formed in 1941 that fought for Vietnamese independence from French imperialist rule and colonialism (Young 2). For a detailed account of Vietnam's reconstruction and reunification after the American War, see Young chapter 15, "After the War (1975–90)."

6. See Witek in *Comic Books as History*, Adams, and Duncan and Smith.

7. Nixon contrasts the immediately graphic images of the 9/11 attacks that were widely displayed in the news media with the less representable forms of slow violence. He maintains that the mainstream media harbors a "representational bias against slow violence" (13).

8. By "ecocritical," I refer to Greg Garrard's definition of ecocriticism in which the study of the relationship between literary or cultural analysis and the physical environment is "an avowedly political mode of analysis" (3).

9. Lisa Lowe defines "hybridity" as cultural intermixing due to histories of often involuntary migration for people of Asian descent in North America (*Immigrant Acts* 67). See Homi Bhabha for his concept of "unhomeliness." As Bhabha suggests, "unhomeliness" is the postcolonial subject's experience of occupying a border position between reference points of cultural identification (e.g., the place of home and origins) and the return of familiar but repressed aspects of home and origins (12).

10. An "emotional flashback" is a term in clinical psychology that refers to a traumatized person's involuntary recurrent memory of an upsetting event. The flashback is a "visual intrusion corresponding to a small number of real or imaginary events, usually extremely vivid, detailed, and with highly distressing content" (Brewin et al. 210).

11. Here I refer to Astrid Erll, who argues for the importance of cultural memory when accounting for contemporary geopolitical matters: "If we want to get our heads around current wars in Afghanistan, Iraq, and on the African continent, the rise of China and India, global warming—and especially around the ways that people make sense of these experiences and from there begin to deal with them (or fail to do so)—then we have to acknowledge that many of the 'hard facts' of what we encounter as 'economy', 'power politics', or 'environmental issues' are at least partly the result of 'soft factors', of cultural processes grounded in cultural memory" (173).

CHAPTER 8

Illustrating Diaspora

*History and Memory in Vietnamese American
and French Graphic Novels*

Catherine H. Nguyen

PREDOMINATELY MEMOIRS, NOVELS, AND short stories, Vietnamese diasporic narratives—and in particular, the second generation's cultural production—now include the graphic novel. In recent years, Vietnamese American and Vietnamese French graphic writers and artists have produced a small though growing body of work in the graphic novel form: GB Tran's *Vietnamerica* (2010), Thi Bui's *The Best We Could Do* (2017), Clément Baloup's multivolume works *Chinh Tri* (2005, 2007) and *Mémoires de Viet Kieu* (*Quitter Saigon*, vol. 1, 2006; *Little Saigon*, vol. 2, 2012; *Les Mariées de Taïwan*, vol. 3, 2017), and Marcelino Truong's *Une si jolie petite guerre* (2012) and *Give Peace a Chance* (2015).[1] Others have appeared with short comics published in major newspapers and journal outlets, such as Doan Bui's short series "Le Vietnam raconté à mes filles" (2015), drawn by Tiphaine Rivièreon on the *Nouvel Obs* site. In the way that graphic novels always have been concerned with the personal and the memoir, Vietnamese diasporic graphic novels also participate in the creation and illustration of personal, familial, community, and intergenerational stories.

With the focus of the collective experience of the Vietnamese diaspora, this comparative paper reads Vietnamese French and Vietnamese American graphic memoirs: Clément Baloup's *Mémoires de Viet Kieu*, volumes 1 and 2, and GB Tran's *Vietnamerica*. Of the available graphic novels and memoirs by Vietnamese diasporic subjects, I choose Baloup and Tran precisely because they engage directly with the notion of history and redefine history and its telling as and through the collective and multiple voices of the Vietnamese diaspora. Moreover, they represent the current work of second-generation transnational Vietnamese French and American writers who are engaging with and retelling their parents' and the first generation's experience in their own words. In this way, they open up their own encounters with their family's stories as direct engagements with memory in the period of postmemory and in the aftermath of war and immigration. Using Baloup's and Tran's work, I argue that the medium of the graphic memoir—of text and image—articulates as well as illustrates individual stories as varied and diverse histories rather than dictating a singular experience and a monolithic history. The graphic artists' interpretation of refugees' and immigrants' experiences of diaspora, I contend, allow for polyphony and multiple illustration of diaspora, contesting a singular history and a reductive image of Vietnamese refugees and immigrants as boat people.

For these Vietnamese diasporic works, the narrative of the graphic memoir is truly a narrative of personal experiences that are rooted in the historical. The Vietnam War serves as the context and background as well as the pretext for the exploration of personal and familial stories. Nevertheless, the graphic memoirs place emphasis not on the Vietnam War as the narrative event but rather on the second-generation diasporic subject coming to learn about others' personal, unique experiences of war and its aftermath in the many elsewheres where Vietnamese diasporic subjects find themselves. In Baloup's and Tran's work, they then work through the memory and experience of war in their moment of postmemory as well as negotiate the intergenerational relationship as second-generation Vietnamese French and Vietnamese American graphic artists.

The stories recorded and illustrated in the graphic memoirs are those that pay witness to the Vietnamese French and American experience of war, displacement, and settlement. Michele Janette categorizes early Vietnamese narratives as "tales of witness," as they are "works based in personal experience and driven by the need to inform, to educate, to correct the record and claim a spot in the American psyche. This is largely a corrective literature, a deliberate intervention into dominate American culture" (xix). While Baloup's and Tran's graphic memoirs are products of the second generation, they specifically take on narratives that participate in Janette's "tales of witness" but in their removed position to receive and inherit such histories. As second-generation Vietnamese diasporic subjects, Baloup and Tran have no direct access to these narratives of life in Vietnam before and around 1975 and narratives of life in the direct aftermath of migration and displacement. Rather than typical "tales of witness" to set the record straight about Vietnamese history, culture, or belief, these stories are now told in order to provide knowledge of and transmit such life experiences. It is the first generation's passing on of these stories to the second; therefore, it is an intergenerational interaction of storytelling and receiving, of testifying and witnessing. Therefore, I contend that these graphic narratives are the collection and documentation of such "tales of witness" through the mode of the graphic memoir and the illustration of such experiences; the graphic memoirs therefore articulate the relationship between the first and second generation and the passing and bequeathing of personal histories.

On one hand, Clément Baloup's *Mémoires de Viet Kieu* situates polyphony within a collection of individual narratives of displacement. Born in northern

France to a Vietnamese father and a French mother, Baloup is part of the second generation of Vietnamese French immigrants. Drawing from his personal background and his father's personal history of immigration, Baloup uses his father as the starting point to his project on documenting as well as depicting the Vietnamese experience in France and in the United States (and later in Taiwan, with the third volume on Vietnamese brides). The connecting thread of these separate stories is the graphic artist, who meets different Việt Kiều (the overseas Vietnamese) and documents their testimony through words and illustration. Because of this, the graphic memoirs jump from the present to the past, as well as from Vietnam to France and America, to pay witness to their individual trials. Baloup's graphic memoirs, then, situates the individual experiences of the diaspora in its many elsewheres.

On the other hand, *Vietnamerica* explores GB Tran's own family and is therefore Tran's rendering of his familial narrative of the Vietnam War and its aftermath through Tran's voyage to Vietnam. *Vietnamerica* brings together the author's own personal search for an understanding of his family's experiences that is not only narrated through the voice of his mother, Dzung, but is also rooted in the experience of his family at large as well as his personal encounters with family members in Vietnam. As such, Tran learns of his father's and mother's lives before and during the Vietnam War, and meets his extended family, many of whom he has never known. Tran therefore is not only the recipient of his family's stories but also the one who documents and participates in the transmission of his family's story as he negotiates his own relationship with his parents and family. With *Vietnamerica*, Tran's graphic narrative, then, opens up to the plurality of experience within one family, highlighting the unique and personal stories that come together by blood, marriage, and travel.

Through Baloup's and Tran's second-generation negotiations and working through family and individual narratives of the Vietnamese diaspora, they (re)-present two directions and articulations for collective memory and history in terms of polyphony and multiplicity in the form of the graphic memoir.

Curating Histories, Collecting Stories: Clément Baloup's *Mémoires de Viet Kieu*

Clément Baloup, a mixed-race Vietnamese French graphic artist, draws on his father's history to receive others' experience of displacement and immigration in his series *Mémoires de Viet Kieu*. Educated at the Ecole européenne supérieure de l'image in Angoulême, France, Baloup developed a style that draws on and emphasizes "graphic and narrative experimentation, the power [*pregnance*] of strong stories with complex adult themes, and the possibility of looking at the world and its reality" ("Artist's Statement" 53). With his series *Chinh Tri* on the Vietnamese anticolonial resistance in France and in Vietnam during the 1920s through the 1940s and then *Mémoires de Viet Kieu* on Vietnamese refugee and immigrant experiences during the 1960s and onward, Baloup realizes this "narrative experimentation" by the switching between monochromatic and robust color schemes as well as with a very complex narrative engagement of the Vietnamese experience of war, resistance, and displacement. In *Redrawing French Empire in Comics* (2013), Mark McKinney draws attention to Baloup's examination of France's and Vietnam's postcolonial connections as well as to his color technique, saying that the "use of color by Baloup, and Jiro too [Baloup's early collaborator], is related to aesthetic considerations, ethnic ones (such as *métissage*) and narrative ones" (136). Moreover, McKinney points to Baloup's technique of "[creating] viewpoints at once subjective and historical" (130). For Baloup, the space and different memories of Vietnam are the constant subject of his graphic novel work, as it is an engagement with his father's as well as his own story. Baloup explains:

Et moi je m'y suis intéressé [au Vietnam] quand j'avais une vingtaine d'années, c'est un intérêt qui a grandi en allant sur place, j'ai eu envie d'en savoir plus, d'expérimenter d'autres choses liées à cette culture. . . . Au début je ne pensais pas que le Vietnam serait au cœur de mon travail mais très vite j'ai commencé à collecter des informations et une documentation importante qui ont présidé à la réalisation de mes albums. (Marie 160)

For me, I became more interested in Vietnam in my twenties and from traveling to Vietnam. There, I wanted to know more and to experiment with this culture. . . . At first, I did not think that Vietnam would be at the heart of my work, but I quickly realized it would be once I had started to gather information and important documentation that would direct the development of my graphic work. (my trans.)

Baloup's engagement with diasporic Vietnamese stories is very much in the plural and through the personal. Through his travels and being there on the ground, Baloup interacts with different Vietnamese French and American immigrants and later documents their stories in illustration and dialogue. As a result, much of Baloup's work interrogates and illustrates the diverse experience, history, and memory of Vietnam.

In this section, I read Clément Baloup's *Mémoires de Viet Kieu* in order to define counterhistory as plural and polyphonic and specifically as counter-*histoires* that are personal, individual stories collected and illustrated by Baloup. The tension between monolithic and plural histories is examined through the (re)-publication history of the introductory volume of the series: *Quitter Saigon*. Furthermore, I draw attention to Baloup's method of collecting personal stories through face-to-face encounters and interviews as well as his portrayal of those conversations as images in the form of the graphic memoir. The collecting and presenting of stories proposes a different understanding of history as defined through the curatorial space of museums; Baloup intervenes in the museum space to highlight illustrated personal stories as a counter to historical projects of documentation and collection. Therefore, I include a discussion of the space of the museum with regard to the presentation and representation of monolithic history and how Baloup offers the alternative space of the graphic memoir, where he curates personal stories of the Vietnamese diaspora.

CURATING HISTORY:
BALOUP'S MUSEUM SPACES AND MEMORY

The opposition of history as stories—*histoires*, in the French—and history as official, monolithic history is what the graphic memoirs attempt to address in Baloup's graphic documentation of the Vietnamese diasporic experience, and the wordplay of *histoires* in French speaks to both history/historical accounts and fictions/imaginative stories. The (re)publication history of *Quitter Saigon*, Baloup's first volume of the *Mémoires de Viet Kieu* series illustrates how *histoires* as stories are required to fit into *histoire* as history, specifically official and officialized histories. As the opening volume to the series, *Quitter Saigon* is required by the publishing house and by the reading public to have historical context and background for the individual stories of Vietnamese displacement and immigration to France. While the very first publication in 2006 (sixty-four pages) does not have any introduction to the three individual narratives of Vietnamese men, the revised second reprint of *Quitter Saigon* in 2010 (ninety-six pages) includes two notable additions: an introductory sequence and a fourth individual narrative. Later in 2013, another revised reprint, the third edition (110 pages) is issued with even more contextual material for the introductory sequence and for the individual stories as well as a collective account of the Vietnamese French of the Centre d'accueil des Français d'Indochine. Despite the additions of more individual and collective stories to *Quitter Saigon*, most significant is the inclusion and the revision of the introductory sequence that attempts to fit the personal narratives that follow—the *histoires* in the plural—into the overall history/*histoire* of Vietnam. The historical background can be informative for an audience ignorant of Vietnamese history and immigration; however, I contend that the imposition of history in the form of the introductory sequence and in a form reminiscent of a textbook juxtaposes against the diverse individual and collective stories of Vietnamese French immigrants.

First included in the second reprint and then revised in the third reprint of *Quitter Saigon*, the introductory sequence provides the historical context and background of both the Vietnamese diasporic experience and Baloup's interven-tion. The first image of both reprints is a detail of Nick Ut's (in)famous photo-graph "The Terror of War" or more commonly known as "Napalm Girl" where a Vietnamese girl is running bare down a road away from the napalm bombing of Trang Bang (*Quitter* 2010 and 2013, 3). The use of a detail of this image to begin the text (in the reprints) is an act of reappropriation by Baloup, where he adds into the illustration of the photograph both contextual information and a critical note: on the top left-hand corner inside the panel is the caption "Tràng Bàng, Sud-Vietnam, été 1972" [Trang Bang, South Vietnam, Summer 1972] and inserted as a text box on the bottom right corner, "S'il y a bien une image inter-nationalement connue de la guerre du Vietnam, c'est celle des enfants qui courent pour échapper au napalm qui brûle leur village" [If there is an internationally recognized image for which the Vietnam War is known, it is the one of the chil-dren running from napalm that had burned their village] (*Quitter* 2010, 3) (see figure 8.1).[2] This added commentary speaks to Baloup's intention of drawing in the reading public with a famous image of the Vietnam War to situate the rest of his work of unknown narratives; Baloup says, "My goal was to make the story as clear as possible for someone who have no idea of the whole historic context, that's why I pay homage to famous photograph in the first pages, so it would ring a bell, call [*sic*] the global imagery and then I could focus on the main plot, the Viet kieu" ("Re: Access to Artist Statement"). The aim of reproducing the famous photograph, then, is to have the reader recall the Vietnam War and the possible narratives coming out of such conflict. Rather than merely reproducing the actual photograph, Baloup chooses to redraw a detail of the photo into a pal-ette of grays and blues and to include his own commentary on the image as the internationally recognized picture of the Vietnam War. This kind of intervention occurs, importantly, in the space of the museum: Baloup's visit to the War Rem-nants Museum in Ho Chi Minh City, Vietnam.

The association with the photograph "Napalm Girl" and the War Remnants Museum is tied to a fraught, controversial history of curating and possible pro-paganda. In her analysis of the War Remnants Museum in *The American War in Contemporary Vietnam*, Christina Schwenkel includes a discussion of the Nick Ut photograph and its display history with the Vietnamese national museum. She highlights the power of displaying such an image in the space of a state museum, which is criticized as a play to "elicit international sympathy for the country" (172). This critique arises from how the "iconicity of this image lies in its affec-tive power, its ability to shock, enrage, and distress the observer. It is rendered sacred insofar as it signifies to the viewer a pure and presumably unmediated representation of the most innocent and vulnerable victims of war: children" (172). Schwenkel draws attention to this critique of the emotional and political

Figure 8.1. Clément Baloup,
*Mémoires de Viet Kieu: Quitter
Saigon*, vol. 1 (2010): 3.

use of the image because the War Remnants Museum is a government-operated museum whose history lies with the Socialist Vietnamese state and its use as a form of national propaganda. The museum was first called the Exhibition House for U.S. and Puppet Crimes when it opened in the direct aftermath of the Vietnam War in September 1975, then later changed to Exhibit House for Crimes of War and Aggression in 1990, and finally settled with its current name, the War Remnants Museum, in 1995. The various name changes through the years mirror the state's changes in their international and economic relations with the United States. The museum's display of "Napalm Girl," then, participates in the perpetuation of discourses of anti-American sentiment and the horrors of war crimes. For Schwenkel, the controversy of the War Remnants Museum's on-and-off display of Nick Ut's photograph highlights how the "image acquired a new register of value and meaning as it traversed borders and entered into new settings" (171); the original image, a photojournalistic document, is now redefined as a mode of state propaganda. With Baloup's appropriation and reproduction of "Napalm Girl" and its display in the War Remnants Museum, he comments on the institutionalized form of history that is produced by the museum space as singular and biased, particularly when he includes images of other exhibits, such as jars of preserved human fetuses affected by Agent Orange, directly after his illustration of "Napalm Girl." Opening *Quitter Saigon* with the iconic image, the graphic memoir begins by situating Vietnamese history and memory within the space of the institutionalized space of the museum. Through this reappropriation of "Napalm Girl," Baloup engages with the museum as a "critical [space] at which visitors assume active roles in questioning cultural-historical truths and claims to objectivity" (Schwenkel 147).

Here, Baloup includes the photograph as part of his own visit to the War Remnants Museum and as a way to open up the introductory historical sequence. With its displays of "Napalm Girl" as well as the jars of Agent Orange fetuses, it is the space of the museum that prompts and sets up the introductory historical sequence that follows. Commenting on how the photographs and images of the American War in Vietnam only constitute one of many events that are a part of Vietnam's violent history, Baloup illustrates panels of Vietnam's modern history of foreign occupation (*Quitter* 2010, 4–7). Intercutting the two full-colored panels where Baloup is present in the space of the museum are gray/blue panels, very much like the illustrative rendering of the "Napalm Vietnam" photograph; these panels then provide the history of foreign presence and occupation of Vietnam (see figure 8.2). They include images of the Vietnam War (Operation Rolling Thunder as well as an American helicopter hovering above rice paddies), the arrival of the French in Vietnam and the start of French colonization, the raising of the Japanese flag to mark the Japanese occupation of Vietnam, the guerrilla warfare of both the First Indochina War and the Vietnam War, and the consequences of war on the Vietnamese population (death, reeducation camps, and the boat people refugees). Each gray/blue panel includes the historical context, often the year and location of the historical event; but more importantly, Baloup stylizes them in a completely different way from the rest of the graphic memoir. The textual inserts are boxy, static, and official in style that contrasts against the conversational style and tone of the interviews that follow, which often has text inscribed directly onto the panel rather than separate text boxes. The vision of history here is rendered in blue, gray, black, and white and in a static style that reinforces the conventional, formal aspect of history.

The entire introductory sequence of Baloup's museum visit and the historical panels are revised in the third publication (2013) in a visual and formal way that concretizes and codifies the historical context as if in a textbook and significantly repositions Baloup into a passive viewer. Before, in the second reprint, the presence of Baloup in colored panels gestures away from the institutionalized history and toward the individual encounter with and critique of such events. In a way, Baloup curates Vietnamese history for the reader by already defining the modern history of Vietnam as a violent history: "Mais ces images terribles [de la guerre du Vietnam] ne consitutent qu'un des épisodes de l'histoire violente qu'a connue le Vietnam durant l'époque moderne" [These terrible images (of the Vietnam War) only constitute but one episode in the violent history of Vietnam in the modern era] (2010, 4). Baloup follows this statement with each other instance of military colonization and occupation (French, American, and Japanese). However, in the third reprint, what was before Baloup's commentary is now reduced to authoritative yet detached information; Baloup's narrative voice is taken away and made into text box captions. This is clearly marked with the shift from Baloup as the curator of the images with commentary text drawn as several speech bubbles to Baloup as a passive observer/museum visitor, whose voice is reduced to one speech bubble. Rather than interacting with the reader, Baloup is now positioned as a passive observer, looking at the exhibits in the same way that the reader looks at the illustrated panels.

The shift in Baloup's agency speaks to the definition of history within the museum space as the mere presentation of historical events. Rather than a critical engagement with historical images and objects as illustrated through Baloup's own interaction with the museum's exhibit, the third reprint shifts history to the object of display and presentation in the museum space. The historical panels in the second reprint have a textual-visual interaction, where informative and critical comments are made in text box inserts inside the image panels. With the third reprint, however, each illustration is separated from its textual description; there is no intimate interaction between word and image (see figure 8.3).

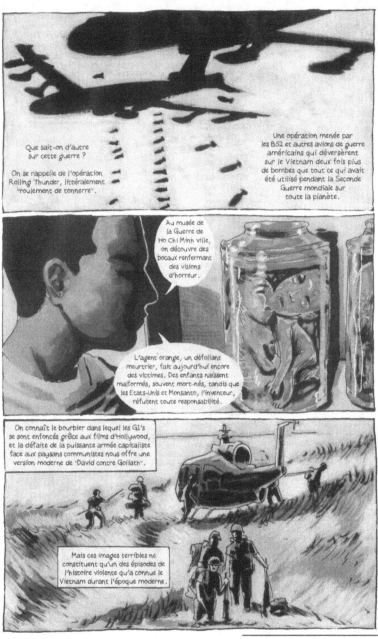

Figure 8.2. Clément Baloup,
*Mémoires de Viet Kieu: Quitter
Saigon*, vol. 1 (2010): 4.

Que sait-on d'autre sur cette guerre ? On se rappelle de l'opération "rolling thunder", littéralement "roulement de tonnerre". Une opération menée par les B.52 et autres avions de guerre américains qui déversèrent sur le Vietnam deux fois plus de bombes que tout ce qui avait été utilisé pendant la seconde guerre mondiale sur toute la planète.

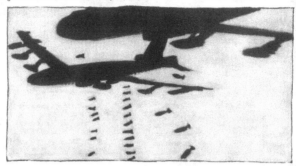

Au musée de la guerre de Ho Chi Minh-Ville, on découvre des bocaux renfermant des visions d'horreur. L'agent orange, un défoliant meurtrier fait aujourd'hui encore des victimes. Des enfants naissent malformés, souvent mort-nés, tandis que les Etats-Unis d'Amérique et Monsanto, l'inventeur, réfutent toute responsabilité.

On connaît le bourbier dans lequel les GI's se sont enfoncés grâce aux films d'Hollywood, et la défaite de la puissante armée capitaliste face aux paysans communistes nous offre une version moderne de "David contre Goliath". Mais ces images terribles ne constituent qu'un des épisodes de l'histoire violente qu'a connue le Vietnam durant l'époque moderne.

Figure 8.3. Clément Baloup,
Mémoires de Viet Kieu: Quitter Saigon, vol. 1 (2013): 4.

The page layout now depicts images with relevant text completely separate; the captions are positioned underneath each panel and regulated to white spaces of the page. While the text, for the most part, remains the same, the effect of the different layout with the text separated from the image makes the introductory sequence more formal, bringing to mind the practice of exhibiting a work with its museum label beside it. In the form of a book, the new layout recalls that of a historical textbook; the interaction between image and text is no longer dynamic as with Baloup's commentary but is now static in its narration of history.

Importantly, these changes in the layout and the reduction of Baloup's speech bubbles seem to be in response to the demands of the reading public and publication market. Baloup comments that the reprints with the additions of the introductory sequence and additional personal/collective narratives come from a desire to improve on his work but also provide materials for a reading public ignorant of the context: "when *Quitter Saigon* was released I had a sense of frustration, that I could have, should have made it better. Also, during signatures [*sic*] and meeting with the audience, readers often told me that they liked the graphic novel but they thought it was too short, they wanted to know more about the Indochina/Vietnam/France story. So basically, they had a frustration!" ("Re: Access to Artist Statement"). The revisions of *Quitter Saigon* highlight the demands of contextualizing the personal narratives in order for the reading public to better comprehend. In a way, the juxtaposition of the textbook appearance of the third reprint's introductory sequence against the illustrated individual stories argues for the different versions of *histoire* as both history and stories, that personal experiences of history are just as significant, if not more, than the historical events.

In the second volume of *Mémoires de Viet Kieu*, *Little Saigon*, Baloup significantly shifts away from the textbook introduction of *Quitter Saigon* to draw and rearticulate his agency. Moreover, Baloup revisits the space of the museum to propose a different kind of curatorship. With *Little Saigon*, Baloup continues with his interviews and encounters with other Việt Kiều, specifically Vietnamese Americans. Unlike the introductory sequence of *Quitter Saigon* that relates the general historical context for Vietnamese immigration, Baloup uses as introductory sequences his visits to various spaces of Little Saigon: a New York restaurant, San Francisco and San Jose in Northern California, Chinatown and Little Tokyo in Los Angeles, and a South Carolina fish market. Providing these instances of travel and excursions, Baloup does away with the overarching historical background of the previous volume and instead focuses on his own particular experience and interactions with various Vietnamese American women and with the larger Asian American communities. As such, this already redefines history as not historical events with notable years and battles but as history as encounters between Baloup and various individuals. Furthermore, this reinstates Baloup with agency; he is active in the conversations from which personal stories are told and in the illustration and collection of these diasporic narratives.

In *Little Saigon*, Baloup reaffirms his definition of curation that is at the heart of his ongoing *Mémoires de Viet Kieu* project with his visit to the Japanese American National Museum. Baloup's act of curating stories by Vietnamese immigrants in France and the United States (and later in Taiwan) is one that considers the individual and personal experience as both history and story. Visiting the Japanese American National Museum, Baloup presents the museum's aim of preserving the past and of passing on memories of Americans of Japanese descent as speaking to his own curating and (re)presentation of diasporic subjects of Vietnamese descent. Baloup depicts his own visit as an active interaction with the museum space and Mae, a museum employee, in a way that opposes the passive representation of the War Remnants Museum.

In *Little Saigon*, the museum is presented as showing more than 130 years of Japanese American history and as bringing to light the presence and the contribution of the Japanese population in the United States. Baloup's museum visit differs from the one in Vietnam; rather than works being presented in a way that is clearly labeled, contextualized, and codified into a specific and singular narrative, this museum visit is framed by the interaction between Mae and Baloup and between Baloup and the museum exhibits. Mae's story is depicted as speech bubbles through various panels where Baloup and Mae walk through the museum and examine paintings, artifacts, and displays. The panels in the Japanese American National Museum follow Mae and Baloup as they work through multiple exhibits and give voice to Mae, who recounts her own ghost story and the history of the Japanese internment, and to Baloup, who poses questions and interacts with Mae and the exhibits. Moreover, any historical context or explanations are illustrated in an oval-shaped text insert that mirrors Mae's speech bubble rather than the square text box captions used earlier in *Quitter Saigon*; in this way, history is linked with interaction in the museum space and with others, constructed as dialogue and the passing of memory instead of static and fixed pages from history textbook.

Rather than a passive, institutionalized history and propaganda of the War Remnants Museum in Vietnam, the history of Japanese American internment is passed down and passed onto others. The transmission and inheritance, the receiving of history and memory, is formulated in terms of ghosts and haunting. While Mae does provide historical details surrounding the Japanese internment during World War II, she opens the museum visit by telling Baloup about her ghost sighting in the museum. Mae tells of how many believe that there is a ghost in the museum and that she did see it one night when working late; at first, she thinks it is just the night guard, but sees a dark shadow by the exit when no one else is present. With no rational explanation for her encounter, Mae importantly ties the ghost to the Japanese American experience of internment, pulling together the spectral with the historical. Explaining the history of the museum, Mae points out that the building was originally a Buddhist center and then the site for processing Japanese Americans during internment. The building, as a historical site in the story of the Japanese internment and now the site for Japanese American history, is, as Mae states: "ce musée est un lieu de mémoire 'privilégié'" [This museum is therefore a "privileged" *lieu de mémoire* (a site of memory)] (*Little Saigon* 135). This kind of framing marks the museum as a privileged site, as a historical site, and as a site for history and memory.

For Mae, the haunting is explained in terms of history and learning about those difficult, unrecognized histories that often are not included in the grand, sweeping narrative of America's open-armed Statue of Liberty and Emma Lazarus's "Give me your tired, your poor / Your huddled masses yearning to breathe free." The spectral therefore becomes a mode through which a historical understanding of the internment can be interrupted and a mode through which the personal narrative can come through. The potential of the ghostly encounter goes against a distant, codified, factual history and therefore offers a possible alternative as the haunting of memory into postmemory, as the experiences of one generation can be passed onto following generations.

The museum as a site for the passing down and on of Japanese American experiences is defined by Baloup as a "'privileged' *lieu de mémoire*." Pierre Nora proposes and constructs the notion of the *lieu de mémoire*, the site of memory/ the place of memory, in relation to collective memory: "Our interest in *lieux de mémoire* where memory crystallizes and secretes itself has occurred at a particular historical moment, a turning point where consciousness of a break with the past is bound up with the sense that memory has been torn—but torn in such a way as to pose the problem of the embodiment of memory in certain sites where a sense of historical continuity persists. There are *lieux de mémoire*, sites of memory, because there are no longer *milieux de mémoire*, real environments of memory" (7). As a site for the (re)presentation of Japanese American history and experience, the museum stands as the site of memory, where others can enter and gain an understanding. Also, the museum itself and its history speak to Nora's *lieux de mémoire* because the building has a history tied to the Japanese American experience and because the creation of the museum comes from and out of the Japanese American community's concern for remembering and commemorating the history and experience of internment. In *Little Saigon*, Baloup includes the history of the building that houses the Japanese American National Museum: it was a Buddhist temple and center before it became the registration and processing center for Japanese Americans being sent to the internment camps during World War II.[3] As a *lieu de mémoire*, the museum is the site of history as well as of memory, where history, historical memory, and memory become accessible through museum exhibits and collections. Furthermore, the formation and creation of the museum comes from a community effort on the part of Americans of Japanese descent—business leaders, community members, and Japanese American World War II veterans—to create a space to remember, commemorate, and pass on a history that would have otherwise been forgotten and elided in the broader American history of multiculturalism. As a *lieu de mémoire*, the Japanese American National Museum, in its history and its aim to preserve and present Japanese American experience, speaks to Baloup's project of collecting, documenting, and illustrating Vietnamese diasporic personal narratives otherwise unknown.

The republication history of Baloup's *Quitter Saigon* reflects the increasing demands of the (French) reading public and the publishing house to provide historical context for the diverse stories that follow. Moreover, the concretization of such history, in terms of formal positioning of text and image, seems to undermine the very distinct, different, and differing personal histories of the Vietnamese French and their experiences of conflict, war, and im/migration. However, Baloup's graphic memoir project proposes the mode of collecting and (re)presenting lived experiences as an act of curating history, as opposed to these fixed textbook illustrations of Vietnamese history. Presenting two different modes of curatorship, Baloup argues for an active engagement with history precisely through the interaction with various Vietnamese diasporic subjects, Viet Kieu from France and the United States. Furthermore, using Mae's ghost story, Baloup places the museum space as the site for the interaction between the living and the dead, the present and the past. Baloup's curating of memory is an act of postmemory, of the second generation's receiving of the first generation's stories.

COLLECTING STORIES: BALOUP'S *MÉMOIRES DE VIET KIEU* PROJECT

While he argues for a different mode of curating history and memory in his representations of museum spaces, Baloup most clearly defines his project as the collecting and recording of individual stories, memories in the form of conversations and testimonies of personal experiences of war and displacement. As such, the bulk of both *Quitter Saigon* and *Little Saigon* are in fact the *Mémoires de Viet Kieu*, the illustration of Baloup's one-on-one encounters and interviews with Vietnamese diasporic subjects and his graphic narration of their distinct lives. This section, therefore, examines the multiplicity and diverse stories of Vietnamese im/migration to France and to the United States that Baloup curates and collects, illustrates and presents.

In his own vision of curating, Baloup views his project as collecting stories and (re)presenting them in a way that is neither journalistic nor didactic. Baloup explains his process, highlighting his personal interaction with the Viet Kieu subject and his transformation of their oral histories into illustrations:

> Ces récits sont donc la transcription en BD d'histoires vraies que l'on m'a person-nellement raconté. Il y a eu une première étape d'entretien avec ces personnes, avec prises de notes sur mon carnet. L'étape suivante, seul dans mon atelier, a été de faire des choix sur ce que j'allais décider de raconter (avec la douloureuse partie qui consiste à couper), puis de ré-écrire les histoires pour qu'elles soient pleinement de la BD (par opposition à un texte illustré didactique ou un reportage journalistique). ("Dessiner: acte resistante")

> These stories are the transcription into comics of true stories that were told to me in person. There was a first phase of interviews with these people, during which I took notes in my sketchbook. The following phase, which I undertook alone in my studio, was to choose what I would or would not tell about them, and then to write the stories so that they would fully be comics, as opposed to a didactic illustrated text. ("Artist's Statement" 58)

In his words, Baloup transcribes each story from his notes and then into illustration in order to impart them to the reader rather than to merely inform the reader. Baloup participates in the passing on of memory; he transmits it through the graphic rendering of individual stories rather than trying to educate the public. Here, Baloup curates these stories as exhibits of personal experience with which the reader can interact through reading and viewing the graphic memoirs.

With Baloup's graphic memoirs, I contend that the plurality and the multiplicity of narratives he presents go hand in hand with his experience of the Japanese American National Museum and against a singular, unifying history that is embodied in the War Remnants Museum. Moreover, I push Baloup even further by arguing that he attempts to construct for the reader the same intimate experience he has when he meets each Việt Kiều and that Baloup illustrates the stories in a way that calls for the reader to listen (here transformed into the act of reading) and to receive, just as Baloup experiences them.

In the two volumes of *Mémoires de Viet Kieu*, Clément Baloup produces a graphic narrative that is not only polyphonic but, more importantly, transnational and diasporic in the representation and depiction of the Việt Kiều in their many Little Saigons.[4] The first volume, subtitled *Quitter Saigon*, illustrates several encounters with Việt Kiều in France who recount their departure from Vietnam. The second volume, *Little Saigon*, takes as a similar starting point the Việt Kiều's displacement from Vietnam as well as their diasporic experiences and settlement but in various cities across America. Here, I argue, the documented and illustrated individual testimonies come to form a polyphonic and plural understanding of the Việt Kiều experience that extends transnationally between France and the United States. Where im/migration is usually transnationally tied between the site of departure and the site of arrival, between Vietnam and France or between Vietnam and the United States, Baloup's graphic narratives bring together the different trajectories of the Vietnamese diaspora, given that Baloup travels around different French provinces to speak with French Việt Kiều in the first volume then visits various cities around the United States to speak with Vietnamese Americans.

Baloup documents through dialogue and illustration his personal encounters with each individual, and these encounters give rise to the Việt Kiều's telling of their experiences and imparting of their stories. The format of these encounters are dialogues and conversations rather than a formal interview; Baloup includes how each person relates to him and he toward them, often in ways that do not directly tie in to the subsequent personal account of diaspora. For example, in *Quitter Saigon* the first narrative belongs to Baloup's father; the scene is one where they are cooking fried shrimp, and Baloup's father starts to talk about his own father. Baloup's father then narrates his childhood in Vietnam and subsequent voyage to France. With the second volume, the preambles are often about finding out about Vietnamese Americans through the avenue of Asian America, such as the Japanese American Museum in Los Angeles and the Laotian area of Oakland. These introductory moments in full color shift to the individual narratives of diaspora in blue/gray monochromatic colors; such a transition positions the reader in the same place as Baloup, as interlocutors to the various Việt Kiều, interlocutors who are attentive and engaged in listening rather than merely documenting or note-taking. Thus, the graphic memoirs do not fall into the pitfalls of ethnography, anthropology, or sociology—fields that often attempt to codify and universalize the individual and individual experiences. Rather, Baloup's graphic narratives are a collection of stories in the way that an anthology would bring together tales of witness and diasporic experience. The very format of conversations between the graphic artist and the Việt Kiều places the audience in a position to receive the testimonies in a visually and narratively direct way so that the personal accounts become the particular and plural histories of the Vietnamese diaspora.

Baloup's one-on-one encounters become the mode to access the stories that go beyond an understanding of history as events, wars, or populations. Using the visual of the graphic narrative, Baloup renders each person as specific and each encounter as distinct. Baloup's direct exchange with each person is illustrated in color, while their stories are illustrated in a dark, monochromatic blue scheme. Each person possesses a singular voice, shown by speech bubbles, and the individual's narratives are recounted in the first person and through in-panel text boxes or direct narration within the panel. The formal presentation of these experiences contrasts against the codified, textbook-like prologue of the third reprint of *Quitter Saigon*. Furthermore, the encounters that Baloup presents are those that do not fall easily within these historical moments of French colonization, Japanese occupation, American military involvement, refugee camps, and the boat people. In *Quitter Saigon* four Vietnamese Frenchmen reflect various and differing experiences: as an unaccompanied minor, as one who escaped persecution and was previously imprisoned in a reeducation camp, and as a Eurasian/mixed-race Vietnamese who had to hide his blond hair, and as one of the early boat people. Baloup also includes a collective narrative of those who were repatriated to France and into Centre d'accueil des Français d'Indochine camps with individual memories of the boat voyage, abuse in the camps, and a summer's outing as the added fifth narrative of *Quitter Saigon*. With *Little Saigon*, Vietnamese American women's stories include the multiple attempts to escape postwar Vietnam, sexual assault and violence in refugee camps, failed marriages, and repeated internal displacement in the United States. In both France and the United States, these stories are not ones that depict the well-known boat people and fit into the easy narrative of immigration and citizenship. What is presented in direct juxtaposition to the historical prologue is the individual and unique experience of Vietnamese history, the personal *histoires*/stories of the Vietnamese in France and in America.

The individual narratives themselves are structured as distinct and are framed and set up by the graphic artist as conversations, but the complete shift into the *je*/French first-person pronoun of the witness him/herself moves away from being framed by an audience and into a more direct form of narration. In doing so, the illustration of the narratives positions the stories as if unmediated by Baloup, as if the individual Việt Kiều were telling the story directly to the reader. The step into the seemingly unmediated individual accounts occurs with the pronoun and with the shift in the visual, where we move from fully colored illustrations of the interview to the blues and grays of the testimony. The *je*/I of the Việt Kiều takes up the agency of narration and also situates the Việt Kiều as witness to his/her personal history.

The notion of witness and testimony is tied to the nature of polyphony as developed in *Mémoires de Viet Kieu*. The title itself signals the multiple nature of what the French word *mémoire(s)* denotes: the first, *mémoire* as memory; the second, *mémoire* as memoirs, the auto/biographical work of memory. Memory here, then, is the specific memory of those who underwent the experience of war, displacement, and relocation, the experience of the Vietnamese diaspora. As such, this memory is not merely an individual memory but one that participates in the discourse of witness and testimony documented by Baloup. Baloup himself positions the work in such a discourse, saying in the acknowledgments of *Quitter Saigon*: "Merci aux protagonistes de ce livre qui m'ont confié leurs souvenirs en toute sincérité" [Thank you to the protagonists of this work who have confided their memories in the most sincere way] (2006, 72; 2010, 95; 2013, 111). *Little Saigon* also takes up this discourse, labeling the work as a "travail de mémoire," a work of memory in the sense of the labor and production of memory through such storytelling (255). That memory is work—to recount and to record as the graphic novels have done—is to situate the storyteller as witness and his/her story as a testimony of his/her personal history given to others.

Baloup's *Mémoires de Viet Kieu* defines memory and memoir in the plural. The first volume, *Quitter Saigon*, was first published with only Vietnamese Frenchmen's stories, rendering the Vietnamese French experience plural but male-dominated. With the publication of the second volume, *Little Saigon*, Baloup includes the female experiences of three Vietnamese American women. Importantly, after the publication of *Little Saigon*, Baloup returns to *Quitter Saigon* to include the collective stories of both men and women in the Centre d'accueil des Français d'Indochine as the fifth and closing chapter. As such, Baloup brings to light the experiences of diaspora in ways that are different, gendered, and nuanced. In the background of all these personal stories is the memory of violence and war; memory is tied to such history but also includes the specific and particular experiences of each diasporic subject. Memory is therefore tied to history, but unlike the institutionalized history of "Napalm Girl" and the gallery of the Agent Orange fetuses in the War Remnants Museum, *Mémoires de Viet Kieu* does not serve to establish these stories as representative of all Viet Kieu and diasporic experience. Rather, Clément Baloup's graphic memoirs present and illustrate how polyphonic the diaspora is, collecting the stories in a way that calls for an attentive ear/eye to read and pay attention to those stories/*histoires*.

Learning the Root(s) of Family History: GB Tran's *Vietnamerica*

Like Baloup, GB Tran belongs to the second generation and engages with the first generation through the form and genre of the graphic memoir. Tran was born in South Carolina in 1976, the first of his family to be born in the United States after his family left Vietnam. As a cartoonist and illustrator, Tran uses the graphic novel form to explore his own journey into his family's past and his parents' journey between Vietnam and the United States. The graphic memoir uses GB's journey to Vietnam with his parents to bring together other familial narratives, including his own parents' lives leaving Vietnam and their return to Vietnam later in the 1990s.[5] As such, *Vietnamerica: A Family's Journey* covers many aspects and the different movements of Vietnamese American life and history: the displacement inside Vietnam during military conflict and war as well as the back-and-forth journeys of Vietnamese Americans to Vietnam.

As one of the first Vietnamese American graphic novels, Tran's *Vietnamerica* has been the subject of many analyses that explore its creative formal features. For Harriet E. H. Earle, *Vietnamerica* exemplifies traumatic analepsis that is grounded in the contrast of two distinct artistic styles: heavy black art and the bright, solid colors of *ligne claire*. This movement between two styles portrays the different stories and temporalities of family history: GB's story alongside and through his parents' stories, his paternal and maternal grandparents' stories, the past and the present. Tran's visual style plays with the hearing and receiving of familial histories and their consequent rendering into illustrations. Significant to this paper is the emphasis of history in Tran's *Vietnamerica*. This distinct visual style allows for what Caroline Kyungah Hong calls "an intricate narrative structured around memories that flow across shifting time and space, in particular through the layering of multiple acts of telling and multiple journeys to Vietnam, not just GB's" (14). *Vietnamerica* allows for a fruitful discussion of history and memory through the lens of family and familial stories.

In GB Tran's *Vietnamerica*, polyphony and plurality are framed by the family narrative, rather than distinct individuals and their personal stories as told and drawn in Baloup's *Mémoires de Viet Kieu*. Timothy K. August argues for the importance of polyphony and plurality in Tran's work, saying, "Tran uses a flattening of time and a multiplicity of perspectives to link the oft-neglected continuities between Vietnamese and Vietnamese American experiences" (165). Using August's reading as a point of departure, I want to focus on how *Vietnamerica* comes to define history in personal terms and history as family history and thus against an understanding of history that is represented by the impersonal, factual textbook. The structure of the graphic memoir moves between the present of the artist's trip to Vietnam and the past of his family's experiences in Vietnam under the different military rules of the French, the Americans, and the Vietnamese communists. Tran includes the narratives of both sides of his family: his father's and his mother's as well as that of his paternal and maternal grandparents. The polyphony of *Vietnamerica* lies in the multiple and various experiences of his grandparents and his parents, and the familial histories are introduced by GB's mother Dzung. As such, the polyphony derives not so much from the multiplicity and plurality of narrators/speakers, as developed in Baloup's work, but rather with the numerous narratives themselves or what Tran defines as "a single history from a collective memory." With *Vietnamerica*, I argue that the graphic memoir form allows for a plurality that provides an alternative and individual discourse of history, like *Mémoires de Viet Kieu*, but now situated within the family as *Viet-*

namerica's subtitle proposes "A Family History" rather than the impersonal and distant as well as official and generalizing narrative of institutionalized history.

In *Vietnamerica*, there are multiple movements of narration despite the narration driven by GB's mother, Dzung. Like Baloup, who illustrates the stories he receives, the graphic artist Tran draws himself within the family auto/biography but does not take on the narrative voice of his familial history to allow for his mother's voice to recount her and the family's experiences. Similar to Baloup's position as interlocutor, GB positions himself as one who receives these family histories but goes further to also participate in his parents' memory work by accompanying them on a return voyage to Vietnam. While GB also holds the position of overall narrator, Dzung is the narrative voice that provides access to the stories of GB's parents and grandparents, their lives in Vietnam and his parents' experience of returning to Vietnam. As such, *Vietnamerica* brings together the family history told through the narrative voice of Dzung and GB's experience of such familial stories through the illustration of the trip to Vietnam.

TEXTBOOK HISTORY: *VIETNAMERICA*'S HISTORICAL ENGAGEMENT

Given the subtitle, "A Family's Journey," *Vietnamerica* places the journey as the central motif for the graphic memoir of GB's family. There are multiple journeys in *Vietnamerica*: his parents' immigration to the United States during 1975, his parents' travels back to Vietnam to visit family and friends, GB's trip to Vietnam, and GB's journey into his family history. The intertwining of personal and familial journey signals how GB is tied to his parents' and his family's history.

GB's story of his own journey to Vietnam for the first time is connected to his parents' story of their chaotic departure from Vietnam in 1975; that is, their family trip to Vietnam is tied to the family's history of leaving Vietnam. In particular, Dzung reads GB into the position of his father, therefore directly situating GB within his own family's history. Rendered distinct by the cursive script, Dzung's voice delivers the first lines of *Vietnamerica*; she asks the question that leads into GB's family history, saying, "You know what your father was doing at your age? He, WE left Vietnam" (3). But these words are not depicted with any personal images; rather, the first page opens up with the image of war and chaos. The first page is formed by three horizontal panels that are dominated by a deep, blood-red color, with each sentence of Dzung's opening lines separately positioned in the two bottom panels (see figure 8.4). The larger top panel has a plane, drawn in black and white, in the top right corner, while the bottom left corner has a dark black column of smoke. The blank space between the two images is full of sky painted in blood red. The bottom two panels have Dzung's text juxtaposed with a vague scene of Saigon and juxtaposes an aerial view of Saigon under smoke with the inside of the cockpit of a military aircraft. The following page goes more

Figure 8.4. GB Tran,
Vietnamerica (2010): 3.

in detail with Dzung's narration and gives further specifics of GB's parents' last moment in Vietnam: "On the evening of April 15, 1975, our family crammed into a U.S. cargo plane bound for America. It was one of the last to take off before the Vietcong bombs destroyed the Saigon airport later that night. That was 30 years ago" (4). Like the first page, Dzung's words are juxtaposed against the black, white, and blue images of herself and her family against the blood-red sky and the black columns of smoke. These images of war and escape reveal the traumatic experiences that Dzung briefly mentions.

Yet Dzung's narration only occurs because of the voyage in the present, where Dzung travels with GB to Vietnam decades later. The third page depicts a completely different image of GB seated between his father and mother on a commercial flight to Vietnam; the colors are not as saturated and pale in comparison to the deep reds and rich blacks of the previous pages. With the spread encompassing war and saturated colors on the left and the tourist travel and pale tones on the right, there is a clear visual juxtaposition between leaving and returning, between war and tourism, and between past and present. The two scenes are clearly opposite yet very reminiscent of each other: one a departure and the other an arrival/return, one during wartime and the other during peacetime; nonetheless, both are tied together through GB and the notion of the journey. Through this juxtaposition or repetitive imagery of airplanes and travel, GB becomes the figure who brings together his family's history with his own discovery of the story of his roots in Vietnam.

GB becomes not only the figure of diasporic return but also that of family history, when Dzung draws the parallel between GB and his father: "Your father was the same age as you are now. Funny coincidence, don't you think?" (5). GB's return to Vietnam is already conflated and tied to the larger family narrative of his family's departure from Vietnam at the end of the war. The literal movement of arrivals and departures is also the figurative narrative movement between the past family history and the present family trip to Vietnam that is to be GB's encounter with the narrative of the family. Throughout the graphic novel, the fluidity of the illustrations between past and present as well as the interjection of the family narrative into GB's personal experience produce the polyphony of the family's multiple narratives: his father's, his mother's, his paternal grandfather's, his maternal grandmother's, and others. Constructed as family stories and familial history, *Vietnamerica* is therefore Tran's inheritance and legacy.

In *Vietnamerica*, Tran specifically defines history against familial history through the recurring image of a history book on the Vietnam War that opposes the illustrated and multiple stories of his paternal and maternal families. After the first few pages that serve as an introduction, *Vietnamerica* continues with a series of chapters or sections, each marked by a blank page and a square illustration.

Figure 8.5. GB Tran,
Vietnamerica (2010): 8.

These blank, colored pages with a single illustrated square stand in for chapter divisions; as the chapters progress, the illustrated square moves from right to left and down the page, thereby marking each of the twelve chapters. The first chapter begins with the illustrated square of a page in a book, on which is inscribed: "To my son, Gia-Bao Tran. 'A MAN WITHOUT HISTORY IS A TREE WITHOUT ROOTS.' —Confucius" (7) (see figure 8.5). The quotation, supposedly attributed to Confucius, argues for a broad understanding of history that grounds man in the way that roots aground a tree.[6] While the saying relates to a specific history, that man needs to understand his (own) history, it is ambiguous enough to speak to a broader, general history: that man needs to understand history or the history of his country to be rooted.

The context of this Confucian inscription, we find out much later, is the dedication that Tri, GB's father, writes inside the cover of the history book *The Vietnam War* (207–8). The book is a large tome in red and yellow and is his father's graduation gift to GB. It is history as codified in a published volume that ties the Confucian notion of man, history, and roots to history in a broad sense: the history of a country, the history of a generation, and history as a history book.

Moreover, it is impersonal: the title written in yellow against a red background and the cover illustrated with an indistinguishable soldier armed with a rifle. The history volume does not have an author and therefore represents a history that is detached and distant. The only specifics are in themselves vague, but the title in English and the typical picture of a soldier seems to point to a Western point of view, one that is perhaps inconsistent with GB's own family's point of view and their personal experience of the Vietnam War.

However, history as embodied by this *Vietnam War* volume is also tied to the individual because it is the gift of knowledge that GB's father bestows on his son. The official history is tied to individual history but only insofar as is the general context and background to the personal history. Here, GB's father gives his son the book in the hope of giving GB an avenue into learning more about his background as a second-generation Vietnamese American. In the ninth chapter, the cover of the history book appears as the image marking the new chapter; the chapter deals with GB's parents' first trip back to Vietnam in 1994 and what they learn about their families and the significant change that has occurred in Vietnam. Even more important is that GB bookends the chapter with close-ups of the history book.

While the textbook image introduces the chapter, it actually begins with GB's helping his mother pack suitcases for the 1994 trip and then ends with GB's receiving the history book as a graduation present. In these near-present 1994 sequences, GB's ignorance is juxtaposed against his parents' learning about their families and about Saigon as Ho Chi Minh City. His refusal to go on the trip with his parents illustrates how GB lacks knowledge about the political and historical context as well as an understanding for his parents' background and experience that prompted their migration from Vietnam to the United States. The history book both opens and closes, and thus bookends, the chapter to provide an avenue, albeit an impersonal one, for GB to begin learning about his own and his parents' historical roots.

Yet this detached and impersonal history is the kind that GB rejects and discards. In the last two pages of the chapter, GB is given the tome by his father. The first panel depicts Tri handing GB his graduation gift. The subsequent panel zooms in on the cover, which is the same image that opens the chapter; then GB stares at the title in disappointment, saying, "Thanks. (I guess)" (206). The scene of the gift is quickly followed by the scene of the book being rejected and indifferently thrown onto a pile of junk; then it is covered by other discarded items and finally tossed into a box for storage (see figure 8.6). The layout of the five panels also illustrate the unimportance of the history book, as three panels set up the forgetting of the volume under a pile of junk and as the last two panels are no longer in the linear layout but are positioned in a downward slant, creating

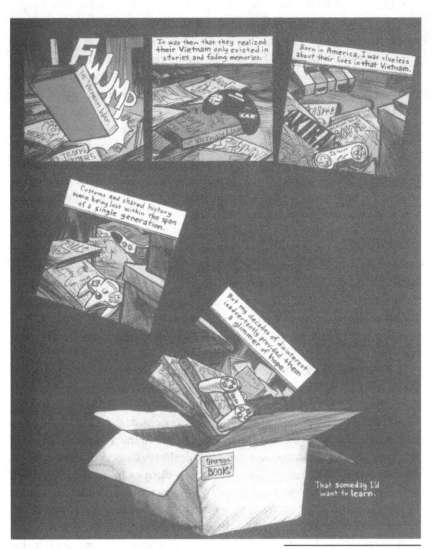

Figure 8.6. GB Tran, *Vietnamerica* (2010): 207.

the trajectory where the panels are tossed, with the history book, into the storage box at the bottom of the page. The throwing away of the history book renders it irrelevant not only for GB but also for the reader. As such, the history book is also rejected as an avenue of knowledge and a way to understand his family's past and history. The graphic novel, moreover, highlights GB's repeated refusal and reluctance to go to Vietnam with his parents because it is the official and published (American) history that produces such disinterest.

The discarded history book nonetheless is also tied to GB's family precisely because of his father's inscription that was first introduced in the first chapter's marker. The context of the dedication—only revealed on the penultimate page of *Vietnamerica*—is on the opening page of the *Vietnam War* volume that was previously cast aside. GB appears to be unpacking in his New York studio and comes across the history book that his father had given him years earlier. The fact that Tri's words are written inside the published volume personalizes the already distant, depersonalized history. That Tri's inscription says "A man without history is a tree without roots" repositions the book history as only an entry point to other histories, specifically his family's own histories. Moreover, the history book along with Tri's inscription actually highlight GB's own lack of knowledge of the Vietnam War in general and of his family's experience of war and conflict.

In opposition to the textual, factual information given by the history book is the experience of Vietnam; the voyage to Vietnam serves as the alternative mode through which GB can learn of his family's history and of Vietnam's history. Significantly, the sequence of the history book is framed by Tri and Dzung's first return voyage to Vietnam, and their trip, in turn, is framed by the discourse of learning. The chapter, whose last two pages deal with GB and the history book, revolves around GB's parents' journey back to Vietnam in 1994, during which they are reunited with close and distant family members and thus learn of life in Vietnam post-1975. In a way, this voyage for GB's parents is a voyage of education, where they come to know about the realities of postwar Vietnam that were not mentioned in smuggled, cryptic, censored letters. The trip as a learning experience is also tied to GB but at first to his lack of interest in and knowledge of Vietnam and his parents' past and their families in Vietnam. The panel right before the graduation gift and history book sequence is of Dzung and Tri as they prepare for trip; Tri says, "Your mother's right. You should go. You might **learn** something" (205, emphasis in original). Here, travel and personal experience define learning one's history and provide an opportunity to learn and understand history beyond the factual, codified history represented by the history book and beyond the Vietnam War. In fact, the narrative that accompanies the depiction of tossing the book aside juxtaposes the two avenues into learning about history, the history book, and the experience of family and travel. GB narrates: "My parents' first trip back together was in 1994, almost two decades after they escaped. It was then that they realized their Vietnam only existed in stories and fading memories. Born in America, I was clueless about their lives in that Vietnam. Customs and shared history were being lost within the span of a single generation. But my decades of disinterest inadvertently provided them a glimmer of hope. That someday I'd want to learn" (206–7). Here, GB points to his own uninformed and unmotivated ways as well as his parents' own learning experience through their return voyage, history is specifically defined as family stories and memories, as cultural customs and "shared history."

Moreover, history is opened up as an opportunity for GB to personally experience his parents' and his extended family's history through a trip to Vietnam and through meeting the family GB has never known. History is defined as accessible through the individual and personal stories of GB's immediate and extended family, rather than the perhaps foreclosed history that is codified and rendered impersonal and detached, as represented by the history book.

ROOTED IN HISTORY: *VIETNAMERICA*'S FAMILY
AND FAMILIAL HISTORY

History, therefore, is not some generalized understanding of historical events; rather, it is the specific, intimate family history. GB clearly rejects a codified, factual history as represented by the history book that is tossed away and offers the familial history as the alternative definition, representation, and understanding of history. Rocío Davis reads graphic memoirs such as *Vietnamerica* as life narratives that "intervene in the contemporary production of memory and the forms contemporary historical writings might take" and points to how the "graphic form [mediates] our access to history through the reconstruction of family stories that are also already historical accounts" (253). Here, Davis positions graphic memoirs as an intervention and an addition to the understanding of what forms historical writings can take. Previously regarded as biased, too personal, or not historically accurate, family stories provide different ways of understanding and approaching history precisely because of their intimate experience of historical events. Davis further argues for an epistemological shift toward family histories as already historical accounts, saying: "By privileging the subject as the object and producer of the historical narrative, graphic texts enact an epistemological shift: knowledge is acquired as much from the facts of history as from lived experience" (254). Using Davis as a point of departure, I read Tran's efforts as positioning the family narrative in the forefront of the telling of history and of historical understanding; furthermore, GB defines the family as rooted in history, both personal and historical, to propose the revision of "a man without history is a man without roots" to "a man without [*family*] history is a man without roots" (my addition and emphasis).

For GB, the dedication in the history textbook characterizes his search for understanding both his family's history and his family's experience of the Vietnam War. His father's words take on personal and familial significance as Tri gives his son a chance to learn about his history and as Dzung narrates GB's grandparents', her husband's, and her own life experiences in Vietnam during military conflict. For *Vietnamerica*, it is not so much that "a man without history is a man without roots," a generalized, impersonal history; rather, GB's graphic narrative revises and familiarizes the Confucian saying to add family as the historical: "a man without [*family*] history is a man without roots."

Furthermore, the image of roots highlights this move toward the family and the familial; *Vietnamerica* repeatedly evokes roots as those of the family tree and, thus, the roots of family history. In fact, a family tree opens and closes *Vietnamerica* illustrated on the inside covers. What we see even before reading the work itself is "The Cast" that depicts both sides of GB's family (see figure 8.7). On one side of the inside cover is GB's paternal family, with his grandparents, their children including GB's father Tri, Tri's first wife and children, and his father's best friend Do. On the other side, the cast is GB's maternal side, with his grandparents and their children including GB's mother Dzung and American family friend Leonard. Although incomplete with regard to the more distantly related family, "The Cast" not only gives the reader a quick reference while reading through the complex family narratives but moreover positions them with relation to one another as families that are forged into the larger, extended family of grandparents, step-aunts and uncles, and even family friends. This family tree, defined as the cast, identifies the relationship between each person and also defines them as actors and storytellers in the telling of their interrelated family histories.

Where "The Cast" serves to introduce the family as historical actors in the familial history, the family tree of GB's maternal side, his *bên Ngoại*, reconfigures the Confucian saying into explicitly "a man without [*family*] history is a man without roots" (see figure 8.8). The tree of GB's mother's family is not drawn in the way that most family trees are typically depicted. While family trees typically use branches to illustrate the growth of the family from one set of ancestors, the family tree drawn by GB is depicted using roots that spread out and deeper with each generation. For the family tree, what is not important is the branches that grow outward and upward, signifying progeny, but rather the roots that extend downward and deep into the earth to ground the family and GB as well. The family tree here is that of Thi Mot, GB's maternal grandmother; her place is therefore the trunk of the family. But each member is the root, with each generation branching out and burrowing deeper. In this way the saying "a man without [*family*] history is a man without roots" is literally depicted: the root that is created by each family member takes hold in the ground; the tree, the family, is grounded, here, in Vietnam, but also in each other. Unlike "The Cast," the family tree of Thi Mot and GB's maternal side depicts each member, regardless of whether he or she appears in the account of *Vietnamerica*. In a sense, the maternal family tree is more complete but also shows how complex family structure is and how varied family experience is. Importantly, the family tree appears when GB first travels back to Vietnam and meets his mother's side for the first time; he is overwhelmed by family but is also grounded by their presence and rapport.

The family roots and consequent family histories are grounded in Vietnam and made possible through GB's personal encounter with his family in Vietnam. Family history is particularly tied to the place of and travel to Vietnam. The appearance of both the history book and Tri's inscription is always tied to packing, with the implied meaning of preparing for new experiences and unpacking objects of memory as well as the work of memory. The first instance is the packing up of GB's belongings, along with the book, into storage at the same time, narratively, that his parents are packing for their first trip back to Vietnam in 1994. This highlights GB's reluctance at that time to explore his parents' past life in Vietnam before 1976. The final appearance of the history book, where the inscription is explicitly shown as written inside the volume, occurs when GB is unpacking in a new apartment in New York (278). In this scene, GB finally opens up the history book that he previously tossed aside indifferently to see his father's inscription. This act of opening up the history book is GB's entrance into his family's history, so much so that GB calls his mother in the panels directly following. He says: "Hi, Mom. It's me. [His mother replies:] Is everything okay? [GB responds:] Yeah, fine. I was just wondering . . . Can I still go to Vietnam with you?" (279). This serves as the final page and final panels of *Vietnamerica* but also the very moment that starts GB's journey to Vietnam that opens the work and GB's journey into his family's history, which is the focus of the entire work. With such a closing, *Vietnamerica* points to the opening up to a different form of history and to a different engagement with memory that is all rooted in the family. That GB's revelation that he would like to learn more about his roots, his family, and his as well as their stories closes *Vietnamerica* positions travel as the means through which he accesses his parents' and his family's history.[7] In point of fact, GB's decision to go with his parents to Vietnam closes the work but is also the departure point for the writing and illustrating of *Vietnamerica: A Family's Journey*.

Vietnamerica, as a family's journey, is one that comes full circle. GB's voyage to Vietnam opens the graphic narrative, and his decision to take that voyage

Figure 8.7. GB Tran,
Vietnamerica (2010):
Front/back inside covers.

Figure 8.8. GB Tran,
Vietnamerica (2010): 62.

closes the work. In the same way, his parents leave Vietnam during the war in the first pages and in the penultimate scene that leads up to the moment where GB decides to join his parents in their journey back to Vietnam. It is a circular movement that highlights the relationship between GB's journey into his family's history and his family's journey as specific, individual, personal stories recounted and relayed by GB's mother, Dzung. This family's journey, moreover, is both the literal travel that is undertaken by GB and his parents to and from Vietnam and the figurative journey of learning of his grandparents', his parents', and even his siblings' (stepsiblings') experiences, memories, and stories of life in Vietnam during the long period of conflicts—the First Indochina War/the anti-French Resistance War and the Vietnam War. It is the inscription that marks both the history book and the graphic narrative that opens up the possibility and understanding of history as one that is personal, rooted in both family and in Vietnam.

Illustrating Diasporas: Conclusions

In the redefinition and the resituating of what history is to the Vietnamese diaspora—from the museum space to first-person narratives and from the history book to family history—both Vietnamese French and Vietnamese American graphic memoirs use the medium to represent graphic memory and to illustrate the diaspora in all of its varied and multiple narratives. What ties both Baloup's and Tran's works together is that an understanding and the representation of such plurality is tied to movement and journeys. For Clément Baloup, the individual witnesses who provide the intimate testimonies of displacement and relocation are encountered only through the graphic artist's own travels around France and the United States to visit them in their particular space of home and residency. *Mémoires de Viet Kieu* reproduces those movements within the texts so that it suggests how one may participate in a movement of displacement to gain a broader yet deeper understanding of the Vietnamese diaspora. For *Vietnamerica*, the movement is one toward the familial roots in the space of Vietnam. The puzzle of figuring out one's roots and history is GB Tran's illustration of the second and later generations' search for understanding and for a place in the history of family and diaspora. In a sense, the diasporic subject can be, in many ways productively, always in movement—between history and story, past and present, one and many, family and diaspora—so that they can articulate in many voices their own *histoires*/stories.

NOTES

1. Translated titles are Baloup's *War* and *Memoirs/Memories of the Viet Kieu, Leaving Saigon, The Brides of Taiwan*; Truong's *Such a Pretty Little War*; and Doan Bui's "Vietnam as Recounted to my Daughters." All Vietnamese French works have only been published in French with the exception of Truong's graphic memoirs, which are translated and published as *Such a Pretty Little War* (2016) and *Saigon Calling* (2017).

2. All translations of Baloup's graphic narratives are mine.

3. The current site of the Japanese American National Museum is a newly constructed pavilion that adjoins the previous building; the pavilion was opened in January 1999. The original building now houses administration and offices (*Japanese American National Museum*).

4. Baloup's third volume of *Mémoires de Viet Kieu: Les Mariées de Taïwan* was published in 2017.

5. To differentiate between authorship and narration, I use Tran when speaking of GB Tran as graphic artist and author and GB to indicate the position of diegetic narrator.

6. A similar quotation is attributed to Marcus Garvey: "A people without the knowledge of their past history, origin, and culture is like a tree without roots." Speaking with Vietnamese family members, I was not able to confirm the quotation as a known Confucian saying or as belonging to Confucius. However, I did learn of a Vietnamese proverb/saying with a similar meaning but very marked in contrast in terms of images: "*Uống nước nhớ nguồn*" ("When you drink water, remember the source"). Here, the link to history is more ambiguous, but the many resonances of rivers and water in Vietnamese culture and language—the country's numerous rivers and streams, the Mekong Delta, as well as the eastern length of the country along the Gulf of Tonkin and the South China Sea and *nước* as meaning both water and nation—opens up for an interpretation that would lend itself toward *Vietnamerica*'s Confucian saying. For a more lengthy discussion of the misattribution, see Hong 16–17.

7. This is not to say that access to family history is only through and in the space and place of Vietnam. Tran suggests that the space and place of the United States is one that relies more on silence and indifference than on sharing or asking about family stories, saying: "My family's unwillingness to share the most basic facts was as much to blame as my decades of disinterest and insensitivity" (98). The parents' struggle to fit in and to earn enough to support the family and the children's growing up in an entirely different environment, culture, and language seem to get in the way of talking about and asking about the family's past life in Vietnam and the family history that continues.

CHAPTER 9

Punking the 1990s

Cristy C. Road's Historical Salvage Project
in Spit and Passion

Angela Laflen

CRISTY C. ROAD'S MEMOIR *Spit and Passion* (2012) recounts how as
an adolescent she came to recognize that there was a "glitch in the things we were
taught rather than the way we are" (45). Evidence of this glitch is that dominant
historical and cultural narratives do not accurately reflect the fact that "there's
a billion kinds of people on earth" (45); instead, Road suggests these narratives
have been carefully edited to exclude people like herself, people marginalized on
the basis of gender, race, and sexuality. *Spit and Passion* also questions whether
it is possible to recover a history that has been edited to silence divergent voices
and experiences. Road answers this question in one way by making her own
coming-of-age in Miami's Little Havana in the 1990s visible and depicting her
silencing as an adolescent. She answers the question in another way by showing
how she learns to "punk" history—primarily through a process of "excorporation," whereby she appropriates and combines diverse materials drawn from the
dominant culture to develop her own contentious politics and to serve as a foundation for her identity. Throughout, Road relies on the unique affordances of
graphic narratives to draw readers into identification with her perspective and to
demonstrate the value of undertaking the kind of historical salvage project that
she models in *Spit and Passion*.

    Spit and Passion takes the form of what Gillian Whitlock has termed an "auto-
graphic," which allows Road to narrate her personal history in ways that would be
impossible in a textual autobiography. This form allows Road to simultaneously
depict the effects of consensus history on her autobiographical avatar Cristy even
as she undercuts consensus history and creates an alternative version of the early
1990s.[1] Autographics have received considerable attention because so many of the
works most responsible for propelling graphic narratives into critical legitimacy
are autobiographical, including Art Spiegelman's *Maus* (1986; 1991), Marjane
Satrapi's *Persepolis* (2003), and Alison Bechdel's *Fun Home* (2006). The unique
way that history can be narrated in autographics has contributed to their critical
and popular success. As Hillary Chute explains in *Graphic Women*, autographics

"use the inbuilt duality of the form—its word and image cross-discursivity—to stage dialogues among versions of the self," to "layer temporalities and narrative positions" and to visualize the process of an author interpreting her own memories (5). In these texts, protagonists have what Joseph Witek refers to in *Comic Books as History* as the "authenticity of an eyewitness" (114), and autographics foreground how the choices and actions of an individual contribute to "large movements of nations and institutions" (152). Consequently, they offer "history with a difference" and rather than "reinforc[ing] a consensus view of American nationalism" frequently focus on stories of those "who were dispossessed and marginalized in American history" (4). Such is the case in *Spit and Passion* as Road makes visible her account of coming of age as a lesbian of color in the 1990s and sheds a critical light on the usually unseen process through which historical narratives are constructed and imbued with authority.

Consensus History and Cultural Homogeneity

Historical narratives draw their authority from resemblance to real life and a level of accuracy, despite ongoing debates among historians and philosophers about the exact nature of historical knowledge.[2] As Simon Gunn explains, scholarly history "is manifest . . . in the pursuit of objectivity, an impossible goal but which is pursued nevertheless in the quest for the complete interpretation, understood as the judgment that cannot be disconfirmed" (39). In *Spit and Passion* Road suggests that one method for achieving a historical judgment that "cannot be disconfirmed" is simply editing out dissenting accounts.

Road's autobiographical avatar Cristy becomes suspicious about the nature of historical knowledge when she realizes that perspectives such as hers are missing from the consensus narratives of American history that she encounters at school, in her Cuban American community, and in the mass media. This consensus history places "an emphasis on the unified and homogenous character of American history" (E. Cheng 118), and it is ideologically conservative, "combin[ing] the idea of American 'Exceptionalism' with steady movement toward more democratic freedom tied to free-market capitalism" (Horton).[3] Focusing on the contributions of "great Americans," consensus history has been criticized for overlooking the work of reform movements and marginalized groups and individuals, and by the 1990s many historians had moved away from consensus history, embracing the "new" social history that sought to narrate history "from the bottom up" rather than by focusing primarily on political and social elites (E. Cheng 118).[4] However, as a junior high student in Miami, Florida, Cristy is entrenched in the conservative, consensus view of American history and culture, and the new social history seems not to have penetrated her community. There is not even evidence of the "history war" raging in American culture at the time.[5] Instead, Cristy's community affiliates itself with nationalistic, heroic visions of American history and culture, interpreting the Cuban American experience through this lens as well. Consequently, Cristy can identify no models of successful lesbian adulthood in her Cuban American community. She *is* familiar with the dominant Anglo-American narrative of coming out, but this model seems to require her to reject her Cuban community and family (since both accept homophobic values), and, as she puts it, "I wanted to be Cubana as much as I wanted to be gay" (Road, *Spit and Passion* 152).

Road has described her purpose for writing *Spit and Passion* as "shed[ding] light on this Latina experience (of holding onto culture) as oppose [*sic*] to just the experience of being queer and scared" ("Queer Latina"). Indeed, this subject has long motivated Road as an artist. Formally trained as an illustrator and with a BFA from the Ringling School of Art and Design, Road has always explored the complexities of her identity through art and writing that she has at times published herself. As a high school student, Road began publishing a fanzine called *Green'zine*, which, although it was originally devoted to the punk rock group Green Day, eventually "transformed into a manifesto about being a hyper-sexual, queer, Latina, abuse survivor, and her journey towards self-acceptance" (Road, *Croadcore*). She published her first autobiography, titled *Indestructible*, in 2006; it is an illustrated memoir that focuses on her high school experiences. Among the issues that Cristy faces as a high school student is the perception by some in her Cuban American community that she is not "Latina enough." She followed *Indestructible* with a semiautobiographical illustrated novel called *Bad Habits: A Love Story* (2008), which focused on "a young bisexual Cuban-American punk rocker living a life of grungy hedonism in New York City" ("Book Review: *Bad Habits*"). Taken together, these works show Road exploring the complex process through which she attempts to balance her ethnicity and her sexuality throughout different phases of her life.

Visualizing a History of Silencing and Exclusion

With *Spit and Passion*, which was published by Feminist Press, Road attained a new level of visibility for her work. In this text she also more directly confronts the process through which historical narratives are created and imbued with authority, ultimately offering her own alternative history of the early 1990s in which her coming-of-age story is central to events during this period. However, she avoids setting up her alternative history as an authoritative, objective account by privileging Cristy's emotional truth over historical accuracy. Road's focus on emotional truth is consistent with her choice of an autographic to narrate her story. As Leigh Gilmore explains, autobiography in general draws "its authority less from its resemblance to real life than from its proximity to discourses of truth and identity, less from reference or mimesis than from the cultural power of truth telling" (3n8), and autographics further separate truth from accuracy due to the "typically exaggerated visual style of the comics" (Chaney, *Graphic Subjects* 4), which highlight their own artifice and do not even try to depict events objectively or chronologically.

Through her autographic, Road visualizes a history that would normally remain unrecorded, especially because Cristy is marginalized within groups that are themselves marginalized (Latinas, punks, and queers), and she uses the multiple layers of narration available in an autographic to explore the complex role that silence plays in Cristy's coming of age. Robyn Warhol usefully describes three levels on which narrative operates in graphic narrative. The first is the verbal level of "the extradiegetic voice-over narration, printed in a font that looks like free hand capital letters, always filling borderless horizontal boxes that run above the panels of the cartoon" (5). The second is the verbal level of the "intradiegetic dialogue, representations of words spoken inside the narrative world, encircled in word balloons and set in the same font as the voice-over" (5). The third is the pictorial level, which in *Spit and Passion* includes reproduced pictures and images drawn from her family archive and popular culture, photographs actually collaged into her own art, and images that depict Cristy's mental state or visceral reaction to narrative events, among others.

The narrative of *Spit and Passion* functions on all three levels but relies more on extradiegetic narration and the pictorial level than on intradiegetic dialogue. This allows Road to capture Cristy's relative silence as an adolescent. This silence indicates the suppression of knowledge about sexuality, and homosexuality in particular, within Cuban American and Anglo-American culture, but it also signals Cristy's refusal to identify with a master narrative of coming out of the closet that she does not feel serves her interests as a Cuban American.

According to Ben Sifuentes-Jáuregui, the trope of silence is complex in narratives by Latino/a queers, denoting repression and oppression as well as self-imposed privacy (4–5). This is true in *Spit and Passion*, and Road devotes considerable storytelling resources to exploring different dimensions of silence. She titles the first chapter in *Spit and Passion* "She Screams in Silence," and Cristy is relatively silent throughout the autographic. Sometimes Road draws attention to this by depicting Cristy with a gag over her mouth. More generally, though, intradiegetic narration is simply absent from the narrative so that characters do not speak to one another. Even when Cristy does vocalize within the narrative, it is often only to herself, as in figure 9.1, which depicts Cristy imagining how she might respond to some of her teachers whom she overhears making homophobic comments.

Figure 9.1. Cristy C. Road, *Spit and Passion* (2012): 136.

In this case, homophobia manifests as silence, as if refusing to speak about homosexuality will negate the threat it is believed to pose to traditional gender and sexual norms.

However, silence is not simply imposed on Cristy by external forces but is also embraced by her at times, so readers must juggle the negative connotations of silence with the positive connotations of self-sought privacy. Such is the case when Cristy refuses to "come out" in *Spit and Passion*, instead choosing to "escape" to the "safety" of her literal closet at home, which by the end of *Spit and Passion* she imagines serving as a chrysalis. Cristy's refusal to come out represents her rejection of what she sees as an Anglo-American master narrative. Road has explained that "the goal of the book is to shed light on the experience of choosing to stay in the closet because of the compromise I'm hesitant to make with my ethnicity" ("Queer Latina"). Her task is to find a way in which she can be both Cuban and queer, and her embrace of silence creates a space within which Cristy crafts her identity as "queerness-through-silence" (Sifuentes-Jáuregui 5).

Since characters are relatively silent within the world of *Spit and Passion*, Road relies heavily on the pictorial level of narration to characterize individuals and to document Cristy's growth through the narrative. For example, Road repeatedly depicts Cristy's eyes popping out of her head; usually Cristy grips them with her hands. These images are an important visual indicator of Cristy's emotional state throughout *Spit and Passion*, but they are not inherently negative or positive and depend on textual context to give them meaning. For example, in figure 9.1 Cristy grips her eyes when she encounters homophobic teachers at her school, but another such image accompanies her first, extremely positive, encounter with punk music. Taken together, images of bodily fragmentation convey a sense that the adolescent Cristy is "coming apart," her sense of herself fragmenting. This fragmentation is both threatening and potentially empowering. This is most clear in figure 9.2, which is an image of Cristy molting, one side of her body having shed its skin. These images of bodily fragmentation and transformation make visible changes that would normally go unseen and perhaps unrecognized, including the bodily changes Cristy experiences as she enters puberty, the psychic transformation she experiences on finding a connection with punk music, and the familial and cultural changes she feels are necessary to reject heterosexism and that she begins to precipitate in *Spit and Passion*. By the end of the memoir, Road suggests that such fragmentation may be necessary—for both Cristy as well as American culture in general. While Cristy's bodily fragmentation signals the possibility that she can construct a new personal history, fragmentation is also central to Road's process of historical salvage as she "breaks apart" dominant narratives to construct her own alternative version of the 1990s.

Figure 9.2. Cristy C. Road,
Spit and Passion (2012): 99.

Through the ways in which she uses the multiple levels of narration, Road draws readers into *Spit and Passion*, requiring them to collude with her to create the meaning of the text. Just as Cristy has to learn to listen for what is not said and to look for what has been rendered invisible in order to craft a usable tradition on which to build her identity, readers of *Spit and Passion* have to similarly learn to read and interpret the trope of silence in the text. This is a key way that Road works to move Cristy's narrative of life on the margins to the center. Although few readers could be expected to share the unique set of factors that contribute to Cristy's identity, we are able to vicariously experience the silencing and marginalization with which she must contend as she comes of age during the volatile period of the 1990s.

The 1990s as a "Special Era"

Though Road's narrative bears similarities to other Latino/a narratives, such as those Sifuentes-Jáuregui discusses, it is also unique due to the combination of personal and political factors that complicate Cristy's coming of age in the early 1990s in Little Havana. In particular, *Spit and Passion* captures the instability of the 1990s as the end of the Cold War and changing gender norms cause upheavals that ripple throughout American culture, from foreign policy to popular culture, and does so through the perspective of a person with an exilic familial history. Consequently, as Cristy comes of age in the midst of social and political instability, she develops a kind of refugee subjectivity and comes to interpret a wide variety of 1990s phenomena through the lens of her family's experiences as Cuban exiles. By highlighting stories of exile—whether that exile is literal or psychic—she suggests that the experience of losing one's home and community might more properly serve as a basis for narrating American history and understanding American culture, rather than those narratives of consensus history built on a myth of American exceptionalism and progress.

Thus, Road's seemingly unique family history is not peripheral to American culture but emblematic of what it means to be American. Although Road does not provide complete biographical details about her family's migration from Cuba to the United States in *Spit and Passion*, she refers to her great-grandmother, Mimita, as a "Cuban exile" and implies that her relatives were among those to flee Cuba during the "golden exile" of the late 1950s and early 1960s, when living with a "stolen culture and identity was, in fact, not compensated with tax-free bonuses and 3-story fountains on their front lawns" (44). Interestingly, even though the events of *Spit and Passion* occur decades after the first generation of Cuban migrants fled to the United States and despite their relative success in the United States, Cristy still seems to perceive of the status of this group and her place within it as tenuous. However, in the context of a number of internal and external pressures facing the Cuban American community in the 1990s, Cristy is perceptive to sense that challenging the norms of the Cuban American community could threaten both the group's hard-won political power and her own status as a member of the group.

Certainly, the position of Cuban Americans became increasingly uncertain in the post–Cold War era of the early 1990s. As Marta Tienda and Susana M. Sanchez explain, "Partly because they were fleeing a socialist state and partly because they did not fit the UN definitions of *refugee*," during the Cold War "Cubans enjoyed a privileged position among the U.S. foreign-born population" (58). Among these privileges "Cuban émigrés were granted visa waivers and parolee status, and were offered a range of services to facilitate their labor market integration, including certification of professional credentials, and college loan programs, and bilingual education" (58). Subsequently, Cuban Americans in Florida attained political power by forming a voting bloc strong enough to elect local and state officials and even influence the presidential election at times. As Susan Eckstein explains, when Cuban Americans switched party loyalties (from Democrat to Republican) in the 1980s, they demonstrated that they would not be motivated by party loyalty but rather by who would offer the best deal to the group. However, maintaining this power required homogeneity among the community.

In the post–Cold War era, the changing priorities of American foreign policy along with the changing demography of the community threatened to lessen the political power of Cuban Americans. American policy toward Cuba became contradictory and confused, and as president, Bill Clinton had a vexed relationship with Cuban Americans. For example, Clinton reversed a long-standing policy of granting Cuban migrants automatic asylum in 1995, and when the Clinton administration authorized the return of Elián Gonzáles to his father in Cuba in 2000, Florida's Cuban Americans responded by turning against Al Gore during the 2000 election, ultimately playing a key role in delivering Florida's electoral votes to George W. Bush (Girard et al. 43–45; Eckstein 135–37). Added to this, a generational divide began to emerge as earlier Cuban migrants who desired to maintain strict sanctions against Cuba clashed with more recent Cuban emigrants who argued that greater contact would undermine the Castro regime more effectively than continued sanctions (Bishin and Klofstad). In the context of these external and internal pressures, Cristy's community is driven to affiliate with conservative Republicans during the 1990s because conservatives more openly supported the tough stance toward Castro that first-generation exiles from Cuba also supported.

Cristy's difficulty in reconciling her ethnicity and sexuality in this historical context stems from the fact that affiliating with Republicans means accepting the political agenda of the conservative evangelical Christians who lead the party, including their focus on issues of gender and sexuality. Evangelicals had become active in politics in the 1980s, playing an important role in the election of Ronald Reagan to the presidency (West xxx), and what came to be known as the new Christian Right "made a significant impact on the American political landscape" throughout the 1980s and 1990s (xxxi). In the 1990s, conservative evangelicals focused particularly on incremental policy changes, seeking partial-birth abortion bans and bans on gay marriage at the state level.

In fact, one of the major political victories for the new Right in the 1990s was passage of the Defense of Marriage Act (DOMA) in 1996. DOMA declared that no state or Indian tribe in the United States would be required to recognize relationships between same-sex couples or recognize same-sex marriages from other states (U.S. Cong. House. Comm. on the Judiciary). For federal government purposes, it defined marriage as a union between one man and one woman as husband and wife and spouse as a person of the opposite sex.[6] Another partial conservative victory was the federal policy "Don't Ask, Don't Tell" (DADT), which went into effect in 1994 and barred openly gay, lesbian, or bisexual persons from military service, while also prohibiting military personnel from discriminating against or harassing closeted homosexual or bisexual service members or applicants.

However, despite conservatives' political victories related to gay rights, they began to lose public support for their initiatives during the 1990s. As Michael Klarman explains, "Despite the fierce political backlash ignited against gay marriage in the 1990s . . . gay rights in general continued to grow," bolstered in part by treatment of these issues within popular culture (70). In *Spit and Passion* Road describes the 1990s as "a special era, manifested through the 15-minute revelations brought to us by 'Vogue' by Madonna, Charytin's exposed cleavage behind her sequined tops, and *Ren & Stimpy*" (12). These glimpses of a more heterogeneous American culture in which gender norms are changing help Cristy recognize that the cultural landscape of the 1990s is not as homogeneous as she has been taught it is, and in this sense the 1990s is "a special era," characterized at once by pervasive homophobic rhetoric and violence and simultaneously by unprecedented acceptance of homosexuality in popular culture. As Klarman explains, "In 1990, only one network television show had a regularly appearing gay character," and "a majority of Americans reported that they would not permit their child to watch a prime-time television situation comedy with gay characters" (73). However, by mid-decade "the most popular situation comedies were dealing with the issue of gay marriage: *Roseanne* in 1995, *Friends* in 1996, and *Mad About You* in 1998. . . . In 1997, after months of rampant speculation, Ellen DeGeneres famously came out in a special one-hour episode of her popular television show, *Ellen*, which was watched by forty-six million viewers" (73).

Incidents of homophobic violence in the 1990s also drew attention to LGBTQ issues and resulted in increased public support for individuals discriminated against on the basis of sexuality; however, the virulence of these incidents indicates how deeply threatening some individuals found changing norms. The most publicized case was the beating death of Matthew Shepard in 1998. Though Cristy is not subject to physical violence in *Spit and Passion*, she does bear witness to how normalized homophobia is in her middle school, where, daily, her classmates question and police one another's sexuality. From them she learns about "the girl who might be 'weird,'" "about the 'bisexual who spread diseases,'" "about the 'disgusting lesbians who do disgusting things in order to attract attention,' about the 'sick people who reject the gender they were assigned at birth,' about 'the disgusting homosexuals who lure you into their haunting grip … by rooming with you in college, sneaking into your pants at the slumber party, and looking at you long enough until you are undressed" (46). Taken together, the messages that Cristy receives about sexuality communicate clearly that "human beings should not be gay if they wanted to survive a day on this earth" (22).

Between the threats of physical danger and community rejection she faces, it is not surprising that Cristy comes to think of herself as a refugee, since she feels systematically excluded from her community. It is also perhaps not surprising that as Cristy seeks a "safe" way to express her feelings of exclusion in the context of youth culture, she finds her way to other cultural outsiders in the form of punk music. By the 1990s punk had been co-opted by consumer culture and was being marketed to adolescents as a way to express rebellion. What is surprising, though, is Road's insistence on the continuing political importance of punk in the 1990s. She even comes to interpret 1990s debates about what it means to be a "real punk" through the lens of her exilic familial history. Ultimately, Road weaves together her personal history, her family history, the larger history of the Cuban American community, and the history of her favorite punk rock band, Green Day, by focusing on each as a story of losing home and community. And depicting these different histories of exile—whether the exile is psychic or actual physical displacement—represents the basis for her alternative history of the 1990s.

What Does It Mean to Be Punk in the 1990s?

Cristy is introduced to punk in junior high by a friend: "Carlito swore I had a problem, something I was not talking about. So he told me to listen to punk rock music" (*Spit and Passion* 40). As her description of this first exposure to punk makes clear, by the 1990s listening to punk rock music, indeed joining the punk subculture, was a well-recognized and largely acceptable way for adolescents to channel their desire to rebel against mainstream culture. Even within Cristy's conservative community, adolescents are permitted to identify with "alternative" musical styles and groups including heavy metal and punk. Although punk was still viewed as an outsider subgroup, by the early 1990s it had become legible as such and was even marketed to youth as an acceptable way to express rebellion. Thus, associating with punk allows Cristy to simultaneously participate in youth culture, express her feelings of dissatisfaction with her conservative community, and disguise her homosexuality.

Though punk emerged in the 1970s as a rejection of capitalistic values, and early punk bands such as the Sex Pistols were anti-authoritarianism and anti-consumerism, the pop punk bands of the 1990s that Cristy idolizes represent the antithesis of the independent spirit of earlier punks. In fact, Cristy's favorite band,

Green Day, perfectly illustrates the co-optation of punk by consumer mass culture in the 1990s. Green Day was originally part of the punk scene at the DIY 924 Gilman Street club in Berkeley, California, and the band's early releases were with the independent record label Lookout! Records. However, in 1994 its major-label debut *Dookie* (released through Reprise Records) became a breakout success and eventually sold more than ten million copies in the United States. The band's commercial success led to controversy about whether the band's musical style and major-label status constituted "true punk." John Lydon, former front man of the Sex Pistols, argued that if Green Day "were true punk they wouldn't look anything like they do" (Melia). Even Green Day's Billie Joe Armstrong acknowledged, "Sometimes I think we've become totally redundant because we're this big band now; we've made a lot of money—we're not punk rock any more. But then I think about it and just say, 'You can take us out of a punk rock environment, but you can't take the punk rock out of us'" ("Green Day"). Critics and scholars have similarly weighed in on what constitutes punk and whether Green Day and other pop punk groups simply manufacture punk, offering only the style without the substance.[7]

Throughout *Spit and Passion*, Road engages these debates about the nature of punk in the early 1990s and considers whether punk's co-optation by consumer culture has destroyed its critical potential. For example, in figure 9.3 Road illustrates the power of MTV to homogenize and negate potentially radical musical expression by depicting a large, three-dimensional MTV logo that has crushed Green Day. This image suggests that MTV "flattens" the critical potential of bands such as Green Day and also that, although MTV is literally constructed out of a variety of alternative musical styles such as "goth" and "metal," it has effectively "closeted" them in order to silence their critiques of capitalism and consumer culture. Through this allusion to closeting Road also pulls debates about punk into her larger consideration of how closeting serves oppressive functions for homosexuals, melding two seemingly dissimilar issues in a way that comes to characterize her narrative style.

Nevertheless, despite the co-optation of punk by consumer culture, Road argues for the continuing importance of punk. She even recasts 1990s debates about what constitutes "true punk" in the context of her larger exilic frame. For example, she writes, "In the end, according to all the books and newspapers, Green Day lost all punk credibility. They could never go back to 924 Gilman St., the club their scene was built around, ever again. . . . I channeled this as if it could be me—losing the Cuban community, which harvested my identity" (*Spit and Passion* 109). Even in figure 9.3, she immediately complicates her visual depiction of the danger of co-optation by MTV by explaining via extradiagetic narration that "popular culture was mostly what was accessible to us people surviving in com-

Figure 9.3. Cristy C. Road,
Spit and Passion (2012): 108.

munities that aren't the highly alternative, highly metropolitan vortexes of big cities" (108). Her point is clear: it is only because Green Day has been co-opted and subsequently cast out of their punk community that they are accessible to her and others on the fringes of American culture. As a result, Green Day's controversial status actually draws Cristy to them since she regards them as fellow exiles.

Moreover, Road insists that punk remains a viable and important way to raise political consciousness by showing how Cristy's discovery of punk fosters her development of a contentious politics. Road recounts how after discovering Green Day, "I could look beyond the older generation's ortho-Catholic socialization and hold tightly, with my dear life, to a new socialization—the one I created through the words of Green Day" (54). Green Day preaches inclusivity; they make Cristy "want to be someone" and "explained a life I wanted to create for myself—an underworld where people like me could exist" (55).[8] The cover of *Spit and Passion* immediately introduces the notion that punk has consciousness-raising abilities as well (see figure 9.4). The cover, which bears a tongue-in-cheek blurb from Green Day's Billie Joe Armstrong promoting the book on the basis that "Cristy C. Road is a badass," gives visual form to the process of consciousness raising as Cristy's head is depicted as literally exploding. Her brain is exposed from the top of a Florida Marlins baseball hat with gray matter falling beside her. Similarly, Cristy's chest is ripped open, her shirt displaying ragged claw marks to expose her heart, over which a large bandage in the shape of an X has been attached. Cristy stands in front of a pile of refuse, out of which hands reach as if for help, and one holds a white flag. Flies buzz around the pile. Despite all of this, Cristy gazes out of the image at the reader with a calm, determined look. She clutches a copy of *Rolling Stone* with a picture of Green Day on the cover, holding it in front of her with both hands almost as if it is a shield. Out of her exposed brain, the Golden Gate Bridge emerges, highlighting the connection to San Francisco, the birthplace of Green Day. This image underscores how the band's music provides a way for her to connect with a larger community—of punks and queers—than she has access to in Miami. As she becomes aware of this larger world and the "billion kinds of people" who inhabit it, Cristy develops a heightened political awareness.

Green Day also points Cristy toward a critical methodology she can use to forge a tradition on which she can build her identity. She particularly admires their appropriational style; even though they no longer produce their own music and it is highly polished as a result, they still cobble together their musical style from a wide variety of sources. She describes pop punk as a "hybrid genre of punk rock influenced by late 70s/early 80s power pop; and the driving rhythms of melodic punk rock" (*Spit and Passion* 53). She admires how Green Day "gath-

Figure 9.4. Cristy C. Road,
Spit and Passion (2012): Cover.

ered their own influences," drawing on "lo-fi alternative rock," "classic metal," and "their own punk rock heroes" (53). This is the kind of critical "bricolage" that has long characterized punk style, as described by its earliest critics such as John Clarke and Dick Hebdige. Punks combine "apparently discrepant styles" that not only invest "objects with new meanings" but also retain "the original meanings as well, even when these [are] contradictory" (Leblanc 40). The point of this "sartorial terrorism" is to protest "against the constraints imposed by conventional norms" and contravene "social standards in an effort to challenge the integrity of the culture that produced them" (41). Punk bricolage also allows punks to combine historical moments in jarring and unexpected ways as they mix older styles of music, fashion, and imagery with present moments and modes. *Spit and Passion* ultimately represents Road's own "historical bricolage" as she mixes together icons, imagery, and folklore from the past and present, from the golden exile to Little Havana to the punk scene in San Francisco, to narrate her coming-of-age story.

DIY History: "Transforming Traditional Values into Radical Ideas"

Cristy protests consensus history and cultural homogeneity by appropriating materials from her family, the Cuban American community, the mass media, and even conservative political culture to craft her own usable tradition. To do so, she chooses to see the materials she appropriates differently. As she puts it, "I could reinvent them. Treasure them in retrospect but smash their unfortunate idiosyncrasies when necessary" (*Spit and Passion* 147). About Catholicism she explains, "I was on a quest to *demystify* the nuts and bolts that transformed the Catholic doctrine into a needle, rather than a celebration" (45, emphasis added). About education: "I wanted to believe there was a *glitch* in the things we were taught rather than the way we are" (45, emphasis added). About the mass media: "The truth was snipped out, like the reconstructed Bible" (110). Her family, too, is subject to this process: "I tried to *disassociate* my family from the evil values they were born into, the values that I believed humanity would eventually reject" (150, emphasis added). Road's decision to interpret the heterosexism of her family, the Cuban American community, and Anglo-American culture as the result of misinformation and miscommunication allows her to see these groups as her allies even if they do not know it. In this way, Road identifies pieces of her culture and family that she can work with to create a usable tradition. Rather than rejecting everything heterosexist outright, Road instead begins a historical salvage project whereby she claims the right to interpret differently than she is supposed to with the goal of "transforming traditional values into radical ideas" (147).

Road relies on a practice that John Fiske, in *Understanding Popular Culture*, calls "excorporation," which is the "'tearing' or disfigurement of a commodity in order to assert one's right and ability to remake it into one's own culture" (13). Fiske explains that "Excorporation is the process by which the subordinate make their own culture out of the resources and commodities provided by the dominant system, and this is central to popular culture, for in an industrial society the only resources from which the subordinate can make their own subcultures are those provided by the system that subordinates them" (13). The commodities that Road excorporates range from mass media offerings to the religious icons that populate her family's home to conservative political materials. While Fiske expresses skepticism about the possibility of using excorporation to effectively resist the dominant system, suggesting that it inevitably leads people to submission to the "system that subordinates them," Road is more optimistic about its possibilities in *Spit and Passion*. She shows that Cristy can put a diverse range of materials—even explicitly homophobic materials—to the service of her critique of conservative ideology without assenting to the oppressive messages of those materials.

For example, Road highlights how religious iconography is subject to transformation despite the fact that the Catholicism practiced in Little Havana is explicitly homophobic. Cristy is particularly taken with La Virgen de la Caridad, the Hispanic image of which was pontifically designated by Pope Benedict XV as the Patroness of Cuba. Road makes clear that although she knows Catholicism, including La Virgen, is implicated in a "social revolution that shackled my organs," she "liked to see it all as my family's art and folklore" (*Spit and Passion* 10). Cristy "decided La Virgen reconstructed the meaning of everything, dismantling the typical doctrines of her followers for the sake of my own salvation. She wasn't a toy anymore—she was an artistic tradition, an ideology that needed work" (35). The top right panel in figure 9.5 illustrates how Road creates a critical bricolage in which she pairs an image of La Virgen with Roseanne Barr and explains that La Virgen "made all those male saints look like homophobes, like Roseanne Barr made all of television look misogynist" (45). In this example, Road creates a surprising juxtaposition to illustrate how she can rework diverse cultural materials to advance her own interpretation and critique.

Through her process of excorporation, Road is even able to make conservative political messages and figures from the 1990s serve the interests of her story and construction of a new history. In this way, she engages consensus history head on—by actually visualizing some of the texts and individuals responsible for creating the dominant narratives that exclude her. For example, a panel in the lower right half of figure 9.5 depicts a stack of books bearing the titles *God Hates Fags*; *The Book of Leviticus, 2nd edition*; *The Federalist Papers*; *In Defense of the Right*; and *Republican Revolution*, but Road positions these on a pedestal labeled

MY GREAT-GRANDMOTHER, MIMITA,
WAS THE MATRIARCH OF THE FAMILY.
I WAS SURE THAT MY FAMILY HAD CREATED
THEIR OWN VERSION OF MIMITA'S VALUE
SYSTEM, IN ORDER TO FIT THEIR MORE
CONVENTIONAL WORLD. I BELIVED MIMITA
WAS SOME SORT OF A PRE-ADOLESCENT
EXPLORER — I THOUGHT SHE WAS
OKAY WITH HOMOS, SHE JUST DIDN'T
TALK ABOUT IT BECAUSE *THE BIBLE*
TOLD HER NOT TO. SHE AND I HAD AN
ELECTRIC PULSE THAT AMPLIFIED
WHEN WE SPOKE. I LIKED TO
BELIEVE EVERY MEMBER OF MY
FAMILY HAD SOME KIND OF DEEP
INTERNAL SYMPATHY FOR HOMOS ...
BECAUSE ISN'T THAT WHAT BEING
A CUBAN EXILE IS ALL ABOUT?

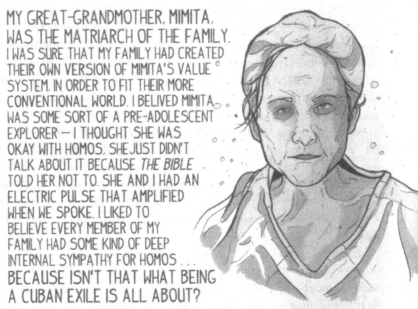

...CLASPING THE ARMS OF YOUR BROTHERS AND SISTERS WHO WERE DISMISSED BY THE COMMUNIST REVOLUTION BECAUSE OF THEIR IDENTITIES?

GRASPING ONTO YOUR BRETHREN WHOSE STOLEN CULTURE AND IDENTITY WAS, IN FACT, NOT COMPENSATED WITH TAX-FREE BONUSES AND 3-STORY FOUNTAINS ON THEIR FRONT LAWNS, NO MATTER WHAT THEY DID WITH THEIR LIVES?

LA VIRGEN MADE THOSE MALE SAINTS LOOK LIKE HOMOPHOBES, LIKE ROSEANNE BARR MADE ALL OF TELEVISION LOOK MISOGYNIST. IT'S LIKE THEY WERE THESE GREATER ENTITIES WHO ADJUSTED TO THE UNDERSTANDING THAT THERE'S A BILLION KINDS OF PEOPLE ON EARTH.

I WANTED TO BELIEVE THERE WAS A GLITCH IN THE THINGS WE WERE TAUGHT RATHER THAN THE WAY THAT WE ARE . . .

BANNED
FOR INACCURACY

SO I NEVER FOUGHT BACK: I JUST SAT BACK, SCARED AND ANGRY AND HOLDING ONTO MYSELF . . .

45

Figures 9.5A and 9.5B.
Cristy R. Road, *Spit and Passion* (2012): 44–45.

"Banned for Inaccuracy" (45). Similarly, throughout the text she reproduces a number of political signs warning that "homosex is a sin" and homosexuals must "repent or perish" (10). By excorporating conservative political messages and including them in Cristy's coming-of-age story, Road simultaneously documents a history of homophobia and questions the extent to which historical and cultural narratives have been edited and manipulated to suit the purposes of those with a stake in maintaining the status quo. In considering the radical potential of La Virgen, for example, Road writes that she might have "honored other women, but we will never know, because so much of her history has already been destroyed by patriarchy" (35). Similarly, she tries to parse what Jesus really taught versus what his "present-day conspirators" want to make him say (18). Although Road cannot necessarily recover the lost history or the truth for herself, she can at least make readers aware that the reality they have been taught is only a construct designed to promote the interests of a few. Through the autographic she can also force mass media, religious, and political materials to signify in ways never intended by their creators as she uses them to narrate the coming-of-age of a young Latina lesbian. In doing so, Road undercuts the power of these materials and subordinates them to her own personal history. In her version of the 1990s, dominant figures and debates matter only inasmuch as they help or hinder Cristy's personal quest for identity.

The strategies that Road uses to create an alternative history of the 1990s also prove useful in reworking her own family's history. In particular, Cristy is drawn to her great-grandmother, Mimita, who fled Cuba for the United States. In the upper left panel in figure 9.5, for example, Road recounts how "I belived [*sic*] Mimita was some sort of pre-adolescent explorer—I thought she was okay with homos, she just didn't talk about it because *The Bible* told her not to" (*Spit and Passion* 44). In fact, she believes that "every member of my family had some kind of deep internal sympathy for homos . . . because isn't that what being a Cuban exile is all about?" (44). In Cristy's historical salvage of Mimita, she becomes Mimita's direct heir since both faced a loss of home. While Mimita was literally exiled from Cuba, Cristy is psychically exiled from her Cuban American community on the basis of her sexuality. Here Road melds historical eras to offer a jarring juxtaposition of American conservatives aligned with Castro. This comparison illustrates how putting stories of exile at the center of her history of the 1990s helps Road uncover surprising similarities between quite different groups. In this alternative history, Cuban Americans, homosexuals, and pop punk bands are joined together by similar exilic experiences, while Castro and American conservatives are united by their willingness to cast people out of their communities on the basis of being different.

In the end, Road's historical narrative of the 1990s is necessarily incomplete, fragmented, and, to some extent, unpolished.[9] Having questioned whether it is possible to recover a history that has been edited to silence divergent voices and experiences, Road concludes that if history is subject to editing and revision, then it is open to her revisionary work as well. By ferreting out stories of exclusion and bricolaging them together in her autographic, Cristy creates an alternative history of the 1990s within which marginalized groups and people become central and dominant events and figures recede to the margins. And if this process is messy and privileges emotional truth over historical accuracy, this also helps Road distinguish her project of historical reconstruction from those highly polished, supposedly objective narratives of consensus history that Cristy finds oppressive.

While Road charges consensus history with "lying about the way things just are" (*Spit and Passion* 98), she acknowledges and draws attention to her own process of reworking her materials. In fact, her autographic recounts exactly the ways that she revises a wide variety of texts and source materials and visualizes the process of an author interpreting her own memories and constructing her own history. The autographic form serves Road in this effort by allowing her to oscillate between "different planes of representation" (Smith and Watson 169) to depict Cristy's experiences coming of age in early 1990s culture and Road's adult, critical interpretation of that time period. And this has the added effect of making the reality in which the adolescent Cristy lives seem strange and false to the reader. Though Cristy is forced to endure the policing of gender and sexuality in her community, and the reader is asked to identify with her feelings of depression and isolation, we are also constantly reminded by Road that not only is Cristy's "reality" a construct but also Cristy herself will break free from it. The effect of this is to simultaneously acknowledge the impact of consensus history and cultural homogeneity on Cristy even as that power is diminished in the eyes of the reader. *Spit and Passion* makes a case for the importance of such strategies even as it employs them to demonstrate how oppressive supposedly objective historical narratives can be for those on the margins and how important it is to make space for subjective experience.

NOTES

1. It has become conventional in critical discussions of autographics to use the author's last name, "Road" in this case, to refer to the author outside the text and the author's first name, "Cristy" in this case, to refer to her in-text avatar. Ann Cvetkovich explains that this practice is consistent with critical discussions of memoir in general (126).

2. For more on the debates about the nature of historical knowledge, see Gunn, chapter 2, and E. Cheng.

3. Although consensus history is associated most with historical practices of the 1950s—before 1960s social history began to emphasize conflict—consensus history continued to be taught at the primary level long after this because of the dynamics of history textbook publishing. See Martin for more on this.

4. Although as Eileen Ka-May Cheng describes, the study of history had fragmented well before the 1990s and has never been as uniform as we might believe (118), *Spit and Passion* demonstrates how history, particularly that taught in elementary and junior high schools, does tend to be uniform and conservative.

5. The early 1990s also saw the eruption of what has been termed "the history wars" as the National History Standards produced by the Center for History in the Schools at UCLA and funded by the National Endowment for the Humanities (NEH) met with strong conservative rejection led by then NEH director Lynn Cheney, Vanderbilt education professor Chester Finn, and a number of other conservative critics and historians. See Nash et al. for a book-length treatment of the controversy over the standards from the perspective of the UCLA faculty who developed them.

6. Ironically, it was an early, local victory in the battle for marriage equality that propelled the national movement against marriage equality. In 1993 a trial court in Hawaii ruled that a state statute prohibiting same-sex marriage violated equal protection as defined by the Hawaii constitution and that the state's argument failed to prove that same-sex marriage had any negative effect on the public. See Gay and Lesbian Advocates and Defenders' "A Short History of DOMA."

7. It is beyond the scope of this essay to list every work that has been devoted to debating the origins and/or definition of punk. For examples of the shape of this debate in the 1990s, see Marcus, Henry, and Nehring. For more recent examples of the debate, see Thompson, Duncombe and Tremblay, and Leblanc.

8. It might be impossible to overstate the importance of punk to Road. It so infuses her work and identity that she even changed her name to the title of a Green Day song. Road's given name is Cristina Carrera; "Christie Road" is the title of a Green Day song.

9. Although *Spit and Passion* enjoyed overall positive reviews (such as Vasquez and Goldsmith), some did note its lack of polish. While some reviewers wished the conclusion were more developed (such as *Publisher's Weekly*'s "Book Review: Spit and Passion"), others felt that the story was too text-heavy and needed to be better edited (such as Camper).

CHAPTER 10

Speculative Fictions, Historical Reckonings, and "What Could Have Been"

Scott McCloud's The New Adventures of Abraham Lincoln

Cathy J. Schlund-Vials

The past conditional temporality of "what could have been" symbolizes a space of attention that holds at once the positive objects and methods upheld by modern history and social science, as well as the inquiries into connections and convergences rendered unavailable by these methods. It is a space of reckoning that allows us to revisit times of historical contingency and possibility to consider alternatives that may have been *unthought* in those times, and might otherwise remain so now, in order to imagine different futures for what lies ahead. This is not a project of merely telling history differently, but one of returning to the past, its gaps, uncertainties, impasses, and elisions.
—Lisa Lowe, *The Intimacies of Four Continents* (175)

I like to think of *The New Adventures of Abraham Lincoln* as a "noble failure." The consensus of comics fans at the time seemed to be that "failure" was description enough. Lately though, fans of the book have been coming out of hiding a bit more often, so maybe history won't be so harsh on it in the long run.
—Scott McCloud, "*The New Adventures of Abraham Lincoln*," scottmccloud.com

PUBLISHED IN 1998, Scott McCloud's *The New Adventures of Abraham Lincoln* represented a substantive "field first" insofar as it innovatively combined Photoshopped backgrounds, computer-generated icons (specifically American flags and the "Great Seal of the United States" from U.S. currency), and manually drawn images.[1] Characterized by McCloud as both his "first attempt at computer-generated artwork" and an unassailable "flop," *The New Adventures of Abraham Lincoln* follows the escapades of ten-year-old African American protagonist Byron Johnson (whose father—a paraplegic war veteran—avers is "the **smartest kid** in **town**!") and his friend Marcie as they attempt to thwart a scheme of celestial proportions involving an extraterrestrial conspiracy, a simulacra version of the sixteenth president, and en masse brainwashing (45). Set in the late 1990s, green-tentacled, one-eyed aliens have created an ersatz version of "Uncle Abe" who suspiciously returns to finish his second presidential term; as the graphic novel unfolds, it is revealed that the imposter Lincoln is a de facto Trojan horse whose campaign for the nation's highest office is fixed to a sinister, world-domination plot.

Consistent with a fictional presidential "reclamation" movement marked by specious name-calling, red-herring arguments about traditional American "values," and highly inaccurate summations of U.S. history, the alien-generated Lincoln and his growing number of supporters-turned-minions distribute American flag transmitters that render listeners incapable of hearing legitimate debate and comprehending reasonable discourse. Inspired at the level of title and plot by Frank Stack's underground comic *The Adventures of Jesus* (1964), which in iconoclastic and anachronistic fashion placed the Christian Messiah in contemporaneous storylines involving encounters with counterculture hippies, antiwar protestors, and police surveillance/brutality, *The New Adventures of Abraham Lincoln* analogously resurrects another version of "Honest Abe" as a central foil for the counterfeit "Liberator."[2] Armed with historical facts and aided by this "real" Lincoln, Byron eventually exposes the aliens' interplanetary plot; in so doing, Byron—in a move befitting an exaggerated comics narrative—valiantly and single-handedly rescues the nation from the perils of authoritarianism and the hazards of demagoguery (see figure 10.1).

McCloud's graphic narrative portrayal of U.S. politics, self-characterized in the introductory epigraph as a "noble failure," has arguably withstood the proverbial "test of time" with regard to its Janus-faced applicability to past/present election campaigns, though such an enduring assessment is, admittedly, formalistically curtailed. According to a critical 2006 *Comics Worth Reading* review, *The New Adventures of Abraham Lincoln* was in the immediate years following its publication a "disappointment" largely due to technological limitations, which resulted in "very minimal cartoony figures over photomanipulated backgrounds with badly integrated visual effects, kind of snazzy for their time but soon clichéd." In the face of these technical imperfections (evident in the comic's inability to fully integrate in print various visual elements with regard to line, contour, shading, and blocking), *The New Adventures of Abraham Lincoln* by and large maintains its political significances (see figure 10.2).

In a 2012 retrospective review of *The New Adventures of Abraham Lincoln*, Colin Smith of *Sequart Organization* surmises:

> Time has been kind to McCloud's art for *The New Adventures of Abraham Lincoln*. His first full-length project to feature work entirely executed on computer, its pages often seemed stiff, still, and lifeless when the book first appeared. The ubiquity of the software which McCloud put to use combined with its over-familiar limitations originally left the tale feeling as if it were something of a vanity project, or an end-of-course exercise, an only-partially successful experiment whose strengths could have been at the very least equaled by more traditional pen'n'paper methods. . . .

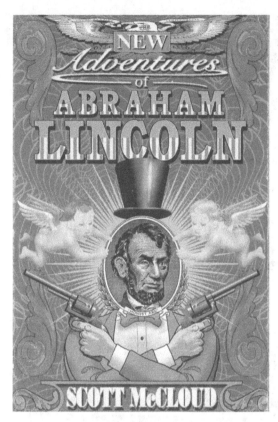

Figure 10.1. Scott McCloud's *The New Adventures of Abraham Lincoln* (1998): cover.

[However, what] once seemed like gimmicky, underachieving pages now carry the same suggestion of a nostalgically idealised, unhealthily sanitized world which a Rockwell parody might, with an air of an America so peculiarly mannered and predictable that it can only be hiding something distinctly unhealthy underneath its uncomfortably artificial surface.

In stressing that "time has been kind" to *The New Adventures of Abraham Lincoln*, Smith privileges a decidedly politicized reading of McCloud's experimental work that accentuates its keen position as a subversive "[Norman] Rockwell parody" that productively uncovers a "nostalgically idealised, unhealthy sanitized world." Denotative of a "sentimental longing or wistful affection for the past, typically for a period or place with happy personal associations" (*Oxford English Dictionary*) and connotative of a time and place that is more imagined than real, Smith's tactical mention of "nostalgia" coheres with *The New Adventures of Abraham Lincoln*'s inventive narrative logics, bringing into simultaneous focus the comic's conspicuous engagements with official U.S. history alongside a still-vexed American present.

Accordingly, Smith's observations about "an America so peculiarly mannered"

Figure 10.2. Scott McCloud,
*The New Adventures of
Abraham Lincoln* (1998): 31.

and delineated by "uncomfortable artificial surfaces" provocatively converge on a reappraisal of McCloud's work as incontestably contingent on two distinct historical-political milieus. Correspondingly situated within a 1990s context of Internet "information highways," "contracts with America," the Monica Lewinsky sex scandal, and President Bill Clinton's subsequent impeachment, McCloud's "failed experiment" reflected on one level in form, tone, and content a polarized, turn-of-the-twenty-first-century governmental imaginary.[3] On another level, and in a more immediate vein, when set against a current political climate marked by vehement Islamophobia, increased unilateralism, reinvigorated anti-black racism, and heightened xenophobia, *The New Adventures of Abraham Lincoln* presciently foreshadows the radical and distressing partisanship part and parcel of post-9/11 U.S. politics.[4] Inadvertently yet provocatively prefiguring forty-fifth president Donald Trump's campaign rallying cry, the fraudulent Lincoln declares, "I want to make America **great** again! I stand for **truth** and **liberty**! And **wholesome all-American goodness!** And **family values!**" (32).[5]

Acknowledging the work's ongoing resonances—and in line with this volume's overriding *historical* focus—of equally compelling note is the extent to which McCloud's graphic narrative strategically utilizes a simultaneously familiar/defamiliarized speculative schema as a means of engaging a larger critique. Such a critique, as this chapter maintains, lays bare the unstable (yet, in the face of vociferous jingoism, seemingly *unshakable*) foundation on which state-authorized narratives of U.S. nationhood, American selfhood, and political personhood are built. To be sure, the critical frames through which McCloud's project is mediated, commencing at the level of presidential history and intersecting with federal politics, incorporate a legible comics genealogy *and* intelligible narrative lineage. To wit, whereas *The New Adventures of Abraham Lincoln* utilizes a similar time-travel focus as the aforementioned *The Adventures of Jesus*, it likewise accesses by way of plot and characterization an established "alternative history" subgenre consistent with past/present American superhero comics and contemporary speculative fiction. A familiar "reboot" conceit of mainstream U.S. comics franchises within the Marvel and DC ("Detective Comics") universes, complementary character histories and parallel plots have been deployed to resurrect fallen heroes, conjure up incongruous narrative arcs (which counter heroic archetypes and militate against established characterizations), and imagine more quotidian life events (such as the problems of regular employment and the complications of more-often-than-not heteronormative marriage).[6]

Shifting from comics to short stories, historiographic essays, and full-length novels, Lincoln's divisive candidacy, mythologized presidency, and tragic assassination, along with the conflict's major battles (such as southwestern Tennessee clashes at Shiloh and the Gettysburg campaign in Pennsylvania), have been popular subjects of twentieth- and twenty-first-century "what if" Civil War narratives; such imaginative accounts function as politically inflected philosophical touchstones on which to map substitute trajectories involving Confederate victory. In turn, these trajectories, not surprisingly, give rise to plots involving either the more progressive dimensions of the Lincoln presidency (particularly in terms of abolition) or the instantiation of southern authoritarianism; this authoritarianism is made apparent in the polemical perseverance of the "peculiar institution" vis-à-vis a state-authorized paternalism and state-sanctioned rights violation integral to the forced enslavement of African Americans. These speculative retellings include works such as Milton Waldman's "If Booth Had Missed Lincoln" (1931); MacKinlay Kantor's *If the South Had Won the War* (1960–61); the 1961 *Twilight Zone* episode "Back There" (focused on Lincoln's assassination); James M. McPherson's essay "If the Lost Order Hadn't Been Lost" (1999); Peter G. Tsouras's edited collection *Dixie Victorious: An Alternate History of the Civil War* (2004); Roger L. Ransom's *The Confederate States of America* (2005); Robert Conroy's *1862* (2006); Harry Turtledove's eleven-book *Southern Victory* series (1997–2007); Seth Grahame-Smith's *Abraham Lincoln: Vampire Hunter* (2010); Billy Bennett's *By Force of Arms* (2012); and Stephen L. Carter's *The Impeachment of Abraham Lincoln* (2012) (among others). Despite differences in plot, and notwithstanding divergences with regard to historical interpretation and hypothetical extrapolation, central to these reimagined contemplations is a past/present, implicit/explicit restaging of Lincoln's fabled status as the so-termed Great Emancipator; such a priori readings in turn foreground alternative imaginings of American futurity via a clear presentism predicted on the concomitant (non)passage of the Thirteenth, Fourteenth, and Fifteenth Amendments (as per the dictates of individualized creative extrapolations).[7]

While *The New Adventures of Abraham Lincoln* ostensibly coheres with the speculative focus of these narrative projections, its deliberate and at times heavy-handed consideration of the parochial present—particularly with regard to public discourse, politics, and race—persuasively undermine dominant-held teleologies concerning racial progress, mainstream assertions about liberatory political participation, and essentializing assessments of U.S. democratic virtue. Within *The New Adventures of Abraham Lincoln*'s emphatically expansive comic imaginary, characters (who are the product of the aforementioned contested present) are afforded a unique audience with the political past and become firsthand witnesses to its multivalent racial (and racialized) legacies. Such destabilizations—made possible through an outlandish alien plot that nonetheless remains grounded in political actuality—are, as this chapter maintains, evident in McCloud's vexed characterizations of the two "Lincolns" who, to varying degrees and divergent ends, fail to live up to the master narrative of U.S. history; they are likewise made visible via *The New Adventures of Abraham Lincoln*'s intrepid protagonist Byron, whose historical skepticism and political cynicism bring to light the persistence of racial conflict and nonresolution of racialized disparity. In so doing, *The New Adventures of Abraham Lincoln*—despite a seemingly "happy ending" that superficially restores via alien defeat and the fake Lincoln's disavowal the "natural order of things"—is a *dystopic* work necessarily circumscribed by a degraded political imaginary; this historically driven imaginary ultimately fails to achieve the emancipatory promises of racial progress embedded in mainstream assessments of the sixteenth president's legacy.

Accordingly, this chapter contends that such dystopic frames potently militate against a noncritical multiculturalism that has become a fundamental tenet of present-day colorblind discourse.[8] Drawing on the evocative reading practices engendered by Lisa Lowe's notion (in the opening epigraph) of a "past conditional temporality" as an analytic through which to "revisit times of historical contingency and possibility to consider alternatives that may have been *unthought* in those times," I argue that crucial to *The New Adventures of Abraham Lincoln*'s diagnostic treatment of past/present U.S. politics is first and foremost its judicious characterization of American history (specifically Abraham Lincoln's position within that history) as a flexible, "reckoning" site on which to "retur[n] to the past, its gaps, uncertainties, impasses, and elisions." To consider those "gaps, uncertainties, impasses, and elisions," this chapter continues with a brief consideration of Scott McCloud's revisionary critical/creative oeuvre as a means of mapping his overall preoccupation with comics as a mixed genre; these cartographic explorations set the stage for McCloud's *The New Adventures of Abraham Lincoln*, which can be categorized as both speculative fiction (defined in this chapter as a broad literary genre encompassing the supernatural, fantastical, and/or futuristic) and graphic narrative (comprehended as an identifiable, "nonexcerpt-able" blended image text form).[9] These formalistic evaluations, which encompass McCloud's use of specific print technologies (namely, Photoshop), presage an examination of McCloud's negotiations with past/present politics vis-à-vis multiple doublings involving characters whose respective names and personifications cohere with a *reiterative* reading of U.S. history. Such reiterations foreground a close reading of *The New Adventures of Abraham Lincoln* and prefigure a concluding return to the historical amnesias and identarian polemics constitutive of a turn-of-the-twentieth-century U.S. racial imaginary.

Fabricated Imaginaries in a Comics Age of Mechanical Reproduction

Undoubtedly, while Scott McCloud's nonfiction works about graphic narrative— particularly *Understanding Comics: The Invisible Art* (1993), *Reinventing Comics: How Imagination and Technology Are Revolutionizing an Art Form* (2000), and *Making Comics: Storytelling Secrets of Comics, Manga and Graphic Novels* (2006)— figure keenly in contemporary scholarship about comics, much less attention has been paid to his creative work. Labeled the "Aristotle of Comics" by Nick Montfort and Noah Wardrip-Fruin in *The New Media Reader* (2003), McCloud's impact as a visual theorist is matched by his creative output, which consistently seeks to revise and reenvision comics form and content (Montfort and Wardrip-Fruin 711). Indeed, McCloud's science fiction/superhero comic series *Zot!* (launched in 1984) represented by way of lighthearted satire a counternarrative to the increasingly dark direction of 1980s superhero comics (such as *Batman: The Dark Knight Returns* [1986] and *Watchmen* [1987]); similarly, McCloud's *Destroy!!* (1986)—which carried the subtitle "the LOUDEST Comic-Book in the UNIVERSE!!!" provided a welcome commentary on the hyperbolic violence in and exaggerated plotlines of mainstream comics. Shifting from graphic narrative to visual form, McCloud has consistently experimented with multiple digital formats: a leading figure in and prominent advocate for e-comics, McCloud has recently explored the web-based possibilities of an "infinite canvas" in narratives such as *The Right Number* (a 2003 multiseries novella) and a comic book he created in conjunction with the 2008 release of Google's web browser, "Google Chrome."[10] Most immediately, McCloud has received considerable acclaim for *The Sculptor* (2015), a work that features protagonist David Smith, a failed artist who makes a deal with a figure named Death; Death gives David the power to sculpt anything on the proviso he has only two hundred days to live.[11]

Whereas Norton and Wardrip-Fruin's above-mentioned characterization of McCloud as the "Aristotle" of graphic narrative coheres with the artist/critic's metaphysical examinations of comics as a distinct genus composed of various subgenres, an equally accurate comparison involves casting him as the "Herodotus of Comics."[12] Such a designation brings to light one of the main foci in this chapter, which time and again returns to McCloud's multivalent engagements with history (inclusive of comics, official presidential narratives, and U.S. race relations). Correspondingly, McCloud's *Understanding Comics* not only provides a critical vocabulary for graphic analysis (e.g., definitions for "icon," "gutters," "pictures," "style," and "clear-lines"); it also establishes a historically organized canon on which to evaluate the form's evolving referential aspects. These allusive lineages, constitutive of innovations in content, characterization, and conceptualization, include the form's more renowned practitioners along with their respective creations (such as Charles Schulz's *Peanuts*, Frank Miller's aforementioned *Batman: The Dark Knight Returns*, Garry Trudeau's *Doonesbury* series, Lynda Barry's *One! Hundred! Demons!*, Art Spiegelman's *Maus*, Steve Ditko's artwork with Marvel, Will Eisner's *Comics and Sequential Art*, R. Crumb's *Zap Comix*, and Osamu Tezuka's *Astro Boy*, to name just a few) (see figure 10.3). On the one hand, this detailed attentiveness to graphic narrative history—which encompasses ancient-world Egyptian pictographs, Japanese manga, newspaper comic

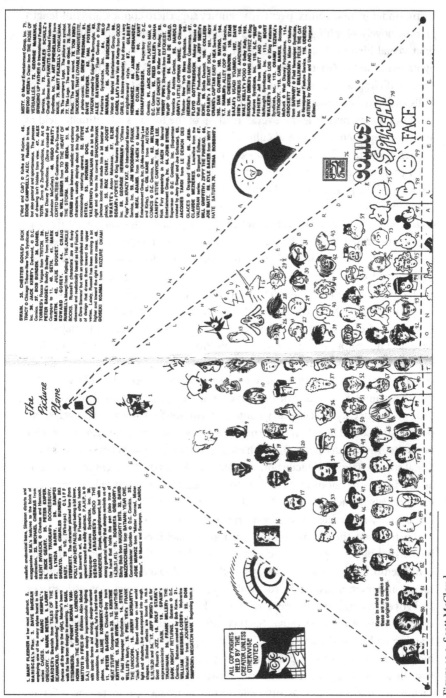

Figure 10.3. Scott McCloud,
Understanding Comics (1993): 52–53.

strips, underground comix, twentieth-century superhero comics, and full-length graphic novels—highlights McCloud's expansive investment in articulating a distinct visual history that takes seriously the form's multiple sites as constituted by its major artists/writers and their multifaceted legacies. On the other hand, McCloud's implicit insistence on genre contiguity, revealed through chronologically ordered assessments that foreground a conspicuous historiographic treatment of comics, buttresses an overall reading of the form as a legitimate field of aesthetic, representational, and cultural inquiry.

Such contemplations of aesthetics and representational politics—which, more often than not, converge on connected experiments with form and content—foreground the past/present schematics of *The New Adventures of Abraham Lincoln*, wherein new visual techniques (redolent in backgrounds and icons generated by Adobe Photoshop) are tactically juxtaposed with traditional formats (manually drawn, penciled/inked characters). This juxtaposition between the mechanized and organic vis-à-vis comics art, in tandem with the novel's specific narratival emplotments, undergirds a discernible fixation on contemporary media practices and late twentieth-century politics. To clarify, while McCloud's initial aim in *The New Adventures of Abraham Lincoln* was aesthetically driven in scope and experimental in execution (as suggested by the artist's stated reliance on Photoshop, Illustrator, and StudioPro, a point stressed in the concluding section, titled "Technical Notes"), the use of late-1990s computer technology nonetheless coincides with the narrative's thematic focus on politically motivated media manipulation and concomitant campaign "spin."[13] Situated adjacent to a turn-of-the-twenty-first-century context of twenty-four hour news cycles, opportunistic "sound bites," and Internet-based reportage (e.g., the aggregate online news site, *The Drudge Report*), which eschews nuanced analysis in favor of sensational superficiality and facile nonscrutiny, McCloud's deployment of Photoshop as key imagistic idiom and chief pictorial medium provocatively reflects and productively refracts *The New Adventures of Abraham Lincoln*'s representational uneasiness with artifice, affectation, and artificiality.

Illustratively, the relative nonintegration of machine-generated images, emblematized by photographic backgrounds that feature the U.S. Capitol, the Lincoln Memorial, "natural" backdrops, architectural exteriors (of homes, monuments, and memorials), and structural interiors (of classrooms, domestic spaces, and governmental auditoriums), renders palpable the evocative *constructedness* of McCloud's graphic narrative. Such constructedness is evident in the comic's framing and three-dimensional use of panel space; Photoshopped backgrounds incorporate a discernible spatial modeling that operates in stark contrast to the two-dimensional figurations of hand-drawn characters. Shadows are added to further an uncanny stereoscopic effect akin to images projected on a "green screen" (known more officially as "chroma key compositing") in present-day film and television.[14] Such technical effects are apparent in a scene that takes place in Dulles International Airport midway through the novel's narrative arc; inked cartoon figures (identifiable as part and parcel of McCloud's unique drawing style) are correspondingly positioned within a 3D-rendered terminal. In particular, these comic personages are located inside a plane that extends along a diagonal sight line, creating a skewed, off-kilter sensibility; such chaotic staging is consistent with a particular moment in the text, wherein the novel's heroic protagonists (inclusive of Byron, Byron's father, Marcie, and the "real Lincoln") must contend with an inimical ambush by the imposter Lincoln's troop of patriotically clad (in red, white, and blue) minions (see figure 10.4).

Figure 10.4. Scott McCloud, *The New Adventures of Abraham Lincoln* (1998): 88.

Shifting from graphic technique to theoretical thematic, McCloud's "assembled" project is, at the level of implementation and with regard to graphic mediation, equal parts simulation and simulacra (apropos the artist's afore-named connections to ancient Greek philosophy); such fabricated sensibilities correspondingly cohere with Walter Benjamin's influential argument in "The Work of Art in the Age of Mechanical Reproduction" (1936), wherein the German critic deconstructs the notion of "authenticity" through mechanistic reproduction.[15] Central to Benjamin's aesthetically driven reasoning is the loss through print reproduction of what he famously terms traditional art's originary "aura"; this "aura" is manifest in essentialized, mythic assessments of "authenticity" vis-à-vis "all that is transmissible from its beginning, ranging from its substantive duration to its testimony to the history which it has experienced" (221). The reproduction of images and their successive mass consumption distances the viewer from a primordial understanding of an aura; such distancing, according to Benjamin, makes possible different contexts and alternative interpretations about the work that carry the potential and embody the promise of revisionary politics (which, depending on the manufacturer/creator, can be both liberatory/progressive or authoritarian/dictatorial in scope). To be sure, such revolutionary contexts and prospects (appropriately promulgated by producers) are principally dependent on medium and remain, notwithstanding reproducibility, historically contingent (for instance, the emergence of cinema as a mass-produced form in the early twentieth century or the midcentury rise of television, which prompted new ways of seeing adapted literary works and quotidian situations).

Respectively, McCloud's contemplation of politics through the "real and the fake"—which defamiliarizes a recognizable medium (comics) via mechanized representation (Photoshop)—occurs through the artist's manipulation of common images that signify long-standing patriotic country-love (such as previously mentioned depictions of flags, icons from U.S. currency, and representations of bald eagles); these manipulations are evident in a sixteen-panel sequence that appears midway in the narrative (see figure 10.5).[16] The first four panels—which feature a moon, an American flag transmitter, Byron's sleeping visage, and an ominous Lincoln portrait—establish a distinct temporality (at night) and encapsulate the contested relationship between protagonist and imposter president. The subsequent twelve panels—which incorporate U.S. iconography, American mass culture (for instance, baseball and a George Washington Pez dispenser), excerpts from past speeches (namely, the preamble to the Gettysburg Address), and lines from "The Star-Spangled Banner"—engender a dizzying compression that on one level replicates Byron's dreamlike state; on another level, and more significantly, such compression coincides with the narrative's overall preoccupation with mass-produced, mass-consumed artifice.

Figure 10.5. Scott McCloud, *The New Adventures of Abraham Lincoln* (1996): 36.

These nationalistic emblems remain historically situated within yet also technologically specific to the mass-produced *The New Adventures of Abraham Lincoln*'s material configurations and narrative arc. Following suit, embedded in its production and entrenched in *The New Adventures of Abraham Lincoln*'s storytelling framework are hackneyed emblems of U.S. nationhood (inclusive of state-sanctioned architecture and state-authorized symbol) that are purposefully rendered *distinguishable* from McCloud's original art counterparts. This critical juxtaposition engenders a fruitful tension between clichéd account and imaginative chronicle. Such an assessment is in part confirmed by the adversarial representation of the two presidents: the imposter Lincoln is sepia-colored and, like the above-discussed Photoshopped backgrounds, appears "super-imposed." These incongruities, which are made even more apparent because of the juxtaposition of monochromatic representation with brightly rendered background, visually accentuate an anachronistic sense that he is in fact "copied" from mid-nineteenth-century photographs.

By comparison, the "real" Lincoln is fully inked and indistinct from the novel's chief characters, which serves to further assimilate him into the novel's narrative arc (see figure 10.6). Revising Benjamin's notion of "aura" to fit the affective contours and politicized registers of Lincoln mythology, both depictions initially and necessarily draw political meaning from their *historic* subject; however, their contradistinguished depictions and oppositional placements in McCloud's graphic narrative, which anticipate and reflect their respective characterizations, constructively distance these representations from their undeniably connective, historically mediated antecedent. Correspondingly at stake in *The New Adventures of Abraham Lincoln*, then, is not so much a representational adherence to the built environment "as it really is" (with regard to a purely *mimetic* impulse or in terms of a naturalistic adherence to representational reality); nor is McCloud's project marked by a conforming preoccupation with Lincoln as "he really was" (e.g., an accurately rendered, complex historic figure). Instead, *The New Adventures of Abraham Lincoln* signals through depictive artificiality an overwhelmingly co-optative political posturing that in the end is truncated, edited, and incomplete. Such posturing is consistent with an American political terrain wherein artifice is privileged over substance. As the next section reveals, such posturing in piecemeal fashion recapitulates official, teleological narratives of the United States while obscuring nefarious motivations and disreputable agendas.

History, Interrupted: *The New Adventures of Abraham Lincoln*

Fixed to a "form-follows-function" receptivity, these inventive frames and contested dynamics set the stage for and largely undergird *The New Adventures of Abraham Lincoln*'s overall reappraisal of contemporary U.S. politics, which—in its

Figure 10.6. Scott McCloud, *The New Adventures of Abraham Lincoln* (1998): 51.

peculiar narratival emplotments and idiosyncratic characterizations—recurrently rehearses U.S. exceptionalism vis-à-vis incomplete, inaccurate, and self-serving elucidations of American history. Such imprecise rehearsals and erroneous retellings foreground a concomitant critique of idealized nationhood and reassessment of American personhood (as defined through political participation and civic engagement); in turn, these notions of U.S. nationalism and selfhood are, as *The New Adventures of Abraham Lincoln*'s characterization and plot bring to light, predicated on potentially disastrous misinterpretations and amnesic misremembrances of the bygone past and its treatment of those who are racial minorities. While it may strike an odd chord to assert that McCloud's *The New Adventures of Abraham Lincoln* is a multiethnic work, given the artist/author's racial background, this chapter in part follows and revises Stephen Hong Sohn's argument in *Racial Asymmetries: Asian American Fictional Worlds* (2014) about Asian American authors whose characters do not reflect their respective ethnoracial backgrounds; as Sohn notes, while Asian American literature remains within the academy a field bound to ethnoracial specificity and "immigrant-centric" themes, such adherences to ethnographic impulses fail to accommodate "works of fiction that trouble critical methodologies through the storytelling perspective" (2). Accordingly, it is precisely McCloud's graphic storytelling perspective—which features as central protagonist an African American subject negotiating the ongoing racial legacies of U.S. history—which make it a relevant revisionary work. To be sure, such critical settings, crucial characterizations, and divisive machinations—convergent on race, politics, and history—are apparent in the comic's opening section, which from the outset establishes the novel's extraterrestrial plot, prefigures its domestic settings (on Earth, in the United States, and in Washington, D.C.), and presages the protagonist's overriding skepticism with regard to manifestly economic treatments of history. These treatments, as the novel time and again makes clear, troublingly eschew academic precision in favor of facetious summary and superficial analysis.

Such dismissals of historical fact, paired with McCloud's synthetic aesthetic, are evident in the comic's opening section. To wit, *The New Adventures of Abraham Lincoln* begins with two panels of varying sizes. The first, much larger than the second, features a Photoshopped representation of the moon (with U.S. flag audaciously placed on its northern axis) and the earth (wherein the United States is portrayed in half shadow); a U.S. astronaut waves to the viewer in the foreground. A date announcement ("**Monday!**") appears above both the astronaut and the earth; an accompanying caption declares, "THE SUN DAWNS ON A MIGHTY NATION!" (1). The second panel, approximately one-fourth the size of the first, shifts the reader's perspective to a more local level, highlighting a typical morning commute to a city named Progress. The next four panels reiterate place-based emphases and confirm that the primary setting of the novel is, in fact, "THE GOOD OLD—U.S. OF A!" Other panels in the series concentrate on a domestic scene (in which a grudging child is being dressed for school by an adult) and focus on the exterior of an educational building (specifically Ben Franklin Middle School). The final panel—wherein a planetary perspective is replicated through another Photoshopped image of the earth (the United States is shown in close-up)—returns, by way of illustrative emphasis, the reader to the first image. While the panels remain by and large geographically united vis-à-vis these location-to-location moments, they fail to adhere with regard to subject (for instance, an ordering in which all aforementioned "outer space" panels are accordingly grouped). As a whole, the panels evocatively disrupt—via divergent perspective points that extend vertically and horizontally while simultaneously encompassing points local, national, and cosmological—a clearly *linear* projection. As a result, McCloud produces in *The New Adventures of Abraham Lincoln*'s initial pages a disordered comics imaginary composed of asymmetrical perspective points; such asymmetries—particularly with regard to the two "planetary" panels that showcase two different "earth" viewpoints—dislocate the viewer while anticipating the doubled frames (and doubled visions) at play in the subsequently anachronistic (or, more accurately, achronological) return of the two Lincolns.

Moving from generalized setting to more specific location, the novel quickly shifts to Ben Franklin Middle School. This institutional space, and the discussion that occurs in this space, further foreshadows the counterfeit Lincoln's inauspicious arrival. The first "institutional" panel, which takes place in a classroom, introduces the reader to the aforementioned Byron Johnson, who, bespectacled with hands folded, is represented via a close-up and bears a more than passing resemblance to his school's namesake (and, not unintentionally, carries the surname of Abraham Lincoln's second vice president and impeached successor, Andrew Johnson).[17] The following panel features an American flag, which hangs, slightly unfurled, in the classroom. This tripartite montage (uncaptioned and lacking speech clouds or thought bubbles) is completed via a return to Byron, who—armed with the same sullen expression—occupies the entirety of a narrowed panel frame (see figure 10.7). This silent three-panel sequence is disrupted by the overly cheery, red-haired Mrs. Murch, who, after morning salutations, asks her class to recite the Gettysburg Address. In response, her students—marked by languid expressions and in bored unison—slowly utter the address's well-known "Four Score and Seven Years Ago" preamble; Mrs. Murch enthusiastically interrupts their recitation, asking, "Aaah, such **grand sentiments!** Such **Wisdom!** Can anyone tell me what these words mean to **you**?" (4–5). Byron is the first to answer Mrs. Murch's decidedly banal query: the protagonist nonchalantly asserts,

Figure 10.7. Scott McCloud, *The New Adventures of Abraham Lincoln* (1998): 3.

"It means eighty-seven years ago."[18] Notwithstanding Byron's rightful rejoinder, Mrs. Murch irritably sentences the resolute protagonist to detention.

Taken together, this twenty-two-panel sequence, wherein Mrs. Murch's assertions of "wisdom" are predicated on an economical reading of the address via its most mundane date assertion, substantively captures McCloud's historically grounded critique, which (to restate) is composed of incomplete renderings of U.S. history that lay bare a wholesale reliance on empty rhetoric over a contemplation of real politics. Indeed, missing from Mrs. Murch's lesson plan and brusque characterization of "wisdom" is a comprehensive or even accurate evaluation of Lincoln's commemorative address, which at the time of its utterance eloquently recast the Civil War as an ideologically significant conflict. Integral to Lincoln's battlefield speech is a *longue durée* assessment of acute human rights violations (via forced enslavement); such characterizations render visible a discernible contradiction with the principles of egalitarianism embedded in the Declaration of Independence (embedded in the assertion that "all men are created equal"). As important, Lincoln's Gettysburg Address, movingly elegiac in scope and highly political in content, was at the time of its November 19, 1863, deliverance intended to remind audience and nation that the preservation of the Union involved profound sacrifice. Returning to *The New Adventures of Abraham Lincoln*'s comic imaginary, the absence of any mention to the nation's slaveholding past, along with Mrs. Murch's concomitant dismissal of Byron's response, strikes an even more telling chord given the protagonist's legibly racialized personhood (as an African American subject).

Such historical amnesias are replicated *and* exponentially amplified via the bizarre speech acts of the imposter Lincoln, who makes his entrance into both plot and text soon after the above-discussed scene. The sham Lincoln takes Byron, Marcie, and an unnamed blond character on a dreamlike tour of U.S. history via a magic American flag carpet ride; the tour commences in what is presumably the Mesozoic Era, given the appearance of what the charlatan executive avers are "**American Dinosaurs**" (15). The tour's historicity and veracity are at once called into question when the trickster Lincoln alleges that Mount Rushmore was a natural rock formation; such wrongheaded assessments continue with the imitation president's claim that Christopher Columbus discovered and brought "**civilization** to the land destined to be the **United States of America**" (18). Other historical inaccuracies involve Ben Franklin's electrical kite experiment (of which Thomas Edison is a key witness); contentions that Lincoln himself fought in the American Civil War; and claims that the Cold War was won with "**Bigger Bombs** and **Better Hygiene**" (24). As critical counterpoint, Byron repeatedly questions the fraudulent Lincoln's fantastical recitation of the historical past. Most telling is an exchange that occurs between the two characters about Columbus's legacy: responding to Lincoln's recapitulation of Columbus's journey to the Americas, Byron states, "**Uh-uh**. He never got further north than the **Dominican Republic** . . . Anyway, he didn't bring '**civilization**.' He just brought a lot of —". Lincoln forcibly interrupts Byron by putting his forearm over his mouth; while silencing the novel's protagonist, the charlatan president nervously states, "**Ha! Ha!** You've still got a lot to **learn**, young man!" (18–19).

These interruptions of historical fact, which time and again involve the humbug Lincoln and his sycophantic followers, persist throughout *The New Adventures of Abraham Lincoln*'s narrative, wherein bombastic assertions and unsubstantiated attacks aurally overwhelm calmly articulated, historically accurate truths. Moving beyond the comic's immediate 1990s imaginary, the phony Lincoln's violent and vehement disinclination to hear Byron's riposte about Columbus's disastrous legacy is alarmingly consistent with a contemporaneous political arena wherein so-termed dark moments in U.S. history (e.g., the forced enslavement of

African Americans, the involuntary relocation and genocidal extermination of Native peoples, the disenfranchisement of women, the compulsory internment/ incarceration of those of Japanese descent during World War II, and systemic discrimination against people of color) are—as per the flattening logics of turn-of-the-twenty-first-century colorblind multiculturalism—tactically disremembered and strategically dismissed. Situated within a problematic forgetful milieu, these interruptive disavowals potently underscore the relative nonexistence of open, progressive discourse, particularly with regard to thoughtful policy discussions and contemplative arguments about past/present racialization.

Illustratively, such discursive failures are most evident in a debate between the two Lincolns, which an unnamed television reporter, à la a heavyweight boxing match, enthusiastically names, "**Lincoln versus Lincoln**!!" According to the reporter, this late twentieth-century matchup proves "the tradition of the **Lincoln-Douglas** debates **lives again!**" Dressed in late twentieth-century attire (blue suit, red tie, and white shirt), the "real" Lincoln is initially confident that "the **people** of this great country can see beneath **shallow facades** and **trickery**" (50). Such an assertion is quickly disabused by what follows via plot and dialogue; his sepia-colored opponent (dressed in nineteenth-century garb and wearing the sixteenth president's iconic top hat) commences the debate by avowing: "**AHEM!! Well**, Mr. So-called 'Abraham Lincoln,' **I believe** in **truth, liberty**, and **the American way! I** fought the **Civil War! I freed the slaves!** I know how to **take charge**, get **tough** on crime, and make America **great** again! My question for **you**, 'sir,' is this: **Who was that woman I saw you with last night?**" (51). Given three minutes to respond by the debate moderator, the authentic Lincoln is visibly flummoxed; as he attempts to answer, the artificial Lincoln—utilizing an all-too-familiar rhetorical strategy—interrupts and quickly manipulates the exchange to his advantage. The true Lincoln, when asked if he has ever been with a woman, replies rather innocently in the affirmative. His fraudulent adversary seizes on this response, averring that "Honest Abe" has damningly admitted to "his indiscretion!!" (51). This mode of exchange—in which fact is countered by interruption and name-calling—is replicated throughout the debate, which takes place over seven pages. Rather than discuss presidential qualifications or political policy, the counterfeit Lincoln continually engages in ad hominem attacks, uses pithy clichés (e.g., "God Bless America"), and asks inconsequential questions intended to garner responses to basic historic "facts" (for instance, Lincoln's mother's maiden name). Notwithstanding the debate's palpable emptiness, and despite the fake Lincoln's overall triviality, he is nevertheless declared the debate victor. Faced with overwhelming audience approval and raucous applause, the "real" Lincoln—disillusioned and disappointed—quietly concedes.

On one level, McCloud's judicious depiction of "style over substance"—largely conveyed via the spurious Lincoln's hyperbolic claims, tangential asides, and personal attacks—incontrovertibly refracts an aforementioned late 1990s imaginary marked by conservative allegations of amoral leadership; such accusations were precipitated in part by the previously mentioned multiple sexual scandals that hit the Clinton administration and were promulgated by an increasingly reactionary Republican Congress. Hence, in its juxtaposed mediation of the first Republican president and his imposter counterpart, *The New Adventures of Abraham Lincoln* renders visible the tremendous ideological shifts within the Grand Old Party, nostalgically recollected as the "Party of Lincoln." Such purposeful doubling— between historical figure and reactionary foil, alongside participatory democratic politics and conservative moral agendas—engenders a principally pointed critique about the superficial state of U.S. affairs at the turn of the twenty-first century. On another level, as a work that is published in the midst of presidential upheaval and impending impeachment, the novel's negotiation of partisan politics necessarily accesses an analogous past that involved radical Republicans and President Andrew Johnson, who—like Clinton—faced impeachment but was ultimately acquitted.[19] While *The New Adventures of Abraham Lincoln* was admittedly published before Clinton's December 1998 congressional arraignment and February 1999 federal exoneration, it nevertheless harnesses by way of plot and characterization a pervasive parochialism constitutive of contemporaneous U.S. politics.

Past Conditional Temporalities

McCloud's novel simultaneously reconsiders and unequivocally rescripts presidential history—inclusive of impeachment and Lincoln's "larger-than-life" historical status—as a means of contemplating and critiquing the discordant one-sidedness of present-day governmentality. Notwithstanding the potent nature of such politicized critique, it is ultimately McCloud's open-ended, racially inflected evaluation of the Great Emancipator's legacy that makes clear the novel's most incisive (and, arguably, most lasting) commentary concerning dominant claims of U.S. exceptionalism that pivot on what has emerged as an indiscriminate multiculturalism. The novel concludes with the true Lincoln's marbleized transformation: the "real" president emerges in statuary form from his elevated perch in the Lincoln Memorial; he and Byron vanquish both extraterrestrial foe and imposter adversary (who, incidentally, is unmasked and revealed to be none other than another historical figure, Benedict Arnold). In addressing the crowds originally gathered to celebrate the ersatz Lincoln's triumphant return to the nation's highest office, the authentic Lincoln begins with a now updated version of the Gettysburg Address preamble: "**ELEVEN SCORE AND TWO YEARS**

AGO . . . !" (115). Initially, what follows is a verbatim recitation of the address, bringing full circle the novel's engagement with it; however, "Honest Abe" halts the recitation and confesses that he doesn't "know how to be . . . [a] symbol" and encourages his awed audience to be vigilant against hollow, symbolic evocations of the past (118–22).

The conclusion of Lincoln's speech in the final pages of McCloud's graphic narrative sets the stage for a provocative exchange between the African American protagonist and sixteenth president. When encouraged by Lincoln to ask "any question," the two share the following exchange (see figures 10.8 and 10.9):

> [BYRON]: Okay, I've got one. What did you think of the 'Negro'?
> [LINCOLN]: I thought they—that **you**—should be **free**.
> [BYRON]: But you never really **believed** we were the equal of whites, did you?
> [LINCOLN]: If I did have any doubts, Johnson, as **many** in my time **had**—then surely knowing you would have put those doubts **forever to rest**.
> [BYRON]: hmm . . . Nice dodge. But there are **some** things you told **Frederick Douglass** . . . that . . .

This dialogue is brought to a sudden close with Lincoln's "return" to a fully marble state; this return is marked by a Photoshopped image of the statue in unmoving profile. Byron's interrogation of Lincoln's racial politics is initially met with a historical relativism that quickly shifts to a present-day revisionism; however, the protagonist's refusal to accept the president's diplomatic response renders discernible through historical skepticism the limits of Lincoln's racial politics.

Byron's allusion to Frederick Douglass accesses a historic meeting between the two men involving the use of African American soldiers during the Civil War; on August 10, 1863, Douglass met with Lincoln to advocate for equal pay and protections for black troops against disproportionate Confederate retaliation. A long-standing critic of Lincoln's administration, Douglass had previously decried the sixteenth president's inaugural address in April 1861 as a speech indicative of a "complete loyalty to slavery in the slave State" (quoted in Beard). Roughly a year later, in September 1862, Douglass disparaged the president's recommendation to Chicago's black clergyman concerning a postbellum colonization of African states. By 1863, Douglass was frustrated by the slow pace of Lincoln's racial policies, to which the president conceded; even so, Lincoln maintained his nonvacillation with regard to improving the lot of both free and enslaved African Americans. The meeting ended with no true resolution: though Douglass was "not entirely satisfied with his views," he was "so well satisfied with the man" that he "determined to go on with the recruiting [of black soldiers]" (quoted in Beard).

Situated adjacent to this historical context, Byron's cross-examination of Lin-

Figure 10.8. Scott McCloud, *The New Adventures of Abraham Lincoln* (1998): 124.

Figure 10.9. Scott McCloud, *The New Adventures of Abraham Lincoln* (1998): 125.

coln's racial motivations, which likewise end unsatisfactorily and in undecided fashion, coheres with *The New Adventures of Abraham Lincoln*'s indefatigable reckoning with the nation's past. Such comic-oriented reckonings, predicated on multiple "historical contingencies" and built on other "alternatives," make urgent the novel's concluding engagement with Lowe's "past conditional temporality." Whereas this fateful exchange between Byron and Lincoln undeniably replays an earlier presidential encounter, it concomitantly engenders a moment *unthought* during the nineteenth century. Byron's trenchant criticism, which hinges on a skepticism with regard to Lincoln's racial politics, potently renders the so-known Liberator silent. It is telling that such silence is represented through the now-marbled and sedentary Lincoln, who has—by the novel's conclusion—been returned via his physical state to the status of mythic, historic icon. Even so, this silence, which interrupts the protagonist's dialogic meditation on past racial dynamics, nevertheless accentuates via abrupt conclusion the ongoing relevance of such race-based queries, prompting in the end an alternative and constructively unsettled reading of both president and nation.

NOTES

1. The Great Seal of the United States involves two distinct images: one features an unfinished pyramid with an eye; the second is a picture of an eagle with the American flag in the foreground.

2. In the introduction to *The New Adventures of Jesus: The Second Coming* (Fantagraphic Books, 2006), R. Crumb avers that Stack's antecedent work, *The Adventures of Jesus* (1964), was the "first of the notorious 'underground comix'" (9). Stack's assumed nom de plume was Foolbert Sturgeon. In the introduction that accompanies *The New Adventures of Abraham Lincoln*, McCloud thanks "the great Foolbert Sturgeon . . . whose underground classic . . . almost certainly inspired the title of this book." McCloud also highlights in his introduction the influences of Tom Hart, Jason Lutes, and Jim Woodring. In so doing, McCloud pays homage to past/present graphic artists and storytellers in a manner consistent with his critical oeuvre.

3. The Contract with America refers to a document released in tandem with the 1994 midterm congressional campaigns by the U.S. Republican Party; authored by Republicans Newt Gingrich (U.S. Representative–Georgia) and Dick Army (U.S. Representative–Texas), the Contract with America outlined conservative policies involving tax reform, governmental reduction, welfare reform, and social services reform. The campaign that ensued is credited with the Republican takeover of the House of Representatives (ending forty years of Democratic control). On December 19, 1998, President Bill Clinton was impeached by the House of Representatives on the grounds that he obstructed justice and committed perjury in denying his affair with White House intern Monica Lewinsky during a sexual harassment case involving Paula Jones. He was acquitted of these two charges by the Senate on February 12, 1999.

4. Such overt political connections within *The New Adventures of Abraham Lincoln* are evident in a scene wherein the imposter Lincoln delivers an address before the U.S. Congress: Newt Gingrich, in introducing the fake president, thanks him for his "**eye-opening tour** and for **returning** to us in our **time of need!**" In response, the alien-generated Lincoln states, "**Thanks,** Newt! Without **fine Republican leaders** like you, we'd be in **much worse shape,** let me tell you" (32).

5. "Make America Great Again" served as Donald Trump's primary campaign slogan in the 2016 presidential election.

6. For example, Marvel published eleven volumes under the auspices of the *What If* series between 1977 and 1984; these issues revised mainstream narrative arcs involving previously dead characters and those from other franchises (e.g., the inclusion of alternative superheroes in *The Avengers*). This frame was continued in the first decade of the twenty-first century with the publication of titles such as "What If Jessica Jones Joined the Avengers?" (2004). From 1942 to 1965, DC Comics published a series of comics titled *Imaginary Stories*, which analogously took place outside established hero narratives; since 1989, DC has featured an *Elseworlds* series that continues such alternative trajectories.

7. The postbellum passage of the Thirteenth, Fourteenth, and Fifteenth Amendments dismantled the tenets of forced enslavement via the abolishment of slavery, the granting of wholesale due process, and the awarding of African American male enfranchisement, respectively.

8. Such "color blindness" disavows systemic racism and instead maintains that the "problem of race" is the "problem" of individual racists.

9. The use of "speculative fiction" in conjunction with *The New Adventures of Abraham Lincoln* is not without controversy, particularly when considered alongside Margaret Atwood's oft-accessed definition about the form. In *Moving Targets*, Atwood contradistinguishes "science fiction" and "speculative fiction" by asserting that the former represents a "fiction in which things happen that are not possible today." By contrast, speculative fiction refers to work that is grounded in events that have happened or ones that could easily happen (such as ecocritical disaster or ubiquitous economic collapse). According to Atwood, "What I mean by 'science fiction' is those books that descend from H. G. Wells's *The War of the Worlds*," which features "an invasion by tentacled, blood-sucking Martians shot to Earth in metal canisters." Speculative fiction "means plots that descend from Jules Verne's books about submarines and balloon travel . . . things that really could happen but just hadn't completely happened when the authors wrote the books." Given the real-time applicability of McCloud's *The New Adventures of Abraham Lincoln*, I maintain that the work—notwithstanding science fiction elements—is ultimately a speculative fiction.

10. The comic was intended to explain the company's new search engine to would-be users. Interestingly, the comic was not originally conceptualized as a web-format work; instead, the work took a print form and was intended for journalists and bloggers. Since its "publication," the comic has been digitized and has circulated in this format. See "The Google Chrome Comic," www.scottmccloud.com/googlechrome, accessed June 2, 2016.

11. Scott McCloud, *The Sculptor* (First Second Books, 2015). According to an advance *Publisher's Weekly* review, *The Sculptor* "makes an early play for graphic novel of the year";

such a positive assessment was echoed by James Martin of the *Telegraph*, who awarded the work four stars out of five. Tim Martin, in his *Guardian* review, averred that McCloud's narrative was "inventive and touching," proving that he could "walk the walk as well as talking the talk."

12. Deemed the "Father of History" by Cicero, Herodotus was a contemporary of Socrates who broke with the Homeric tradition of epic storytelling by focusing on history as a subject worthy of investigative analysis.

13. In the section titled "Technical Notes," McCloud outlines in seven steps the process through which the comic was created. In particular, McCloud includes drafts and examples from the published work. Of particular note are McCloud's detailed descriptions of 3D modeling, lettering, tracing, and layering (inclusive of computer-generated and penciled images). As McCloud writes, "Thanks to the vagaries of print technology, I wound up with some extra pages, so for those of you who are interested in this sort of thing (or just have a little too much time on your hands) here's a basic outline of my working method. Note: There are all kinds of geeky little details that I haven't included. If you're an aspiring comics artist thinking of taking the plunge into computers, send a self-addressed stamped envelope and I'll send you a cold impersonal form letter with a complete breakdown of my working method plus several nervous, incessant reminders that *my* way is not necessarily the *right way*" (*New Adventures*).

14. Chroma key compositing is a postproduction technique that layers two images or video streams together to form a unified picture.

15. The mention of "simulacra" is admittedly and more accurately connected to Platonian philosophy.

16. The use of the "real and the fake" alludes to Frank Chin's infamous critique of Maxine Hong Kingston's inauthenticity vis-à-vis her published creative nonfiction in his essay "Come All Ye Asian American Writers of the Real and the Fake" (1991).

17. Lincoln's first vice president was Hannibal Hamlin (1861–65).

18. The "four score and seven years ago" preamble referred specifically to the July 4, 1776, Second Continental Congress's adoption of the Declaration of Independence.

19. President Andrew Johnson was the first president to face impeachment. On February 24, 1868, the president was impeached by the House of Representatives because of his refusal to abide by the Tenure of Office Act (1867); this act required the president to seek the Senate's advice and consent on cabinet appointments. President Johnson had removed Secretary of War Edwin McMasters Stanton from office and subsequently faced eleven charge articles. After three separate congressional votes, the president was acquitted of all charges on May 26, 1868.

CHAPTER 11

Fractured Innocence in G. Neri and Randy DuBurke's *Yummy: The Last Days of a Southside Shorty*

Katharine Capshaw

IN SEPTEMBER 1994, the cover story of *Time* magazine focused on the short life of a child gang member, Yummy Sandifer. Titled "Murder in Miniature," the article developed two opposing narratives about the nature of Yummy, an African American child from Chicago who murdered another young person and who was eventually executed by his gang leaders. According to *Time*, Yummy was either "a ripening thug" or a child with "a sweeter side," an example of the degradation of the inner cities or its last glimmer of innocence. For *Time*, Yummy became emblematic of the troubles of urban communities. The language of the article uses Yummy to generalize about black urban youth and its potential: "Before they grow up, these children can become walking weapons. One very mean little boy didn't grow up, so he became an icon instead. The crimes he committed—and those he suffered—shook the country's conscience in a way that violent acts with far larger body counts no longer do" (Gibbs 56). In truth, the country had been primed with narratives of the supposed intractability of urban violence since the late 1980s. Whether in coverage of the 1992 Los Angeles riots or in the proliferation of Hollywood movies about gangs, such as *Colors* (1988), *Boyz n the Hood* (1991), *New Jack City* (1991), *Juice* (1992), and *Menace II Society* (1993), American culture was immersed in stories about black urban gang life, and Yummy's loss seemed both an extreme articulation of the degradation of the inner cities and its ultimate typification. Reflecting on this historical moment of intense public assessment of inner city dynamics, G. Neri and Randy DuBurke's young adult graphic novel *Yummy: The Last Days of a Southside Shorty* (2010) considers the conflicting estimations of black male youth and aims through the form of comics to depict the insufficiency of narrative framing of racialized subjects in the 1990s. The 2010 novel recreates a historical moment fraught with bias, contradiction, and political utilitarianism.

A partially obscured image of an African American boy's face appears on the cover *Yummy: The Last Days of a Southside Shorty*. The child seems to peer over the title, his eyes shaded but staring directly out to meet the reader's gaze. His head and forehead take up half the cover and are rendered with a grainy gentleness. Speckles of ink float off of the boy's soft hair, forming a dark aureole around his head, a detail that emphasizes both the child as art object and the illustrator's hand in creating the image. The title of the novel runs across the mouth of the child, blocking our access to the full expression on the child's face and rendering him silent, guarded, and mysterious. The cover of the novel signifies many of its concerns, for engaging the gaze of this mouthless, obscured, shaded child, we are prepared to consider the novel's central attention to the failures of representation of black male childhood. Yummy's inaccessibility in this cover image, coupled with the soft granularity of DuBurke's visual style, mark the child subject as unknowable but sought after, as obscured but desired in the same moment. As we come to discover through the course of the book, this cover image was remediated from the only extant photograph of the eleven-year-old child: his mug shot. As a novel, *Yummy* is concerned with the role of photography as the physical record of this child's history, as a marker of his legibility within the public eye. An expression of state power, a mug shot inexorably locates the black child in criminality. By remediating that image on the cover, DuBurke launches the novel's pursuit of the "truth" around Yummy Sandifer and claims representational instability as the novel's governing aesthetic.

The author's note that begins the novel insists on the narrative as historically situated and the child subject as genuine. Neri explains, "Robert 'Yummy' Sandifer was a real person. He was born in 1983 and lived in the Roseland area of Chicago. At just eleven years old, Yummy became a poster child for youth gang violence in America after a series of tragic events led to his appearance on the cover of *TIME* magazine in September 1994" (3). The novel proceeds to describe Yummy's life as an abused child. Born to a teenage mother (a prostitute) and a father later incarcerated for drug violations, Yummy is beaten by his parents with electrical cords and scarred with cigarette butts, moved in and out of foster care, left with an inattentive grandmother, and finally embraced by a new family, the Black Disciples gang, because as a child he could evade serious jail time for criminal offenses. In attempting to prove his worth to the Black Disciples, Yummy accidentally shoots a fourteen-year-old girl, Shavon Dean, and spends time on the run from the police. Ultimately, in order to stop the police hunt, Yummy's gang family murders him and leaves his body in a railroad tunnel. The narrative is focalized through another eleven-year-old boy, Roger, whose brother is a member of the gang. Neri writes that he created Roger "to guide us, a means of trying to make sense of the madness that hit Roseland in the summer of 1994" (3). Roger's voice appears on the page much more often than his image, as the audience is placed into the role of scrutinizing Yummy in order to "make sense" both of his criminality and the landscape of the inner city during a historical moment of urban despair.

By offering paratextual material from the author, the novel works from the idea of history as a pursuit of memory. Walter Benjamin comments on the impossibility of historical stability in his "Theses on the Philosophy of History," explaining that "the true picture of the past flits by. The past can be seized only as an image [that] flashes up at the instant when it can be recognized and never seen again. . . . To articulate the past historically does not mean to recognize it 'the way it really was.' It means to seize hold of a memory as it flashes up at a moment of danger" (255). Neri frames his pursuit of the subject of Yummy Sandifer through images from *Time* magazine, news coverage, and the mug shot; but his impetus in claiming Yummy and the 1990s as a history to tell comes from personal memory. The author's note that closes the novel explains, "When Yummy's story first broke, I was teaching in South Central Los Angeles. Some of my students came from dysfunctional homes; some had siblings or parents in jail; some had family members who had been killed in the gang wars. . . . I remember following Yummy's story day by day" (95). Yummy becomes an image "which flashes up," to use Benjamin, in Neri's imagination, coming to stand not only for one particular child's story represented in the media but also for a larger cultural experience of the inner city that Neri witnessed as teacher.

Instead of personal memory alone, Yummy's story registers through images circulated in newspapers and magazines, and it is that story Neri both followed in the 1994 moment and continues to follow and recreate through memory. Yummy's history stands in for the history of the inner city in the 1990s, one that Neri and DuBurke, both African American men, wish to complicate for their contemporary young readership. In fact, the assumption of a child reader for the novel propels this historical narrative into the future as well as into the past. Neri and DuBurke use Roger, a child observer of Yummy, to dramatize the question of identification in the novel, for if Roger looks to Yummy as a potential version of his own life, the author also brings into relief the connection between the readership and Yummy; Neri addresses the reader in the "Author's Note," saying, "Make up your mind that you will not let your life end like Yummy's" (95). Yummy becomes a possible negative road map for a young reader, a narrative of becoming that assumes the young reader might walk in Yummy's shoes. Hillary Chute reminds us that "graphic narrative offers compelling, diverse examples that engage with different styles, methods, and modes to consider the problem of historical representation" ("Comics as Literature?" 457); Neri and DuBurke remember Yummy, research his representation through magazines and newspapers, project his life story into potentiality for the child reader, and offer a remediated version of both memory and event.

In telling of the life and death of a child gang member, Neri and DuBurke challenge the process by which male bodies become incorporated into public visual narratives; ultimately these public narratives become historical "truth," especially when considering the stigmatizing moment of the mid-1990s. Neri and DuBurke's novel thus reflects on the construction of history through nationally palatable narratives of black male identity. As an observer of Yummy, Roger seeks to understand him through the representational binaries: Is he a thug or a regular kid? Is his participation in the gang, the Black Disciples, a choice, or was his path to gang membership inevitable? Roger yearns to see Yummy as a child; in one four-panel page appearing after Shavon's murder, the images trace Yummy running through a dark tunnel, ducking to hide from a police car, and hiding inside a Dumpster. Roger narrates: "In no time the police were looking for Yummy. They called it a manhunt. But I called it a boy hunt . . . 'cause that's what he was" (45). The novel in total becomes a "boy hunt," an impossible struggle to reject Yummy's criminality and to claim him through the terms associated with child innocence. This tension between manhood and boyhood, between maturity and innocence, becomes the focal point for questions in the novel about black male youth—its value, its social legibility, its representational malleability. My argument here will begin by briefly discussing the moment of the mid-1990s in terms of representation of urban communities, and then I will move into a consideration of the purposeful destabilization of representation in the novel.

While many urban communities in the 1990s were beset by gun violence, drug escalation, and gang warfare, the media staged further aggression against black communities through representation of supposed black animality, ungovernability, and self-destruction. As Nikhil Pal Singh explains of this moment, "Invidious racial imagery of a black underclass—comprised of wild youths and welfare queens—became an effective right-wing tool to advance broad attacks on tax-supported government services and transfer payments aimed at ameliorating the social conditions of the working poor and unemployed" (10). Pessimism about the current and future state of black communities placed the blame for the state of urban neighborhoods not on the retraction of governmental social supports or the loss of public sector and manufacturing jobs or racist housing practices or unequal educational systems or any of the systemic causes of the deprivations of the inner cities, but on the failure of individual responsibility and the nuclear family.[1] As James Kyung-Jin Lee describes in *Urban Triage: Race and the Fictions of Multiculturalism*, "Cities and their residents suffered economic, political, and cultural hemorrhage so great that it constituted nothing less than a great urban crisis of terminal proportions" (xiv). But public stigmatization took shape around "welfare queens" and, to a great degree, public fear of black youth gang members.

It seems salient that President Bill Clinton used Yummy's death in order to launch neoliberal social policy. In his September 10, 1994, radio address, Clinton references Yummy's death in creating a National Gang Violence Prevention Week and, importantly, employs the child's loss as endorsement of Clinton's landmark crime bill, the Violent Crime Control and Law Enforcement Act, which was signed into law the following week. In the radio address, Clinton describes the act's effectiveness through its severe response to youth criminality: "It'll punish hardened young criminals with stronger penalties, and it will expand boot camps, drug courts, and other sanctions to stop first-time offenders from beginning lives of crime." Contemporary critics recognize that this bill, the most expansive crime act in American history, encouraged the mass incarceration of African American men, as Michelle Alexander describes in *The New Jim Crow*: "The bill created dozens of new federal capital crimes, mandated life sentences for some three-time offenders, and authorized more than $16 billion for state prison grants and expansion of state and local police forces" (56). Further Clinton policies in the 1990s aggressively persecuted communities of color: the Personal Responsibility and Work Opportunity Reconciliation Act purported to end "welfare as we know it" through changes that included a five-year limit and permanent exclusion of individuals convicted of felony drug crimes, such as marijuana possession; and the "one strike and you're out" initiative in public housing excluded and expelled people with criminal convictions, leading to homelessness and familial instability (57). Clinton's radio address also uses Yummy's loss to emphasize individual responsibility (rather than, say, structural assistance for urban communities): "We have to show our children before they enter gangs that they already belong to a community larger than themselves, in which they can feel important and serve a larger purpose. On Monday, here at the White House and at sites all across America, we'll kick off AmeriCorps, our national service effort. AmeriCorps is America at its best, people rolling up their sleeves and assuming responsibility to make our country better." The history Neri and DuBurke engage involves policy that responded to black communities through increased policing and incarceration, the withdrawal of public supports, and an emphasis on individual accountability and social isolation.

This is the landscape in which Yummy emerged into public consciousness. In Southside Chicago in the summer of 1994, his short life seemed to emblematize all the failures of the black community and was characterized through narratives that blame the disintegration of the black family and the poor behavior of adults around the child. Neri and DuBurke deploy three strategies in rewriting historical memory of the 1990s by working against the idea of a stable, knowable subject in Yummy Sandifer: the dialectical insistence on both Yummy's innocence and corruption, textual and visual remediation of public narratives, and the inadequate promise of the nuclear family as a solution to structural economic and racist deprivations.

Robin Bernstein's influential formulation of racialized innocence permits a consideration of the way the black male child subject both invokes and explodes the frameworks that shape ideas about childhood. Bernstein argues that the civil rights movement "elevated to common sense the idea that children do absorb political ideologies" but that contemporary articulations of childhood innocence smuggle in nineteenth-century associations with white virtue and disposable black bodies (242). As a graphic novel, *Yummy* employs the visual to depict these fractured points of view—of childhood at once politicized, pure, and abject—on Yummy's relationship to innocence. The narrative unsettles knowledge about black youth by repeatedly offering a visual dialectic of corruption and innocence. Our first engagement with Yummy begins with a panel containing an image of a chocolate bar emerging from a pocket (see figure 11.1). This is followed by an image of a hand ripping it open and finally an image of Yummy brutally biting into the chocolate. Thus we begin in consumption of candy, an indisputable signifier of childhood, coupled with Roger's narrative voice defining him through childhood nicknames: "His real name was Robert, but the kids in the neighborhood called him Yummy on account of he liked cookies and sweets so much" (7). But Yummy aggressively tears off the wrapper and bites fiercely into the candy, suggesting the violent characteristics that sit in tension with the narrator's insistence on his childishness. Further, the angle of the candy bar in Yummy's mouth is echoed by the position of the joint in the mouth of the older gang member in the panel that follows, connecting the two figures visually. Yummy stands under the elbow of the towering gang member, the child's eyes looking up with worry. The narration focuses on Robert's identification with Yummy: "He was my age, 11 years old. He was just a little guy, what we call a shorty, 4 feet tall and maybe 60 pounds heavy" (7). The description spotlights the physical evidence of his youth, while the image makes clear his tiny stature.

Neri and DuBurke follow this panel with one that closes up on Yummy's face, forcing the reader to peer into the shaded eyes and to question the stability of his categorization as innocent. Yummy's eyes are almost completely dark, and the toughness of his gaze contrasts pointedly with the ingenuous worry of the previous panel. The narration argues against the limitations of his size: "But sometimes he sure didn't act like it [a child]" (7). Neri and DuBurke recognize that black male children are imagined through the binary of innocent and thug and offer Yummy as a pointed example of the insufficiency of such traditional narratives; he is physically small but psychologically bold. He is a shape shifter, baby faced in one image and hard in the next. Both modes are insufficient, for Yummy is unknowable through these simplistic oppositional narratives. Michael

Figure 11.1. G. Neri (writer) and
Randy DuBurke (illustrator),
*Yummy: The Last Days of a
Southside Shorty* (2010): 7.

A. Chaney argues that "a great deal of what we might call, with reservation, an African American graphic novel aesthetic riffs on a historical archive of racist visualization" ("Is There" 73). Here, even in the most direct figuration of Yummy's gang identity, DuBurke shades and evades rather than engaging racist stereotype. He will not offer a version of the opposite pole to innocence that participates in caricature. Instead, his renderings of Yummy as "thug" insist on inscrutability rather than satirical play with stereotype.

In fact, the narrative calls us to study Yummy's face throughout in order to know him better, like Roger, who wonders about Yummy when he is on the run from the police. While the narrative at this point speaks literally about locating Yummy, the images often refuse face-on engagement with him. In a set of five panels Roger imagines Yummy's experience as a fugitive; he wonders about Yummy hiding under a bed or a bridge or even "in my own backyard" (17), and the sequence ends with Yummy's half-obscured face, focusing on eyes that look out with worry. His face is large but hidden, again insisting on the way DuBurke draws us close to scrutinize Yummy but forecloses easy visual access. When describing Yummy's escape from a juvenile detention facility, the narrative emphasizes Yummy's power alongside his elusiveness (see figure 11.2). He almost flies over the fence in the first panel, casts an enormous shadow in the second, scales walls in the third, and moves secretly past other boys in the last sequence to end up in his bed in his grandmother's house. Here DuBurke mobilizes the superhero tradition in comics in order to engage tropes of childhood. Adilifu Nama in *Super Black: American Pop Culture and Black Superheroes* explains that "whether fully realized or faintly sketched, black superheroes in comic books, cartoons, television series, and films are innovative figures that not only reimagine black folk but also stand outside dichotomous ideological constructs concerning American race relations. . . . They have also provided an escape from conventional representations of black racial identity" (154). DuBurke uses the superhero motif to escape the confines of pejorative representation of black male figures, here placing Yummy ultimately into the embrace of childhood. In the final panel, Yummy's face is entirely shaded, and the visual signifiers of innocence and youth—Mickey Mouse, the teddy bear, basketball hero worship—are offered light and clarity. The tip of a triangle moves from the middle panel to point to Mickey Mouse, over sleeping Yummy's head, emphasizing the idea of Yummy as innocent child. The line "It was the only home he knew" (31) insists both on the failure of that home—this is the place where "there were so many kids Yummy could disappear for days and nobody'd notice" (24)—and that it is the "home" that frames and insists visually on his youth and innocence.

Neri and DuBurke follow this sequence of images with the other "home" Yummy occupies with the Black Disciples. The multiple frames in this sequence

Figure 11.2. G. Neri (writer) and
Randy DuBurke (illustrator),
*Yummy: The Last Days of a
Southside Shorty* (2010): 31.

allow DuBurke to offer vacillating visual associations for Yummy. Roger brings Yummy to the headquarters of the Black Disciples where he meets its leader, Monster, a formidable character (as his name indicates) who dominates the gang through fear and intimidation. The narration moves between presenting Yummy as assertive and decisive ("I wanna be a Black Disciple!" [35] Yummy demands) and as naïve and incapable (Monster tells him to hold up his hand for the pledge, then says, "Your other right hand," as Yummy stares ingenuously up into his face) (see figure 11.3). When Yummy takes the pledge to the gang, DuBurke completely shades his eyes; in the top left panel of figure 11.3 they are blank, dark, and hard. But when in the panels that follow Monster slices Yummy's hand to perform a blood brother handshake, Yummy is wide eyed, his rounded face set in full light in contrast to the darkly shaded, joint-smoking Monster who slices his own hand cavalierly. Yummy reads almost like a toddler at the end of this sequence, his size exaggeratedly small, and he hugs Monster when Monster says, "Now we family. You work for us" (37). In this sequence, DuBurke signals to the young adult reader the infantilizing result of giving over one's power to a corrupt authority figure, one who invokes the power of "family," becoming a distorted father figure to the diminished child. When Monster gives Yummy a gun, the child replies, "Nobody never gave me nothin' before" (37). Whereas in the escape from juvenile detention, DuBurke focuses expressly on Yummy's youth, here the fusion of gang identity with Yummy's imagined place in the family becomes especially unsettling. The visual vacillation between innocence and corruption suggests our unstable perspective on his motivations, and finally DuBurke represents Yummy's movement into this "family" as an extension of the child's fundamental innocence. An expression of gentle gratitude in the hug with Monster is a profound moment of limitation; gang identity fuses articulations of innocence and of corruption in constructions of Yummy, precluding the idea that Yummy is simply a child who loves superheroes and his teddy bear. While he cannot rest entirely in innocence, his violence becomes an expression of familial devotion. The discomforting collision of these two poles enable DuBurke and Neri to meditate on the failure of representation to explain fully Yummy's involvement in violence and to articulate the lived sensibility of a child gang member.

When Yummy shoots into a crowd of gang enemies and accidentally kills Shavon, we see again the movement from darkness and inscrutability into the revelation of Yummy's boyish face. Yummy approaches the group of "his so-called rivals playing football" (40), and DuBurke places him initially with his back to the viewer, so that it is difficult even to distinguish Yummy from the other young people. When Yummy reaches for the gun, he faces out from the panel, his eyes completely obscured in black and his masklike face small and inscrutable. On the following page, when Yummy shoots Shavon, the blast from the gun is

Figure 11.3. G. Neri (writer) and
Randy DuBurke (illustrator),
*Yummy: The Last Days of a
Southside Shorty* (2010): 36.

figured as a white explosion that covers nearly all of Yummy's body. A close-up of Yummy pulling the trigger renders Yummy entirely in blackness, save a single eye that stares out to meet the viewer's gaze. In committing the criminal act, Yummy is in a way unfigured, a black outline of violence absent of particularizing detail. This style insists on the singularity of the "thug" identity, its monolithic solidness, as well as the inaccessibility of details of Yummy's criminal desire. We cannot know him or see him as anything but the black mass of "thug" when he commits violence.

This obscured face of corruption ultimately gives way to surprise, recognition, and softness (see figure 11.4). In a four-panel page, Yummy approaches Shavon. First he is entirely the figure of darkness, but visually emphasized as small in contrast with Shavon's legs stretching across the bottom of the panel. In the next panel, we see the back of Yummy's head as he looks down at the girl on the street. The last two panels balance a close-up of the victim with a close-up of Yummy, his questioning voice calling her name, "Shavon . . ." (42). His round cheeks and wide-open eyes recall the baby face of the gang initiation scene (see figure 11.5). Continuing the emphasis on his youth, the next series of panels puts the over-sized gun in contrast to the back of Yummy; in figure 11.5, the gun is nearly twice the length of Yummy's head and both are cross-hatched, setting them in relief and emphasizing the size distortion that accentuates Yummy's smallness. We then face Yummy, who takes a defensive stance with his hand in the air, and in the final panel Yummy leaves the gun on the ground and appears again on the run, in motion. Through this sequence DuBurke mobilizes the constructions attached to Yummy; the child begins as thug enveloped in darkness and impenetrability, transforms into innocent whose rounded face is stunned by Shavon's death, and finally into mystery child on the run, the subject of Roger's "boy hunt." As Derek Parker Royal argues, "Because time is spatialized in graphic narrative, where readers see the character development across panels, comics can underscore the fluidity of ethnic identity" ("Introduction: Coloring America" 10). Neither available construction of black male childhood—innocent or criminal—adequately accesses Yummy's character, as Neri and DuBurke make clear in the continual flux of representation.

If these one-dimensional categories prove inadequate to understanding urban youth, the novel also pursues media representations in order to destabilize historical "knowledge" about black communities. Neri and DuBurke remediate elements of the news coverage in order to fragment the narrative of Yummy's life. Roger, the narrator, asserts midway through the text, "I tried to find out who the real Yummy was" (63), in part so that he can chart his own sense of futurity, in part to reclaim his brother (who is also a gang member), and in part to understand his neighborhood. First, Roger collects opinions, including those

Figure 11.4. G. Neri (writer) and
Randy DuBurke (illustrator),
*Yummy: The Last Days of a
Southside Shorty* (2010): 42.

Figure 11.5. G. Neri (writer) and
Randy DuBurke (illustrator),
*Yummy: The Last Days of a
Southside Shorty* (2010): 43.

of his mother and father, whose responses depict the two poles of public opinion on Yummy. The parents appear in the middle of the page in a long rectangular panel that stretches from margin to margin. Three panels in black appear above them at the top of the page and three more below them at the bottom. The parents' opinions float in speech bubbles across the top and bottom of the page: his father says, "I blame his parents! They made that Yummy into a monster. Beat him since he was a baby. That's like packing dynamite. You hit it one too many times, and it'll blow." The mother's opinions reach across the black frames in speech bubbles at the bottom of the page: "I heard he was on a waiting list to be sent out of state because there was nowhere else to put him. So they just stuck him back out on the street. Didn't give him therapy or direction. Just a 'get out of jail free' pass" (57). In the layout of this page, the opinions become nearly decoupled from the parents, floating above and below them in panels of darkness. The effect here is to depict the transformation of opinion into narrative, for, as Roger writes down the ideas he gathers, the ideas take on space of their own and lose their tethering to a particular individual or context. The blame for Yummy's situation, whether on the family or the state, becomes a cliché circulating in the open space of the text.

The narrative then samples from news coverage of Yummy's death, with language taken directly from the *Time* article "Murder in Miniature" and from the *Chicago Tribune* in order to demonstrate the transformation of news coverage into public discourse (see figure 11.6). The first voice we hear is derived from that of an academic, an expert on gangs; the *Time* article states, "George Knox, a gang researcher at Chicago State University, believes Yummy was sent on a specific mission of revenge sparked by a drug feud or a personal insult." *Time* then quotes Knox: "'If it was just an initiation ceremony, he'd do it from a car. But to go right up to the victims, that means he was trying to collect some points and get some rank or maybe a nice little cash bonus" (59); we see that while Neri and DuBurke present an authority figure in the middle of the panel, there is no specifying information to identify the particular individual or localize the source of the opinion. The second panel also contains remediated coverage; while the *Time* article locates these quotations as coming from Cook County public guardian Patrick Murphy and Cook County circuit judge Thomas Sumner, here the combination comes from a single, white authority figure.[2] In DuBurke's illustrations, both adult male figures seem to be closed-mouthed, even as the speech bubbles float above their heads. This strategy further displaces the language of the newspaper from particular sites of authority. Even Roger's voice in the text box combines the sources of these quotations, saying, "Everyone had an opinion" (61), a gesture that levels the authoritative voices into a single mass and somewhat dismisses their perspectives as personal outlook. In terms of the transmutation

Figure 11.6. G. Neri (writer) and Randy DuBurke (illustrator), *Yummy: The Last Days of a Southside Shorty* (2010): 61.

of news coverage into a graphic novel, we also note the significance of framing. Figure 11.6 is paneled like the bars of a cell, an especially significant move given the three figures are agents of the state. The third panel pictures a woman who identifies as Yummy's lawyer and tries to connect with him by seeing him as a child, bending over to call him a "little pumpkin" (61).[3] This perspective bears a little more visual weight, as the woman's face is unobscured, her body is larger and more central than those of the male figures, and her lips part as though she is speaking the words. In this way the page subtly endorses the lawyer's estimation of Yummy's child status.

The next page continues to amass public assessments of Yummy (see figure 11.7), including information drawn from psychiatric evaluations. The top two panels represent the materialization of psychological reports on Yummy; the first language is taken from *Time*'s coverage of Yummy's psychological assessment, and the second is taken from the narrative voice of the article. The bottom of this page contains the voices of politicians. The first provides a close-up, distorted image of the face of the mayor of Chicago, Richard Daley, who notoriously stood over the body of Sandifer and offered the insufficient explanation that he "fell through the cracks" and his inadequate retrospective projection of what might have been if the state had done its job (see Daley). The second and third panels render the president, Bill Clinton, whose radio address on September 10, 1994, used Yummy's death to endorse neoliberal social policy. By examining Clinton's original speech, it becomes apparent that Neri and DuBurke refuse to represent the stigmatization of the black family. Clinton's original address contains the following about children in cities:

> All too many are growing up without the values of mainstream society, without knowing the difference between what's right and wrong, and without believing that it makes a difference whether they do right or wrong. . . . The number of gang homicides has nearly tripled since 1980 in Robert and Shavon's hometown. And all across America, too many decent people have felt the anguish of losing a child to the meanness of the streets. At younger and younger ages, boys and girls are turning to gangs and to guns. For a child without an involved family, a gang offers a feeling of belonging. For a young person without options for tomorrow, a gang offers a sense of purpose. For anyone born in a home barred and chained off from danger, life on the streets seems like a taste of freedom they've never known.

Clinton's language bears a sense of near inevitability to black child gang involvement and places responsibility for that development on the shoulders of the black family. Clinton offers first the generalization about children growing up "without the values of mainstream society," then he moves to describing children "without an involved family," and he concludes by describing children "in a home barred and chained off from danger" as also heading toward gang violence. No matter whether the black child's family fails him or protects him, gang life appears inevitable. In their remediation of Clinton's speech, Neri and DuBurke purposefully excise defamations of the black family, focusing instead on the facts of homicide rates and the idea of freedom offered by the streets. In the lower right panel, the end of this sequence, Roger's hand clicks off the radio, indicating the black boy's refusal to engage further the defamations of authority figures and the government. Concluding with the politicians and Roger's decision to turn off the media seems entirely apt, as Roger takes control of the narrative, reflecting on the multiple public iterations of Yummy's identity. Here we note, too, that for a young adult audience the novel suggests the need for a critical and reflective perspective on public narratives of black youth. Young people, Neri and DuBurke seem to suggest, have the power both to piece together the stories that describe black urban life and to refuse those stories by turning to the authority of lived experience.

Roger interprets Yummy through his personal experience on the terrain of childhood (see figure 11.8). In figure 11.8, Roger fuses the multiple Yummys, his body covering most of the page. He contains various conceptions of Yummy, each of which insist on the gang member's status as a child and reshape criminality to reflect Roger's experience in the school yard. Roger wonders whether the "real" Yummy was the child who stole from him or the kid who smiled at him. By shutting off the adult media and governmental assessments of Yummy, Roger can assert his own frame of reference as a young person, encompassing and embracing Yummy visually within his own black body spread across the page. In the last image, at the bottom right, Roger imagines himself as a double of Yummy. This move reflects Neri and DuBurke's construction of a child reader who imagines himself through Yummy's story. The lines of darkness fall across Yummy's face, anticipating later images of the child in hiding, peeking out from his sites of refuge through venetian blinds. Here Roger's body becomes the darkness, the safe place of hiding, for Yummy as defined as a youth and as similar to the narrator. In contrast to the voices of media and authority that immediately preface this page, the body of Roger, holding his pencil in order to work out his own opinion about Yummy, becomes a refuge for black innocence.

Neri and DuBurke return to a reflection on the way public discourse shapes expectations for black child life by framing Yummy publically through his mug shot. We first see the mug shot on television as Roger and his family watch coverage of the killing. As opposed to the shifting evocations of Yummy's character offered by DuBurke, the mug shot pins him down in the media as debased. It is visually contrasted with the image of Shavon as eighth-grade graduate, which follows the mug shot by just a few panels and also appears on the television screen.

Figure 11.7. G. Neri (writer) and
Randy DuBurke (illustrator),
*Yummy: The Last Days of a
Southside Shorty* (2010): 62.

Figure 11.8. G. Neri (writer) and
Randy DuBurke (illustrator),
*Yummy: The Last Days of a
Southside Shorty* (2010): 63.

Later in the narrative, public articulations of Yummy intersect with private memorial when we learn that at Yummy's funeral this is the only extant image of the child. The mug shot appears as a placard, blown up and sitting on an easel, next to Yummy's coffin. Like the remediation of news coverage, the novel reshapes the signification of the image. Instead of criminality, the mug shot at the funeral suggests the lack of love, of parental attention, offered Yummy and places him even more squarely into the position of neglected child.

A full-page image follows the mug shot panels, one that again samples the language of the *Time* magazine article, creating an image that reshapes documentary photography and journalism to reanimate the historical record and engage the current moment (see figure 11.9). Much of the language on the page derives directly from "Murder in Miniature," which describes the fact that mothers in the community brought their children to look at Yummy in the coffin in order to discourage them from joining gangs. Roger employs the language of one of the children in the *Time* article who is afraid of falling into the coffin because of his mother's urgent pushing. However, the child in the *Time* article emphasizes the finality of Yummy's loss: "'Some kids said Yummy looked like he was sleeping, but he didn't look like he was sleeping to me.' What exactly then did he look like? 'Kind of like he was gone, you know?'" (55). In Neri and DuBurke's version, Roger instead concludes the page with the vision of Yummy "like a little kid sleeping" (87), emphasizing a more sentimental, less severe perspective on the body of the child, willing him into sweet, peaceful slumber. The teddy bear in the coffin underlines the effect.

With this touch DuBurke, in fact, reshapes the central image from the *Time* coverage, placing children around Yummy and the stuffed animal alongside him as did the magazine. But the image in the *Time* essay depicts children physically much closer to the body, with fingers outspread to touch Yummy's face. These are not gestures of affection, however, but as the article describes, child hands seek out "stitches on his face where the bullets fired into the back of his head had torn through." Just as Neri and DuBurke diminish the child's perspective on the loss of Yummy from the original, here they eliminate the gruesome scrutiny of his wounds, evidencing the children's visceral attachment to the violence inflicted on Yummy's body. As Chaney reminds us, "Informed by historical structures of spectacle, the display of black bodies undergoes a process of media negotiation in graphic novels by black authors and writers" ("Drawing" 176). We see Neri and DuBurke rendering Yummy through the lens of innocence, finally, rather than through corruption. Nancy Pedri suggests scholars have not theorized in enough depth about the role of a range of visual modes to the graphic novel: "Given the growing number of graphic narratives that incorporate a variety of different types of images into their visual track, investigations into intermodality and its

Figure 11.9. G. Neri (writer) and
Randy DuBurke (illustrator),
*Yummy: The Last Days of a
Southside Shorty* (2010): 87.

implication for the reading of graphic narratives need to be expanded beyond an overarching approach to the interaction of drawn images and written words" (2). Considering the remediation of the documentary photograph in *Yummy* permits us to recognize the authors' purposeful reshaping of the narratives available to black childhood. Instead of yoking images of the guileless innocent with the thug, as J. William Spencer reminds us is the typical mode of media reporting on youth criminality,[4] in the funeral scene Neri and DuBurke reshape the historical record, emphasizing both the personal through Roger's sympathetic identification with Yummy and an idealized instantiation of Yummy frozen in death and in a state of childhood innocence perhaps only permanently accessible to black children when they are imagined through loss.

Neri's personal investment in this historical moment is apparent since he taught in South Central Los Angeles schools at the time of Yummy's murder. In fact, he reiterates the preacher's words (from figure 11.9) in his concluding author's note: "So, was Yummy a cold-blooded killer or a victim? The answer is not black-and-white. Yummy was both a bully *and* a victim—he deserves both our anger and our understanding. Other answers, however, may be clearer. Like the preacher at Yummy's funeral said: make up your mind that you will not let your life end like Yummy's. Easier said than done, no doubt. But if you can find a way to make the choice of life, then other decisions may be easier. Choose wisely" (95). Neri and DuBurke see a continuity between the past and present and experience history with the stakes of the present in mind. I would suggest, however, that in grappling with the criminality of the subject, Neri is more invested in youth than in Yummy's criminality, calling him a "bully," as on the school yard, and rejecting the extreme of "cold-blooded killer." The note's didacticism tilts the text toward an instrumentalist perspective on history, one that starts from Benjamin's idea of narrating history as a "means to seize hold of a memory as it flashes up at a moment of danger" but pushes the idea of history as a flash of memory, and image, toward a moralism that depends on the innocence of a (dead) black child and urges contemporary youth to prize their own lives similarly (255).

If Yummy's characterization tilts toward innocence in the end, who is to blame for his loss? A central issue for the novel as a historical narrative of the mid-1990s is the role of the family to gang violence. Min Hyoung Song in *Strange Future: Pessimism and the 1992 Los Angeles Riots* explains that conservatives attributed the decline of the inner cities in part to "the corruption of the nuclear family" (19), a factor that Neri and DuBurke consciously engage in depicting the life of an eleven-year-old. Invoking and ultimately disrupting the idealization of a nuclear family, a "home," that Yummy seeks to access, Neri and DuBurke combat the idea that a two-parent, heteronormative family would be an easy solution for the deprivations experienced by urban youth.

In the moments before being picked up by the Black Disciples and murdered, Yummy asks a neighbor and her family if they will pray with him. Yummy says, "Dear Lord . . . I don't know why everyone hates me so much. I just wanna go home. Can't you take me home, God? I didn't mean to hurt Shavon." The neighbor joins him, saying, "Lord, please watch for his soul. He is too young to know better, and he never had guidance from anybody. Amen" (72). There is no home on earth for Yummy, his call, "Can't you take me home, God?" answered in his death. The neighbor ties his lack of culpability to his rootlessness, and at this point it seems as though Neri and DuBurke are arguing for family as a solution for gang youth. The narrative extends this embrace of family in the scene of Yummy's death in the railroad tunnel, for Yummy's last word ingenuously, hopefully calls for the head of his new "family": "Monster?" (82). The novel ironically invokes home and family as a fundamental need for black youth.

But in the example of Roger's brother, Gary, the book undermines the idea of the nuclear family as a straightforward solution to gang violence. On the last pages of the book, Gary, a member of Yummy's gang, meets his parents and Roger at the site of Shavon's memorial. He appears diminished to Roger, transformed from brute to penitent son: "He didn't look so tough anymore" (92). When Gary's father asks, "What about the Disciples?" Gary responds, "I just wanna come home is all," and the father answers, "Let's go home then" (93). Gary's redemption is predicated on a return to the supposed safety of his two-parent family. The book seems to reify the rationales offered by government and media in the 1990s, that the solution to the problems of the inner city rests on personal, individual, moral choices. In some sense, then, the end of the book seems to make material the idea that the heteronormative nuclear family is the city's salvation. But DuBurke's visual cues are much more ambivalent. On the last page of the novel we hear Roger's insistence on "fighting for" family; but interspersed between his words are panels that depict the South Side Chicago skyline. This last page focuses initially on the two-parent/two-child family, then narrows in on the boys and places buildings between the two figures. The neighborhood literally moves in between Roger and his brother in the penultimate panel, with both faces half obscured and Gary looking away, peering outside the confines of the family car (see figure 11.10). The last panel, then, arrives in tension and indecision, as the hopeful language chafes against the final image, which erases the family and pictures the neighborhood entirely. As Royal explains about the significance of layout to ethnic graphic novels, "So the spaces of graphic storytelling—the word balloons, the frame of the individual panels, the gutter (the 'blank' space between panels), the strip (the horizontal ban of panel arrangement), and the page layout itself—foreground relational perspective between and among individual subjects. Such visual strategies are an essential component of multiethnic graphic narrative, writing that by its very nature relies upon themes of cultural context and contingency to generate meaning" ("Introduction: Coloring America" 10–11). In terms of *Yummy*, the relationship between the figures and skyline stresses the landscape of social complication. Roseland gets the last visual word, so to speak, and the book rests in a structural critique of the neighborhood rather than of the supposed failures of black families.

These final pages also destabilize the idea of "home" as the safe haven of a heteronormative two-parent family by echoing conspicuously the opening sequence to the novel. Roger begins the novel by constructing "home" as Roseland—his neighborhood—not his nuclear family. He contrasts the public image of Chicago, land of Oprah Winfrey and the Bulls, with that of Roseland, where children risk being shot at night. Roger explains: "Sometimes it feels like a war movie. But this ain't no movie. This is my neighborhood—Roseland—home sweet home" (6). The panel at the bottom of the page is dominated by a sign reading "Welcome to Roseland," with a line through "Roseland" and the word "Hell" scrawled under it. This is also the neighborhood in which Shavon dies just outside her two-parent family's house. This death sequence offers particularly potent critique of the idea that the family insulates against gang violence. In the first two panels, Shavon's parents burst out of the doorway to the family's home, their mouths open with shock. The second panel pictures Shavon's mother in grief. Framed tightly lengthwise, the image cuts off the sides of the mother's head in order to focus on her wide-open mouth and the halo of black ink spreading upward from the top of her hair, a sign of the encroaching darkness of grief and an echo, perhaps, of her daughter's blood spatter. The three-panel page concludes with the parents set entirely in blackness, cradling their dead child. Arguing both that the city contains intact families and that the nuclear family cannot protect young people from violence, Neri and DuBurke forestall any straightforward political reading of the history of the inner cities, offering instead a structural critique of the neighborhood itself as a site of violence. Just as Neri and DuBurke are more concerned with the failure of narrative paths in depicting Yummy than actually delving into his psychology, the novel does not pursue the economic, social, and political reasons for the neighborhood's violent dynamic. Instead, the last panel of the novel offers us the skyline rather than the neighborhood's inner life, as we stand outside and face the insufficiency of narrative to understanding fully the moment of the 1990s in America's cities.

At Yummy's funeral, Roger's father throws into the trash the *Time* magazine issue that contains "Murder in Miniature" and features Yummy's mug shot on its cover. "This is the only way someone from our neighborhood is ever gonna be on the cover of 'TIME,'" he suggests (89), a move that highlights the novel's argument for the insubstantiality of the historical record in telling the history of

Figure 11.10. G. Neri (writer) and
Randy DuBurke (illustrator),
*Yummy: The Last Days of a South-
side Shorty* (2010): 94.

urban youth. By depicting *Time* in the trash can, Neri and DuBurke insist on the role of the imagination in recreating historical memory and also echo the notion of child agency evidenced in the moment when Roger turns off the voices on the television and radio and turns to his own authority. As Chute argues, "Graphic narrative suggests that historical accuracy is not the opposite of creative invention; the problematics of what we consider fact and fiction are made apparent by the role of drawing" ("Comics as Literature" 459). *Yummy* also reminds us, as Chaney notes, of "the graphic novel's mechanics for recirculating, re-framing, and re-animating" ("Drawing" 180) in order to make explicit the constitution and shaping of history. *Yummy* uncovers the way in which we typically read black childhood through conflicting concepts, constructions that reveal the unsteady value of black children's lives in American culture. The novel involves the young reader, too, in critically examining those constructions and in embracing child narrative authority. *Yummy's* story makes clear the limitations of historiography, arguing that black male childhood becomes legible through only a few unsatisfactory narrative pathways: either naïve innocence, profound violence, or death.

NOTES

1. Regarding pessimism, Min Hyoung Song characterizes the era as follows: "This was a moment with little optimism about the future, a general sense of futility about the possibility for positive change, and, as such, a *vulnerability* to arguments for greater state repression as a necessary defense against the triptych sign of national decline (the diminished economic fortunes of a white middle-class, the daily misery of poor urban blacks, and alien invasion)" (25). Nikhil Pal Singh explains, "In a sweeping rollback of civil rights–era jurisprudence, in the 1990s the U.S. Supreme Court overturned minority-business set-aside programs, minority voter redistricting efforts, and court-ordered desegregation mandates. Meanwhile, the new Democratic administration of President Bill Clinton went his predecessors one better, promising to 'end welfare as we know it.' Both the legal decisions and the policy shift were filtered through the logic of neo-liberal discipline that vehemently opposes government intervention into the 'natural' workings of the marketplace, implicitly reopening an expanded field for the play of 'private' racist beliefs and practices" (11).

2. From Nancy Gibbs's "Murder in Miniature": "'If ever there was a case where the kid's future was predictable, it was this case,' says Cook County public guardian Patrick Murphy. 'What you've got here is a kid who was made and turned into a sociopath by the time he was three years old.' . . . 'I see a lot of Roberts,' says Cook County Circuit Judge Thomas Sumner, who handled charges against Yummy for armed robbery and car theft. 'We see this 100 times a week,' says Murphy" (57).

3. From Gibbs's "Murder in Miniature": "Ann O'Callaghan, a lawyer and assistant public guardian, met Yummy once, last December in court. She was astounded by his size and

demeanor. 'Some of these kids we represent are ominous characters. But I had to bend over, and I was like, "Hi! My name is Ann, and I'm your lawyer." I couldn't believe it.' Yummy wasn't the least bit intimidated by the courtroom. 'It was like he was just sitting there waiting for a bus'" (58).

4. Spencer argues that "media constructions of violent youth . . . couple images of depravity with images of youthful innocence" (60).

CHAPTER 12

Art Spiegelman and the Caricature Archive

Jennifer Glaser

AS A NUMBER OF CRITICS have noted, Art Spiegelman's decision to use animals to represent national, racial, and ethnic identity in *Maus* (1986, 1991) dramatizes both the role of the animal in the long history of anti-Semitic caricature and the ethical (and representational) problems attendant to racial essentialism.[1] Few scholars have extended this analysis of race or racial carica- ture into Spiegelman's post-*Maus* work. From his critique of racism in Robert Crumb's representation of African American identity to his investment in the aftermath of the Danish Muhammad and French *Charlie Hebdo* cartoon con- troversies, Spiegelman has manifested a profound engagement in investigating the relationship between comics and race, as well as the prominence of racial caricature in the history of comics. This essay looks at the role of what I call "the caricature archive" in the artist and critic's work from his animalian compositions in *Maus* to his work in *In the Shadow of No Towers* (2004) and in his later critical writings about caricature and race. In conducting this overview of Spiegelman's career, I provide a wider meditation on the complex inheritance of caricature for comics artists, arguing that this grappling with the history of racial (and often racist) visual representation is a constitutive feature of the comics medium and one that makes it uniquely situated to highlight the continuing importance of the visual to how we imagine and interpret race.

Prominent critics, from Hillary Chute to Charles Hatfield, have asked how we might evaluate comics and graphic narrative as a medium apart from other media, rather than merely another genre of literature or visual art.[2] One an- swer to this multivalent question is that comics are inscribed with history, every stroke of the drawing pencil shadowed by an unavoidable past composed of the choices made by previous artists. Comics are, by their very nature, palimpsests, artifacts of the caricature archive as much as they are products of the present. As a cartoonist who strategically employs caricature in his own work and a cartoon historian who explores the role of caricature in the work of other artists, Spiegel- man draws our attention to this defining characteristic of comics and its power to shed light on race, representation, and the continuing power of stereotype in contemporary culture.

Spiegelman has been criticized in recent years for "no longer drawing comics," most notably by his friend and fellow comics artist R. Crumb. I would argue that, although he no longer draws as many comics as he once did in the conventional sense, he maintains an even more important role in the evolution of the medium: that of a historian in the field of cartooning. If his work in *Maus* was archival in part because it drew on extensive research into the Holocaust, as well as the material remnants of his family's personal history, his more recent work has drawn him into a different set of archives—this one aesthetic.[3] Spiegelman's long-standing preoccupation with formal questions, beginning with his exploration of the limitations of the comics medium in the underground journal *Raw*, is intimately tied with an overarching historicizing impulse in his work that provides us, as critics, with a means of seeing the deeply political work that comics can do—particularly around issues of race and representation. Spiegelman is adamant that comics artists be aware of their aesthetic antecedents, as well as the ways in which comics, as an art of exaggeration, trades in stereotype. As the artist put it in a 2000 interview, "Almost by definition, cartooning tends to use stereotypes, you're dealing with a recognizable iconic picture. It ends up saying, 'yes, those Chinese are really good at laundry, ha.' But it doesn't tell you how to get past that. Much harder to take that stereotype and do some kind of judo to it that actually undoes it. And when you do, then you're in dangerous territory" (Spiegelman, "Art Spiegelman" 221). By insisting on self-reflexivity and historical awareness in his art, Spiegelman finds a way for stereotype—and its visual cousin, caricature—to become "dangerous" to the very assumptions on which it relies for its power.

Maus, Race, and Caricature

No appraisal of Spiegelman's investment in race or caricature can avoid the centrality of *Maus* to his oeuvre. *Maus*, serialized in *Raw* from its second issue onward, was published as a stand-alone volume in 1986 (with the appropriate subtitle of "My Father Bleeds History"), with the second volume following in 1991. The first volume sets up the narrative's main characters: Art's Auschwitz-survivor father, Vladek; his beloved, now-dead mother, Anja; and cartoonist Art, as well as the triangulated tension between the three that will propel the story forward. If much of book 1 of *Maus* revolves around an absent archive—specifically Art's mother's diaries that were destroyed by Vladek after her suicide—in "And Here My Troubles Began," *Maus*'s second book, Spiegelman offers his readers another archive, one that is a panoramic history of his own aesthetic and ethical processes. One way to read book 2 of *Maus* is as a metacommentary on book 1, a proto-*MetaMaus* of sorts. In addition to the famous images of Spiegelman and his drawing table balanced precariously atop the bodies of those who died in the camps, Spiegelman provides a variety of other images that highlight his own agency and role as artist in the second volume of *Maus*, published five years after the first appeared to widespread acclaim (*Maus* Book II, 41).

The opening pages of book 2, in which he provides a lengthy account of his process and the role of animal avatars within it, are particularly important to the wider world of *Maus* and Spiegelman's development as an artist within it. Spiegelman gives the reader a peek at his spiral-bound sketchbook, its lined pages featuring images of a striped-shirt-clad moose, poodle, frog, rabbit, and mouse (11) (see figure 12.1). In a panel that overlaps the sketchbook, Art's wife, Françoise, here depicted as a mouse, as she has been throughout the pages of *Maus*, book 1, enters the scene and asks her husband what he is doing. "Trying to figure out how to draw you," he replies (11). Traditionally, these opening pages have been read as an attempt to expose and satirize the architecture of national, religious, and racial thinking. Spiegelman's comic meditation on whether to represent his wife and artistic collaborator, Françoise, as a mouse like himself (despite not having been born a Jew), a frog (as a caricature of her French heritage), or any one of a host of other animals dramatizes the absurdity of essential concepts of identity. Françoise believes she should be depicted as a mouse, but Art worries that she can't be a "true" mouse because of her French, Christian heritage. When Françoise suggests a "bunny rabbit," Art demurs, saying, "The bunny rabbit is too sweet and gentle . . . I mean the French in general. Let's not forget the centuries of anti-Semitism. . . . I mean, how about the Dreyfus affair? The Nazi collaborators?" (11). Françoise avers: "But if you're a mouse, I ought to be a mouse too. I converted didn't I?" (11). Françoise and Art's conflict over questions of representation exposes the pitfalls of Spiegelman's decision to allegorize groups of people as different species of animals (as well as his awareness of these pitfalls). Moreover, their argument suggests that Spiegelman's ideas about how to represent national identity collide with the idea of Jewishness as a racial identity, one that locates Jewishness in matrilineal descent, rather than consensual relations, such as marriage or conversion, a tension at the heart of *Maus* as well as Nazi racial policy.[4]

In the hands of master ironist Spiegelman, the exegesis in the scenes is undermined by the images that surround it. After all, the drawings make it clear that Spiegelman's choice has already been made. The conversation between Art and Françoise takes place in the present tense of the page, but, since both artists are portrayed as mice, it renders the conversation as part of the book's (and the author's) own history. At the same time, I would contend that these famous pages also represent and provide a gloss on another history, this one a distinctly visual one. This passage marks a turning point in Spiegelman's commitment to explor-

Figure 12.1. Art Spiegelman,
Maus, book 2 (1991): 11.

ing not only the limits of the comics form but also its aesthetic and compositional history. Thinking of this scene as an example of Spiegelman's engagement with comics history—particularly, the history of caricature and its role in comics—allows us to reevaluate one of the central conceits in the Holocaust narrative: Spiegelman's use of animals to represent Germans, Jews, and Poles. This choice has been at the center of conversations about *Maus* since its publication.

Other comics artists, such as Harvey Pekar, have criticized Spiegelman's choice to use animals to represent the conflict. In 1986, soon after book 1's publication, Pekar wrote: "I do not have general objections to anthropomorphism, but I do object to the way Spiegelman uses it. Art stereotypes nationalities, Orwell doesn't. Orwell's pigs don't represent a whole nation." Arguing against such criticism, Hatfield suggests that the animal metaphor works by "defamiliarizing the already familiar details of the Holocaust" (140). Spiegelman himself has contextualized the animal metaphor via the Nazi portrayal of Jews as vermin in propaganda of the time, such as the anti-Semitic film *Der ewige jude* (The Eternal, or Wandering, Jew), which opens with an image of pestilent rats running amok before moving to discuss the similar pathology of the bestial Jew (Spiegelman and Chute 114) (see figure 12.2). In contrast to Orwell's more archetypal use of bestial allegory in *Animal Farm*, Spiegelman's animal metaphors are rooted in history, used with a nod to particular instances of visual representation.

While Spiegelman's work has long been read through this interest in the archive of anti-Semitic propaganda, it has not been placed within the artist's particular interest in the history of comics and visual culture. We can read the opening scene of *Maus*'s second volume not simply as another example of Spiegelman's self-reflexivity but, instead, as a manifestation of his particular interest in the caricature archive and its repercussions for artists, such as Spiegelman himself, who are interested in working against the flattening effect of racial caricature. In a 2001 interview with Lawrence Weschler, Spiegelman averred that "if Maus is about anything . . . it's the critique of the limitations—the sometimes fatal limitations—of the caricaturizing impulse. I did my damnedest not to caricature anybody in this book—and anybody who caricatures my efforts in any other lights, that's their problem, not mine" ("Pig Perplex" 233). As we will explore, this "caricaturizing impulse" has a particular importance in comics (and, particularly, American comics) history.

Throughout *Maus*, Spiegelman strategically uses caricature—the Polish pigs (dubbed "*schwein*" by Germans), the Jewish vermin—so as to expose "the sometimes fatal limitations of the caricaturizing impulse," particularly in German visual propaganda of the period. However, Spiegelman's focus on racial caricature in *Maus* extends beyond his exploration of Nazi racial caricature into the particular history of race—and racial stereotype—in American representation. Famously,

Figure 12.2. Mjölnir [Hans Sch-
weitzer], poster for the film *Der
ewige Jude* [The Eternal or Wandering Jew], directed by Fritz Hippler,
1940, U.S. Holocaust Memorial
Museum, courtesy of Museum für
Deutsche Geschichte.

he highlights the painful disjuncture between Vladek's experience as a victim of Nazi racism and his experience of race in America. In one scene, Françoise and Art drive Vladek to get groceries, and they pick up a hitchhiker on the way home (see figure 12.3). The hitchhiker, an African American man (drawn as a black dog to symbolize both his racial and national identity), terrifies Vladek, who spends the entire ride home anxiously waiting for the man to steal his groceries. During the drive home, the hitchhiker sits in the back seat framed by his position in between Françoise, Art, and Vladek—and their varying expectations of his behavior. When Françoise angrily comments on Vladek's racism, saying, "How can you, of all people, be such a racist! You talk about blacks the way the Nazis talk about the Jews," Vladek remarks, "I thought really you are more smart than this, Françoise. It's not even to compare the shvartsers and the Jews!" (99).

Vladek is not the only one to note—and resist—the comparison between Jews and African Americans that *Maus* makes. Given that so much of *Maus* takes place in America, as Art attempts to make sense of his own place in Vladek's story and the Jewish (American) narrative of the Holocaust, it is difficult not to read Spiegelman's magnum opus as being as much about Jewish American identity and race as the experience of Jews in Europe during the Holocaust. In his penetrating critique of identity politics, *The Trouble with Diversity*, Walter Benn Michaels singles out *Maus* (along with Philip Roth's *The Plot against America*) as a work that problematically racializes Jews in America. He writes that "in Spiegelman's America, every immigrant group—German cats, Polish pigs, even blacks—has been assimilated, with the exception of the Jews! The German cats are now dogs, the Polish pigs are now dogs, blacks are black dogs, but the Jews are still mice. It's almost as if the Nazi racial system were an American rather than a European phenomenon" (53). This move, according to Michaels, displaces African American suffering onto the bodies of Jews and reifies Jewish uniqueness.[5] Michaels reads the serial work as a form of unethical appropriation, marking the artist as one of a species of Jewish artists bent on borrowing African American otherness to cement Jewish uniqueness in America.

Michaels's critique is fascinating but shortsighted, for a number of reasons. It suggests that Spiegelman was not conscious of the ways in which *Maus* mixes Nazi and American racial politics and ideology. However, in recent interviews, in the foreword to the rereleased *Breakdowns*, and in *MetaMaus*, his retrospective glance at the creation of *Maus*, Spiegelman makes it clear that the history of race and racial caricature in America shadowed Vladek's story from its inception. He relates that the idea for using mice for *Maus* "started with me trying to draw black folks" (Spiegelman and Chute 111). When cartoonist Justin Green asked him to submit comics to an anthology of animal-centered comics, called *Funny*

Figure 12.3. Art Spiegelman,
Maus, book 2 (1991): 99.

Aminals, Spiegelman decided that he "could do a strip about the black experience in America, using an animated cartoon style. I could draw Ku Klux Kats and an underground railroad and some story about racism in America" (112). These images would use the exaggerated minstrel style of many early American cartoons in a manner that influenced the cartoonish style of the caricatures in *Maus*.

In the foreword to the reprint of *Breakdowns: Portrait of the Artist as a Young %@)&*!*, published in 2008, Spiegelman devotes two strips, "Pop Art" and the cheekily named "Mouse: Birth of a Notion," to telling how *Maus* came to employ animals as its central device. Although also described in *MetaMaus*, Spiegelman's collaboration with Chute, in *Portrait* it has the added emotional resonance of being framed as a story that Spiegelman tells his own disinterested young son, Dash. This strip is important in the Spiegelman oeuvre not only because it relates *Maus*'s natal myth but also because it links *Maus* to a uniquely American visual and racial history, while illustrating the profoundly archival and self-reflexive nature of Spiegelman's work. Pointing to an immense statue of Vladek, Art tells his son, "Hey! See that thing back there? It's a monument I built to my father . . . I never dreamed it would get so big!" (12). "It all started when my pal, Justin Green, invited me to do a short strip for an underground comic called *Funny Aminals*" (12). Above an image of Crumb's disturbing and lascivious cover, we hear the opening of Spiegelman's story: "Robert Crumb himself was gonna do the cover . . . this was a big deal" (12). This invocation of Crumb is not insignificant. Apart from being the anointed father of the underground comix movement and a powerful influence on Spiegelman and other comics creators of the time, Crumb plays a part in the vexed racial history of contemporary comics, as we have seen. The title of the next strip, "Mouse: Birth of a Notion," appears over an African American caricature that resembles early depictions of African Americans in newspaper strips, such as Winsor McCay's Jungle Imp in *Little Nemo* (12).

Visiting filmmaker Ken Jacobs's class at Harpur College in Binghamton, New York, in 1971, Spiegelman comes upon an idea for "Funny Aminals" (13). Jacobs screens silent films of actors in blackface, enacting the grossest racial stereotypes, alongside early American cartoons, such as Walt Disney's Mickey Mouse. Jacobs's words are superimposed over two panels of cinematic images (see figure 12.4). "So, what's the difference between those anthropomorphic animals and these subhuman minstrels?" he asks, while standing in front of an image of actors in blackface playing music and wearing tiny hats and buffoonishly large ties (13). Just beneath this image, his disembodied voice floats above an image of Mickey Mouse to aver: "And this jazz age Mickey Mouse is just Al Jolson with big ears."

Spiegelman is shown dashing out of the classroom, his eyes big, the image

Figure 12.4. Art Spiegelman, *Breakdowns: Portrait of the Artist as a Young %@&*!* (2008): 13.

of Mickey Mouse still dwarfing him. Excitedly, he decides on the topic of his strip for *Funny Aminals* and shouts: "—race in America! . . . cats with burning crosses! . . . lynched mice! . . . Ku Klux Kats!" (13). Moments later, this reverie is interrupted when Spiegelman encounters a black man, who has heard his ranting about Ku Klux Kats and shoots the artist a confused look. Interestingly, at this encounter with a black body, Spiegelman comes up against the limits of his own racial imagination. In the next panel, which shifts from full color into a melancholic black and gray, Spiegelman is being trailed by rats. "Shit! I know bupkis about being black in America! Bupkis," he says. Beneath this image and word bubble, Spiegelman places a rectangular insert—written in an editorial tone—with the words: "Then Hitler's notion of Jews as vermin offered a metaphor closer to home" (13). It is significant that "the birth of a notion" is the title of the strip and its subject. The vignette itself is a tale of origins that borrows from film history and explicitly nods to the "miscegenated" origins of both American cartooning and American film history. Ken Jacobs makes a link between blackface performers, such as Al Jolson, and iconic twentieth-century American cartoons, most notably Mickey Mouse. What neither Jacobs nor Spiegelman acknowledges here are the links between blackface performance and Jewish identity. Spiegelman abandons the idea of exploring race in America in *Funny Aminals* because he purports to know "bupkis" about "being black in America." As Michael Rogin argues persuasively in *Blackface, White Noise*, many Jewish performers, such as the celebrated actor Al Jolson, donned blackface precisely so as to cement their whiteness in an American racial landscape predicated on the black-white binary. Moreover, Spiegelman's idea to create a strip devoted to the "Ku Klux Kats" nods further to the relationship between race and film history in America—in this case by referencing the controversial blackface film "classic" *Birth of a Nation*, which marries national mythology with a tortured hagiography of the Klan.

It is not by accident that a half-page panel, featuring a large image of Ken Jacobs, looms over the artist's relation of the story of *Maus*'s birth. As the panel suggests, Jacobs helped frame Spiegelman's artistic trajectory. Shown looking at the reader through a viewfinder that frames his own eye and perspective, Jacobs, Spiegelman writes, "taught me how to look at art . . . and to see myself as some sort of artist!" (3). Beneath the large, photorealistic portrait of Jacobs is a smaller, more cartoonish image of Spiegelman and Jacobs at an art museum, looking at a work of Cubist art. Here, Jacobs is shown to quite literally frame how his protégé sees art, gesturing to the painting and saying, "stop being such a slob-snob, Art. Just think of the paintings as giant comics panels!" This suggestion points to the ways in which, as Spiegelman writes, his teacher taught him "how to look at art." It also emphasizes that Jacobs allowed Spiegelman to think of comics on the same plane as high art, analogizing the frame of the canvas to that of the panel.

This question of medium is of central importance, however. Michaels's evaluation of *Maus* as merely appropriating African American identity never acknowledges that it is constructed in a different medium from the other works he critiques in his writing against identity politics. Namely, he fails to see that the medium of comics contains within it the possibility of dramatizing and self-reflexively critiquing the stakes of (visual) representation. Both Jared Gardner and Hillary Chute have argued that comics is a profoundly archival medium. If we take Chute's point that "the form of comics is a locus of the archival, a place where we can identify an archival turn," we might also label comics as a medium that carries within it not only the possibility to represent historical events but also to represent a deeper visual inheritance—that of the caricature archive—as well (Chute, "Comics as Archives"). Spiegelman represents and plays with this compromised inheritance throughout *Maus*, particularly in his unpacking of the very animal caricatures he uses to represent the various "races" in the text. Although he continues to employ caricatures in book 2 of *Maus*, he emphasizes their constructed nature by showing that his characters are not really animals but human beings wearing animal masks. The masks they wear, the masks imposed on them by the outside world, are often too small to fit them, allowing their complex humanity to spill over the boundaries of the flattened caricature mask (see figure 12.5).

Time flies...

Figure 12.5. Art Spiegelman,
Maus, book 2 (1991): 41.

The Caricature Archive and the History of Comics
before and after the Comics Code

Placing caricature at the very center of the comics tradition is itself not a new
move. As early as 1987, in "Comics and Catastrophe," an appraisal of the seri-
ousness of comics in the wake of *Maus*'s publication, Adam Gopnik argued that
modern comics "are the relatively novel offspring of an extremely sophisticated
visual culture. The caricature, from which all other kinds of cartooning descend,
first appears around 1600 in Italy, within the circle of Bernini and the Caracci—
and then not as a popular form, a visual slang, but as an in-ground dialect, an
aristocratic code" (29). Gopnik was interested in how the exaggerated language of
comics worked on its readers. To Gopnik, "our mistaken beliefs about cartooning
testify to the cartoon's near magical ability, whatever its real history, to persuade
us of its innocence. Even though cartoons are in fact recent and cosmopolitan, we
respond to them as if they are primordial. If we could understand why this happens, we might begin to understand the special cognitive and even biological basis
of our response to the form" (30). Despite comics' relative modernity, according
to Gopnik, this primordial response arises from the cartoonist's aptitude with the
caricature form first developed by fine artists of the seventeenth century.

Caricature has always inhabited a paradoxical position within comics and cartooning—as both a tool of high art and popular culture, a mode of political subversion and a mockery of the already marginalized. A hundred years or so after
Bernini and his circle popularized caricature, Jews and other archetypical others
were often its victims. As Sander Gilman points out in his landmark exploration
in *The Jew's Body*, since the Enlightenment, attempts to locate Jewish difference
from the larger European body politic were largely aimed at the purported difference of the Jew's body. Frequently taking pictorial form, representations of Jewish corporeal difference—of Jews with exaggerated or enlarged features, such as
noses, feet, and hands, were commonplace. Late nineteenth- and early twentieth-
century comics traded in similar stereotypes, both of Jews and of other others. As
Spiegelman was to explore in his later work on comics history in *In the Shadow of
No Towers* and his Comix 101 lectures, the early innovators of the American newspaper comics strip, such as Winsor McCay and Frederick Burr Opper, employed
highly charged and often racialized caricature to explore the role of American
others in the turn-of-the-century social landscape. Editorial cartoonists, such as
Thomas Nast, often turned their drawing pens to depicting immigrants to the
United States as beasts and buffoons. The Irish, once viewed as inhabiting an
intermediary position in America's racial binary, were often drawn as apelike in a
manner that replicated stereotypical images of black Americans.

Comics depictions of African Americans were particularly brutal and borrowed their racial vocabulary from minstrelsy, a popular entertainment that combined blackface with offensive stock characters, such as the mammy, the buck, and the pickaninny.[6] As Jeet Heer makes clear in a column for the *Comics Journal* called "Racism as a Stylistic Choice," many of the most influential early newspaper cartoonists, such as Winsor McCay, had an interest in blackface that predated their caricatured depiction of African Americans in their work. Heer writes that "in 1911, there was a curious incident where it looks as if Winsor Mc-Cay and a friend dressed in blackface and attacked a man they thought was trying to blackmail the cartoonist's wife Maude McCay. . . . The use of blackface in this incident sheds some very interesting light on McCay's racial politics, showing how they grew as part of the broader minstrel culture he participated in through the dime museum and on vaudeville." Moreover, McCay was not the only early newspaper cartoonist who had one foot in minstrel culture. "Because they were popular entertainers, other pioneering comic strip cartoonists partook of the broad culture of minstrelsy and corked up at some point in their lives, including George Luks and Jimmy Swinnerton" (Heer). Interestingly (and, perhaps, controversially), Heer, although critical of these early comics artists, also identifies caricature as central to the art of comics more generally—part of "the style" of some of its most adept early artists, such as George McManus. According to Heer, "the very forcefulness and confidence of McManus' line-work combined with his considerable talent for delineating monstrous facial features made his apelike Africans all the worse."

Later, comics' role in the circulation of racial stereotype was at the center of one of the most challenging moments in comics history—the midcentury introduction of the Comics Code. Psychoanalyst Fredric Wertham's *Seduction of the Innocent* (1954) is famous for its sweeping critique of the comics industry, focusing particularly on comics' repercussions for the "innocent" youth who made up the majority of comics readership. Wertham's work—and the congressional inquiry it spawned—inspired one of the darkest moments in the annals of recent comics history. In the wake of the psychoanalyst's criticism, the comics industry adopted a Comics Code that censored many of its most talented artists, leaving what Spiegelman calls in one of his strips only "relatively insipid comics on the newsstands" (*Breakdowns* 10). For our purposes, however, what proves most interesting about Wertham's work is not its pervasive postwar anxiety about juvenile delinquency and violence or its concerns about the repercussions of depictions of so-called deviant sex on its child readership but instead its assertions about the essentially racist nature of comics.

Wertham spends pages of *Seduction of the Innocent* meditating on how "comics expose children's minds to an endless stream of prejudice-producing images. This influence, subtle and pervasive but easily demonstrable by clinical psychological methods, has not only directly affected the individual child, but also constitutes an important factor for the whole nation" (100). Not surprisingly, Wertham goes on to situate this problematic representation of race and racial conflict in American comics against the nation's Cold War moment. He writes that "the United States is spending at present millions of dollars to persuade the world on the air and by other propaganda means that race hatred is not an integral part of American life. At the same time, millions of American comic books are exported all over the world which give the impression that the United States is instilling race hatred in young children" (100).[7] His anticomics crusade is often mocked—rightly—for being continuous with McCarthyism and other attempts to sanitize American culture into an idealized fantasy of postwar prosperity and health. However, critics of Wertham rarely acknowledge either the ways (however few) in which the psychoanalyst was *right* about comics or the fact that his own origins affected his reading of the art form's dangers.

Born in Nuremberg, Germany, in 1895 to a haute bourgeoisie Jewish family, Wertham (originally Wertheimer) escaped the Nazi peril only because he moved to the United States in 1922 after working in a prominent Munich psychiatric clinic ("Fredric Wertham"). Part of a generation with understandably deep suspicions about mass culture and its role in the dissemination of violent or racist imagery, it is not entirely surprising that Wertham would target comics for criticism.[8] The language he employs in his critique of the form is telling in this regard. In one extended passage, he writes that for young readers of comics "there are two kinds of people: on the one hand is the tall, blond, regular-featured man sometimes disguised as a superman (or superman disguised as a man) and the pretty young blonde girl with the super-breast. On the other hand are the inferior people: natives, primitives, savages, 'ape men,' Negroes, Jews, Indians, Italians, Slavs, Chinese and Japanese, immigrants of every description, people with irregular features, swarthy skins, physical deformities, Oriental features" (101). Wertham's mention of "the tall, blond, regular-featured man sometimes disguised as a superman" invokes not only the iconic superhero created by DC Comics in 1938 but also the language of *Übermenschen* that Nazi ideologues borrowed from Nietzsche in their pursuit of Aryanization. The language of "inferiority," as well as Wertham's assertion that "the brunt of this imputed inferiority in whole groups of people is directed against colored people and 'foreign born,'" also recalls language surrounding the recent experiences of Jews and other minorities in Europe (101).

Although Spiegelman directly addresses Wertham in one of his post-*Maus* autobiographical comics strips, he does so not to acknowledge this link between the psychoanalyst's experience and that of his parents, who were roughly Wertham's age and social class, but in order to suggest the complexity of his relationship to

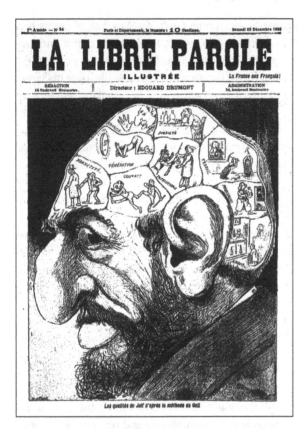

Figure 12.6. Emile Courtet, *La Libre Parole* (1893), cover, courtesy of The Jewish Museum.

his father, Vladek, whose thriftiness led him to buy young Art old comics without realizing they were the racy pre-Code comics Wertham and other experts had decried (see figure 12.6). Nonetheless, it is necessary to historicize Wertham as someone with ties to wartime Germany and one of the first figures in comics to recognize the powerful—and sometimes dangerous—role that caricature retains within it. Not surprisingly, given Wertham's training in psychoanalysis, he was also deeply concerned with the psychosexual implications of comics and the way in which they married racial caricature with ideas about gender and sex. His writing about this topic also echoes Nazi-era caricatures of the lascivious Jewish man and his threat to Aryan womanhood, as well as American caricatures of dangerous black male sexuality and objectified/exoticized black women. He writes that "the depiction of racial stereotypes in sadistic actions makes a great impression on children. . . . In many comic books dark-skinned people are depicted in rapelike situations with white girls" (103).

Wertham was not the first critic (or the first psychologist) to make this association of comics with racist caricature or psychosexual undertones—to see how "a psychiatric question becomes a social one" (103). As Marc Singer points out, Frantz Fanon, in *Black Skin, White Masks* (1952), noted how comics and cartoons upheld colonial fantasies about black racial inferiority that seeped into the minds of the children who read them. Fanon uses comics to illustrate his larger point about the mechanism of internalized self-hatred in colonial cultures. If, as Fanon suggests, "the Tarzan stories, the tales of young explorers, the adventures of Mickey Mouse . . . are written by white men for white children," what effect do they have on children of color (124)? "And the Wolf, the Devil, the Wicked Genie, Evil, and the Savage are always represented by Blacks or Indians; and since one always identifies with the good guys, the little black child, like the little white child, becomes an explorer, an adventurer, and a missionary 'who is in danger of being eaten by the wicked Negroes,'" Fanon notes (124–25).

The colonized were not the only ones to internalize these stereotypes. For comics artists of the American underground, most notably R. Crumb, the vernacular of caricature remained central. In the documentary *Comic Book Confidential*, R. Crumb tacitly acknowledges that (often racist) caricature was foundational to underground comix as he defined them. The 1960s witnessed artists who were intent on pushing against the repressive apparatus of the industry's Comics Code, mirror image of the larger attempt to straitjacket American expression during the 1950s. Central to this movement was, according to Crumb, an impetus to "break every taboo first. Get that over with." He describes that process of taboo-breaking as involving "drawing racist images, any sexual perversion there is, make fun of authority figures, get past all that and really get down to business." Crumb's interest in breaking taboos around depicting both race and sex were at the heart of the artist's early career as a social satirist in visual form. However, as Spiegelman has pointed out, the artist's later portrayals of African American identity in caricatured form risked overt racism. From a 1995 interview given in the wake of Crumb's controversial "Taking Over" strip to his meditation on Maus's origins in *MetaMaus*, Spiegelman has repeatedly remarked on the paradox in Crumb's work, suggesting that the artist was trying to do important political work in his earlier representation of race but may have gone too far in his representation of African American bodies. According to Spiegelman, he himself avoided representing African American identity in comics form because he "realized that it could be received as one more example of the trope that Crumb had consistently mined with Angelfood McSpade and other willful racist caricatures: the return of the repressed—all that insulting imagery that had been flushed out of the mainstream culture but existed in the back of everybody's lizard brain—now brought back in a kind of Lenny Bruce 'Is there anybody I haven't insulted yet?' spirit, with the hope that if you say the word 'nigger' over and over again, you remove its sting" (*MetaMaus* 113). In his own work, Spiegelman has staked out a particularly useful position between Crumb's id-filled play with racial stereotype and the calls for censorship of offensive imagery that have occurred in the wake of the Muhammad and *Charlie Hebdo* cartoon controversies. Not surprisingly, Spiegelman's response to these thorny questions of representation has been to locate his work—and the work of various artists working within the cartoon idiom—in the medium's history, exploring the inescapable role of caricature in cartooning while also using it to expose and undermine the stereotypes that give caricature its offensive force.

Spiegelman and Caricature Culture after *Maus*

Spiegelman expands on this exploration of the political work that comics do in his later visual work. The majority of *In the Shadow of No Towers* (2004), Spiegelman's narrative of the experience of life in the aftermath of the fall of the Twin Towers in Lower Manhattan on 9/11, is given over to the story of how Spiegelman and his wife, Françoise, experienced the 2001 tragedy and their frantic search for their daughter, whose school was located, literally, in the shadow of the towers. In the course of this narrative, Spiegelman also explores the turmoil in America's political scene after Bush's fraught election in 2000, as well as anxieties about terrorism and the attendant Islamophobia after 9/11. Throughout the text, however, an alternate history bleeds through this larger trauma narrative: that of classic comics and comics artists' own approach to the representation of both violence and otherness, often via the device of caricature. On the first page of the oversized volume, alongside images of the damaged towers, he provides a faux nineteenth-century etymology for the oft-used post-9/11 rhetorical trope of "the other shoe dropping" by adapting an early newspaper comics drawing style into a strip called "etymological vaudeville" (1). Pages later, he introduces a duo of characters he dubs "The Tower Twins," based loosely on the early newspaper comics figures the Katzenjammer Kids. The Tower Twins' identical cartoonish faces are presented against the backdrop of the burning towers or, in one memorably macabre strip, as victims of the American obsession with oil (see figure 12.7). Many of the critics who have written about *In the Shadow of No Towers* have rightly looked at how Spiegelman's fragmented, bricolage technique can be read as a response to the trauma of 9/11. As Kristiaan Versluys suggests, *In the Shadow of No Towers* is, among other things, Spiegelman's attempt to find a form commensurate to the task of representing the unrepresentable, just as it was in *Maus*. In her reading of the text, Laura Beadling usefully complicates this argument, suggesting that Spiegelman's post-9/11 work brings together two histories—that of early twentieth-century comics and early twenty-first-century America after the attack on the Twin Towers. With this in mind, she argues that

Spiegelman included strips from the heyday of newspaper comics in order to highlight their sometimes-racist representation of various new American others and draw a connection to growing nativism and anti-Arab sentiment in the post-9/11 United States. I would extend Beadling's reading by emphasizing that, in *In the Shadow of No Towers*, Spiegelman was interested not just in personal or global history but also in formal, compositional history precisely to show that history can be rewritten (or redrawn) by artists who are self-critical and aware of the repercussions of their use of images.

Spiegelman's narrative is, literally, encased in and framed by the archive—the inside front cover of *In the Shadow of No Towers* is a reproduction of the *New York World* from 1901 in the aftermath of McKinley's assassination. The theme of the historical archive, as well as that of the newspaper, recurs through Spiegelman's preoccupation with the origin of contemporary comics in the bygone history of newspaper strips. At the end of *In the Shadow of No Towers* he presents a lengthy history of comics via both scholarly exegesis and images in a section he calls "The Comic Supplement." Spiegelman writes that in the aftermath of 9/11 "the only cultural artifacts that could get past my defenses to flood my eyes and brain with something other than images of burning towers were old comic strips; vital, unpretentious ephemera from the optimistic dawn of the 20th century. That they were made with so much skill and verve but never intended to last past the day they appeared in the newspaper gave them poignancy; they were just right for an end-of-the-world moment" (11).

As Spiegelman points out, the earliest newspaper comics were spurred by the circulation war between Joseph Pulitzer and William Randolph Hearst. Readers of Pulitzer's *New York World* were greeted by the artist Richard Outcault's full-color "Hogan's Alley," which "depicted a gang of street urchins in a Lower Manhattan ghetto. Like a cheerfully sociopathic Hogarth, Outcault drew scenes of political and social commentary that teemed with brickbat violence, antic animal torture and the gleeful racism of the day" (11). "Hogan's Alley spotlighted one shanty-Irish guttersnipe in a bright yellow nightshirt, a Yellow Kid, whose popularity made him not just the comics' first star but also America's first 'hot licensing property'" (11). From this exploration of the Yellow Kid and his imitators, Spiegelman moves to discuss comics from the famous Katzenjammer Kids to Frederick Burr Opper's Happy Hooligan strip and Winsor McCay's Little Nemo comics.

In the excerpt from the Happy Hooligan strip he chooses to include in *In the Shadow of No Towers*, the character appears in a kind of blackface. In the strip, called "Is This Abdullah, the Arab Chief?" "the hapless hobo, described by Opper as 'Misfortune's favorite son,' trades his tin can in for a turban to become

Figure 12.7. Art Spiegelman, *In the Shadow of No Towers* (2004): 4.

Abdullah Hooligan, a dark-skinned circus clown who provokes his camel and gets tossed into . . . a tower of acrobats!" (12). Published in August 1911, just a few years before the destruction of the Ottoman Empire, Opper's cartoonish Arab chief spoke to American anxieties about class and racial mobility and the first sustained wave of Arab immigration to the United States. In the strip, the Happy Hooligan is doubly caricatured. Already appearing as apelike in a manner that recalled early twentieth-century American caricatures of the Irish, here he dons blackface (figure 12.8).[9] As Spiegelman makes clear, Windsor McCay's Little Nemo, too, relied on racial stereotype, featuring, as it did, the grossly caricatured African figure of "A Jungle Imp" to accompany Nemo on his nighttime journeys. Spiegelman even reads Osama bin Laden into Herriman's Krazy Kat, writing, "This is deep stuff, and after the attack it hit me like a ton of bricks; it proposed that since every Eden has its snake, one must somehow learn to live in harmony with that snake! I'm still working on it" (12). The author's wholesale journey through early newspaper comics becomes an attempt to work out how our own post-9/11 world can approach otherness—the snake within Eden. His particular focus on how cartoonists used animal avatars, such as Krazy Kat, to work out distinctly human(-istic) concerns also has great resonance for

Figure 12.8. Art Spiegelman, *In the Shadow of No Towers* (2004): 12.

understanding Spiegelman's earlier work on *Maus* and its relation to race and American caricature—a topic the comics artist has revisited multiple times in recent years.

This theme—the seduction of the other and the complexity of representation—is a theme he comes back to again and again in interviews and in his art. Writing of his time at the *New Yorker*, he shares: "I had a cover that was first accepted and then rejected with horror by the *New Yorker* at the tail-end of the O. J. Simpson trial. I drew something that portrayed 'the race card' since this was exploited repeatedly by O. J.'s lawyers during the trial" (Spiegelman, "Art Spiegelman" 221). The cover worried the magazine's editors because of its employment of the vocabulary of racist caricature. But, according to Spiegelman, "The idea of showing O. J. with a minstrel face was not about reaffirming that 'all blacks are watermelon eating coons,' but a way of showing that he was playing himself up as a black victim. It's a paint job, as much a mask as the Klan mask on the Los Angeles Police Department. One thing that makes it so complicated is that I'm not black, therefore I don't have the same right to say certain things; though, in the same issue of the *New Yorker*, Maya Angelou describes the O. J. trial as a minstrel show" (221). These anxieties about who has the "right to say certain things" might seem merely an artifact of identity politics. However, in Spiegelman's work as artist and cartoon historian, it becomes the engine for exploring the limits of visual representation and the dual-edged inheritance of the caricature archive. As he says in his *Harper's* article on the use of caricature in the Danish cartoon wars, "It takes skills to use such clichés in a way that subvert or expand this impoverished vocabulary" ("Drawing Blood" 45). Luckily for us, Spiegelman has such skills.

Spiegelman, Cartooning, and Caricature in the Public Sphere

In 2005 the Danish newspaper *Jyllands-Posten* wrote to members of their country's newspaper illustrators' union, asking its members if they wanted to contribute cartoons featuring the prophet Muhammad. This project, purportedly begun as an exercise to see if illustrators would engage in self-censorship out of fear of Islamic reprisal, ended up causing a massive controversy. The newspaper published twelve editorial cartoons, most of which depicted Muhammad in highly unflattering caricature or compromising situations. The response from the global Muslim world was swift, and protests turned increasingly ferocious. The question of whether the cartoons should have been published—and whether they were published only in order to mock and tease members of an aniconic faith—was debated by many writers and intellectuals.

In 2006, in the wake of what he called the "Danish cartoon wars," Spiegelman argued that the offensive depictions of the Prophet Muhammad inspired by the journal *Jyllands-Posten*, however repugnant, needed to be *seen* to be demystified. Part of that process of demystification for the artist was the integration of the images into a longer history of caricature. In an article on the controversy in *Harper's*, he asserts that "cartoon language is mostly limited to deploying a handful of recognizable visual symbols or clichés. It makes use of the discredited pseudo-scientific principles of physiognomy to portray character through a few physical attributes and facial expressions" ("Drawing Blood" 45). Although Spiegelman does not explicitly note the relationship of this definition of cartooning to the widely accepted writings of Scott McCloud on the topic, it is clear that his description is related to what McCloud has called the iconic natures of comics art. In his celebrated *Understanding Comics*, McCloud argues that comics are unique in the way they encourage reader participation and interpretation. Part of that investment on the part of the reader comes from the importance of the gutter, the space between panels, in comics. More important to McCloud's sense of comics, however, is the manner in which artists strategically employ the blankness of the cartoon, as opposed to more photorealistic portraiture, to encourage readers to identify with the characters they are depicting. In contrast to McCloud's definition, however, "cartoon language," as Spiegelman portrays it, works to distance readers from the subject being depicted.

Throughout his *Harper's* piece, "Drawing Blood," Spiegelman places the violence of the Muhammad images produced by Western artists for the Danish contest within the long history of caricature. The article is a study in ambivalence. Although Spiegelman makes it clear that he believes it is important not to censor the images, he also thinks that the cartoons produced in Denmark largely fail as satire—as did the cartoons produced by artists in response to an Iranian contest to satirize the Holocaust in the wake of the controversy. Spiegelman takes the often anti-immigrant *Jyllands-Posten* to task for trying to create exactly the sort of vehement response from the Muslim community that eventually occurred. Unlike many newspapers and magazines, including the *New York Times*, however, *Harper's* and Spiegelman insist on reproducing and critiquing the Muhammad images that have caused such an uproar. According to Spiegelman, it is precisely necessary to interact with these images in order to destabilize them and the force of their insult.[10] This approach to the controversy, which Jeet Heer calls "the best article on the Danish Muhammad controversy," arises from Spiegelman's profound respect for the medium and history of comics, as well as his belief, manifested as early as his "Cracking Jokes" strip of 1975, that jokes (visual or otherwise) aren't funny unless they challenge authority in some way.

In 2015 questions about violence and caricature arose again—this time in response to the shooting of eleven people employed by the French satirical magazine *Charlie Hebdo*. The magazine had long been in the crosshairs of Islamic fundamentalists angry about the publication's aggressive secularism, its nasty depictions of Muhammad and Islam, and its mockery of France's Muslim community. In the wake of the killings Spiegelman again addressed these issues of caricature, cartooning, and violence. Not long after the shootings at the *Charlie Hebdo* offices in Paris, he gave an interview to *Democracy Now*, controversially titled "Cartoonist Lives Matter." Here Spiegelman argues that cartoons "should make a mess, by God." Spiegelman talks of going to a demonstration in support of the *Charlie Hebdo* cartoonists who were murdered by terrorists:

> I felt really like in a minority, not because I'm a secular Jew, but because I'm an American in this demonstration that was mostly the French, feeling this very viscerally. And so, among all of the shouts of "Nous sommes Charlie Hebdo! Nous sommes Charlie Hebdo!" I'm there going, "Cartoonists' lives matter! Cartoonists' lives matter!" And this had to do specifically with that mandate to say the unsayable. It's an important thing in order to be able to focus you on what needs to be said, if you want to be talking about the primacy of language, of verbal language.

Here, Spiegelman pits the popular refrain of "we are Charlie Hebdo" against the statement that "cartoonists' lives matter." Both phrases evoke the digital hashtags that developed in the wake of the shooting of Michael Brown in Ferguson, Missouri, the growth of "Black Twitter" and the Black Lives Matter movement, and the push to identify with a variety of imperiled groups via the "We are all X" hashtags. Spiegelman pits this call for universal identification against his own, more particular identity as a cartoonist whose purpose is to "say the unsayable."

Asked in the same interview by Amy Goodman about how to view *Charlie Hebdo*, given their investment in often gross and offensive caricature, "this issue of afflicting the afflicted and how often cartoons are used to keep people down, whether we're talking about the caricatures of African Americans or black Americans during the times of lynching or Jews made out to look like shysters, or, of course, Muslims," Spiegelman says,

> the problem lies . . . not in the anti-Semitic or the black caricatures, but the impossibility of people in certain class and societal situations to not be able to make themselves felt. So let's focus on that problem rather than on the insult that comes with the rest of it, because maybe I'm just a cockeyed optimist, but I believe that if you get enough thought out there, eventually it actually does sift into what makes more sense. . . . And the things that don't make sense that are built on these unpleasant race caricatures only work because we recognize them.

Spiegelman's belief that we must see and "recognize" "unpleasant race caricatures" in order to subvert them is continuous with his longtime investment in understanding and representing the history of comics and cartoons via the comics archive.

Recently, anthropologist Ann Laura Stoler has noted that "among historians, literary critics and anthropologists, archives have been elevated to new analytic status with distinct billing, worthy of scrutiny on their own" (*Along the Archival Grain* 44). This so-called archival turn is characterized by "the move from archive-as-source to archive-as-subject" (44). Nowhere does this turn to the archive have more resonance than in comics studies. In recent years, scholars from both within and outside the boundaries of comics studies have begun to assess the profoundly archival nature of the comics medium. In an analysis of the role of comics (and comics artists) as collectors of historical ephemera in a digitally mediated age, Jared Gardner remarks that "archives are everywhere in the contemporary graphic novel" ("Archives" 787). Ann Cvetkovich's pivotal reading of the queer archive constructed by Alison Bechdel in her graphic memoir, *Fun Home: A Family Tragicomic* (2006) marks a sustained attempt to grapple with the profoundly archival nature of the comics medium. This turn is important because comics are archival on multiple levels. As Cvetkovich has noted in her reading of *Fun Home*, many autobiographical comics artists (quite literally) draw from their own personal archive in the making of their comics. Bechdel's particular case of "archive fever" surrounds her choice to recreate the various documents, private and public, narrative and visual, that made up her childhood in rural Pennsylvania. But, as Chute notes in her assessment of her collaborative work with Art Spiegelman in *MetaMaus*, comics are archival in ways that transcend what critic Gillian Whitlock has called the "autographic."[11] Chute comments that "graphic narratives not only thematize archives—for instance, the cartoonist's work of finding and collecting is an actual plotline of Maus—but further, because of the pictorial, word and image format of their pages, they are able to actually incorporate or physically represent concrete archives (thus the famous three photographs, two from the war era, that Spiegelman places within Maus)" ("Comics as Archives"). As *MetaMaus* and its accompanying CD-ROM make painstakingly clear, *Maus* is a deeply archival work that has arisen from Spiegelman's research into the Holocaust as well as his lifelong interest in the makeshift pamphlets and other ephemera left behind by survivors. In addition to the extensive archive of Nazi propaganda on which Spiegelman drew for *Maus*, he also manifests throughout *Maus* and the rest of his ouevre a deeper engagement with the American caricature archive. Spiegelman has evinced this commitment to exploring aesthetic history, and the inheritance it leaves for future artists, since his earliest work. More recently, in *In the Shadow of No Towers* and his new introduction to *Breakdowns*, Spiegelman has maintained that commitment to looking at the ways in which comics is an art form constituted by its self-reflexive relationship to the caricature archive.

NOTES

1. Critics such as Joseph Witek and Michael Rothberg have analyzed the role of animals in *Maus*.

2. Hatfield and Chute take up the issue of comics as a unique medium most persuasively in *Alternative Comics* and *Graphic Women*, respectively.

3. *MetaMaus* reviews this archival material (and includes much of it on CD)—from the self-published Holocaust pamphlets produced by survivors that Spiegelman's parents collected after the war to the scholarly resources he used to recreate the world of the camps.

4. Throughout *Maus*, Spiegelman also draws attention to the limits of his choice via his use of masks and masking. When Polish Jews, including Vladek and Anja, wish to "pass," they don pig masks. Spiegelman himself wears a mouse mask throughout much of book 2 of *Maus*, suggesting the contingency of his own Jewish identity.

5. In his earlier work, *The Shape of the Signifier*, Michaels articulates a similar critique of *Maus* as participating in what critic Hilene Flanzbaum has called the "Americanization of the Holocaust."

6. Recent critical anthologies, such as Sheena C. Howard and Ronald L. Jackson's *Black*

Comics: The Politics of Representation, attempt to redress the gap in comics scholarship by studying African Americans as subjects, rather than objects, of representation.

7. Wertham's assertion that America was desperate to appear less racist as part of a Cold War strategy is a particularly apt one. Later scholarship has shown that the gains of the civil rights movement, including Supreme Court cases such as *Brown v. Board of Education*, benefited from fears that America's deep racism would make the Soviets more appealing to people around the world.

8. Theodor Adorno's oft-critiqued savaging of the danger of mass cultural forms arises from a similar place.

9. Opper was self-conscious about his own participation in the art of caricature, but, like Spiegelman, he saw it as a somewhat inevitable aspect of cartooning, writing about the role of caricature in his essay "Caricature Country and Its Inhabitants" (1901).

10. In a series of tweets, Jeet Heer has noted how Spiegelman has carved out a position between Crumb's extreme taboo-breaking in matters of caricature and the sort of censorship advocated by some critics of the Danish cartoonists.

11. In Chute's *Graphic Women*, she outlines the importance of the autographic nature of comics to its power in relating narratives of trauma. In contrast to many mass-mediated works, comics contain the hand (and, often, the handwriting) of the artist. This term was originally theorized by Gillian Whitlock in her work "Autographics: The Seeing 'I' of the Comics."

BIBLIOGRAPHY

Adams, Jeff. *Documentary Graphic Novels and Social Realism*. Peter Lang, 2008.

"Addressing Ebony White—Was Will Eisner Racist?" *Comics Cube*, 26 May 2010, comicscube.com/2010/05/addressing-ebony-white-was-will-eisner_26.html. Accessed June 2017.

Aldama, Frederick Luis. "Multicultural Comics Today: A Brief Introduction." Aldama, *Multicultural Comics*, pp. 1–25.

———, editor. *Multicultural Comics: From Zap to Blue Beetle*. University of Texas Press, 2010.

———. *Your Brain on Latino Comics: From Gus Arriola to Los Bros Hernandez*. University of Texas Press, 2009.

Alexander, Michelle. *The New Jim Crow: Mass Incarceration in the Age of Colorblindness*. New Press, 2010.

Ammons, Elizabeth, and Valerie Rohy, editors. *American Local Color Writing, 1880–1920*. Penguin, 1998.

Anderson, Ho Che. *King: A Comics Biography of Martin Luther King, Jr.* Fantagraphics Books, 2005.

Anderson, John Jacob. *A Manual of General History: Being an Outline History of the World from the Creation to the Present Time*. Clark & Maynard, 1876.

Armstrong, Julie Buckner. "Civil Rights Movement Fiction." *Cambridge Companion to American Civil Rights Literature*. Edited by Julie Buckner Armstrong, Cambridge University Press, 2015, pp. 85–103.

Armstrong, Julie Buckner, and Amy Schmidt, editors. *The Civil Rights Reader: American Literature from Jim Crow to Reconciliation*. University of Georgia Press, 2009.

Atwood, Margaret. *Moving Targets: Writing with Intent, 1982–2004*. House of Anansi Press, 2005.

August, Timothy K. "Picturing the Past: Drawing Together Vietnamese American Transnational History." *Global Asian American Popular Cultures*. Edited by Shilpa Davé, LeiLani Nishime, and Tasha Oren, New York University Press, 2016, pp. 165–79.

Babic, Annessa Ann, ed. *Comics as History, Comics as Literature: Roles of the Comic Book in Scholarship, Society, and Entertainment*. Reprint edition. Fairleigh Dickinson University Press, 2015.

Baloup, Clément. "Artist's Statement." Trans. Mark McKinney. *European Comic Art*, vol. 8, no. 1, Spring 2015, pp. 52–68.

———. "Dessiner: acte resistante" ["Drawing: An Act of Resistance"]. Speaker Series, 18 Mar. 2015, Illinois State University, Normal, Ill. Lecture.

———. *Mémoires de Viet Kieu: Little Saigon*. Vol. 2, La Boîte à Bulles, 2012.

———. *Mémoires de Viet Kieu: Les Mariées de Taïwan*. Vol. 3, La Boîte à Bulles, 2017.

——. *Mémoires de Viet Kieu: Quitter Saigon.* Vol. 1, La Boîte à Bulles, 2006.

——. *Mémoires de Viet Kieu: Quitter Saigon.* 2006. Vol. 1, La Boîte à Bulles, 2010.

——. *Mémoires de Viet Kieu: Quitter Saigon.* 2006. Vol. 1, La Boîte à Bulles, 2013.

——. "Re: Access to Artist Statement." Received by Catherine H. Nguyen, 25 Jan. 2016.

Baloup, Clément, and Matthieu Jiro. *Chinh Tri: La Choix de Hai.* Vol. 2, Seuil, 2007.

——. *Chinh Tri: Le Chemin de Tuan.* Vol. 1, Seuil, 2005.

Barker, Martin. *Comics: Ideology, Power and the Critics.* Manchester University Press, 1989.

Barthes, Roland. *S/Z: An Essay.* Translated by Richard Miller, Hill & Wang, 1974.

Beadling, Laura. "Twin Turns: Art Spiegelman's *In the Shadow of No Towers* and History." *Graphic History: Essays on Graphic Novels and/as History.* Edited by Richard Iadonisi, Cambridge Scholars, 2012, pp. 37–54.

Beard, Rick. "When Douglass Met Lincoln." *New York Times,* 9 Aug. 2013, opinionator. blogs.nytimes.com/2013/08/09/when-douglass-met-lincoln/?_r=0. Accessed 10 June 2016.

Beaty, Bart. *Comics Versus Art.* University of Toronto Press, 2012.

Bechdel, Alison. *Fun Home: A Family Tragicomic.* Houghton Mifflin, 2006.

Beck, C.C., artist. "Captain Marvel Rides the Engine of Doom." Penciled by Pete Costanza, written by Bill Parker. *Whiz Comics,* no. 12, Jan. 1941. *The Shazam! Archives,* illustrated by C. C. Beck, vol. 1, DC Comics, 1992, pp. 159–70.

Benjamin, Walter. *Illuminations: Essays and Reflections.* Edited by Hannah Arendt, translated by Harry Zohn, Schocken, 1969.

——. "Theses on the Philosophy of History." 1940. Benjamin, *Illuminations,* pp. 253–64.

——. "The Work of Art in the Age of Mechanical Reproduction." Benjamin, *Illuminations,* pp. 217–52.

Bennett, Jane. *Vibrant Matter: A Political Ecology of Things.* Duke University Press, 2010.

Berger, John. *Ways of Seeing.* Penguin, 1972.

Berlatsky, Eric L. *The Real, the True, and the Told: Postmodern Historical Narrative and the Ethics of Representation.* Ohio State University Press, 2011.

Bernstein, Robin. *Racial Innocence: Performing American Childhood from Slavery to Civil Rights.* New York University Press, 2011.

Bhabha, Homi K. *The Location of Culture.* Routledge, 1994.

Bickley, R. Bruce, Jr. *Joel Chandler Harris: A Biography and Critical Study.* University of Georgia Press, 1978.

Bierbaum, Tom, et al. *Legion of Super-Heroes,* no. 33, Sept. 1992, DC Comics, 1992.

Bierce, Ambrose. *The Collected Works of Ambrose Bierce . . . : The Devil's Dictionary.* Vol. 7, Neale, 1911.

Bishin, Benjamin G., and Casey A. Klofstad. "The Political Incorporation of Cuban Americans: Why Won't Little Havana Turn Blue?" *Political Research Quarterly,* vol. 65, no. 3, Sept. 2012, pp. 586–99.

"Book Review: *Bad Habits: A Love Story.*" *Publisher's Weekly,* 25 Sept. 2008, publishersweekly .com/978-1-59376-215-5. Accessed 25 April 2017.

"Book Review: *Spit and Passion.*" *Publisher's Weekly,* 1 Oct. 2012, p. 82.

Bordelon, David. "Picturing Books: Southern Print Culture in Howard Cruse's *Stuck Rub-*

ber Baby." *Crossing Boundaries in Graphic Narrative: Essays on Form, Series and Genre.* Edited by Jake Jakaitis and James F. Wurtz, McFarland, 2012, pp. 107–22.

Braziel, Jana Evans, and Anita Mannur. "Nation, Migration, Globalization: Points of Contention in Diaspora Studies." *Theorizing Diaspora: A Reader.* Edited by Braziel and Mannur, Blackwell, 2003, pp. 1–22.

Breckenridge, Janis, and Madelyn Peterson. "Lila Quintero Weaver's *Darkroom: A Memoir in Black and White*: Envisioning Equality." *Confluencia: Revista Hispánica de Cultura y Literatura,* vol. 29, no. 1, Fall 2013, pp. 109–25.

Brewin, Chris R., et al. "Intrusive Images in Psychological Disorders: Characteristics, Neural Mechanisms, and Treatment Implications." *Psychological Review,* vol. 117, no. 1, 2010, pp. 210–32.

Brotherman: Dictation of Discipline. Brotherman Comics, brothermancomics.com/. Accessed 30 April 2017.

Brozo, William G., et al. *Wham! Teaching with Graphic Novels across the Curriculum.* Teachers College, 2014.

Bui, Doan, writer. "Le Vietnam raconté à mes filles." Illustrated by Tiphaine Rivière, *Nouvel Obs,* 16 Jul. 2015–13 Aug. 2015.

Bui, Thi. *The Best We Could Do: An Illustrated Memoir.* Abram ComicArts, 2017.

Bullard, Robert D. *Dumping in Dixie: Race, Class, and Environmental Quality.* 3rd ed., Westview Press, 2000.

Bureau of Census. Fourteenth Census of the United States: 1920. U.S. Department of Commerce, Washington, D.C. www.census.gov/library/publications/dicennial/1920/volume-4/41084484.4ch04.pdf. Accessed 3 Dec. 2014.

Byerman, Keith. "Black Voices, White Stories: An Intertextual Analysis of Thomas Nelson Page and Charles Waddell Chesnutt." *North Carolina Literary Review,* vol. 8, 1999, pp. 98–105.

Cadden, Mike. "'But You Are Still a Monkey': *American Born Chinese* and Racial Self-Acceptance." *Looking Glass: New Perspectives on Children's Literature,* vol. 17, no. 2, 2014, lib.latrobe.edu.au/ojs/index.php/tlg/article/view/477/427. Accessed 1 Dec. 2016.

Caminero-Santangelo, Marta. *On Latinidad: U.S. Latino Literature and the Construction of Ethnicity.* University Press of Florida, 2007.

Camper, Cathy. "Book Review: Spit and Passion." *Lambda Literary,* 25 Dec. 2012, lambdaliterary.org/reviews/12/25/spit-and-passion-by-cristy-c-road/. Accessed 12 Aug. 2015.

Caron, Tim. "'Black and White and Read All Over': Representing Race in Mat Johnson and Warren Pleece's *Incognegro: A Graphic Mystery.*" *Comics and the U.S. South.* Edited by Brannon Costello and Quiana J. Whitted, University of Mississippi Press, 2012, pp. 138–60.

Chakrabarty, Dipesh. "The Climate of History: Four Theses." *Critical Inquiry,* vol. 35, no. 2, 2009, pp. 197–222.

Chaney, Michael A. "Drawing on History in Recent African American Graphic Novels." *MELUS,* vol. 32, no. 3, special issue: Coloring America: Multi-Ethnic Engagements with Graphic Narrative, 2007, pp. 175–200.

———, editor. *Graphic Subjects: Critical Essays on Autobiography and Graphic Novels*. University of Wisconsin Press, 2011.

———. "Is There an African American Graphic Novel?" *MLA Approaches to Teaching the Graphic Novel*, ed. Stephen Tabachnick, 2009, pp. 69–75.

Chao, Fred. *Johnny Hiro: Half Asian, All Hero*. Tom Doherty, 2009.

Cheng, Anne Anlin. *The Melancholy of Race: Psychoanalysis, Assimilation, and Hidden Grief*. Oxford University Press, 2001.

Cheng, Eileen Ka-May. *Historiography: An Introductory Guide*. Continuum, 2012.

Chin, Frank. "Come All Ye Asian American Writers of the Real and the Fake." *The Big Aiieeeee! An Anthology of Chinese American and Japanese American Literature*. Edited by Frank Chin et al., Plume Press, 1991, pp. 1–93.

Chiu, Monica, editor. *Drawing New Color Lines: Transnational Asian American Graphic Narratives*. Hong Kong University Press, 2015.

Choy, Philip P., Lorraine Dong, and Marlon K. Hom, editors. *The Coming Man: 19th Century Perceptions of the Chinese*. University of Washington Press, 1995.

Chute, Hillary L. "Comics as Archives: Meta*MetaMaus*." *e-misférica*, vol. 9, no. 1–2, 2012. hemisphericinstitute.org/hemi/en/e-misferica-91/chute. Accessed 4 Dec. 2015.

———. "Comics as Literature? Reading Graphic Narrative." *PMLA*, vol. 123, no. 2, 2008, pp. 452–65.

———. *Graphic Women: Life Narrative and Contemporary Comics*. Columbia University Press, 2010.

———. Review of *Our Cancer Year*, by Harvey Pekar and Joyce Brabner; *Janet and Me: An Illustrated Story of Love and Loss*, by Stan Mack; *Cancer Vixen: A True Story*, by Marisa Acocella Marchetto; *Mom's Cancer*, by Brian Fies; *Blue Pills: A Positive Love Story*, by Frederik Peeters; *Epileptic*, by David Beauchard; and *Black Hole*, by Charles Burns. *Literature and Medicine*, vol. 26, no. 2, 2007, pp. 413–29. *Project Muse*, muse.jhu.edu /article/242732. Accessed 24 Aug. 2015.

Clark, J. Spencer. "Encounters with Historical Agency: The Value of Nonfiction Graphic Novels in the Classroom." *History Teacher*, vol. 46, no. 4, 1 Aug. 2013, pp. 489–508.

Clark, Noelene. "'Boxers & Saints': Gene Yang Blends Chinese History, Magical Realism." *Los Angeles Times*, 10 Sept. 2013, herocomplex.latimes.com/books/boxers -saints-gene-yang-blends-chinese-history-magical-realism/#/0. Accessed 30 Sept. 2015.

Clarke, John. "Style." *Resistance through Ritual: Youth Subcultures in Post-War Britain*. 1993. Edited by Stuart Hall and Tony Jefferson, 2006, pp. 175–91.

Clinton, William Jefferson. "The President's Radio Address: September 10, 1994." *Clinton Digital Library*, 10 Sept. 1994, presidency.ucsb.edu/ws/index.php?pid=49062. Accessed 3 Sept. 2015.

Cohen, Paul A. *History in Three Keys: The Boxers as Event, Experience, and Myth*. Columbia University Press, 1997.

Cohn, Jesse. "Mise-en-Page: A Vocabulary for Page Layouts." *MLA Approaches to Teaching the Graphic Novel*. Edited by Stephen Tabachnick, 2009, pp. 44–57.

Coleman, Jeffrey Lamar, editor. *Words of Protest, Words of Freedom: Poetry of the American Civil Rights Movement and Era*. Duke University Press, 2012.

Comic Book Confidential. Directed by Ron Mann, Cinecom Pictures, 1989.

Cong-Huyen, Anne, and Caroline Kyungah Hong. "Teaching Asian American Graphic Narratives in a 'Post-Race' Era." *Teaching Comics and Graphic Narratives: Essays on Theory, Strategy and Practice.* Edited by Lan Dong, McFarland, 2012, pp. 80–93.

Conway, Michael. "The Problem with History Classes." *Atlantic,* 16 Mar. 2015, theatlantic .com/education/archive/2015/03/the-problem-with-history-classes/387823/. Accessed 30 Sept. 2015.

Costello, Brannon. *Plantation Airs: Racial Paternalism and the Transformations of Class in Southern Fiction, 1945–1971.* Louisiana State University Press, 2007.

Costello, Brannon, and Qiana J. Whitted, editors. *Comics and the U.S. South.* University Press of Mississippi, 2012.

Cousins, Paul M. *Joel Chandler Harris: A Biography.* Louisiana State University Press, 1968.

Crumb, R. Interview with Steve Bell. *Guardian,* 18 Mar. 2005, theguardian.com/film/2005 /mar/18/robertcrumb.guardianinterviewsatbfisouthbank. Accessed 4 Dec. 2015.

Cruse, Howard. "The Long and Winding Stuck Rubber Road." *Howard Cruse Central,* howardcruse.com/howardsite/aboutbooks/stuckrubberbook/longroad/. Accessed 30 July 2015.

———. Personal interview with Julie Buckner Armstrong. 13 Dec. 2014.

———. *Stuck Rubber Baby.* 1995. Vertigo, 2010.

Cvetkovich, Ann. "Drawing the Archive in Alison Bechdel's *Fun Home.*" *WSQ: Women's Studies Quarterly,* vol. 36, no. 1, 2008, pp. 111–28.

Daley, Richard. "Quotes of the Day." *Chicago Tribune,* 1 Sept. 1994, chicagotribune.com /news/chi-daley-quotes-20110429-story.html. Accessed 5 Aug. 2015.

Davé, Shilpa. "Spider-Man India: Comic Books and the Translating/Transcreating of American Cultural Narratives." *Transnational Perspectives on Graphic Narratives: Comics at the Crossroads.* Edited by Daniel Stein et al., Bloomsbury Academic, 2013, pp. 127–43.

Davis, Rocío G. "Layering History: Graphic Embodiment and Emotions in GB Tran's *Vietnamerica.*" *Rethinking History,* vol. 19, no. 2, 2015, pp. 252–67.

de Certeau, Michel. *The Writing of History.* Translated by Tom Conley, Columbia University Press, 1988.

DeLoughrey, Elizabeth, and George B. Handley. "Introduction: Toward an Aesthetics of the Earth." *Postcolonial Ecologies: Literature of the Environment.* Edited by DeLoughrey and Handley, Oxford University Press, 2011, pp. 3–39.

Dickel, Simon. "'Can't Leave Me Behind': Racism, Gay Politics, and Coming of Age in Howard Cruse's *Stuck Rubber Baby.*" *Amerikastudien/American Studies,* vol. 56, no. 4, special issue: American Comic Books and Graphic Novels, 2011, pp. 617–35.

Dittmer, John. *Local People: The Struggle for Civil Rights in Mississippi.* University of Illinois Press, 1995.

Dong, Lan. "Asian American Graphic Narratives: An Introduction." Unpublished manuscript authored by Monica Chiu et al. Typescript.

Donohoe, Janet. *Remembering Places: A Phenomenological Study of the Relationship between Memory and Place.* Lexington, 2014.

Dooley, Bridget G. "Stories in Cultures, Compassion in Stories: How Embedded Narrative Functions within Yang's *Boxers* and *Saints*." *inkt|art*, 19 May 2014, inktart.org/2014/05/19/stories-in-cultures-compassion-in-stories-how-narrative-functions-within-yangs-boxers-and-saints/. Accessed 30 Sept. 2015.

Dunbar-Nelson, Alice. "The Pearl in the Oyster." 1900. *The Works of Alice Dunbar-Nelson*, vol. 3, Oxford University Press, 1988, pp. 51–64.

Duncan, Randy, and Matthew J. Smith. *The Power of Comics: History, Form and Culture.* Continuum, 2009.

Duncombe, Stephen, and Maxwell Tremblay, editors. *White Riot: Punk Rock and the Politics of Race.* Verso, 2011.

Earle, Harriet E. H. "Traumatic Analepsis and *Ligne Claire* in GB Tran's *Vietnamerica*." *Comics Grid: Journal of Comics Scholarship*, vol. 4, no. 1, 2014, pp. 1–4.

Eckstein, Susan. "The Personal Is Political: The Cuban Ethnic Electoral Policy Cycle." *Latin American Politics and Society*, vol. 51, no. 1, Mar. 2009, pp. 119–48.

Eisner, Will. *Comics and Sequential Art.* Poorhouse Press, 1985.

———. *Graphic Storytelling and Visual Narrative.* Norton, 2008.

———. "Never Too Late." Interview by Andrew D. Arnold. *Time*, 19 Sept. 2003, content.time.com/time/arts/article/0,8599,488263,00.html. Accessed 26 July 2012.

El Refaie, Elisabeth. *Autobiographical Comics: Life Writing in Pictures.* University Press of Mississippi, 2012.

Erll, Astrid. *Memory in Culture.* Translated by Sara B. Young, Palgrave Macmillan, 2011.

Esherick, Joseph W. *The Origins of the Boxer Uprising.* University of California Press, 1987.

Eskew, Glenn T. *But for Birmingham: The Local and National Movements in the Civil Rights Struggle.* University of North Carolina Press, 1997.

"Exclusive: Gene Luen Yang Announces New *Boxers and Saints* Graphic Novels." *Wired*, 23 Jan. 2013, wired.com/2013/01/exclusive-gene-yang-announces-new-boxers-and-saints-graphic-novels/. Accessed 30 Sep. 2015.

Fanon, Frantz. *Black Skin, White Masks.* Translated by Richard Philcox, Grove, 2008.

Fine, Theresa. "*Incognegro* and Portrayals of Lynching." *Graphic History: Essays on Graphic Novels and/as History.* Edited by Richard Iadonisi, Cambridge Scholars, 2012, pp. 109–20.

Fiske, John. *Understanding Popular Culture.* 1989. Routledge, 2010.

Flanzbaum, Hilene, ed. *The Americanization of the Holocaust.* Baltimore: Johns Hopkins University Press, 1999.

Ford, Stacilee. "'Maybe It's Time for a Little History Lesson Here': Autographics and Ann Marie Fleming's *The Magical Life of Long Tack Sam*." *Drawing New Color Lines: Transnational Asian American Graphic Narratives.* Edited by Monica Chiu, Hong Kong University Press, 2014, pp. 125–43.

Forman, Ross G. "Peking Plots: Fictionalizing the Boxer Rebellion of 1900." *Victorian Literature and Culture*, vol. 27, no. 1, 1 Jan. 1999, pp. 19–48.

"Fredric Wertham." *American National Biography*, anb.org/articles/14/14-01160.html. Accessed 4 Dec. 2015.

Gabilliet, Jean-Paul. *Of Comics and Men: A Cultural History of American Comic Books.* Translated by Bart Beaty and Nick Nguyen, University of Mississippi Press, 2010.

Gardner, Jared. "Archives, Collectors, and the New Media Work of Comics." *Modern Fiction Studies*, vol. 52, no. 4, Winter 2006, pp. 787–806.

———. *Projections: Comics and the History of Twenty-First-Century Storytelling.* Stanford University Press, 2012.

———. "Same Different: Graphic Alterity in the Work of Gene Luen Yang, Adrian Tomine, and Derek Kirk Kim." Aldama, pp. 132–47.

Garrard, Greg. *Ecocriticism.* Routledge, 2012.

Gay and Lesbian Advocates and Defenders. "A Short History of DOMA." *GLAD*, 3 Mar. 2009, glad.org/doma/. Accessed 15 Oct. 2015.

General Code of the City of Birmingham, Alabama. Mitchie, 1944.

Gibbs, Nancy R. "Murder in Miniature." *TIME*, 19 Sept. 1994, pp. 54–60.

Gilly, Casey. "Gene Luen Yang Explores Chinese History with 'Boxers & Saints.'" *Comic Book Resources*, 16 Sept. 2013, cbr.com/gene-luen-yang-explores-chinese-history-with-boxers-saints/. Accessed 30 Sept. 2015.

Gilman, Sander. *The Jew's Body.* Routledge, 1991.

Gilmore, Leigh. *The Limits of Autobiography: Trauma and Testimony.* Cornell University Press, 2001.

Girard, Chris, et al. "Exile Politics and Republican Party Affiliation: The Case of Cuban Americans in Miami." *Social Science Quarterly*, vol. 93, no. 1, Mar. 2012, pp. 42–57.

Gloeckner, Phoebe. *A Child's Life and Other Stories.* 1998. Frog Books, 2000.

Goellner, Caleb. "Gene Luen Yang on the History and Art behind 'Boxers & Saints.'" *Comics Alliance*, 3 Sept. 2013, comicsalliance.com/gene-luen-yang-on-the-history-and-art-of-boxers-saints-interview/. Accessed 30 Sept. 2015.

Goldman, Andrea S. *Opera and the City: The Politics of Culture in Beijing, 1770–1900.* Stanford University Press, 2012.

Goldsmith, Francisa. "Book Review: *Spit and Passion*." *Booklist*, no. 1, 15 Jan. 2013, p. 74.

Gomez, Rain Prud'Homme C. "Crossin' the Log: Death, Regionality, and Race in Jeremy Love's *Bayou*." *Undead Souths: The Gothic and Beyond in Southern Literature and Culture.* Edited by Eric Gary Anderson et al., Louisiana State University Press, 2015, pp. 211–23.

Gonda, Kenji. "Passing to Authenticity." *Eigo Seinen/Rising Generation*, vol. 154, no. 7, 2008, p. 415.

Gopnik, Adam. "Comics and Catastrophe." *New Republic*, 22 June 1987, pp. 29–33.

Gordon, Ian. *Comic Strips and Consumer Culture, 1890–1945.* Smithsonian Institution Press, 1998.

Gray, Jonathan W. *Civil Rights in the White Literary Imagination: Innocence by Association.* University Press of Mississippi, 2013.

"Green Day: We're Still Punks." *Contactmusic*, 12 Oct. 2005, contactmusic.net/green-day/news/green-day-were-still-punks. Accessed 25 Sept. 2015.

Green, Justin. *Binky Brown Meets the Holy Virgin Mary.* Last Gasp, 1972.

Groensteen, Thierry. *Comics and Narration*. Translated by Ann Miller, University Press of Mississippi, 2013.

———. *The System of Comics*. 1999. Translated by Bart Beaty and Nick Nguyen, University Press of Mississippi, 2007.

Grooms, Anthony. *Bombingham*. 2001. One World/Ballantine, 2002.

Gunn, Simon. *History and Cultural Theory*. Routledge, 2006.

Gustines, George Gene. "Black and White and Graphic All Over: A 1930s Tale of Race, Passing and Pain." *New York Times*, 3 Mar. 2008, mobile.nytimes.com/2008/03/03 /books/03gust.html. Accessed 3 June 2009.

Halberstam, David. *The Fifties*. New York: Random House, 1993.

Hall, Jacquelyn Dowd. "The Long Civil Rights Movement and the Political Uses of the Past." *Journal of American History*, vol. 91, no. 4, 1 Mar. 2005, pp. 1233–63.

Harris, Joel Chandler. *Nights with Uncle Remus: Myths and Legends of the Old Plantation*. Osgood, 1883.

Harvey, Robert C. *The Art of the Comic Book: An Aesthetic History*. University Press of Mississippi, 1996.

Hatfield, Charles. *Alternative Comics: An Emerging Literature*. University Press of Mississippi, 2005.

Hebdige, Dick. *Subculture: The Meaning of Style*. Routledge, 1979.

Heer, Jeet. "Racism as a Stylistic Choice and Other Notes." *Comics Journal*, 14 Mar. 2011, tcj.com/racism-as-a-stylistic-choice-and-other-notes/. Accessed 5 Sept. 2015.

Henry, Tricia. *Break All Rules! Punk Rock and the Making of a Style*. UMI Research, 1989.

Hobson, Fred. *But Now I See: The White Southern Racial Conversion Narrative*. Louisiana State University Press, 1999.

Hong, Caroline Kyungah. "Disorienting the Vietnam War: GB Tran's *Vietnamerica* as Transnational and Transhistorical Graphic Memoir." *Asian American Literature: Discourses and Pedagogies*, vol. 5, 2014, pp. 11–22.

Horton, Paul. "The New History Wars Part II: A Classroom Simulation." *Living in Dialogue*, 14 Oct. 2014, livingindialogue.com/new-history-wars-part-ii-classroom -simulation/. Accessed 10 Aug. 2015.

Howard, Sheena C., and Ronald L. Jackson, II, editors. *Black Comics: Politics of Race and Representation*. Bloomsbury, 2013.

Huntley, Horace, and John W. McKerley, editors. *Foot Soldiers for Democracy: The Men, Women, and Children of the Birmingham Civil Rights Movement*. University of Illinois Press, 2009.

Iadonisi, Richard, editor. *Graphic History: Essays on Graphic Novels and/as History*. Cambridge Scholars, 2012.

Jaffe, Meryl. "Using Graphic Novels in Education: *Boxers & Saints*." *CBLDF* (Comic Book Legal Defense Fund), 31 Oct. 2013, cbldf.org/2013/10/using-graphic-novels-in-education -boxers-saints/. Accessed 30 Sept. 2015.

Janette, Michele, editor. *Mỹ Việt: Vietnamese American Literature in English, 1962–Present*. University of Hawaii Press, 2011.

Japanese American National Museum. Japanese American National Museum, 2016, janm.
org/. Accessed 15 Jan. 2016.

Johnson, E. Patrick. "'Quare' Studies, or (Almost) Everything I Know About Queer Studies
I Learned from My Grandmother." *Black Queer Studies: A Critical Anthology*. Edited
by E. Patrick Johnson and Mae G. Henderson, Duke University Press, 2005, pp. 124–57.

———. *Sweet Tea: Black Gay Men of the South*. University of North Carolina Press, 2008.

Jones, Gerard. *Men of Tomorrow: Geeks, Gangsters, and the Birth of the Comic Book*. Per-
seus, 2004.

Jones, Suzanne W. *Race Mixing: Southern Fiction since the Sixties*. Johns Hopkins University Press, 2006.

Joseph, Peniel. "Waiting till the Midnight Hour: Reconceptualizing the Heroic Period
of the Civil Rights Movement, 1954–1965." *Souls: A Critical Journal of Black Politics,
Culture, and Society*, vol. 2, no. 2, 2000, pp. 6–17.

Joyce, James. *Ulysses*. 1922. Simon & Brown, 2013.

Kanigher, Robert, writer. *Lois Lane: Superman's Girl Friend*. Penciled by Werner Roth,
inked by Vince Colletta, no. 106, National Periodical Publications, Nov. 1970.

Kelley, Brian. "Teachers' Guide with Common Core State Standards Connections:
Boxers & Saints by Gene Luen Yang." First Second Books, geneyang.com/docs
/BoxersSaintsTeachersGuide.pdf. Accessed 30 Sept. 2015.

King, Martin Luther, Jr., "Letter from a Birmingham Jail." 16 Apr. 1963. Martin Luther
King, Jr. Research and Education Institute, Stanford University, okra.stanford.edu
/transcription/document_images/undecided/630416–019.pdf. Accessed 20 Aug.
2015.

King, Richard H. "Politics and Fictional Representation: The Case of the Civil Rights
Movement." *The Making of Martin Luther King and the Civil Rights Movement*. Edited
by Brian Ward and Tony Badger, Washington Square, 1996, pp. 162–78.

Kiyama, Henry (Yoshitaka). *The Four Immigrants Manga: A Japanese Experience in San
Francisco, 1904–1924*. Berkeley, Calif.: Stone Bridge Press, 1998.

Klarman, Michael J. *From the Closet to the Altar: Courts, Backlash, and the Struggle for
Same-Sex Marriage*. Oxford University Press, 2013.

Knüsel, Ariane. "'Western Civilization' against 'Hordes of Yellow Savages': British Perceptions of the Boxer Rebellion." *Asiatische Studien/Etudes Asiatiques*, vol. 62, no. 1, 2008,
pp. 43–83.

Lankford, Tom. "Crackdown on Sex Perverts Ordered for City by Connor." *Birmingham
News*, 8 Aug. 1962, A28.

Lawrence, Mark Atwood. *The Vietnam War: A Concise International History*. Oxford University Press, 2008.

Layman, John, and Rob Guillory. *Chew: Taster's Choice*. Vol. 1, Image Comics, 2013.

Leblanc, Lauraine. *Pretty in Punk: Girls' Gender Resistance in a Boys' Subculture*. Rutgers
University Press, 1999.

Lee, James Kyung-Jin. *Urban Triage: Race and the Fictions of Multiculturalism*. University
of Minnesota Press, 2004.

Lee, Robert G. *Orientals: Asian Americans in Popular Culture*. Temple University Press, 1999.

Lévi-Strauss, Claude. *The Savage Mind*. Translated by George Weidenfeld, University of Chicago Press, 1966.

Lewis, John, and Andrew Aydin, writers. *March*. Illustrated by Nate Powell, vol. 1, Top Shelf Productions, 2013.

———. *March*. Illustrated by Nate Powell, vol. 2, Top Shelf Productions, 2015.

———. *March*. Illustrated by Nate Powell, vol. 3, Top Shelf Productions, 2016.

Liu, Jonathan H. "Interview: Gene Yang Talks *Boxers & Saints*." *GeekDad*, 9 Sept. 2013. geekdad.com/2013/09/gene-yang-boxers-saints/. 30 Sept. 2015.

Loss, Robert. "Profluent Lingering, Trauma and Subjectivity in Mat Johnson and Warren Pleece's *Incognegro*." *International Journal of Comic Art*, vol. 15, no. 2, 2013, pp. 528–45.

Love, Jeremy. *Bayou*. Zuda Comics, 2007–2010.

———. *Bayou*. Vol. 1, DC Comics, 2009.

———. *Bayou*. Vol. 2, DC Comics, 2010.

———. "Jeremy Love's American Style." *Graphic Novel Reporter*, interviewed by John Hogan, graphicnovelreporter.com/authors/jeremy-love/news/interview-060209. Accessed 8 Aug. 2015.

———. Lecture. Comics Studies in the South Symposium, 25 Oct. 2013, University of South Carolina, Columbia, S.C.

Lowe, Lisa. *Immigrant Acts: On Asian American Cultural Politics*. Duke University Press, 1996.

———. *The Intimacies of Four Continents*. Duke University Press, 2015.

Lye, Colleen. *America's Asia: Racial Form and American Literature, 1893–1945*. Princeton University Press, 2005.

Marcus, Greil. *Lipstick Traces: A Secret History of the Twentieth Century*. Harvard University Press, 1989.

Marie, Vincent. «Clément Baloup: *Mémoires de Viet kieu* ou la puissance d'évidence des images.» *Albums—des Histoires dessinées entre ici et ailleurs: Bande dessinée et immigration 1913–2013*. Edited by Vincent Marie and Gilles Ollivier, Musée de l'Histoire de l'Immigration/Futuropolis, 2013, 160–63.

Marshall, Kerry James. *Rythm Mastr: A Superhero Tale*. K. J. Marshall, 1999.

Martin, Douglas. "Norma Gabler, Leader of Crusade on Textbooks, Dies at 84." *New York Times*, 1 Aug. 2007.

Martin Luther King and the Montgomery Story. Fellowship on Reconciliation, 1957, crmvet. org/docs/ms_for_comic.pdf. Accessed 21 June 2016.

Mayer, Petra. "'Boxers & Saints' & Compassion: Questions for Gene Luen Yang." *NPR*, 22 Oct. 2013, npr.org/2013/10/22/234824741/boxers-saints-compassion-quesions-for-gene -luen-yang. Accessed 30 Sept. 2015.

McCloud, Scott. *The New Adventures of Abraham Lincoln*. Homage Comics, 1998.

———. "The New Adventures of Abraham Lincoln." *scottmccloud.com*, scottmccloud. com/2-print/older/abe/index.html. Accessed 4 Feb. 2015.

———. *Understanding Comics: The Invisible Art*. Harper, 1994.

McDowell, Deborah E. *Leaving Pipe Shop: Memories of Kin*. Scribner, 1996.

McKinney, Mark. *Redrawing French Empire in Comics*. Ohio University Press, 2013.

McWhorter, Diane. *Carry Me Home: Birmingham, Alabama: The Climactic Battle of the Civil Rights Revolution*. Simon & Schuster, 2001.

Mehta, Binita, and Pia Mukherji. Introduction. *Postcolonial Comics: Texts, Events, Identities*. Edited by Mehta and Mukherji, Routledge, 2015, pp. 1–26.

Melia, Daniel. "John Lydon Calls Green Day 'Plonk' Not 'Punk.'" *Gigwise*, 9 Feb. 2006, gigwise.com/news/13310/john-lydon-calls-green-day-%22plonk%22-not-%22punk%22. Accessed 1 Oct. 2015.

Mendlesohn, Farah. *The Rhetorics of Fantasy*. Wesleyan University Press, 2008.

Metress, Christopher. *The Lynching of Emmett Till: A Documentary Narrative*. University of Virginia Press, 2002.

———. "Making Civil Rights Harder: Literature, Memory, and the Black Freedom Struggle." *Southern Literary Journal*, vol. 40, no. 2, 2008, pp. 138–50.

Michaels, Walter Benn. *The Shape of the Signifier*. Princeton University Press, 2004.

———. *The Trouble with Diversity*. Henry Holt, 2006.

Miodrag, Hannah. *Comics and Language: Reimagining Critical Discourse on the Form*. University Press of Mississippi, 2013.

Misztal, Barbara A. *Theories of Social Remembering*. Open University Press, 2003.

Mitchell, Koritha. "Love in Action: Noting Similarities between Lynching Then and Anti-LGBT Violence Now." *Callaloo, vol.* 36, no. 3, 2013, pp. 688–717.

Monteith, Sharon. "Civil Rights Fiction." *The Cambridge Companion to the Literature of the American South*. Edited by Monteith, Cambridge University Press, 2013, pp. 159–73.

———. "Civil Rights Movement Film." *Cambridge Companion to American Civil Rights Literature*. Edited by Julie Buckner Armstrong, Cambridge University Press, 2015, pp. 123–42.

Montfort, Nick, and Wardrip-Fruin, Noah. *The New Media Reader*. MIT Press, 2003.

Moore, Alan, and Dave Gibbons. *Watchmen*. 1987. DC Comics, 2014.

Morrison, Toni. "A Humanist View." Black Studies Center public dialogue. Part 2, 30 May 1975. Portland State University's Oregon Public Speakers Collection, pdxscholar.library.pdx.edu/orspeakers/90/. Accessed 3 May 2015.

———. *Playing in the Dark: Whiteness and the Literary Imagination*. Vintage, 1992.

Mozzocco, J. Caleb. "Interview: Gene Luen Yang on *Boxers & Saints*." *School Library Journal*, 19 Sept. 2013, blogs.slj.com/goodcomicsforkids/2013/09/19/interview-gene-luen-yang-on-boxers-saints/. Accessed 30 Sept. 2015.

Nama, Adilifu. "Introduction." *Black Kirby: In Search of the Motherboxx Connection*. Edited by John Jennings and Stacey Robinson, Black Kirby Collective, 2013, p. 11.

———. *Super Black: American Pop Culture and Black Superheroes*. University of Texas Press, 2011.

Nash, Gary, et al. *History on Trial: Culture Wars and the Teaching of the Past*. Knopf, 1997.

Neale, Jonathan. *A People's History of the Vietnam War*. New Press, 2003.

Nehring, Neil. *Flowers in the Dustbin: Culture, Anarchy, and Postwar England*. University of Michigan Press, 1993.

Neri, G., writer. *Yummy: The Last Days of a Southside Shorty*. Illustrated by Randy DuBurke, Lee & Low, 2010.

"The New Adventures of Abraham Lincoln." *Comics Worth Reading*, 17 June 2017, comicsworthreading.com/2006/06/17/the-new-adventures-of-abraham-lincoln/. Accessed 12 May 2016.

Nixon, Rob. *Slow Violence and the Environmentalism of the Poor*. Harvard University Press, 2011.

Nora, Pierre. «Between Memory and History: Les Lieux de Mémoires.» *Representations*, vol. 26, no. 1, 1 Apr. 1989, pp. 7–24.

Norman, Brian. *Neo-Segregation Narratives: Jim Crow in Post–Civil Rights American Literature*. University of Georgia Press, 2007.

Norman, Brian, and Piper Kendrix Williams, editors. *Representing Segregation: Toward an Aesthetics of Living Jim Crow, and Other Forms of Racial Division*. State University of New York Press, 2010.

Oh, Sandra. "Sight Unseen: Tomine's *Optic Nerve* and the Politics of Recognition." *MELUS*, vol. 32, no. 3, special issue: Coloring America: Multi-Ethnic Engagements with Graphic Narrative, 2007, pp. 131–56.

Olson, Ray. "Stuck Rubber Baby." *Booklist*, 1 Sept. 1995, p. 27.

O'Malley, Bryan Lee. *Scott Pilgrim: Scott Pilgrim's Precious Little Life*. Vol. 1, Oni Press, 2012.

Opper, Frederick B. "Caricature Country and Its Inhabitants." *Independent*, vol. 53, 1901, pp. 778–81.

Payne, Charles M. *I've Got the Light of Freedom: The Organizing Tradition and the Mississippi Freedom Struggle*. University of California Press, 1995.

Pedri, Nancy. "When Photographs Aren't Quite Enough: Reflections on Photography and Cartooning in *Le Photographe*." *ImageTexT*, vol. 6, no. 1, 2011, english.ufl.edu/imagetext/archives/v6_1/pedri/. Accessed 29 July 2017.

Pekar, Harvey. "Blood and Thunder: Harvey Pekar and R. Fiore." *Comics Journal*, April 1990, tcj.com/blood-and-thunder-harvey-pekar-and-r-fiore/. Accessed 22 March 2013.

Peterson, James Braxton. "Birth of a Nation: Representation, Nationhood, and Graphic Revolution in the Works of D. W. Griffith, DJ Spooky, and Aaron McGruder et al." Aldama, pp. 105–19.

Pollack, Harriet, and Christopher Metress, editors. *Emmett Till in Literary Memory and Imagination*. Louisiana State University Press, 2008.

Praytor, Jim. Telephone Interview with Julie Armstrong. 15 Dec. 2014.

Rancière, Jacques. *The Emancipated Spectator*. Translated by Gregory Elliot, Verso, 2009.

Richards, Gary. "Everybody's Graphic Protest Novel: *Stuck Rubber Baby* and the Anxieties of Racial Difference." Costello and Whitted, pp. 161–83.

Rifas, Leonard. "Race and Comix." Aldama, pp. 27–38.

Road, Cristy C. *Bad Habits: A Love Story*. Soft Skull, 2008.

———. *Croadcore: The Art of Cristy C. Road, 1998–2015*. croadcore.org. Accessed 12 Aug. 2015.

———. *Indestructible: Growing Up Queer, Cuban, and Punk in Miami*. Microcosm, 2006.

———. "Queer Latina Punk Artist Cristy C. Road: The Interview." Interviewed by Heidi

Andrea. *Autostraddle*, 25 Jan. 2013, autostraddle.com/queer-latina-punk-artist-cristy
-c-road-the-interview/. Accessed 12 Aug. 2015.

———. *Spit and Passion*. Feminist, 2012.

Roan, Jeanette. "Tasting Is Knowing: *Chew*, Food, and Disgust." Association for Asian
American Studies Annual Conference, 25 Apr. 2015, Evanston, Ill. Presentation.

Rodriguez, Clara E. "Racial Themes in the Literature: Puerto Ricans and Other Latinos."
Hispanic New York: A Sourcebook. Edited by Claudio Iván Remeseira, Columbia University Press, 2010, pp. 183–200.

Rogin, Michael. *Blackface, White Noise: Jewish Immigrants in the Hollywood Melting Pot*.
University of California Press, 1996.

Romano, Renee C., and Leigh Raiford, editors. *The Civil Rights Movement in American
Memory*. University of Georgia Press, 2006.

Rothberg, Michael. "'We Were Talking Jewish': Art Spiegelman's 'Maus' as 'Holocaust'
Production." *Contemporary Literature*, vol. 35, no. 4, 1994, pp. 661–87.

Royal, Derek Parker. "Drawing Attention: Comics as a Means of Approaching U.S. Cultural Diversity." *Teaching Comics and Graphic Narratives: Essays on Theory, Strategy and
Practice*. Edited by Lan Dong, McFarland, 2012, pp. 67–79.

———. "Introduction: Coloring America: Multi-Ethnic Engagements with Graphic Narrative." *MELUS*, vol. 32, no. 3, special issue: Coloring America: Multi-Ethnic Engagements
with Graphic Narrative, 2007, pp. 7–22.

Russell, Thaddeus. "The Color of Discipline: Civil Rights and Black Sexuality." *American
Quarterly*, vol. 60, no. 1, 2008, pp. 101–28.

Sánchez González, Lisa. *Boricua Literature: A Literary History of the Puerto Rican Diaspora*. New York University Press, 2001.

Satrapi, Marjane. *Persepolis: The Story of a Childhood*. Translated by Mattias Ripa and
Blake Ferris, Pantheon, 2003.

Schlund-Vials, Cathy J. "Drawing from Resistance: Folklore, Race, and *Secret Identities: The
Asian American Superhero Anthology*." *Amerasia Journal*, vol. 39, no. 2, 2013, pp. 2–24.

———. "Ecological Imaginations, the Vietnam War, and Vietnamese American Literature."
Asian American Literature and the Environment. Edited by Lorna Fitzsimmons et al.,
Routledge, 2014, pp. 111–25.

Schuyler, George. *Black No More: Being an Account of the Strange and Wonderful Workings
of Science in the Land of the Free, A.D. 1933–1940*. 1931. Northeastern University Press,
1989.

Schwenkel, Christina. *The American War in Contemporary Vietnam: Transnational Re-
membrance and Representation*. Indiana University Press, 2009.

Sears, James. *Lonely Hunter: An Oral History of Lesbian and Gay Southern Life, 1948–1968*.
Westview Press, 1997.

Seetharaman, Suresh, et al. *Spider-Man India*. Vol. 1, Marvel Comics, 2005.

Shah, Nayan. *Contagious Divides: Epidemics and Race in San Francisco's Chinatown*. University of California Press, 2001.

Siegel, Jerry, and Joe Shuster. *Superman*. No. 1, Action Comics, 1933.

Sifuentes-Jáuregui, Ben. *The Avowal of Difference: Queer Latino American Narratives*. State
University of New York Press, 2014.

Sims, Guy A., (author) and Anyabwile, Dawud, illustrator. *Brotherman: Dictator of Discipline*. Big City Comics, 1990.

Singer, Marc. "'Black Skins' and White Masks: Comic Books and the Secret of Race." *African American Review*, vol. 36, no. 1, 2002, pp. 107–19.

Singh, Nikhil Pal. *Black Is a Country: Race and the Unfinished Struggle for Democracy*. Harvard University Press, 2004.

Smith, Colin. "On *The New Adventures of Abraham Lincoln*, by Scott McCloud." *Sequart Organization*, sequart.org/magazine/11175/on-the-new-adventures-of-abraham-lincoln-by-scott-mccloud/. Accessed 12 May 2016.

Smith, Sidonie, and Julia Watson. "Introduction: Situating Subjectivity in Women's Autobiographical Practices." *Women, Autobiography, Theory: A Reader*. Edited by Smith and Watson, University of Wisconsin Press, 1998, pp. 3–52.

Smith, Zack. "Award-Winning BOXERS AND SAINTS—Gene Luen Yang's Two-Perspective Historical GN." *Newsarama*, 29 Jan. 2014, newsarama.com/20181-award-winning-boxers-and-saints-gene-luen-yang-s-two-perspective-historical-gn.html. Accessed 30 Sept. 2015.

Sohn, Stephen Hong. *Racial Asymmetries: Asian American Fictional Worlds*. New York University Press, 2014.

Sollors, Werner. *Neither Black nor White yet Both: Thematic Explorations of Interracial Literature*. Harvard University Press, 1999.

Solomon, Dan. "One-Two Punch: Gene Luen Yang's 'Boxers' and 'Saints' Duo Takes on the Boxer Rebellion." *Austin Chronicle*, 20 Sept. 2013, austinchronicle.com/arts/2013-09-20/one-two-punch/. Accessed 30 Sept. 2015.

Song, Min Hyoung. *The Children of 1965: On Writing, and Not Writing, as an Asian American*. Duke University Press, 2013.

———. "'How Good It Is to Be a Monkey': Comics, Racial Formation, and *American Born Chinese*." *Mosaic*, vol. 43, no. 1, 2010, pp. 73–92.

———. *Strange Future: Pessimism and the 1992 Los Angeles Riots*. Duke University Press, 2005.

Song of the South. Directed by Harve Foster, Walt Disney Productions, 1946.

Sontag, Susan. *On Photography*. Picador, 1977.

Spencer, J. William. "It's Not as Simple as It Seems: Ambiguous Culpability and Ambivalent Affect in News Representations of Violent Youth." *Symbolic Interaction*, vol. 28, no. 1, Feb. 2005, pp. 47–65.

Spiegelman, Art. "Art Spiegelman: Walking Gingerly, Remaining Close to Our Caves." Interviewed by Natasha Schmidt. 2000. *Art Spiegelman: Conversations*. Edited by Joseph Witek, University Press of Mississippi, 2007, pp. 220–22.

———. *Breakdowns: Portrait of the Artist as a Young &@*!*. Pantheon, 2008.

———. "Cartoonist Lives Matter: Art Spiegelman Responds to Charlie Hebdo Attack, Power of Cartoon." *Democracy Now*, 8 Jan. 2015, democracynow.org/2015/1/8/cartoonists_lives_matter_art_spiegelman_responds. Accessed 3 Jan. 2016.

———. "Drawing Blood: Outrageous Cartoons and the Art of Outrage." *Harper's*, June 2006, vita.it/static/upload/dra/drawing_blood-copy.pdf. Accessed 3 Jan. 2016.

———. *In the Shadow of No Towers*. Pantheon, 2004.

———. *Maus: A Survivor's Tale: My Father Bleeds History*. Pantheon, 1986.

———. *Maus II: A Survivor's Tale: And Here My Troubles Began*. Pantheon, 1991.

———. "Pig Perplex." Interviewed by Lawrence Weschler. 2001. *Art Spiegelman: Conversations*. Edited by Joseph Witek, University Press of Mississippi, 2007, pp. 230–33.

Spiegelman, Art, and Hillary L. Chute. *MetaMaus: A Look inside a Classic*. Pantheon, 2011.

Spurgeon, Tom. "CR Sunday Interview: Gene Luen Yang." *Comics Reporter*, 17 Nov. 2013, comicsreporter.com/index.php/cr_sunday_interview_gene_luen_yang/. Accessed 30 Sept. 2015.

Stoler, Ann Laura. *Along the Archival Grain: Epistemic Anxieties and Colonial Common Sense*. Princeton University Press, 2010.

———. "'The Rot Remains': From Ruins to Ruination." *Imperial Debris: On Ruins and Ruination*. Edited by Ann Laura Stoler, Duke University Press, 2013, pp. 1–35.

Stoltz, Eric. "Saint Vibiana, the Patron of Nobodies." *Cathedrals of California*. 17 Sep. 2007. Website no longer available.

Stone, Amy L., and Jane Ward. "From 'Black People Are Not a Homosexual Act' to 'Gay Is the New Black': Mapping White Uses of Blackness in Modern Gay Rights Campaigns in the United States." *Social Identities*, vol. 17, no. 5, 2011, pp. 605–24.

Strömberg, Fredrik. *Black Images in the Comics: A Visual History*. Fantagraphic, 2003.

Tchen, John Kuo Wei, and Dylan Yeats, editors. *Yellow Peril! An Archive of Anti-Asian Fear*. Verso, 2014.

Thompson, Stacy. *Punk Productions: Unfinished Business*. State University of New York Press, 2004.

Tienda, Marta, and Susana M. Sanchez. "Latin American Immigration to the United States." *Daedalus, the Journal for the American Academy of Arts and Sciences*, vol. 142, no. 3, 2013, pp. 48–64.

Toomer, Jean. *Cane*. 1923. Norton, 2011.

Tran, GB. *Vietnamerica: A Family's Journey*. Villard, 2010.

Truong, Marcelino. *Give Peace a Chance: Londres 1963–1975*. Editions Denoël, 2015.

———. *Saigon Calling: London 1963–1975*. Translated by David Homel, Arsenal Pulp Press, 2017.

———. *Such a Lovely Little War: Saigon 1961–1963*. Translated by David Homel, Arsenal Pulp Press, 2016.

———. *Une si jolie petite guerre: Saigon 1961–1963*. Editions Denoël, 2012.

United States. Cong. House. Committee on the Judiciary. *Defense of Marriage Act*. 104th Cong. Pub. L. 104–199. GPO, 1996. *The Library of Congress, Thomas*, congress.gov /bill/104th-congress/house-bill/3396/text. Accessed 25 April 2017.

Ut, Nick (Huỳnh Công Út). "Terror of War (Napalm Girl)." *Vietnam Napalm 1972* Collection. 8 Jun. 1972. Associated Press/AP Images, apimages.com/Collection/Landing /Photographer-Nick-Ut-The-Napalm-Girl-/ebfc0a860aa946ba9e77eb786d46207e. Accessed August 2015.

Vargas, Zaragosa. *Crucible of Struggle: A History of Mexican Americans from Colonial Times to the Present Era*. Oxford University Press, 2011.

Vasquez, Tina. "Book Review: *Spit and Passion*." *Bitch Magazine: Feminist Responses to Pop Culture*, no. 58, 2013, pp. 59–60.

Versaci, Rocco. *This Book Contains Graphic Language: Comics as Literature*. Continuum, 2007.

Versluys, Kristiaan. "Art Spiegelman's *In the Shadow of No Towers*: 9-11 and the Representation of Trauma." *Modern Fiction Studies*, vol. 52, no. 4, Winter 2006, pp. 980–1003.

Wanzo, Rebecca. "Black Nationalism, Bunraku, and Beyond: Articulating Black Heroism through Cultural Fusion and Comics." Aldama, pp. 93–104.

Ward, Brian, editor. *Media, Culture, and the Modern African American Freedom Struggle*. University Press of Florida, 2001.

Warhol, Robyn. "The Space Between: A Narrative Approach to Alison Bechdel's *Fun Home*." *College Literature*, vol. 38, no. 3, 2011, pp. 1–20.

Weaver, Lila Quintero. *Darkroom: A Memoir in Black and White*. University of Alabama Press, 2012.

Wertham, Fredric. *Seduction of the Innocent*. 1954. Main Road, 2004.

West, John G., Jr. "Introduction: Religion in American Politics." *Encyclopedia of Religion in American Politics*. Edited by Jeffrey D. Schultz et al., Oryx, 1999, pp. xiii–xxxii.

White, Hayden. "Interpretation in History." *New Literary History*, vol. 4, no. 2, 1 Jan. 1973, pp. 281–314.

———. "The Value of Narrative in the Representation of Reality." *Critical Inquiry*, vol. 1, no. 1, 1980, pp. 5–27.

White, Walter. *Flight*. 1926. Negro Universities Press, 1969.

———. *A Man Called White: The Autobiography of Walter White*. 1948. University of Georgia Press, 1995.

Whitlock, Gillian. "Autographics: The Seeing 'I' of the Comics." *Modern Fiction Studies*, vol. 52, no. 4, 2006, pp. 965–79.

Whitt, Margaret Earley, editor. *Short Stories of the Civil Rights Movement: An Anthology*. University of Georgia Press, 2006.

Whitted, Qiana J. "Of Slaves and Other Swamp Things: Black Southern History as Comic Book Horror." Costello and Whitted, pp. 187–213.

Wiggins, Robert L. *The Life of Joel Chandler Harris: From Obscurity in Boyhood to Fame in Early Manhood*. Pub. House Methodist Episcopal Church, 1918.

Wilson, Anthony. *Shadow and Shelter: The Swamp in Southern Culture*. University Press of Mississippi, 2006.

Wilson, G. Willow, and Adrian Alphona. *Ms. Marvel Volume 1: No Normal*. Marvel, 2014.

Witek, Joseph, editor. *Art Spiegelman: Conversations*. University Press of Mississippi, 2007.

———. *Comic Books as History: The Narrative Art of Jack Jackson, Art Spiegelman, and Harvey Pekar*. University Press of Mississippi, 1989.

———. "Comics Modes: Caricature and Illustration in the Crumb Family's *Dirty Laundry*." *Critical Approaches to Comics: Theories and Methods*. Edited by Matthew J. Smith and Randy Duncan, Routledge, 2011, pp. 27–42.

Wolk, Douglas. *Reading Comics: How Graphic Novels Work and What They Mean*. Da Capo Press, 2007.

Wong, Alia. "History Class and the Fictions about Race in America." *Atlantic*, 21 Oct. 2015, theatlantic.com/education/archive/2015/10/the-history-class-dilemma/411601/. Accessed 29 July 2017.

Wong, David H. T. *Escape to Gold Mountain: A Graphic History of the Chinese in North America*. Arsenal Pulp Press, 2012.

Wonham, Henry B. *Playing the Races: Ethnic Caricature and American Literary Realism*. Oxford University Press, 2004.

Wright, Bradford W. *Comic Book Nation: The Transformation of Youth Culture in America*. Johns Hopkins University Press, 2001.

Yang, Gene Luen. *American Born Chinese*. First Second, 2006.

———. *Animal Crackers*. SLG Publishing, 2010.

———. *Boxers*. First Second, 2013.

———. "The Boxers and the Power of Pop Culture." *GeneYang.com*, 20 Feb. 2013, geneyang.com/boxers-and-pop-culture. Accessed 30 Sept. 2015.

———. "How Chinese Opera and American Comics Are Alike." *GeneYang.com*, 27 Feb. 2013, geneyang.com/how-chinese-opera-and-american-comics-are-alike. Accessed 30 Sept. 2015.

———. "Interview: Gene Luen Yang on *The Shadow Hero*." *Nerdist*, nerdist.com/interview-gene-luen-yang-on-the-shadow-hero/. Accessed 27 June 2015.

———. *Saints*. First Second, 2013.

Yang, Gene Luen, and Sonny Liew. "The Blue Scorpion and Chung." *Secret Identities: The Asian American Superhero Anthology*. Edited by Jeff Yang et al., New Press, 2009, pp. 63–74.

———. *The Shadow Hero*. First Second, 2014.

Yang, Gene Luen, and Thien Pham. *Level Up*. First Second, 2011.

Yang, Gene Luen, et al. "The 'Asian Invasion': An Interview with Gene Luen Yang." *Lion and the Unicorn*, vol. 38, no. 1, 2014, pp. 123–33.

Yang, Jeff, et al., editors. *Shattered: A Secret Identities Book: The Asian American Comics Anthology*. New Press, 2012.

———. *Secret Identities: The Asian American Superhero Anthology*. New Press, 2009.

Young, Marilyn B. *The Vietnam Wars, 1945–1990*. Harper Perennial, 1991.

CONTRIBUTORS

FREDERICK LUIS ALDAMA is Arts and Humanities Distinguished Professor of English and University Distinguished Scholar at The Ohio State University. Known for his work in Latino/Latina American postcolonial literature, cognitive science, art, music, film, and comics books, he is author, coauthor, and editor of thirty books. He is also the founder and director of LASER (Latinx Space for Enrichment Research).

JULIE BUCKNER ARMSTRONG is professor of literature and cultural studies at the University of South Florida St. Petersburg, where she teaches courses in African American, American, and women's literatures. She has authored and edited multiple publications on the literature of civil rights and racial justice, including the *Cambridge Companion to American Civil Rights Literature* (Cambridge University Press, 2015); *Mary Turner and the Memory of Lynching* (University of Georgia Press, 2011); *The Civil Rights Reader: American Literature from Jim Crow to Reconciliation* (University of Georgia Press, 2009); and, with Susan Hult Edwards, Houston Roberson, and Rhonda Williams, *Teaching the American Civil Rights Movement: Freedom's Bittersweet Song* (Routledge, 2002). She is currently working on a collection of essays, *Birmingham Stories*, about everyday people and places in the iconic civil rights movement city where she was born.

KATHARINE CAPSHAW is professor of English at the University of Connecticut (Storrs). She is also affiliate faculty for the Africana Studies Institute at UConn. The former editor of the *Children's Literature Association Quarterly*, Capshaw has published more than two dozen essays in journals and academic books on race and children's literature and culture. She has lectured nationally and internationally on the subject of black childhood. She is the author of *Children's Literature of the Harlem Renaissance* (Indiana University Press, 2004) and *Civil Rights Childhood: Picturing Liberation in African American Photobooks* (University of Minnesota Press, 2014). Her coedited (with Anna Mae Duane) anthology of essays, *Who Writes for Black Children? African American Children's Literature before 1900* (University of Minnesota Press), appeared in 2017. She is at work on a new book on the Black Arts movement and childhood.

MONICA CHIU is professor of English and American studies at the University of New Hampshire. She specializes in Asian American studies and, more recently, graphic narratives. After teaching at the University of Hong Kong as a Fulbright Scholar, 2011–12, Chiu edited *Drawing New Color Lines: Transnational Asian American Graphic Narratives* (Hong Kong University Press, 2014). Her essays on graphic narratives appear in *Asian American Literature: Discourses and Pedagogies* and *English Language Notes*. Her most recent monograph in Asian American studies is *Scrutinized! Surveillance in Asian North American Literature* (University of Hawai'i Press, 2014).

MARTHA J. CUTTER is professor of English and Africana studies at the University of Connecticut. From 2006 to 2014 she served as editor of *MELUS: Multi-Ethnic Literature of the United States*, and from 2004 to 2006 she was the editor of *Legacy: A Journal of American Women Writers*. She has three published books: *Unruly Tongue: Language and Identity in American Women's Writing* (University of Mississippi Press, 1999), *Lost and Found in Translation: Contemporary Ethnic American Writing and the Politics of Language Diversity* (University of North Carolina Press, 2005), and *The Illustrated Slave: Empathy, Graphic Narrative, and the Visual Culture of the Transatlantic Abolition Movement, 1800–1852* (University of Georgia Press, 2017). She has also published more than thirty-five articles on American multiethnic literature.

JENNIFER GLASER is associate professor of English at the University of Cincinnati, where she teaches courses on contemporary American fiction, race, ethnicity, and visual culture. Her book, *Borrowed Voices: Writing and Racial Ventriloquism in the Jewish American Imagination*, was published in 2016 by Rutgers University Press. She has published or has publications forthcoming in venues such as *PMLA*, *MELUS*, *Safundi*, *ImageTexT*, *Early American Literature*, *American Literature*, the *New York Times*, the *Faster Times*, *Literature Compass*, and the *LA Review of Books*, as well as an anthology of essays from Random House. She is also at work on a new monograph about seeing race in comics.

TAYLOR HAGOOD is professor of American literature at Florida Atlantic University. His publications include *Faulkner, Writer of Disability* (Louisiana State University Press, 2014); *Secrecy, Magic, and the One-Act Plays of Harlem Renaissance Women Writers* (The Ohio State University Press, 2010); and *Faulkner's Imperialism: Space, Place, and the Materiality of Myth* (Louisiana State University Press, 2008) as well as articles and reviews in such journals as *African American Review*, *American Literature*, *College Literature*, *European Journal of American Culture*, *Literature Compass*, *Mississippi Quarterly*, *Modern Fiction Studies*, *Studies in Popular Culture*, *Southern Literary Journal*, and *Walt Whitman Quarterly Review*. He edited *Critical Insights: The Sound and the Fury* (Salem Press, 2014), coedited the forthcoming collection *Undead Souths: The Gothic in Southern Literature and Beyond* with Eric Gary Anderson and Daniel Cross Turner, and is a collaborative editor on the Digital Yoknapatawpha Project. Formerly a Fulbright Gast professor at Ludwig-Maximilians-Universität-München in Munich, Germany, he currently serves as a research ambassador for the Deutsche Akademischer Austausch Dienst/German Academic Exchange Service.

CAROLINE KYUNGAH HONG is associate professor of English and the director of graduate studies in English at Queens College, City University of New York. She is currently finishing a book on Asian American comedy and has published work on Asian American literature and pop culture, including articles on Asian American graphic narratives. She is the current cochair of the Circle for Asian American Literary Studies.

ANGELA LAFLEN is associate professor of English and codirector of women's studies at Marist College in Poughkeepsie, New York. She teaches in the areas of literature and gender, digital writing, and technical communication. She has presented her work at meetings of the Modern Language Association, American Comparative Literature Association, and the Conference on College Composition and Communication, and her work has appeared in *Mosaic: A Journal for the Interdisciplinary Study of Literature*, *Modern Language Studies*, and *Computers and Composition*, among other journals. Her work focuses on gender issues, contemporary women's writing, digital literacy, and online pedagogy. She is author of *Confronting Visuality in Multi-Ethnic Women's Literature* (Palgrave Macmillan, 2014) and coeditor of *Gender Scripts in Medicine and Narrative* (Cambridge Scholars, 2010). Her current work investigates narratives of the body's interior that problematize and contest the dominant biomedical view of the body.

CATHERINE H. NGUYEN is a PhD candidate in comparative literature at UCLA and completed an MA as a Fulbright France scholar at the Université de Provence. Her dissertation examines how diasporic Vietnamese narratives of adoption as particular forms of immigration reveal and work against the disavowal of imperialism, war, and loss in American and French literatures. She is also the managing editor and the French-language edition editor of diacritics.org, a critical blog on Vietnamese and Vietnamese diasporic production.

JEFFREY SANTA ANA is associate professor of English and affiliated faculty in Asian and Asian American studies and women's, gender, and sexuality studies at Stony Brook University. He is the author of *Racial Feelings: Asian America in a Capitalist Culture of Emotion* (Temple University Press, 2015). He has published articles on Asian American and multiethnic literatures in *Signs*, *positions*, and *Journal of Asian American Studies*. His essay "Emotions as Landscapes: Specters of Asian American Racialization in Shaun Tan's Graphic Narratives" was published in the collection *Drawing New Color Lines: Transnational Asian American Graphic Narratives* (Hong Kong University Press, 2014), edited by Monica Chiu. He is currently writing a book manuscript titled *Transpacific Environmental Imagination: Ecologies of Memory in the Asian-Pacific Diaspora*. His book conceives of an ecologies of memory to explore diasporic Asian Pacific works that recall and speak in defense of ancestry, place, and the natural world, a remembering that articulates a transnational perspective to mediate environmental crisis and human-induced climate change.

JORGE SANTOS is assistant professor of English at the College of the Holy Cross and specializes in twentieth-century ethnic American literature, particularly in the intersections between race and religious experience. He earned his PhD at the University of Connecticut in 2014. He has presented at conferences across the country, and he was awarded the Aetna Critical Writing prize in 2014 for his work on Rhode Montijo's comic book *Pablo's Inferno*, which has recently been accepted for publication in *ImageTexT*. He is currently working on a book titled *Graphic Memories of the Civil Rights Movement* as well as publications on narratives dealing with the traumas of Japanese American internment.

CATHY J. SCHLUND-VIALS is professor of English and Asian/Asian American studies at the University of Connecticut; she is also the director of the Asian and Asian American Studies Institute at UConn. She is author of two monographs: *Modeling Citizenship: Jewish and Asian American Writing* (Temple University Press, 2011) and *War, Genocide, and*

Justice: Cambodian American Memory Work (University of Minnesota Press, 2012). Her work on visual culture, popular culture, and graphic narrative has appeared in a number of collections and journals, including *Modern Language Studies*, *Drawing New Color Lines* (edited by Monica Chiu), *Amerasia*, *Life Writing*, *Looking Back on the Vietnam War* (edited by Brenda Boyle and Jeehyun Lim), and *positions*. She has also coedited a number of collections, which include *Disability, Human Rights, and the Limits of Humanitarianism* (Ashgate, 2014), *Keywords for Asian American Studies* (New York University Press, 2015), *The Beiging of America: Personal Narratives about Being Mixed Race in the Twenty-First Century* (2Leaf Press, 2017), and *Asian America: A Primary Source Reader* (Yale University Press, 2017). She recently edited *Flashpoints for Asian American Studies* (Fordham University Press, 2017) and serves as a series editor—with Rick Bonus and Shelley Lee—for Temple University Press's Asian American History Culture initiative.

INDEX

Page numbers in *italics* indicate illustrations. Specific works are generally under the name of the author(s).

348 • INDEX

Jet, 117, 118

Jews and Judaism: blackface performance and Jewish identity, links between, 303–4; *Der ewige jude* (The Eternal or Wandering Jew; 1940 movie), 298, *299*; Golden Age of comics, Jewish creators in, 103–4nn3–4; history of comics, caricatured and stereotyped throughout, 306, 308, *309*; Spiegelman's *Maus*, 2, 4, 5, 15, 91, 108, 110, 217, 246, 294, 295–304, *297*, *301*, *305*, 311

Jim Crow South, x, 2, 11–12, 57, 106–7, 109, 113. *See also* Johnson, Mat, and Warren Pleece, *Incognegro*; Love, Jeremy, *Bayou*

Jiro, Matthieu, 185

Joan of Arc: in Weaver's *Darkroom*, 144, *145*; in Yang's *Saints*, 62, 64–65, 72, 77, 79, 82–83

Johns, Geoff, and Grant Morrison, 52 (2006–7), viii

Johnson, Andrew, 259, 265n19

Johnson, E. Patrick, 124

Johnson, James Weldon, *Autobiography of an Ex-Colored Man* (1912), 39n5

Johnson, Mat, and Warren Pleece, *Incognegro* (2008), ix, 11–12, 18–38; depictions of skin color / race in, 18, *19*, 24–31, *26*, *27*, *29*, *30*, 39n10; female-to-male gender passing, 39n8; intertextuality with earlier passing literature, 18–19, 20–24; multiple racial alliances, openness to, 20–22; performance, race as, 24; plotline, 18; scholarly study of, 38n2; shade and shadow in, 21–22, *30*, 31, 37; split persona / dual identity, use of, 37; stereotypical portrayals of black or passing individuals and, *19*, 31–38, *34*, *35*, *36*, 39–40n16; as writerly versus readerly text, 19, 20, 24

Johnson, Mat, *Loving Day* (2015), 38n1

Jolson, Al, 302, 303

Jones, Gerard, 88, 103nn3–4

Jones, Paula, 263n3

Joyce, James, *Ulysses* (1922), 6, 17n5

Juice (1992 movie), 266

Jyllends-Posten Muhammad cartoon controversy (2005), 15, 294, 311, 315–16, 319n10

Kane (Kahn), Bob, 103n3

Kang, Jeevan J., Suresh Seetharaman, and Sharad Devarajan, *Spider-Man: India* (2004–5), 92

Kantor, MacKinlay, *If the South Had Won the War* (1960–61), 244

Katchor, Ben, *The Jew of New York* (1998), viii

Katzenjammer Kids, 311, 312

Keller, George Frederick, *99*, 100

Killins, John O., *'Sippi* (1967), 110

Kim Phúc, Phan Thị, and "Napalm Girl" photo, 6, 187–89, *188*, 200

King, Martin Luther, Jr., 6–7, 8, 106, 112, 116, 126, 127n8; "Letter from a Birmingham Jail" (1963), 8

King, Richard H., 111

King Kong, 105n20

Kingston, Maxine Hong, 1, 265n16

Kirby, Jack, 67, 100, 105n18

Kirkman, Robert, *Invincible* (2003), viii

Kitchen Sink (press), 91

Kiyama, Henry (Yoshitaka), *The Four Immigrants Manga* (1931), 85n1

Klarman, Michael, 226

Knox, George, 280

Ku Klux Klan, 9, 23, 24, 57, 60n7, 302, 303, 304

Kurtzberg, Jake, 103n3

Laflen, Angela, 14, 217, 340–41

Larsen, Nella, *Passing* (1920), 39n5

Last Gasp (press), 91

Latino/a and Hispanic Americans: activism, mid-twentieth century, 155–56n1; negotiating black/white binary racial identity, 129, 139–47, *141*, *143*, *145*, 156n2. *See also* Road, Cristy C.: *Spit and Passion*; Weaver, Lila Quintero, *Darkroom*

Layman, John, and Rob Guillory, *Chew* (2009–16), vii, 102–3

Lazarus, Emma, 195

Lee, Bruce, 92

Lee, Harper, *To Kill a Mockingbird* (1960), 110

Lee, James Kyung-Jin, *Urban Triage* (2004), 269

Lee, Robert E., 55

Lee, Robert G., 94

Lee, Spike, 127n10

Lee (Lieber), Stanley, 103n3

Legendary Weapons of China (1982 movie), 86n5

Lévi-Strauss, Claude, 47

Lewinsky, Monica, 243, 263n3

Lewis, John, Andrew Aydin, and Nate Powell, *March* (2013–16), 6–11, 17n3, 17n6, 110

LGBTQ community: DADT ("Don't Ask, Don't Tell") campaign, 126–27n2, 226; female-to-male gender crossing/passing, 39n8; "new" civil rights movement of, 126–27n2; 1990s as special era for, 225–27; same-sex marriage, 14, 127n2, 225–26, 238n6. *See also* Cruse, Howard: *Stuck Rubber Baby*; Road, Cristy C.: *Spit and Passion; and specific events*

Liebowitz, Jack, 103n3

lieux de mémoire, concept of, 195–96

Liew, Sonny. *See* Yang, Gene Luen, and Sonny Liew

Lincoln, Abraham: Carter's *The Impeachment of Abraham Lincoln*, 244; Gettysburg Address, 250, 255–56, 257, 259–60, 265n18; Grahame-Smith's *Abraham Lincoln: Vampire Hunter*, 244; Waldman's "If Booth Had Missed Lincoln," 244. *See also* McCloud, Scott: *The New Adventures of Abraham Lincoln*

local-color and dialect writing, 44

Lockpez, Iverna, *Cuba* (2010), viii

model minority, Asian Americans viewed as, 89, 91, 93, 98

Monkey King (Chinese mythocultural figure), 62, 97, 104–5n16

monotone versus color in comics, 60n8

Montfort, Nick, and Noah Wardrip-Fruin, *The New Media Reader* (2003), 245

Montieth, Sharon, 110, 112–13

Montijo, Rhode, *Pablo's Inferno* (1999–2001), vii

Moore, Alan, and Dave Gibbons, *Watchmen* (1986–87), 90, 104n5, 246

Morales, Robert, and Reginald Hudlin, *Truth* (2004), viii

Morris, Willie, 127n4

Morrison, Grant, and Geoff Johns, 52 (2006–7), viii

Morrison, Toni: *Beloved* (1987), 16; "A Humanist View" (1975), 1, 38; *Playing in the Dark* (1993), 119

MTV, 228, 229

Mukherji, Pia, and Binita Mehta, *Postcolonial Comics* (2015), 3

multiethnic graphic novels. *See* history, memory, and multiethnic graphic novels

Murphy, Patrick, 280, 292n2

Nama, Adilifu, 104n15; *Super Black* (2011), 3, 273

"Napalm Girl" photo, 6, 187–89, *188*, 200

Nast, Thomas, 306

National Book Award in Young People's Literature, 61

National Endowment for the Humanities (NEH), 238n5

National Gang Violence Prevention Weel, 270

National History Standards, 238n5

National Review, 100

Native Americans: African Americans and, 51–52, *52*; Chicano Americans and, 156n2

nature in Tran's *Vietnamerica. See* Tran, GB, *Vietnamerica*

Navarro, Rafael, *Sonambulo* (1996), ix

NEH (National Endowment for the Humanities), 238n5

Neri, G., and Randy DuBurke, *Yummy* (2010), 14–15, 266–92; black urban gang life, male identity, and communities in American culture, 266, 269–71, 282–83; child readership, construction of, 268, 283, *285*, 286–88, *287*; cover art, 266–67; family and home, destabilization of ideas of, 288–92, *291*; media coverage and public discourse, use of, 268, 277–86, *281, 283*, 290–92; memory, history as pursuit of, 268; mug shot of Yummy, use of, 267, 268, 283–86, 290; murder of Shavon Dean by Yummy, 267, 269, 275–77, *278*, 283, 290; paratextual author's notes on historicity of story,

267–68, 288; racialized innocence and corruption in, 271–77, *272, 274, 276, 278, 279*, 286–88, *287*

New Adventures of Abraham Lincoln, The. See under McCloud, Scott

New Jack City (1991 movie), 266

New York Post Sunday Magazine, 8

New York Times, 316

New York Times Magazine, 8

New York World, 312

New Yorker, Spiegelman's O. J. Simpson cover for, 314–15

Nguyen, Catherine H., 14, 182, 341

9/11, 311–12

Nitz, Jai, *Kato, Origins* (2010), viii

Nixon, Rob, 13, 159–60, 166, 181n7

Norris, Frank, 105n19

nostalgia: of Love's *Bayou*, 41, 42–48; of McCloud's *New Adventures of Abraham Lincoln*, 241–43

Nouvel Obs, 182

Obama, Barack, 7, 8, 17n6, 127n2

O'Callaghan, Ann, 292–93n3

Okubo, Miné, *Citizen 13660* (1946), 85n1

Olson, Ray, 109

O'Malley, Brian Lee, *Scott Pilgrim* (2004–10), 92

"one drop" rule, 23, 25, 28–29, 39n9

Opper, Frederick Burr, 306, 319n9; *Happy Hooligan* (1900), vii, 312–14, *314*

Orange, James, 150

Orientalism, ix, 13, 65, 73, 87–89, 92–94, 97

Orwell, George, *Animal Farm* (1945), 298

Osama bin Laden, 313

Osceola (Seminole chief), 51

Outcault, Richard, *Hogan's Alley* (1894–96), 105n18, 312

Page, Thomas Nelson, 44–45, 46

Parks, Rosa, 126

passing. *See* Johnson, Mat, and Warren Pleece, *Incognegro*

Pedri, Nancy, 286

Pekar, Harvey, 298; *American Splendor* (1976–2008), 91, 108. *See also* Witek, Joseph, *Comic Books as History*

performance: blackface, 33, *34*, 302–4, 307, 312–13; in Cruse's *Stuck Rubber Baby*, 107, 123; history, *March* as performative version of, 11; in Love's *Bayou*, 42, 44, 46, 47, 56; minstrel shows, 12, 32, 56, 302, *303*, 307, 314–15; in Neri and DuBurke's *Yummy*, 275; race as, in Johnson and Pleece's *Incognegro*, 24; in Tran's *Vietnamerica*, 163; in Weaver's *Darkroom*, 147; in Yang and Liew's *Shadow Hero*, 89, 90; in Yang's *Boxers* and *Saints*, 66, 70, 71, 72

Printed in the USA
CPSIA information can be obtained
at www.ICGtesting.com
CBHW010247100824
12999CB00013B/613